The Presidency of
ANDREW
JACKSON

AMERICAN PRESIDENCY SERIES

Donald R.McCoy, Clifford S. Griffin, Homer E. Socolofsky
General Editors

George Washington, Forrest McDonald
John Adams, Ralph Adams Brown
Thomas Jefferson, Forrest McDonald
James Madison, Robert Allen Rutland
John Quincy Adams, Mary W. M. Hargreaves
Andrew Jackson, Donald B. Cole
Martin Van Buren, Major L. Wilson
William Henry Harrison & John Tyler, Norma Lois Peterson
James K. Polk, Paul H. Bergeron
Zachary Taylor & Millard Fillmore, Elbert B. Smith
Franklin Pierce, Larry Gara
James Buchanan, Elbert B. Smith
Andrew Johnson, Albert Castel
Rutherford B. Hayes, Ari Hoogenboom
James A. Garfield & Chester A. Arthur, Justus D. Doenecke
Grover Cleveland, Richard E. Welch, Jr.
Benjamin Harrison, Homer B. Socolofsky & Allan B. Spetter
William McKinley, Lewis L. Gould
Theodore Roosevelt, Lewis L. Gould
William Howard Taft, Paolo E. Coletta
Woodrow Wilson, Kendrick A. Clements
Warren G. Harding, Eugene P. Trani & David L. Wilson
Herbert C. Hoover, Martin L. Fausold
Harry S. Truman, Donald R. McCoy
Dwight D. Eisenhower, Chester J. Pach, Jr., & Elmo Richardson
John F. Kennedy, James N. Giglio
Lyndon B. Johnson, Vaughn Davis Bornet
James Earl Carter, Jr., Burton I. Kaufman

The Presidency of

ANDREW
JACKSON

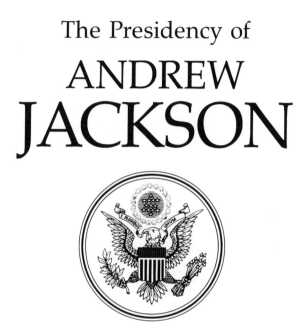

Donald B. Cole

UNIVERSITY PRESS OF KANSAS

To my grandchildren,
Nathan, Andy, Matt, Tim, Nessie,
Madeline, and Sam

© 1993 by the University Press of Kansas
All rights reserved

Published by the University Press of Kansas (Lawrence, Kansas 66049),
which was organized by the Kansas Board of Regents
and is operated and funded by Emporia State University, Fort Hays State
University, Kansas State University, Pittsburg State
University, the University of Kansas, and Wichita State University

Library of Congress Cataloging-in-Publication Data

Cole, Donald B.
The presidency of Andrew Jackson / Donald B. Cole.
p.   cm.—(American presidency series)
ISBN 0-7006-0600-9
1. Jackson, Andrew, 1767–1845.
2. United States—Politics and government—1829–1837.
I. Title.   II. Series.
E382.C69   1993
973.5'6—dc20   92-43377

British Library Cataloguing in Publication Data is available.

Printed in the United States of America

10 9 8 7 6 5 4 3 2 1

The paper used in this publication meets the minimum requirements
of the American National Standard for Permanence of Paper
for Printed Library Materials Z39.48-1984.

CONTENTS

FOREWORD

The aim of the American Presidency Series is to present historians and the general reading public with interesting, scholarly assessments of the various presidential administrations. These interpretive surveys are intended to cover the broad ground between biographies, specialized monographs, and journalistic accounts. As such, each will be a comprehensive work which will draw upon original sources and pertinent secondary literature, yet leave room for the author's own analysis and interpretation.

Volumes in the series will present the data essential to understanding the administration under consideration. Particularly, each book will treat the then current problems facing the United States and its people and how the president and his associates felt about, thought about, and worked to cope with these problems. Attention will be given to how the office developed and operated during the president's tenure. Equally important will be consideration of the vital relationships between the president, his staff, the executive officers, Congress, foreign representatives, the judiciary, state officials, the public, political parties, the press, and influential private citizens. The series will also be concerned with how this unique American institution—the presidency—was viewed by the presidents, and with what results.

All this will be set, insofar as possible, in the context not only of contemporary politics but also of economics, international relations, law, morals, public administration, religion, and thought. Such a broad approach is necessary to understanding, for a presidential administration is more than the elected and appointed officers composing it, since its work so often reflects the major problems, anxieties, and glories of the nation. In short, the authors in this series will strive to recount and evaluate the record of each administration and to identify its distinctiveness and relationships to the past, its own time, and future.

The General Editors

PREFACE

In the preface to his biography of Andrew Jackson, published in 1860, James Parton posed the enigma of the man:

> The first of statesmen, he never devised, he never framed a measure. He was the most candid of men, and was capable of the profoundest dissimulation. A most law-defying, law-obeying citizen. A stickler for discipline, he never hesitated to disobey his superior. A democratic autocrat. An urbane savage.

Ever since this assessment, historians have tried to unravel the mystery of a man whom, in Parton's words, "two thirds of his fellow-citizens deified, and the other third vilified." Although the interpretations have varied greatly, the writers have almost always portrayed Jackson as bigger than life, so dominant a figure that his era was named for him. No other American—not even Washington or Lincoln or Franklin D. Roosevelt—has been accorded this honor. Parton himself wrote that Jackson's will "tyrannized . . . over his friends, over Congress, over the country." Writing more than a century later, Jackson's foremost biographer, Robert V. Remini, concludes his life of the Old Hero with the words of Herman Melville, "Thou great democratic God! . . . Thou who didst pick up Andrew Jackson from the pebbles; who didst hurl him upon a warhorse; who didst thunder him higher than a throne!" Even writers who have emphasized ideas more than the man have presented Jackson as someone who knew what he was doing. He has been pictured alternately as one who led the people "out of captivity and bondage," or was responsible for the "Rise of Liberal Capitalism," or adhered to the states'-rights tradition.[1]

In this book I present a different Jackson, a man less sure of himself than imagined, a man more controlled by the political and economic forces of his age than the reverse. Brought to the presidency by a broad coalition of conflicting interest groups, Jackson was involved in constant battles not only against his opponents but also among his supporters. One by one leaders of the coalition rose and fell—John C. Calhoun, John H. Eaton, Louis McLane—leaving Amos Kendall and Martin Van Buren as the men of influence during Jackson's second term. The greatest accomplishment of his administration was not an act proposed by Jackson but the rise of a new institution, the mass political party. The dominant theme of his presidency was his inconsistent and unsuccessful battle to resist the market revolution, which was transforming America. Though he believed in states' rights and yearned for a bygone Arcadia, he was also entranced by the prosperity and the rise of commerce brought on by the market economy. His ambivalence toward the new politics and the new economy and the ambivalence of his followers is the story of this book.

In reaching these conclusions I am indebted to many Jacksonian scholars but to three in particular. Although I do not carry my analysis of Jackson's uncertainties as far as James C. Curtis, I have been guided by the insights in his *Andrew Jackson and the Search for Vindication*. My thinking has also been stimulated by Marvin Meyers's portrayal of the Jacksonian "effort to recall agrarian republican innocence" in *The Jacksonian Persuasion: Politics and Belief*. Throughout the book I have been helped in many ways by the works of Robert V. Remini.[2]

Two scholars whose views differ from mine have helped me immensely in preparing this study. Richard B. Latner read and commented on an early version, and Richard E. Ellis did the same for the first half of a later draft. Daniel Feller also provided a careful reading of an early draft. My debt to John J. McDonough of the Library of Congress, for his advice, his editing, and his friendship, knows no bounds. Nor do my obligations to my late friend and neighbor Richard F. Niebling, who edited and cared about the manuscript. The general editors of the American Presidency Series, Donald R. McCoy, Clifford S. Griffin, and Homer E. Socolofsky, reviewed the manuscript thoroughly and offered many constructive suggestions. I am especially grateful to Jacqueline Thomas and the staff of the Phillips Exeter Academy Library, who have always made the library my second home. And Tootie knows how much I owe to her. The book is dedicated to our grandchildren, who would have liked the Old Hero.

Part 1

THE JACKSON COALITION, 1829–33

1

★ ★ ★ ★ ★

AN ANXIOUS REPUBLIC

The mood at Andrew Jackson's plantation, the Hermitage, was gloomy as the president-elect tried to compose a letter. His mind, he sighed, was "so disturbed" that he could "scarcely write." Less than a month earlier he had sat through the night at his wife's bedside, trying to bring Rachel, who had died of a heart attack, back to life. Sixty-one, but "twenty years older" after that night, he had just completed arrangements for her tomb and was awaiting the arrival of the steamboat that would start him on the way to his inauguration. Forty-eight hours later, on 19 January 1829, Jackson set off from Nashville down the Cumberland River.[1]

The sudden death of his beloved Rachel had only served to renew the anger and frustration that had consumed Jackson after losing the presidency to John Quincy Adams four years earlier. Although he had won a plurality of the popular and electoral votes in 1824, Jackson had been defeated in the House of Representatives when three states that had voted for him went over to Adams along with three others that had been carried by Henry Clay. When Adams appointed Clay secretary of state, Jackson was outraged and accused the two of a "corrupt bargain." The charge was unfair because Clay had good reason to back Adams, who agreed wholeheartedly with Clay's national economic program, but from that moment Jackson used the charge as the basis of his campaign for election in 1828.

The cry of corruption had made the campaign one of the nastiest in American history. The Jacksonians had denounced Adams for squandering money on a billiard table and other luxuries for the President's House, as the White House was then called, and made the preposterous charge that Adams had "procured" a woman for the czar of Russia while serving there as minister. Not to be outdone, the Adams supporters had dug up as much scandal about Jackson as they could, starting with his irregular marriage. On moving to Nashville in 1788 Jackson had boarded with the widow Rachel Donelson, who also had her daughter and son-in-law, Rachel and Lewis Robards, under her roof. The young couple had already been separated once because of Lewis's fits of jealousy. Now when Rachel seemed to show an interest in the new boarder, her husband departed in a rage for Kentucky. Learning later that he was planning to return, Rachel fled to Natchez, taking Jackson along for protection. After word came that Robards had obtained a divorce, Andrew and Rachel promptly married but soon discovered that Robards had not satisfied all the requirements for a divorce. The Jacksons continued to live together and remarried in 1793 when the divorce became final. In the campaign the Adams side accused the Jacksons of having lived in sin, forcing Jackson into an elaborate defense.[2]

Isolated at the Hermitage, Rachel Jackson had been unaware of these stories, but while shopping in Nashville soon after Jackson's victory she came across one of the pamphlets defending her against accusations of bigamy. A private, deeply religious woman, who lived only for her home and her husband, she was already frightened at the prospect of going to Washington. Now she became emotionally disturbed and developed pleurisy, and the heart attack followed. Jackson blamed her death on Adams, Clay, and his other opponents.

As the citizens of Washington awaited the president-elect's arrival, their state of mind was no less somber than his. The prominent society leader Margaret Bayard Smith wrote that Secretary of the Navy Samuel Southard, who had jousted with Jackson during the campaign, looked "wretched," and Treasury Secretary Richard Rush "totally seclude[d] himself." When she called on Secretary of State Henry Clay, she found him sleeping, covered by a cloth "like a black pall," and was "shocked" by his pale appearance, "his eyes sunk in his head and his countenance sad and melancholy." On the eve of the inauguration she still reported no gaiety, parties, or parades, only "dullness" and "gloom."[3]

Mrs. Smith suggested one reason for the gloom when she remarked that after the inauguration many "excellent families" would be lost to Washington society. She was referring to Jackson's campaign promise to sweep many of the incumbent civil servants out of their positions. On his way to Washington he underscored the promise by fastening two hickory brooms to the prow of his steamboat. If he carried out the threat, a great change would take place, for as the presidency had passed from one member of the Virginia dynasty to another and on to Adams, there had been few removals from federal office. As a result a secure, self-satisfied establishment had grown up in the nation's capital. Now its citizens were afraid that their anxious community might be disrupted.[4]

Mrs. Smith and her friends were also anxious because they had a low opinion of Andrew Jackson. Since he had spent altogether barely a dozen months in Washington, mostly as senator from 1823 to 1825, they knew little about him firsthand and had to base their expectations on the stories that preceded him. During his early career Jackson had often acted violently. In his youth he had a habit of "slobbering" at the mouth when he spoke, a problem that worsened when he became angry. As he grew up he developed a strict code of honor and a tendency to personalize disputes, leading to as many as eight duels. He had killed Charles Dickinson in one of them after being badly wounded and had acted as second in two others, in one of which the distance between the duelers was only ten feet. He had engaged in a notorious brawl with Thomas Hart Benton in a Nashville hotel. Because of his personality he had made many enemies, including such prominent men as Clay and the generals John Sevier and Winfield Scott. Mrs. Smith speculated that Rachel's death removed the one person who had been able to "control the violence of [Jackson's] temper [and] sooth [sic] the exacerbations of feelings always keenly sensitive and excessively irritable."[5]

Jackson's record as a military commander was also the source of many lurid tales. In the war against the Creeks in 1813–14 he had arbitrarily executed six militiamen and had quelled a mutiny by threatening to shoot the first soldier who started for home. After the Battle of New Orleans he had been fined $1,000 for contempt of court in refusing to recognize a writ of habeas corpus. Aware that the public pictured him "with a Tomahawk in one hand, and a scalping knife in the other" when he was elected to the Senate in 1823, he took conscious steps to appear "calm [and] dignified." Although Jackson's courtly behavior as a senator did much to improve his reputation, many people still had a bad impression of him in 1829.[6]

Some observers wondered whether Jackson would live out his term of office. His duel with Dickinson had left him with a bullet dangerously close to his heart, which so infected his lungs that he coughed continually, often spitting up blood. After the brawl with Benton he came away with a bullet lodged in his left arm and almost died from loss of blood, which soaked through two mattresses. Throughout his entire political career he suffered from recurrent bouts of dysentery, severe swelling of his legs, frequent stomachaches, and painful headaches, some of which resulted from his regular doses of medicines loaded with lead and mercury. By 1829 his once powerful six-foot-one-inch body had wasted to 140 pounds. Obsessed with his health and sometimes depressed, he talked and wrote frequently of dying.[7]

Other Americans, however, did not share the gloom that hung over the president-elect and the capital. They had long admired Jackson because of his frontier exploits and especially his victory over the British at New Orleans in 1815. The words of the popular ballad "The Hunters of Kentucky," sung repeatedly in the 1828 campaign, reflected the strong grip that Jackson held on American folklore:

> But Jackson he was wide awake, and
>   wasn't scared with trifles,
> For well he knew what aim we take
>   with our Kentucky rifles;
> So he marched us down to "Cyprus Swamp";
>   The ground was low and mucky;
> There stood "John Bull," in martial pomp,
>   *But here was old Kentucky.*

Because of his toughness and iron will Jackson's followers called him "Old Hickory" or sometimes the "Old Hero," making him the first president to have a nickname. They came out by the thousands to march for him, vote for him, and cheer him on his way to Washington, and they were planning to storm the capital for his inauguration. Even men such as Ralph Waldo Emerson and the merchant Philip Hone of New York, who disapproved of Jackson, admitted that his popularity made him the commanding figure of the era.[8]

As the inauguration drew closer, it was uncertain whether Jackson would turn out to be the frontier ruffian that Margaret Bayard Smith's set dreaded or the stalwart Old Hero that his followers so admired. The doubt was magnified because no one knew how he stood on the pressing issues of the day. His record in local politics and as a senator was unclear, and during the election campaign he had said little about his beliefs.

Sen. Daniel Webster summed up the uncertainty when he wrote to his brother Ezekiel:

Gen. J. will be here abt. 15. Feb.
Nobody knows what he will do; when he does come.
Many letters are sent to him; he answers none of them.

His friends here pretend to be very knowing; but, be assured, not one
of them has any confidential communication from him.
Great efforts are making to put him up to a general sweep, as to all
offices. . . .
The present apparent calm is a suspension of action—a sort of syncope
arising from ignorance of the views of the President elect.
My opinion is
That when he comes, he will bring a breeze with him.
Which way it will blow, I cannot tell.
He will either *go with the party,* . . . or else, he will . . . *be President upon
his own strength.* . . .
My *fear* is stronger than my *hope.*[9]

People wanted to know how the new president would act because
ever since the Battle of New Orleans the country had been changing
so dramatically that there was little certainty or agreement about any aspect of American life. The roots of the changes reached deep into the
eighteenth century when the rise of early trade and commerce began
to transform the agrarian economy of the British colonies. Although
the American Revolution was hardly a social revolution, the forces that
it unleashed ate away at the traditional economy and society. More
middle-class Americans were elected to office, the governments in turn
were more responsive to public opinion, paper money was issued, slaves
were freed in the North, pioneers resumed their movement westward
unrestrained by the British Proclamation Line, and more American
ships, freed from British controls, began to ply the seas. The War of 1812
only furthered the trend by encouraging the rise of manufacturing in
New England.

After the war a revolution in transportation accelerated the changes.
During the turnpike era after 1800, improved toll roads had already cut
the time from Boston to New York from seventy-four hours to thirty-
three hours; steamboats between New York and Rhode Island promised
further cuts. The steamboat also reduced the journey from New York to
Albany from seven days to ten hours. On the Mississippi the steamboat
shortened the time up river from New Orleans to Louisville, which had
been three months by keelboat, to one or two weeks. The steamboat that
carried Jackson down the Cumberland and up the Ohio and the roads
over which he traveled from Pittsburgh to Washington were part of this
transformation. Jackson's election in 1828 coincided with the most revolutionary transportation change of all, the coming of the railroad.

An important byproduct of the transportation revolution was the
increased speed of communication. Hezekiah Niles, editor of the Baltimore *Niles' Register,* announced with delight that it took only one hour

and forty-two minutes to deliver copies of President Jackson's first annual message to Baltimore and only fifty hours to carry it all the way to Cincinnati. A comparable surge occurred in the number of newspapers, which had grown from about 90 in 1789 to about 800 in 1829. The spread of newspapers in the United States far outstripped that in Europe. By the 1830s, for example, one newspaper a week was printed for every four inhabitants in Pennsylvania compared with one for every thirty-six in England.

The transportation revolution was part of the larger market revolution. Steamboats and canals reduced costs and increased the flow of produce between the Mississippi Valley and the Atlantic and across the ocean to Europe. The old self-sufficiency disappeared as farmers produced surplus crops for markets in the rising cities and towns of America and the ports of Europe. Factories in mill cities such as Waltham and Lowell, Massachusetts, added textiles and other products to the flow of goods. In 1800 there had been only six cities with more than 10,000 in population; in 1830 there were twenty-three. For the first time the United States had a metropolis—New York—with a population of 200,000.[10]

The economic expansion brought on an increased demand for money to finance the new enterprises. Since the United States government coined only a limited amount of money, entrepreneurs turned to the states. The Constitution denied the states the right to issue paper money, but state legislatures got around the prohibition by chartering private banks (called state banks) that issued their own bank notes. Although these notes were not legal tender, they were widely accepted. As a result, between 1811 and 1830 the number of state banks in the United States rose from 88 to 330 and the amount of bank notes in circulation from $23 million to $61 million. The latter figure included some $13 million in notes of the Second Bank of the United States, chartered by the federal government. Sales of public land, which were closely related to the expansion of banking, climbed during the same period from 575,000 acres a year to almost 2 million acres a year.[11]

As the production of goods began to move out of the home and into the factory, the lives of American workers changed accordingly. Drawn by the new opportunities, men and women left their homes to live in the mill cities, where they were joined by increasing numbers of immigrants. Immigration, which had never exceeded 10,000 a year before 1825, was never less than 30,000 a year after 1831. In 1828 over 12,000 people came from Ireland alone. The impersonal environment of the factory changed the status of labor, and a labor movement began to appear. The Mechanics' Union of Trade Associations of Philadelphia in 1827 was the first of a group of urban trade councils that soon grew into the

National Trades Union. Philadelphia was also the birthplace of the Workingmen's party in 1828, the only such labor party in American history, which spread quickly to other cities. The arrival of four prominent radicals—Frances Wright, Robert Dale Owen, George Henry Evans, and William Leggett—in 1828-29 sparked the Workingmen's movement in New York City. Wright, for example, called attention to the changes taking place by rejecting contemporary fashion and appearing in a tunic.[12]

American society, never static to begin with, could not resist the economic revolution. Women's lives were reshaped as the new manufacturing system took sons and husbands away during the day or longer, leaving women in charge of the home. The decline in the white birthrate, which fell by one-quarter in the first half of the century, added to women's sense of control. But women paid a price for these gains as the belief spread that they were not suited for the new occupations. A new concept grew of separate spheres, according to which men should go out into the business world and women should stay at home. Although women continued to have choices and played a large role in their communities, they lost much of their opportunity to compete with men for jobs in the outside world.[13]

The rise of the textile industry, which made clothing of all sorts readily available, altered styles so that class distinctions in dress for men began to disappear. Fashionable men no longer wore cocked hats and wigs or tied their hair in a queue, and pantaloons replaced knee breeches. James Madison was the last president to wear his hair in a queue and James Monroe the last seen in knee breeches. Nor were men as likely to don special garments when they went out in the evening. The changes in women's styles were equally rapid but less democratic, for hoop skirts, stomach boards, and stays—worn mostly by upper-class women—were becoming fashionable.[14]

Improvements in transportation and communication contributed to the fall of old religious denominations and the spread of new ones. As Oliver Wendell Holmes later described in his "One-Hoss Shay," Congregationalism fell apart under the attacks of Unitarianism, which had invaded the Harvard Divinity School in 1805. Even the liberal doctrines of the Unitarians were too strict for Emerson, who resigned his pulpit in 1832 because he could not bring himself to celebrate the Lord's Supper. With this act Emerson freed himself for a career in writing and lecturing that in time made him a symbol for the age of individualism.

New or invigorated evangelical denominations grew rapidly in the early nineteenth century, eclipsing traditional churches such as the Anglican and the Presbyterian. The Baptist church spread quickly to the Southwest; Methodism grew from 55,000 members in 1790 to 500,000 by

1830. The Disciples of Christ made similar inroads among the Presbyterians. The most influential evangelical movement, the Second Great Awakening, began with a series of revivals on the frontier in 1797 and reached a high point under Charles G. Finney in the 1820s and 1830s. After receiving a license from the Presbyterian church in 1824, the tall, personable Finney began a crusade to save souls in New York, Pennsylvania, and Massachusetts. Using the "anxious bench" and other new devices to draw his listeners, often in tears, into the service, he began to win over entire towns.[15]

Religious ferment was strongest in western New York along the Erie Canal, which has been dubbed the "Burned-Over District" because its people became so fired up by revivals and social reforms. Mormonism had its start there in 1827 in Palmyra, when Joseph Smith announced that he had uncovered golden plates containing a history of American Indians identified as the lost tribe of Israel. In 1830 Smith organized the Mormons officially as the Church of Jesus Christ of Latter-Day Saints and attracted several thousand converts in the first few years. Anti-Masonry also flourished in the Burned-Over District. In 1826 the disappearance of a member of the Masons, who had threatened to publish revelations about the order, led to the rise of the Anti-Masonic movement, which spread throughout the Northeast. Though not a religion, Anti-Masonry aroused the sort of emotional fervor associated with evangelism.

The evangelical movement produced social reforms such as Sabbatarianism, temperance, and public education. Sabbatarianism was much on people's minds in January 1829, for its advocates were engaged in a nationwide drive to preserve the old morals by closing businesses, taverns, and the post offices on Sundays. One of the leaders of the movement, the Reverend Ezra Stiles Ely of Philadelphia, wrote Jackson at the Hermitage that month, urging him not to travel on the Sabbath on his trip to Washington. The letter arrived after Jackson had left, but the president-elect had bowed to the Sabbatarians anyway by delaying his departure until Monday.[16]

A significant shift in sectional power added to the country's divisions. The addition of Florida and the Louisiana Purchase had greatly expanded the area south and west of the original thirteen states. As the population of the United States rose from 5 million in 1800 to 13 million in 1830, the states west of the Appalachians had increased their share from 7 percent to 28 percent while those on the Atlantic coast had lost proportionately. Particularly hard hit was the state of Virginia, whose population had fallen from 18 percent to 8 percent of the Union. In the election of 1804 Virginia ranked first in electoral votes; by 1832 it had dropped to third, behind New York and Pennsylvania and barely ahead of Ohio. Between 1817 and 1829 land values in Virginia had been cut in half, and exports were down from $9 million to $3 million. The Old Dominion had not yet paid the full price politically. Although the Virginia dynasty had ended, three Virginians still served in the cabinet or on the Supreme Court: Attorney General William Wirt, Chief Justice John Marshall, and Associate Justice Bushrod Washington. But this favored position was not likely to last. A letter writer in the *Richmond Enquirer* complained accurately that his state was "rapidly declining in the scale of the Union."[17]

Also fearful were planters in South Carolina, who had seen their economic situation worsen during the 1820s. The South Carolinians placed the blame squarely on tariff duties, which had risen steadily since the War of 1812. One of them called tariff protection a system of "fraud, robbery and usurpation," designed to "stretch the purse of the manufacturer" and "impoverish the planter," who would have to pay higher prices for imported goods. The South Carolinians became more disturbed in 1828, when Congress passed the so-called Tariff of Abominations, raising the duties on woolen and cotton cloth and also on raw wool, hemp, and iron.[18]

The tariff strengthened the hand of radicals in South Carolina, who were beginning to call for the right of a state to nullify an unconstitutional act of Congress. At the request of the radicals, South Carolina's leading statesman, John C. Calhoun, prepared an "Exposition," outlining the theory of nullification; but since Calhoun was to be vice-president under Jackson as he had been under Adams, he kept his authorship secret. Even after the Exposition had been edited by a committee, members of the South Carolina legislature considered it so extreme that they refused to endorse it. They did, however, adopt a sharply worded "Protest" against the protective tariff in December 1828 and printed 5,000 copies of the Exposition for public consumption. On reading the two documents, many people wondered if South Carolina was contemplating secession.

Concern over the future of slavery lurked behind some of the opposition to the tariff. In the years following the American Revolution moderates had dominated the debate over slavery in both the North and the South. Northerners were content to abolish slavery in their part of the country, leaving the problem in the hands of the southerners. Many of the latter were so embarrassed by slavery that they followed the lead of Thomas Jefferson in questioning the institution. After the War of 1812 northern and southern reformers united in efforts to colonize free blacks in Africa.

But the climate of opinion began to change. The debate over slavery in Missouri in 1820 was so divisive that Jefferson wrote that the question, "like a fire bell in the night, awakened and filled [him] with terror." In 1824 the Ohio legislature presented resolutions to Congress calling for the emancipation of slaves who would agree to colonize, and in 1827 the American Colonization Society requested federal aid for such deportations. A year later the basis for the abolitionist movement was laid when Benjamin Lundy, the publisher of the Baltimore *Genius of Universal Emancipation*, took a walking tour of the North and became acquainted with Arthur Tappan and William Lloyd Garrison. That same year the free black David Walker moved from North Carolina to Boston and published *Walker's Appeal . . . with a Preamble to the Coloured Citizens of the World*, which called on blacks to revolt.[19]

In the face of these activities southerners began to suspect the entering wedge of abolitionism. Robert J. Turnbull of South Carolina denounced the colonization proposal as a "NEST EGG, placed there by Northern abolitionists," which would become a "Pandora's Box." The South Carolina legislators had this view in mind when they wrote in their Protest that their state was "wholly dependent" on agriculture because of "her climate, situation and peculiar institutions. . . . The valuable products of her soil [were] among the very few that [could] be cultivated with any profit by slave labor." And on Lundy's return to Baltimore, slave traders assaulted him and left him almost dead.[20]

The transformation of the United States in the decade and a half before Jackson became president was pervasive and accelerated so rapidly that Americans reacted emotionally, sometimes violently. The changes offered great opportunity and yet were so alarming that Americans divided over whether to embrace them or resist them. As in their reaction to Andrew Jackson, many Americans responded with enthusiastic approval, but others drew back with fear and anxiety.

These two points of view were apparent in the response to the new materialism. In America work and moneymaking had seemingly become a way of life. The French traveler Michel Chevalier wrote that "from the moment he gets up, the American is at his work, and he is absorbed in it till the hour of sleep. He never permits pleasure to distract him." Americans were swept up in a consumer revolution as luxuries, especially those for the household, flooded the markets. "The women," said another traveler, the Baron de Montlezun, "spend their days shopping; that is their favorite occupation." This frenzied search for well-being, ever since the hallmark of Americans, enthralled those seeking to get ahead, who believed that anything was possible for the individual in this new world. The New York City booster Mordecai Noah boasted in

1817 that Americans enjoyed "more national happiness and individual prosperity than . . . any people on the face of the globe." The Congregational minister Lyman Beecher, however, preached in 1829 that "the greater our prosperity the shorter its duration, and the more tremendous our downfall." Beecher and others like him were afraid that the old republican virtues of the Revolution were being lost.[21]

Americans also found the transportation revolution and the technology that accompanied it a mixed blessing. When Congressman Andrew Beaumont of Pennsylvania learned that the United States patent office had burned and that hundreds of models had been lost, he saw no need to worry. "Build a building as large as the President's House," he boasted, "& the Yankees will fill it with models in two years." But others were not so optimistic. On hearing that the *Pulaski* had sunk with the loss of almost 200 lives, Benjamin Brown French, an assistant clerk in the House of Representatives, lamented, "Something must be done, or steam navigation had better never have been discovered—it will prove, to the human race rather a curse than a blessing." Even Hezekiah Niles had to report soberly that 76 out of 321 steamships on the western waters had been lost because of accidents. Steamboat explosions became so frequent that pessimists used them as a metaphor for the coming destruction of material progress.[22]

As the number of banks and the amount of bank notes multiplied after the War of 1812, the lines were drawn between the entrepreneurs who wanted more banks, more money, and more speculation in land and the more traditional agrarian folk who dreaded the results. The latter seemed vindicated when the Panic of 1819, brought on by speculation in land and mismanagement by the Bank of the United States, caused state banks to fail, sweeping savings and property away from thousands of Americans. The suffering was particularly severe in the West, causing several states to pass relief laws to stay foreclosures and leading to a "Relief War" in Kentucky over the constitutionality of such laws.

The social changes elicited similar divisions. Although many Americans welcomed the new mode of dress, some did not. Two assistant clerks in the House of Representatives were so alarmed that they carried on a serious conversation about it one evening. "The change to the present fashion of pants," said one, "threw this country back a hundred years." Not required to don the old full dress, a man no longer felt "the responsibility of behaving like a gentleman." Other social disagreements were far more divisive: Sabbatarians versus those people who wanted to work and make money on the Sabbath, Anti-Masons versus Masons, abolitionists versus slave owners.[23]

In 1825 two remarkable events emphasized the gap between anxious, backward-looking Americans and those more exuberant and forward-looking. On 8 September the Marquis de Lafayette completed a year-long tour of the United States in which he helped celebrate the fiftieth anniversary of the American Revolution. According to Niles, "No one like Lafayette" had ever before "*re-appeared* in any country." It was almost as though he had returned from the dead. As they poured their adulation on the old general, anxious Americans sought to reassure the world and themselves that they were still committed to the ideals of the Revolution. At the laying of the cornerstone for the Bunker Hill Monument in June 1825, Lafayette sat with the other old soldiers of the Revolution as Daniel Webster advised his listeners to "let the sacred obligations which have devolved on this generation, and on us, sink deep into our hearts." Many Americans feared that their compatriots had forgotten these obligations.[24]

On 4 November 1825, a short time after Lafayette had departed, a line of boats carrying prominent businessmen and government officials reached New York City after completing the long journey from Buffalo along the Erie Canal and down the Hudson River. As the boats paraded into New York Harbor, DeWitt Clinton poured a keg of water from Lake Erie into the Atlantic Ocean, symbolizing the completion of the Erie Canal. By bringing prosperity to upstate New York and by helping to make New York City a metropolis, the canal represented one of the first great triumphs of the economic revolution and encouraged hopes for more.[25]

The obvious clash between these two perceptions of America and its future was reflected in state and national politics. As the market revolution unfolded in the Jackson era, Americans responded in a variety of ways. Almost all Americans retained a common faith in the republican ideals of the Revolution, usually called republicanism—distrust of power, especially when lodged in a central government, fear of corruption, belief in liberty, equal rights, patriotism, and civic virtue—but they disagreed on how these ideals related to the market revolution. At one end of the spectrum were those individuals who yearned for the old agrarian society based on the common good, feared the dangers resulting from economic change, and put the rights of the states over the power of the central government. They tended to look backward, believing that the spread of paper money, banking, speculation, and commercial activity would encourage corruption and lead to more wealth for a privileged few and the loss of republican liberty for the rest. At the other end were those people who stood for a commercial, manufacturing, free-enterprise society based on individual self-interest, embraced economic change, and were nationalistic enough to let the central government foster the economy with tariffs and other benefits. They tended to look forward, believing that the market revolution would lead to more wealth for everyone, thus preserving republican liberty for all. At the risk of oversimplifying, the "agrarian-minded" were at one end of the spectrum, the "commercial-minded" at the other. Americans—especially politicians—took positions somewhere between these philosophical poles.[26]

Since the federal government was becoming increasingly involved in the economy, it was imperative that the American people know where their new president stood between these poles. Would he resist change or embrace it? The continuing battle between these two extremes would have a profound effect on American politics and would do much to shape the politics of Jackson's presidency. But as Webster pointed out in his letter to his brother, no one knew how the new president would act.

Compounding the uncertainty, the country's political system was also undergoing a revolution. Between 1815 and 1830 a dozen states had revised their constitutions or written new ones. In the process they had removed religious qualifications for voting, lowered or eliminated property and taxpayer qualifications, and transferred the choice of presidential electors from the legislatures to the people. Although the people chose the electors in only half of the states in 1812, they chose them in all but two of the twenty-four states in 1828. As a result over a million Americans voted for president in 1828, compared with barely a third of that number in 1824. The changes were far from complete. No women and only a tiny percentage of free blacks could vote, and property and taxpayer qualifications continued in Rhode Island, Connecticut, New Jersey, Virginia, South Carolina, and Louisiana well beyond the 1830s. And the high turnout in 1828 did not indicate a sudden democratic outpouring. In most of the states a higher percentage of the eligible voters had turned out in earlier state elections. Nonetheless, in 1828 almost all white adult males could vote, and over half of them did so in the presidential election. The changes did much to justify the phrase "the age of the common man."[27]

It was also rapidly becoming the age of the new-style politician, the prototype being Martin Van Buren. Adaptable and pragmatic rather than ideological and dogmatic, always ready to compromise, and a superb political organizer, the "Little Magician" rose rapidly to power in the factional politics of New York. His state party, headed by the Albany Regency, was a well-disciplined organization held together by patronage, a party press, and a fierce sense of party loyalty. As Sen. Silas Wright, who had risen through the ranks, later expressed it, "the first man we see *step to the rear,* we *cut down* . . . they *must* not falter or they perish." By 1821 Van Buren and the Albany Regency had gained control of New York.[28]

In winning New York Van Buren had pushed aside DeWitt Clinton, who had dominated the politics of the state for twenty years as governor and as mayor of New York City. The charismatic Clinton—called the "Magnus Apollo"—epitomized the old-style upper-class politician, to whom the people deferred and who ruled through personality and family connections. His uncle, George Clinton, had governed New York during the Revolution and later served as vice-president under Jefferson and Madison. Both George and DeWitt Clinton ran for president. The triumph of the middle-class Van Buren over the aristocratic Clinton vividly demonstrated the shift from the old, stable ideals of the eighteenth century, in which the gentry controlled office, toward the new, unstable political liberalism of participatory democracy. Clinton's sudden death on 11 February 1828 cleared the way even further for Van Buren in New York.

The Albany Regency not only built a new type of state political party, but it also created a new rationale for parties. According to the old ideal, parties, or factions as they were called, endangered the nation by dividing it. James Madison and George Washington had warned about "the mischiefs" and "the baneful effects" of factions in Federalist Number 10 and in the Farewell Address. In the new theory parties were a positive good because they brought the people into government and protected the state against the rising menace of selfish individualism. No longer were parties an abuse of power; they now offered the only means for a free society to check the abuse of power. By seeking to preserve community virtue the new concept continued the ideals of the Revolution, but by assuming that divisions in society were inevitable, the concept accepted the enlightened self-interest that was central to the market revolution.[29]

The new politics and the widespread social and economic changes combined to create a new political party system. After the War of 1812 the collapse of the Federalist party brought an end to the old system of Federalists and Jeffersonian Republicans. In the Era of Good Feelings that followed, party distinctions blurred as the Republicans, now often called National Republicans, adopted many of the Federalist programs. One of these was the Second Bank of the United States, which became so powerful that it was commonly referred to as "the Bank." The seeds of a new party system were sown when Congressman John Randolph of Virginia, Sen. Nathaniel Macon of North Carolina, and other southern Old Republicans began to question the constitutionality of these national

16

programs and to demand a return to Jeffersonian states' rights. They were also alarmed at the efforts of northerners to restrict the spread of slavery during the Missouri Compromise in 1820. After the Panic of 1819 more seeds were sown when western farmers led by Thomas Hart Benton, now a senator from Missouri, and editors Amos Kendall and Francis P. Blair in Kentucky, blamed the Bank for the depression. Their hostility merged with the existing agrarian protest against the spread of the new commercial economy.[30]

Van Buren represented a group of northerners who shared the views of the Old Republicans. Elected to the Senate in 1821, he went to Washington determined to "revive the old contest . . . and build up a party" based on the old Jeffersonian alliance of New York and the South. Allying himself with the Old Republicans, he backed Secretary of the Treasury William Harris Crawford of Georgia for president in 1824 and when Crawford was defeated set about organizing an opposition to President Adams. Starting with his own core of northern and southern Crawford men, he formed an alliance with the followers of John C. Calhoun, who, despite being vice-president, was opposed to Adams, and then drew in Jackson supporters in Pennsylvania and the West. In 1827 he wrote Old Republican Thomas Ritchie, asking him to join in forming a Jackson party. Ritchie, the editor of the *Richmond Enquirer,* was also the head of the Richmond Junto, the leading political organization in Virginia. Van Buren told Ritchie that they would unite "the planters of the South and the plain Republicans of the North." Shrewdly blending modernism and nostalgia, he said that they must combine Jackson's "personal popularity with the portion of old party feeling yet remaining."[31]

In the election of 1828 the Jackson organization was led by two central committees, one in Nashville headed by Jackson's land partner John Overton and another in Washington chaired by banker John P. Van Ness. Van Buren, who was also running for governor of New York, coordinated a caucus of the leading Jacksonians in Congress, while Sen. John H. Eaton of Tennessee, who had run Jackson's campaign in 1824, prepared publicity, answered charges, and traveled about stirring up support for the Old Hero.[32]

The Jacksonians enthusiastically embraced new modes of politicking. They used their congressmen's franking privilege to lower mailing costs and yet still spent almost $1 million during the campaign. They exploited the popularity of Old Hickory by organizing hickory clubs and erecting hickory poles. With the popular vote now decisive, the party press became all important. The Jacksonian editors were an aggressive, rather odd-looking group: the coarse Duff Green of the Washington *United States Telegraph,* the lame Isaac Hill of the *New-Hampshire Patriot,* the thin and tubercular Amos Kendall and the angular Francis P. Blair of the *Argus of Western America* in Frankfort, Kentucky. With their slashing style they spread the stories portraying Adams as a corrupt, spendthrift man and defended Jackson against accusations of adultery and cruelty. In answering the charge that Jackson had murdered a dozen men, Hill replied, "Pshaw! Why don't you tell the whole truth? On the 8th of January, 1815, he murdered in the coldest blood 1,500 British soldiers for merely trying to get into New Orleans for Booty and Beauty." With such sarcastic, often unbridled sallies the Jackson editors outdid their opponents.[33]

Van Buren and Eaton devised a campaign that stressed the candidate while avoiding or glossing over issues. To keep the pugnacious Jackson from speaking out of turn they insisted that he follow the established custom of staying at home. In two unusually blunt letters Van Buren told Jackson not to reply to attacks and not to come to Washington. Jackson followed the advice and contented himself with vague references to reform, promising to remove corrupt officials and to restore republican virtue and the power of the people when he was elected. Meanwhile Eaton portrayed him as a latter-day Cincinnatus, who preferred the Hermitage to the President's House, a popular image that was well summed up by the *Albany Argus*:

> The Soldier Boy
> of the First War of Independence
> The Veteran Hero
> of the Second;
> Now the Honest, Unassuming Farmer of Tennessee.[34]

The wisdom of the strategy became apparent when the results were in. Jackson gained a sweeping victory, winning almost 650,000 votes to barely 500,000 for Adams and carrying every state in the South and the West as well as Pennsylvania and most of New York. He set off for Washington with a solid popular mandate. Many of those Americans voting for Jackson were drawn by the image of the Old Hero, others by the excitement of the Jackson campaign, and some because they hoped to share in the spoils. Jesse Hoyt of the Albany Regency wrote that Van Buren would have to satisfy the "just expectations" of the party faithful.[35]

Contrary to the general impression, issues also played a part in the election. Although specific positions were avoided as much as possible, National Republicans were generally forced to defend Adams's nationalistic commercial program, while a majority of Jackson's supporters preferred a return to states'-rights agrarian policies. Jackson was backed by a broad coalition of groups based on confusing combinations of economic, ideological, sectional, and personal interests. His western supporters, for example, were divided over the Bank. He was originally brought forward for the presidency by a probanking commercial-minded clique in Tennessee led by Eaton and Overton, the richest man in the state. A much larger group of westerners—agrarians like Benton, Kendall, and Blair—backed Jackson because they thought he would fight the Bank and also lower the price of public land.

In the South the nullifiers, including Calhoun, were not sure of Jackson but were willing to give him a chance to show what he could do for their section. Like most southerners they wanted to defend slavery, lower the tariff, put an end to federal internal improvements, and remove the Indians still remaining east of the Mississippi. If he disappointed them, some southerners were prepared to have their states nullify acts of Congress. Old Republican southerners agreed on the goals but not on the means. Unwilling to go as far as the nullifiers, they wanted Jackson and Van Buren to unite the Northeast and Southeast in the name of strict construction of the Constitution.

In the Northeast, Old Republicans such as Van Buren were sympathetic to the South but were less committed to strict construction of the Constitution than their southern allies. Still another Jackson group— the farmers and small manufacturers of the Middle Atlantic states and Ohio—were more in tune with the new nationalistic commercial programs than most Jacksonians. Many of them were drawn to Jackson by the high tariffs put on hemp, wool, and iron products by the Jacksonian Congress in the tariff of 1828. Some of them, including Van Buren's friend Sen. Louis McLane of Delaware, were among the former Federalists supporting Jackson. Within these often overlapping groups, Jacksonians were ideologically inconsistent and often swayed by changing interests. Van Buren, for example, who was ordinarily for states' rights, joined McLane and Eaton in supporting tariff protection in 1828. The Jackson coalition was so unwieldy that Daniel Webster doubted that it would hold together. Jackson's friends, he wrote, had "no common principle—they [were] held together by no common tie," and the general lacked the "character . . . to conduct his measures by his own strength."[36]

Much depended on Jackson. Those who voted for him did so largely because they believed him to be a patriotic man of the people, a simple down-to-earth farmer, with Jeffersonian Republican beliefs. But would he live up to this image? In his earlier years he had soured on much of the new market capitalism as a result of having been almost ruined financially in a land deal when an associate, whose bank notes he had endorsed, went bankrupt. From then on he had resisted banks, bank notes, debts, speculation, and other aspects of the new economy, fearing that they would destroy his ideal of an egalitarian agrarian society. After the Panic of 1819 he had sided with the opponents of the Bank. Yet at the same time he was being supported by probanking politicians in Tennessee. During the 1828 campaign, furthermore, he had seemed to support a commercial economic program by pointing to his Senate votes in favor of the tariff and internal improvements. Jackson also continued to dabble in land speculation and as a plantation owner was realizing handsome profits from the expanding new economy. How these contradictory positions would translate into economic policies was unclear. Van Buren, for one, had reservations about how closely the Old Hero hewed to the Old Republican line. Although Jackson had been "well grounded" in Jeffersonian doctrines, Van Buren feared that they had gathered "rust" during the course of his military campaigns.[37]

Jackson's views on party politics, especially the use of the spoils system, were also uncertain. During the Era of Good Feelings he had opposed the new political ideas, urging Monroe to lay party feeling aside in making political appointments; but on joining forces with Van Buren, he had had second thoughts. "I am no politician," he conceded, "but if I were a politician, I would be a New York politician." Jackson's talk about removing corrupt officials led to anxious speculation. As Webster had pointed out in his letter to his brother, no one knew whether Jackson would try to establish a party government based on the spoils system or *"be President upon his own strength."*[38]

Amid the uncertainty the defeated Adams men viewed the results of the election with horror. James Heaton of Ohio deplored the "feverish excitement . . . produced by designing and dishonest men" that had led the people "into error." Once he had assumed that the government was so balanced that it could not be thrown "out of gear"; now he feared for the "permanent existence" of the United States. Some supporters of Adams such as Thurlow Weed of New York were already emulating the Jackson men, but on the whole the Adams party was reluctant to adopt the new methods. In the area of political strategy, it was less forward-looking than the Jackson party.[39]

Even with the new political techniques, the new national party system that Van Buren was seeking had barely begun to emerge. The Jackson and Adams organizations would grow in time into the Democratic and Whig parties, forming the second American party system, but that development was still several years away. Modern political parties with well-organized constituencies in all the states, nominating and electing members of Congress and holding national conventions to nominate a president, did not exist. In 1828 the terms "Democratic" and "Whig" were not in use, as both sides considered themselves Republicans. Those individuals who supported Jackson were called the "Jackson party," or "Democratic Republicans," or "Jacksonians"; those for Adams were known as the "Adams party," or "Republicans," or, increasingly, "National Republicans." To confuse the issue even more, many voters considered themselves Clay men or Calhoun men. Reacting to the fluid political situation, Hezekiah Niles commented, "We are pretty soon, it seems, to have another great political controversy, though the names of the persons on whom parties are to be rallied are not yet determined."[40]

Confusion loomed in Washington, for Jackson was about to take over an executive branch of government that was dominated by Adams men. In addition, the Supreme Court was filled with justices appointed by Jackson's predecessors. Congress was hard to gauge. In theory Jacksonians would have majorities in both houses, but the numbers were not reliable because in areas where Jackson was popular candidates sometimes ran as Jackson men to get elected but could not be counted on in Congress.[41]

Although the president-elect seemed to be more of an agrarian Old Republican than a commercial-minded nationalist in 1829, neither Daniel Webster nor anyone else could tell which way the wind would blow once Jackson took office. Nor could they be sure whether he would act the part of ruffian or hero. Yet clearly he would have to take positions on the two most important developments of the 1820s, the market revolution and the new politics. Thus the American people looked ahead to the presidency of Andrew Jackson with a mixture of enthusiasm and anxiety.

2

AN UNCERTAIN PRESIDENT

As Jackson's steamboat made its way up the Ohio River, throngs gathered to greet him at every stop. There was no difficulty picking out the Old Hero. The shock of gray, almost white, hair, the tall, erect carriage, the worn body made him easily identifiable even from afar. Up close the deep brow, the strong cheekbones, the firm mouth, and the deep-set blue eyes never failed to convey an aura of strength. Frances Trollope caught a glimpse of him when he went ashore at Cincinnati. "He wore his grey hair carelessly, but not ungracefully arranged," she wrote, "and, in spite of his harsh gaunt features looks like a gentleman and a scholar." Although Jackson responded to the crowds, the journey never became a triumphal procession; absorbed in his grief, he allowed no formal celebrations.[1]

Waiting for Jackson in Washington was Sen. John H. Eaton. After serving briefly in the War of 1812, Eaton had returned to Tennessee, where he developed a close, almost filial, relationship with Jackson, publishing his biography and marrying one of his wards. The marriage and the subsequent death of his wife made him a wealthy man. Appointed to the Senate in 1818, he immediately won Jackson's gratitude by defending him against charges of improper behavior in invading Florida. Jackson's debt mounted as Eaton ran his campaigns in 1824 and 1828. With eleven years in the Senate, the good-looking, rather dashing Eaton was second only to Benjamin Ruggles of Ohio in seniority. When Eaton first came to Washington, he roomed at the boardinghouse of William O'Neale and soon started a long affair with O'Neale's daughter Margaret

O'Neale Timberlake, whose husband, a navy purser, was often at sea. Gossip about the two turned ugly in 1828 when Timberlake died abroad— some said he slashed his own throat because of Peggy's behavior. Despite the talk, however, Eaton married Peggy Timberlake on New Year's Day 1829. Now he was awaiting Jackson's arrival apprehensively, for his marriage was being roundly criticized and ridiculed.

Eaton was also concerned about the political "maneuvering" going on within the coalition, especially the rivalry between Calhoun and Van Buren over which man would become the president's heir apparent. Congressman James Buchanan of Pennsylvania had pointedly remarked: "Disguise it as we may, the friends of Van Buren and those of Calhoun are becoming very jealous of each other." The two rivals, both forty-six, were poles apart in appearance and in personality. Van Buren, the consummate politician who had grown up in New York politics, was plump and short, pleasant-looking but far from handsome. Bland and suave, he had gently and cautiously maneuvered his way toward the top, making few enemies in the process. Calhoun, on the other hand, a man of brilliant intellect and sober righteousness who had grown up amid the traditions of South Carolina, was trim and tall, with brown hair and rugged features that made him decidedly handsome. A driven, humorless man, he too had worked his way forward, believing that he deserved to become president, and had made many enemies in the process. Unlike Jackson, neither man was likely to stir the emotions of the people or to be mastered by his own emotions.[2]

When Jackson reached Pennsylvania, Calhoun's followers were prepared to give him a military escort through the state, but friends of Van Buren, wary of the vice-president, blocked the proposal. The Calhoun men also planned a celebration to greet Jackson when he arrived in Washington. Eaton, who favored Van Buren, feared that any festivities would hurt the Little Magician, who was away in New York carrying out his recently assumed duties as governor, while Calhoun was on hand and could take part. Eaton also knew that the grieving Jackson wanted nothing to be made of his arrival. For these reasons he sent a carriage to Rockville, Maryland, that brought Jackson into the capital on 11 February with no fanfare. One witness described "a plain carriage drawn by two horses followed by a single black servant, & preceded by perhaps 10 horsemen who had perhaps joined it by accident on the road."[3]

Jackson arrived in a Washington that had not escaped the economic revolution. In the years since the government had moved to the city in 1800 the population had grown from 3,000 to 19,000, making Washington the ninth largest city in the United States. Since the War of 1812 the road north to Baltimore had been much improved, and to the south the three bridges across the Potomac, burned by the British in 1814, had been rebuilt; just within the year the Chesapeake and Ohio Canal and the Baltimore and Ohio Railroad had been started, promising even better transportation in the future. Five banks, one college, and at least half-a-dozen schools attested to the vigor of the city. Jackson could count on the close scrutiny of three major newspapers, the *Daily National Intelligencer* and the *National Journal*, both of which had supported Adams, and his own party organ, the *United States Telegraph*.

Yet even with its growth, the city was still largely a cluster of buildings on either side of Pennsylvania Avenue between Capitol Hill and the President's House, hemmed in by a steep ridge to the north and a noisome canal and swamp to the south. Since the streets were neither paved nor lighted, citizens moving about the city faced the unpleasantness of a sea of mud or a cloud of dust by day and the added danger of darkness and thieves at night. Fine homes were beginning to appear, especially near the President's House, but members of Congress most often roomed and ate in the many boardinghouses that had sprung up on Capitol Hill and along Pennsylvania Avenue. Visitors who could afford it patronized three hotels on the avenue. On his arrival Jackson moved into the largest and newest of these, John Gadsby's National Hotel, four stories high, which boasted 200 rooms and had been open barely a year.[4]

The major task facing the new president was to replace the bitterness and the uncertainty of the campaign with unity and order. He needed to brush aside his own gloom and uncertainty as well as the uneasiness enveloping the capital by showing magnanimity toward his opponents, by taking firm control of the coalition that had elected him, and by clarifying his position on the market revolution and the new concept of political parties. Jackson had won a great popular mandate and could afford to be magnanimous. He had ample time in which to get started since Congress would not reconvene until early December. He was also fortunate in not having a foreign-policy crisis awaiting him, as had been the lot of his predecessors John Adams and James Madison, or a financial panic or a war, which would plague his successors Martin Van Buren and Abraham Lincoln.

His task, however, was daunting, for Jackson, the first president since Jefferson to take over after a change of parties, was also an outsider in Washington. Jackson's brief tenure in the Congress had done little to make him comfortable in the capital. While a senator in 1823 he had complained to Rachel that there was "nothing done here but vissitting [*sic*] and *carding each other.*" A few months after arriving in Washington in 1829 he felt the same way, telling his friend Samuel Swartwout of New

York, *"Our society wants purging here."* Washington society, in turn, expected the worst from the new president, with his reputation as a military man and his promise to clean out the government.[5]

Jackson had an immediate chance to reduce the political bitterness by following the usual protocol and making a courtesy call on President Adams. Since this was the first time that a succeeding president had not been in Washington when elected, the matter of a courtesy call took on special significance. But Jackson continued to blame Adams for Rachel's treatment during the campaign and was too angry to make the call. Even after Adams tried to restore civility by sending Jackson a friendly message about the transition, the president-elect would not budge. When it finally became clear that Jackson would not call, Adams decided to retaliate by refusing to attend the inauguration. Twenty-eight years earlier, in somewhat different circumstances, his father had made the same decision.

During the next nine months Jackson had many opportunities to assert control over his coalition—choosing his advisers and the cabinet, delivering his inaugural address, responding to the crisis that had arisen over Eaton's marriage, and making his appointments to federal offices. In choosing his advisers Jackson acted the part of an outsider by depending on his Tennessee friends and relatives. Living with him in the President's House would be Andrew J. Donelson and his wife Emily, who with their two-year-old son had accompanied him from Tennessee. Andrew, who was Rachel's nephew and another of Jackson's wards, had graduated from West Point and had served under Jackson in the Florida War before becoming his private secretary. He would continue in that capacity while Jackson was president, though officially he was a secretary in the General Land Office. Emily, who was her husband's first cousin, was to act as the president's hostess. The young Donelsons, both of whom were under thirty, brought a warmth and liveliness to the President's House that Jackson craved. A third Tennessean, Jackson's former quartermaster Maj. William B. Lewis, was given the job of second auditor of the Treasury and asked to serve as a presidential adviser. The broadshouldered Lewis, a member of the original Jackson clique and at forty-four twice a widower, would also move into the President's House. The Donelsons would find it hard to work in harmony with Lewis, who represented a rival faction in Tennessee. Emily Donelson, for example, later derided him as nothing but a "sycophant," who had moved in with the president to "save himself all expense."[6]

Jackson rewarded another group of his western followers by appointing Amos Kendall of Kentucky as an adviser and making him fourth auditor of the Treasury. After growing up in Massachusetts and graduating from Dartmouth, Kendall moved to Kentucky, where he came under the influence of Henry Clay, first as a tutor for Clay's children and then as editor of the *Argus of Western America*. Taking the same antibanking position as Jackson during the Panic of 1819, he eventually broke with Clay and helped Jackson carry Kentucky in 1828. Taciturn and conscientious, the thirty-nine-year-old Kendall was the antithesis of the voluble, easygoing Lewis. When the two were asked to choose between the positions of second and fourth auditor of the Treasury, Lewis said bluntly that he wanted the job with the least work while the hardworking Kendall volunteered for the one with the most work. Each got his wish.[7]

With Eaton in the Senate, Calhoun continuing as vice-president, and Kendall soon to be a presidential adviser, three of the groups making up the coalition were well represented in Washington. Though not on hand himself, the Old Republican Van Buren could count on the presence in the capital of James A. Hamilton of New York, the son of Alexander Hamilton. One of the Middle Atlantic nationalists, Sen. Louis McLane, was also on hand and was being mentioned for the cabinet.

Jackson, however, bypassed all but one of these men in selecting his cabinet, relying on Eaton, who had the experience in Washington that the president-elect lacked, as well as on two other Tennesseans, Lewis and Sen. Hugh Lawson White. Jackson pointedly ignored both Van Buren and Calhoun, neither of whom had been early Jackson men. Determined to have a close friend in the cabinet in whom he could confide, he decided to make one of the two Tennessee senators his secretary of war. Of the two, White, who came from eastern Tennessee, had the better legal mind and was more highly respected, but Eaton was closer to Jackson. When Jackson left the decision up to the two men, Eaton outmaneuvered White. In a cleverly composed letter to White on 23 February, Eaton suggested, without much evidence, that Jackson preferred him, and White bowed out. Eaton brought a strong voice for the Bank, tariff protection, and Indian removal to the cabinet.[8]

In picking his postmaster general Jackson first decided to retain the incumbent, Calhoun's friend John McLean of Ohio, who had deserted Adams and had supported Jackson in the election. McLean agreed to continue in his office until he suddenly realized that he would be expected to turn out a number of his friends to make way for Jacksonians. He then asked to be removed from the cabinet, and Jackson, perhaps interested in ridding himself of a western political rival, nominated him for a seat that had recently opened on the Supreme Court. To replace McLean, Jackson appointed Kendall's friend William T. Barry, once dean of the law school at Transylvania University in Kentucky, who had been promised the seat on the Supreme Court. Barry, who had been narrowly defeated for governor of Kentucky in 1828, had led the Relief party in the state after the Panic of 1819. Despite his impressive credentials, he had not shown much administrative ability in four years as lieutenant governor. One Kentuckian who knew him well said that he was "not fit for any station which require[d] great intellectual force or moral firmness." Jackson, however, was drawn to Barry, who had gone west across the mountains at an early age just as he had. He also knew that Barry and Kendall had done yeomen's service in delivering Kentucky's electoral votes. So Barry had been picked for the Supreme Court seat and then good-naturedly agreed to change places with McLean.[9]

In selecting the secretaries of state and Treasury Jackson rewarded the northern elements in his coalition. It came as no surprise that he offered the first post to Van Buren, for the Little Magician's role in the campaign as well as the importance of New York made his selection almost inevitable. After some delay, he accepted—with the understanding that James A. Hamilton would serve as interim secretary for a few weeks while Van Buren wound up his affairs as governor. Though a professed Old Republican, Van Buren was too pragmatic to be bound by ideology. For secretary of the Treasury Jackson turned to Pennsylvania, where he had a choice between Congressman Samuel D. Ingham and former congressman Henry Baldwin. A Yale graduate and legal scholar, Baldwin was better educated than Ingham, who had been forced to go to work at the age of fourteen. Hamilton called Ingham "not fitted" to be secretary, and Jackson's biographer James Parton was later to remark sarcastically that Ingham had not been a "speaking member" of Congress. Although Jackson was personally attracted to Baldwin, who had once fought a duel, he had political reasons to choose Ingham, who had worked hard during the campaign and was more moderate on the tariff than the protectionist Baldwin. In the end Jackson bowed to pressure from the Pennsylvania congressional delegation, which insisted on Ingham. Although far from being a nullifier, Ingham was the one solid Calhoun man in the cabinet.[10]

Jackson's strong support in the South made it essential that the remaining two places go to southerners. Responding to that pressure, he appointed two socially prominent plantation owners, Sen. John Branch of North Carolina as secretary of the navy and Sen. John M. Berrien of Georgia as attorney general. Although neither was especially well qualified for his position, they were both popular figures with long careers in their home states. Branch was also a close friend of Eaton and Jackson, and Berrien was backed by Lewis and was an advocate of Indian removal. Both men, furthermore, had once had ties with the Crawford wing of the coalition. Supporters of states' rights, slavery, and low tariffs, they were good representatives of the South and would be closer to Calhoun than to Van Buren.[11]

Jackson had done a reasonable job of balancing the varied interests of his coalition in his cabinet. With members chosen from six different states representing almost all sections of the country, he had secured good geographic balance. Only New England and the Northwest had been overlooked. By naming one probanking nationalist, Eaton, a moderate Pennsylvania nationalist, Ingham, a western agrarian, Barry, and three states' righters, Van Buren, Branch, and Berrien, he had provided ideological balance as well. Jackson furthermore saw to it that neither Van Buren nor Calhoun dominated the cabinet by naming only one Calhoun man, Ingham, and only one Van Buren man, Eaton, other than the Little Magician himself. Since none of the new cabinet officers except Van Buren was a strong political figure, Jackson avoided the situation that had plagued Monroe, whose ambitious cabinet officers elbowed each other to become the next president.

Even with these virtues, the new cabinet received little approval. The outpouring of criticism that greeted the announcement of the cabinet showed the impossibility of satisfying all elements of the coalition. The Virginians were particularly disturbed because they saw their fears of losing influence in the government coming true. They had hoped to have Sen. Littleton W. Tazewell appointed secretary of state, but Jackson rebuffed them, saying that Virginia had held more than its share of offices in the past. The failure of Jackson to appoint a Virginian and the death of Justice Bushrod Washington later in the year left John Marshall as the only Virginian in the cabinet or on the Supreme Court. The Old Republicans in Virginia were incensed by the lack of representation. Thomas Ritchie wrote that the cabinet was not the sort that "dazzles and overcomes its enemies," and almost two months after the cabinet had been announced, the "uproar" had not subsided in the Old Dominion.[12]

Similar discontent surfaced among the nullifiers of South Carolina. When they had tried to influence Jackson, they had been told that they were too extreme on the tariff. And when Calhoun himself came in to lobby, the new president brought him up short by declaring that his rival Van Buren must first be consulted. After the announcement, one South Carolinian "denounced" the new cabinet, and another predicted that Van Buren would be "cut[ting his] throat" if he joined such a weak group.[13]

Nor was Van Buren pleased. Though delighted to be secretary of state, he was distressed that none of his special friends—particularly Louis McLane—had been appointed. He had also wanted someone from Virginia because of his ties with Old Republicans in that state. Van Buren's supporters were even more disappointed, one of them—Elias Kent Kane of Illinois—wondering whether Calhoun had helped pick the cabinet. While on his way to join the administration in mid-March, Van Buren heard nothing but tales of woe. He could not even escape by going to bed, for in New York City Sen. Levi Woodbury of New Hampshire came up to his hotel room to complain that no one from New England had been chosen. In Philadelphia Sen. Edward Livingston of Louisiana voiced fears that the foreign diplomats would hold the new administration in "contempt," and at New Castle, Delaware, Van Buren escaped McLane's "excited harangue" only by boarding the stagecoach. Sen. Samuel Smith in Baltimore was no less pessimistic. Not surprisingly, Van Buren was sick and exhausted when he arrived in Washington.[14]

Even in Tennessee there was dissatisfaction. Jackson's one-sided victory in his home state in 1828 only served to mask a long-standing rivalry between one faction led by John Overton, which had long supported Jackson, and another led by Andrew Erwin and former governor William Carroll. The Erwin faction resented that Eaton and Lewis of the Overton group had had so much influence in selecting the cabinet. Carroll complained that Jackson had offered him nothing, even though they had "fought side by side," and that Eaton and Lewis were getting the "fat offices." Neither of the two advisers was popular among Tennessee politicians, who considered them simply cronies of the president. In the week before the cabinet was officially announced, members of the Tennessee congressional delegation came to Jackson to protest his appointments, especially that of Eaton. They had no success.[15]

Although he could not have been expected to please everyone, Jackson still deserved some of the criticism. By listening only to his Tennessee advisers and rejecting the advice of other supporters, he showed his parochialism and did little to take control of his coalition. He ignored several important geographic segments and went out of his way to antagonize Old Republicans in Virginia and nullifiers in South Carolina. Moreover, by appointing five members of Congress, Jackson overlooked other backgrounds, such as commerce and journalism, that would have made his cabinet less insular. Madison, Monroe, and John Quincy Adams had averaged only one appointment from Congress. Jackson had also appointed a weak cabinet. The opposition's claims that it was "the Millennium of Minnows" or "a compound of embicility [sic], tyranny and hypocrisy" were too harsh, but as a body it was far inferior to previous cabinets. It included only one man of stature—Van Buren—compared with four such men under Monroe—Adams, Calhoun, Crawford, and William Wirt—and three under Adams—Clay, Wirt, and Richard Rush. All of these men ran for president—except Rush, who ran for vice-president. Jackson could easily have appointed a more talented cabinet.[16]

By picking such mediocre men in such a parochial way Jackson underscored his position as an outsider and lent credence to the charges of his opponents. During the process he also showed none of the magnanimity that the situation required, and at times he even acted vindictively. For example, to some observers it appeared that he had insisted on cabinet members who shared his antipathy for Clay. Five of the six appointees satisfied this test. Eaton was the source of the "bargain and corruption" charge against Clay, and on the basis of the charge Branch and Berrien had voted against Clay in the Senate when he was nominated for secretary of state. Barry deserted Clay because of the charge and ran as an anti-Clay candidate for governor of Kentucky, and Ingham spread the charge wholesale during the presidential election. The only cabinet member not conspicuously hostile to Clay was the only strong one—Van Buren.[17]

In his occasional comments while selecting the cabinet Jackson gave no evidence that he was interested in healing wounds or in seeking unity. Instead he appeared defensive and unsure. He told James A. Hamilton, for example, that he owed the Virginians nothing. In a similar vein he remarked that he planned to appoint someone from North Carolina because the Tarheel State had never had a cabinet member and deserved the honor more than its "more showy neighbors," presumably Virginia and South Carolina. Jackson also revealed great anxiety when Van Buren hesitated over whether to give up his governorship. On 23 February, four days after Jackson had settled on the membership of the cabinet, he still had not heard from Albany and showed his anxiety by asking Hamilton several times if Van Buren would accept.[18]

Furthermore, Jackson did not exercise much control over his subordinates while he was putting together his cabinet. First, he gave too much power to the often sloppy Lewis and Eaton. In writing Eaton on one occasion, Van Buren was so worried about his friend's "habitual carelessness" that he arranged to have one of his sons draw up the letter so that the handwriting would not show that it was from Van Buren himself. He confessed that he was afraid that Eaton might leave the letter in "one of the Committee rooms folded up in a petition in behalf of some good fellow." Jackson let Eaton and White decide on their own which of them should be secretary of war and stood by while Eaton outwitted White. Next, he let Eaton and Lewis select Branch and Berrien, neither of whom was well qualified. He also surrendered control by letting the Pennsylvania delegation dictate the choice of Ingham. In considering the reappointment of John McLean to the Post Office he was asking for trouble; already disloyal to Adams, the ambitious McLean would probably have been disloyal to Jackson. The general made matters worse by permitting McLean to change positions with the incompetent Barry.[19]

While the cabinet was being picked, people were pouring into Washington, transforming it temporarily from a hostile community braced for an outsider president into the people's capital. Never before had the young nation witnessed such a spectacle as the scene on 4 March 1829. Inaugurations—even Washington's and Jefferson's first—had been rather tame events. After Jefferson's was over, for example, there was little celebration; the new president had merely returned inconspicuously to his boardinghouse for supper. But this time the city was overrun by tens of thousands. Webster reported in amazement: "I never saw any thing like it before. Persons have come 500 miles to see Genl Jackson; & they really seem to think that the country is rescued from some dreadful danger." The hordes of visitors placed an enormous burden on a community that had a population of less than 20,000. Boardinghouse owners charged visitors who could find a space twenty dollars a week, three times the going rate. Those less fortunate slept where they could, even "on the floors in tap rooms." Firewood, already expensive because of a cold winter, sold for twelve dollars a cord, eggs for eighty cents a dozen.[20]

Inauguration day dawned warm and sunny, even though the Potomac remained frozen over. At 11:00 A.M. a contingent of soldiers from the Revolution and the Battle of New Orleans met Jackson in front of the National Hotel to escort him on foot to the Capitol. Margaret Bayard Smith, no democrat herself, caught the democratic emotions of the day as she stood on the south terrace of the Capitol and strained to catch a glimpse of the Old Hero making his way up Pennsylvania Avenue. "Even from a distance," she recalled, "he could be discerned from those who accompanied him, for he only was uncovered (the Servant in presence of his Sovereign, the People)." "Ah," exclaimed others, more swept up in the spirit of the day than she, "there is the old man and his gray hair, there is the old veteran, there is Jackson." After forcing his way through the crowds and into the Capitol, Jackson went to the Senate chamber to see the new senators sworn in. Here the caustic publisher Anne Royall also caught the democratic spirit of the occasion describing Jackson in his severe black suit as the plainest dressed man in the room.[21]

In deference to the people the inauguration, for the first time, was held outdoors on the east portico of the Capitol, which until 1981 became the traditional site for these ceremonies. When Jackson finally appeared on the portico at noon, a great shout went up from the crowd and all heads were instantly uncovered. Aware of his role, Jackson then thrilled the 20,000 spectators by bowing before taking his seat—the servant bowing before his sovereigns.

In his inaugural address Jackson failed to take advantage of the democratic setting. He made no call for majority rule, rotation in office, or other democratic changes. He did not tell the people his position on the market revolution or try to unite them behind his administration. Making no effort to mend wounds, he offered no invocations to unity such as Jefferson's call for Americans to "unite with one heart and one mind" or his claim that "we are all Republicans, we are all Federalists."[22]

Instead Jackson gave a defensive address designed to reassure his critics and hold together his coalition. Prepared originally at the Hermitage by Overton, Lewis, and his other Tennessee advisers, it bore their cautious, conservative imprint. To the Old Republicans he offered economy in government and the end of the national debt. For those people who feared his martial ways, he promised not to enlarge the military establishment. To attract his more nationalistic followers he advocated "internal improvements and the diffusion of knowledge," while calling for equal treatment to "agriculture, commerce, and manufactures." The only threatening part of his address came when he repeated his campaign pledge to devote himself to "the task of reform," which would require "the correction of those abuses" that had corrupted the "freedom of elections" and had placed "power in unfaithful or incompetent hands."[23]

Because Jackson's weak voice was inaudible in the outdoors few people actually heard the address, but those who read it seemed to like it. The *London Morning Post*, for example, was pleased with the president's "moderation and wisdom" in promising "to preserve peace and to cultivate friendship" with foreign nations. The Old Republican *Richmond Enquirer* praised the reference to economy but was unhappy about the support for internal improvements. Even the disappointed South Carolinian, James Hamilton, Jr., called the speech "chaste, patriotic, sententious, and dignified" and, perceptively, one that "expose[d] no weak flanks." The Washington bureaucracy, however, could have found no comfort in his reference to "reform."[24]

After Jackson had finished his address and received the oath of office, he bowed once more to the people. "Had the spectacle closed here," wrote Margaret Bayard Smith, "even Europeans must have acknowledged that a free people . . . was majesty," but the crowd could no longer be contained. They broke through the rope separating them from the president, forcing him to flee back into the Capitol. "The *Majesty of the People* had disappeared," Smith wrote primly, replaced by "a rabble, a mob." Jackson too was transformed; he mounted a handsome white charger and assumed once again the role of military hero. The crowd followed him back to the President's House, where they stormed through the building, soiling carpets and sofas and destroying several thousand dollars worth of cut glass and china. Men and women received bloody noses as they fought for the refreshments and had to be lured from the house by tubs of punch placed on the lawns. The president, almost crushed by the mob, escaped out the back way. Already alarmed by the call for reform, the Washington establishment saw its worst fears confirmed by the wanton destruction of property.[25]

Immediately after the people had departed, Jackson was thrust back into his role as outsider when the Peggy Eaton affair brought him face to face with Washington society. As soon as the Eatons had married, unpleasant stories had begun to multiply. Brig. Gen. Richard K. Call, once a Jackson aide, admitted that he had propositioned Peggy while he was boarding at O'Neale's. The Reverend John N. Campbell, minister of the Presbyterian church that the president attended, had heard from a doctor who had since died that Mrs. Timberlake had suffered a miscarriage in 1821 after Timberlake had been away for a year. It was also asserted that Major Eaton and Mrs. Timberlake had registered at a hotel in New York as man and wife.[26]

The marriage and the stories quickly became political issues. When the Tennessee congressmen had come to protest Eaton's appointment to the cabinet, they had been particularly critical of the marriage. Then on inauguration day the wives of Calhoun, Branch, Ingham, and other administration officials snubbed Peggy Eaton at the inauguration and at the ball in the evening. A few days later when the Eatons paid a social call on the Calhouns, Floride Calhoun received them politely but told her husband the next day that she had "determined not to return Mrs. Eaton's visit." The matter struck close to the President's House, for hostess Emily Donelson also refused to call upon the Eatons. The situation worsened when John Eaton asked Mrs. Donelson to reconsider, remarking in a patronizing fashion that she was "young and uninformed."[27]

Jackson became fully aware of the rumors when he received a letter from the Reverend Ezra Stiles Ely in Philadelphia, written on 18 March. The busybody Ely, who had already told Jackson not to travel on the Sabbath, had been in Washington for the inauguration but had apparently not been willing to confront the Old Hero at that time. In the letter Ely outlined the charges against the Eatons and even suggested that Rachel Jackson had disapproved of Peggy.[28]

In responding to these charges Jackson personalized the entire affair. He reproved Ely for not speaking to him "personally," saying he would have told the clergyman about the "foulest and basest means" his opponents were using to attack Eaton. Furious that Rachel had been "introduced into this affair," Jackson emphatically denied that she had disapproved of Mrs. Timberlake. A Mason himself, the president could not believe that Eaton would have had "criminal intercourse" with a fellow-Mason's wife. If Mrs. Timberlake had been registered as Mrs. Eaton it was only because the hotelkeeper had made a mistake. He concluded by reminding Ely that they should "guard virtuous female character with vestal vigilance."[29]

Jackson took the affair so personally partly because he had boarded at O'Neale's himself and was well acquainted with everyone involved. When Eaton had decided to marry Peggy after Timberlake's death, Jackson had naively urged him to go ahead in order to put a halt to the gossip. The parallels between the criticism of the Eatons and the attacks on himself and Rachel during the campaign were obvious. Insisting that his opponents were trying to intimidate him into removing Eaton from the cabinet, he vowed that he "would sink with honor to [his] grave before [he] would abandon" his friend. Jackson could not let the matter rest. He could not resist discussing it in scores of letters to friends such as John Overton, Samuel Swartwout, and Gen. John Coffee. Official business took a back seat as the president dispatched agents to check on stories and kept Lewis busy collecting information defending the Eatons.[30]

On 1 September Campbell finally summoned sufficient courage to call on the president and reveal that he was the source of the story about the miscarriage. After a long, angry exchange Jackson concluded that if he could prove that Timberlake had been in Washington during the year 1821 Mrs. Eaton would be exonerated. He and Lewis rushed to the Eatons' quarters the next day to examine Timberlake's books, which seemed to prove that he had been in Washington that entire year. Armed with that information, Jackson called a cabinet meeting for the evening of 10 September, which was attended by Ely, Campbell, Lewis, Donelson, and all members of the cabinet except Eaton. The president refuted the charges, stressing that Timberlake had been in Washington in 1821, and when Campbell changed the date of the miscarriage to 1826, shouted him down. Ely, who had been to New York for his own investigation, conceded that he had found nothing to convict Major Eaton, only to have Jackson interrupt that Mrs. Eaton was not guilty either. "She is," he declared to the stunned cabinet, "chaste as a virgin!" Walking home that evening, Ingham and Van Buren took opposing sides on the affair but agreed that nothing had been settled.[31]

During the winter of 1829–30 while Congress was in session, the

"Eaton malaria," as Van Buren dubbed it, became even more virulent, and neither side showed any inclination to back down. The strong-minded Mrs. Eaton acted so belligerently that she became known as Bellona, the goddess of war. Jackson made his position clear by resigning from the Reverend Mr. Campbell's church. Then, in an effort to reduce the hard feelings, he and Van Buren escorted two of Mrs. Eaton's critics, Mrs. Ingham and Emily Donelson, to the presidential dinner that opened the social season, but the coldness of the cabinet wives continued. Soon thereafter Van Buren invited the principals to two parties of his own and talked his bachelor diplomat friends Sir Charles R. Vaughan of England and Baron Paul Krudener of Russia into hosting two others. But the parties failed to end the controversy. None of the cabinet wives attended either of Van Buren's dinners, and Mrs. Eaton caused a scene at one after colliding with the wife of Gen. Alexander Macomb. The wife of Chevalier Huygens of the Netherlands created an incident herself by leaving Baron Krudener's dinner abruptly when she found herself seated next to Mrs. Eaton.[32]

Jackson was now so disturbed that he drew up a stern ultimatum for his wayward cabinet members. If any of them, he declared, had "entered into the combination charged, to drive major Eaton from my cabinet," that person had committed "an indignity and insult" against the president and "had better withdraw" from the cabinet. His listeners denied any part in a conspiracy, but the ostracism of Mrs. Eaton continued. By June 1830 her determination had begun to weaken, and she had retreated so far from society that she even turned down an invitation from the president. Although the Eaton affair gradually faded, it still dragged on for another year.[33]

During the long struggle the members of the president's official family had divided over the Eatons in roughly the same way that they were reacting to Van Buren. The Calhouns, Inghams, Branches, Donelsons, and the widower John M. Berrien and his daughter refused to have anything to do with the Eatons. John Quincy Adams called them the "moral party." Of this group only Ingham was supporting Calhoun, but they were all suspicious of Van Buren. Opposing them was the "frail sisterhood," consisting of Van Buren, Eaton, Lewis, Barry, and Kendall. Of this group Barry and Kendall, especially the latter, were less committed to Van Buren than the others, but they were all against Calhoun. Barry, who had lived with the Eatons when he had first arrived, was grateful to Peggy for having nursed his son through a serious illness and to John for having put his "servants, carriage and horses" at Barry's command. Van Buren was Eaton's political friend and as a widower had no one to turn him against Peggy. Lewis, who was also a widower and who had defended the Jacksons against similar charges in the election campaign, found it easy to do the same for the Eatons. The puritanical Kendall admitted that Peggy was "too forward" but said that the other rumors were lies.[34]

With this sort of division, participants and observers naturally interpreted the Eaton affair in political terms. Jackson first accused his old political opponent Henry Clay of creating the squabble in order to destroy his administration, but by the end of 1829 he was blaming Calhoun. Jackson's change in attitude coincided with his increased admiration for Van Buren. With the Calhouns opposing Peggy Eaton and Van Buren defending her, the secretary of state had risen rapidly in Jackson's estimation. The sharp-eyed Margaret Bayard Smith noted that Van Buren had become the "constant riding, walking and visiting companion" of the president. Suffering from badly swollen legs and fearful that he might soon die, Jackson wrote a careful letter to John Overton on 31 December identifying the New Yorker as his successor. Van Buren, he wrote, was "every thing that I could desire him to be . . . frank open, candid, and manly." Jackson accused Calhoun, on the other hand, of orchestrating a conspiracy against him and Van Buren. Barry agreed, saying that Calhoun's friends were trying to drive Eaton out of the cabinet because he was "more friendly to Mr. Van Buren than to Mr. Calhoun."[35]

Critics of Van Buren, however, tended to blame him for the affair. James Parton firmly established this view when he wrote in 1860 that "the political history of the United States, for the last thirty years, date[d] from the moment when the soft hand of Mr. Van Buren touched Mrs. Eaton's knocker." The author Henry Wikoff, who visited Washington soon after the Eaton affair, also blamed it on the Little Magician. The president, he wrote, had fallen "under the influence of [the] dextrous intriguer" Van Buren.[36]

There is no question that, politically, the "Eaton malaria" was a godsend for Van Buren. It not only helped turn Jackson against Calhoun, but it also weakened the position of the Tennesseans Eaton and Donelson. Yet to say that Van Buren or Calhoun engineered the affair in order to get rid of the other is going too far. The cautious Van Buren was never that bold, and political conspiracies were not the proud Calhoun's style. Van Buren was, however, inordinately clever at turning events to his own advantage, and the Calhouns were trapped in the affair by their eminence in Washington society. Van Buren came out the winner.

Other observers were inclined to see the affair as a battle between entrenched Washington social leaders and Jacksonian outsiders, who considered Washington society immoral. Like Jackson, Kendall too thought Washington needed reforming. When he came to the city in winter 1829, he wrote his wife that if there was "more extravagance, folly, and corruption anywhere in the world than in this city," he did not wish to see it. Washingtonians, on the other hand, looked down upon and feared the sometimes rough Jacksonians who had descended upon them.[37]

William T. Barry was the first to connect the Eaton affair with a social clash in the capital. There was in Washington, he wrote, "an aristocracy . . . claiming preference for birth or wealth." When Mrs. Eaton, "the daughter of a Tavern-keeper . . . , moved into the fashionable world," this "touched the pride of the self-constituted great." Barry was close to the mark. Jackson would have been furious if he had overheard Margaret Bayard Smith's friends when they first learned of the marriage between Mrs. Timberlake and Major Eaton. Peggy, they said, was not of "an inspiring character" and would make "a suitable lady in waiting" for Rachel Jackson since "birds of a feather will flock together." Later they joked about Rachel Jackson's habit of smoking a pipe. The president was angry enough as it was when Susan Decatur, the widow of naval hero Stephen Decatur, sent him a letter repeating one of the lurid rumors about the Eatons.[38]

Although there were important political and social overtones to the Eaton affair, the best way to examine it is to focus on Jackson, for if he had not taken it so seriously there would never have been an affair at all. In the history of the presidency the "Eaton malaria" is unique. No other president spent most of his first two-and-a-half years in office trying to protect the reputations of a cabinet member and his wife. The degree to which the episode dominated the presidency cannot be fully appreciated without reading Jackson's correspondence. About half of Jackson's published letters between his inauguration and September 1831 concern either the Eaton affair or the related subject of Jackson's deteriorating relationship with Calhoun. Jackson's violent, emotional words—"intrigue," "conspiracy," "intimidate," "cruelly," "treachery"—show how deeply he cared about what was a trivial matter far beneath the dignity of the president. Jackson believed that evil men—Calhoun and others— were conspiring to hurt men of virtue—Eaton and Van Buren. And, more significantly, he believed that the conspiracy was aimed at destroying his administration.[39]

The intensity of Jackson's response suggests that Jackson was defending himself more than he was defending the Eatons, behavior that would certainly not have been out of character. An orphan at a young age, a self-made man, he grew up sensitive to slights and insults, seeming to make a career out of defending his honor. He arrived in Washington angry and depressed by the treatment of Rachel during the campaign and her sudden death. The flagrant rejection of his friend's wife seemed to be a renewal of the attacks upon his own wife. Dangerously ill and talking of dying, Jackson, not surprisingly, reacted violently.

Jackson feared losing his Tennessee friends, on whom he relied for emotional support. One of them, Eaton, had been attacked and might have to leave the government. Others such as the members of the Tennessee congressional delegation and friends in Nashville had turned against Eaton. Jackson could not even count on Rachel's family, the Donelsons. He was driven to tears when Andrew J. Donelson scornfully lashed out at Eaton and "Lewis and Co." He remarked that he was "surrounded by his judases—such as Daniel," referring to Donelson's brother, who was also against the Eatons. More than once Jackson spoke mournfully of "a house divided."[40]

The president also feared that he was losing control, not only over his family and friends but also over his cabinet and his coalition. In a revealing outburst to Andrew J. Donelson he said that forty members of Congress had asked him if he was still "at the head of the Government." Angry and unsure, he told Donelson that he would "shew the world" that he was. Concerned that he would be considered a weak president, he spoke and acted in ways that raised doubts. Instead of taking control and disarming his enemies he had increased tensions by allowing himself to be consumed by the Peggy Eaton affair.[41]

He also increased tension by his many removals of public officials. Since Jackson had campaigned on the issue of reform, promising to remove corrupt and incompetent officers, and had repeated the promise in his inaugural, hopes and fears ran high about the prospect of mass removals. Margaret Bayard Smith wrote that everyone in the government was "filled with apprehension" at the "rumour of a general proscription. . . . men whose all depends on the decision, await it in fear and trembling." The opposition *Daily National Intelligencer* described one clerk who "from mere fear of removal, cut his throat from ear to ear" and another who "went raving crazy." When approached by a nervous friend in search of a job, Kendall told him not to be embarrassed, for "every man you meet is on the same business." On his arrival in Washington Van Buren was immediately besieged by "a crowd of applicants for office." Jackson himself reported that the "crowds of hungry expectants" left him no time to write his friends. He avowed that if only he "had a tit" for every one of the thousands of applicants "to suck the Treasury pap, all would go away well satisfied."[42]

The drama was so high and the issue so important that observers then and historians ever since have debated the way in which the Jacksonians dealt with the situation. Jackson and his defenders insisted that they were simply replacing unworthy officials in a democratic way. In his first annual message the president called it "rotation" in office, saying that it was "a leading principle in the republican creed." Arguing that few could hold office for "any great length of time" without becoming corrupt, he proposed limiting appointments to four years. "The duties of all public officers," he wrote, were "so plain and simple that men of intelligence" could easily perform them. His opponents, however, called the process the "spoils system," insisting that the Jacksonians were interested only in putting their party followers in office. Starting with James Parton in 1860 anti-Jackson historians have blamed the Old Hero for replacing a system based on merit with one based on partisanship.[43]

Jackson introduced his rotation in office as soon as he was inaugurated, sending seventy-six names to a special session of the Senate held 4–17 March to confirm appointments. To ensure that there were no hitches, he submitted only the names of his cabinet officers and other mostly uncontroversial candidates, such as John McLean for the Supreme Court. He also had the three senators who were joining the cabinet—Eaton, Branch, and Berrien—keep their Senate seats for a few days so that they could vote on some of the early nominations. As a result all of his nominees were confirmed, with a debate over only four.[44]

As soon as the Senate adjourned, Jackson broadened his attack on incumbents by seeking out corrupt officials. In his "Outline of Principles," drawn up on 23 February, the president had instructed his cabinet officers to remove all those individuals who had used their positions to interfere with "the freedom of state elections" or whose "moral habits" made them poor "examples of fidelity & honesty." Led by an eager Kendall the new administration soon uncovered a number of corrupt officeholders. A certain amount of corruption was not surprising; as land sales, customs collections, and other federal enterprises increased, it had become all too easy for public officials to borrow government funds for their own private use. When their speculations went bad, their accounts were sometimes in arrears when examined. The Jacksonians later claimed that in the first year and a half they had removed officials who had defaulted to the amount of $457,000; Kendall reported a shortfall of $280,000 in the Treasury Department alone. These amounts were not unusually high—less, for example, than under Monroe or later under Van Buren—but Jackson felt vindicated by the removals.[45]

The case of Tobias Watkins attracted the most attention. Watkins, a Clay man, had held the auditorship in the Treasury Department that was given to Kendall. When Watkins fled abruptly, he was brought back, put on trial, and found guilty of being $3,300 short in his accounts. Not only the administration newspaper the *United States Telegraph* but also the opposition *Niles' Register* and *Daily National Intelligencer* carried running accounts of the trial.[46]

While the administration was harrying a few defaulters out of office, it was also replacing hundreds of other officials, the vast majority of whom had not been corrupt and whose incompetence had not been proven. These large-scale removals and the appointments of controversial figures such as Kendall, Lewis, and Isaac Hill of New Hampshire led to outrage and protest. The opposition newspapers carried long lists of recess appointments, which would not come before the Senate until Congress convened in December. In addition to defending Watkins, the same newspapers published the complaints of some of those men removed, including William Slade of Vermont, who had been sacked unceremoniously in the State Department. Even the Jacksonian *Richmond Enquirer* carried a questioning lead article entitled "Etiquette and Appointments to Office."[47]

As the controversy grew, so did the impression that the Jacksonians were sweeping the incumbents out of office. By the end of the first year opposition senator John Holmes of Maine was claiming that Jackson had removed 1,921, or almost 20 percent, of some 11,000 federal officials. On the basis of this number, which was passed on and even enlarged for the rest of the century, Jackson's critics accused him of starting the spoils system. After visiting Washington in 1832, Alexis de Tocqueville wrote that "at every new election the fate of all the Federal public officers [was] in suspense." In his biography of Jackson in 1860, James Parton cited Holmes's figures to accuse the president of creating the spoils system. Parton denounced Jackson for "debauching the government" and entitled one of his chapters, "Terror among the Office-Holders."[48]

The critics should have known better. Three weeks after Holmes's assertion, Duff Green, speaking for the administration, attacked the senator's figures. Green followed through in September with an article in the *Telegraph* setting the number of removals at 919, or less than 10 percent, a figure that has never been seriously challenged. In the 1850s Thomas Hart Benton in his *Thirty Years' View* corrected Tocqueville's distorted interpretation. The latest student of the subject has estimated the removals at only 9 percent and the recent tendency has been to play down the concept of a Jacksonian spoils system.[49]

Yet even if the lower figure is correct, Jackson's program of removals viewed in the context of the times constituted an important break with the past and marked the beginning of a system of party patronage. Jackson was the first president to make removals a matter of policy. Jefferson had dismissed many Federalists, but he disapproved of large-scale partisan removals and made no public announcements. Jackson's removals, furthermore, came after a long period of inactivity—particularly the removal of civil officials appointed directly by the president. In the twenty years before Jackson, the three presidents combined had removed only 66 in this category. Jackson removed 252 of 610, or 45 percent.

Jackson's removals were all the more dramatic because he acted so quickly. John Adams made no civil appointments during his first month in office and Thomas Jefferson made only four, but Jackson made sixty-eight in the first nine days alone. Most of Jackson's removals came during his first year in office, when he removed more officials in one year than all preceding presidents had in the previous forty. Outside of Washington Jackson's removals seemed greater than they actually were because they were so concentrated in the Northeast, the stronghold of the Adams party, where the spoils system was already established. Of the 491 deputy postmasters removed in 1829 and 1830, 143 were from New England, 131 from New York, and 79 from the other Middle Atlantic states, a total of 353, or 72 percent. Most of the large postmasterships were affected, or as James Parton expressed it, "nearly all . . . that were worth having."[50]

The changing times also contributed to the importance of the removals. As the country had grown, the number of officials working for the government had grown with it— from about 3,000 in 1801 to almost 11,500 in 1831. In Washington alone the number employed in the legislative, executive, and judicial branches had risen from 145 to 344. More and more of these individuals were living in Washington. At the start of the century few public officials brought their families to the rough new capital, but three decades later the number had grown. As a result Jackson's dismissals affected families as well as individuals. So many houses were put up for sale in 1830 that a temporary decline in property values occurred in the city.[51]

Jackson's tendency to appoint members of Congress, already apparent in his cabinet selections, was also alarming. The practice had long been deplored—even by Jackson himself—because it encouraged corruption by eroding the separation between the legislature and the executive. To discourage such abuse the Founding Fathers had inserted a specific clause in Article One of the Constitution stating that

> no Senator or Representative shall, during the Time for which he was elected, be appointed to any civil Office under the Authority of the United States, which shall have been created, or the Emoluments whereof shall have been encreased during such time.

Jackson violated the spirit if not the letter of this clause. There was great criticism, therefore, when the administration appointed forty-one members of Congress to office in the first five years.[52]

The appointment of newspaper editors was even more shocking. Since newspapers were often unprofitable and debt-ridden, editors rarely ranked high on the economic or social ladders. Forced to spend much of their time doing odd printing jobs to make ends meet, they were commonly looked down upon as artisan printers by their social superiors. Senators John Tyler of Virginia and Josiah S. Johnston of Louisiana referred to them scornfully as mere "printers"; Sen. Samuel Bell of New Hampshire called them "skunks." When the Jacksonians gained control of the Senate in 1827, they elected Duff Green of the *Telegraph* to replace Joseph Gales and William W. Seaton of the *Intelligencer* as printer—the first time that a change in political control had led to a change in that office. After the election of 1828 the Jacksonian newspaper editors stormed Jackson's quarters to demand similar rewards. According to one possibly apocryphal tale, two dozen of them called on Jackson to present their demands. Leading the way, the exuberant Mordecai Noah of the *New York Courier and Enquirer* hesitated and turned to the thin, bent-over Isaac Hill of the *New-Hampshire Patriot,* saying, "Hill, you are the ugliest of the clan, of a hungry aspect enough. I am fat and plump: you shall lead us on, and as soon as the old president sees this picture of starvation, he will surrender at once."[53]

Jackson did surrender. During the next two years the State Department shifted 71 percent of the contracts for printing the federal laws from opposition newspapers to Jackson newspapers. In addition fifty-nine "editors of the foulest presses," as John Quincy Adams called them, received government jobs. Some were given positions in the Land Office or the Treasury Department; others were appointed as postmasters and a few as port collectors, making them powerful figures in their communities. Among the more important were Kendall, Hill, who was named second comptroller in the Treasury Department, and Elijah Hayward of Ohio, who became the commissioner of the General Land Office. There were many protests, mostly from those individuals who feared that the independence of the press would be undermined. One of the most vociferous critics was the aristocratic Thomas Ritchie of the *Richmond Enquirer,* a Jacksonian himself but socially more acceptable than most of the other editors. Father Ritchie, as he was called, wrote a sharp letter of protest to Van Buren and asked him to pass it on to the president. "We lament," he wrote, "to see so many of the Editorial Corps favored with the patronage of the Administration . . . which will have the effect of bringing the vaunted Liberty of the Press into . . . contempt."[54]

Ultimately, the Jackson administration must take the responsibility for starting the party patronage system because the policies begun under the Old Hero continued—and became more widespread—after he left office. From that time on whenever the party in power changed, the percentage of removals steadily climbed. This was particularly noticeable among the civil officials appointed directly by the president. The percentage of removals in this group rose from 45 percent under Jackson to almost 50 percent under Tyler, to almost 60 percent under Zachary Taylor, and exceeded 90 percent under Abraham Lincoln. Even when the party in power remained the same, the new president began to feel obliged to make removals. When Democrat James Buchanan replaced Democrat Franklin Pierce in 1857, William L. Marcy of the Albany Regency, a great spoilsman himself, remarked ruefully, "Strange things have been enacted here during the last three weeks. Pierce men are hunted down like wild beasts." As a result of these increasingly harsh patronage policies a demand for civil-service reform arose in the 1870s.[55]

Even though observers had good reason to believe that they were witnessing the start of a spoils system, Jackson himself did not think in those terms. At times he seemed sincere in his belief that he was simply following his democratic reform policy of rotation in office. Soon after taking office, for example, he told Susan Decatur that he could not remove a certain official until the man's "incompetency" had been fully established. As he later recalled, he intended to "grant offices to none but such as was honest and capable."[56]

But Jackson did not always base his appointments on merit and frequently appointed friends, relatives, and old soldiers to office. In answering criticism from Ritchie on this score the president said that surely the editor would not have him "proscribe" his friends, "merely because they are so." He was unable to find a place for Robert J. Chester, the husband of Rachel's niece Elizabeth Hays, but he did manage to nominate Elizabeth's brother Stockley for surveyor general. He refused to replace Solomon Van Rensselaer of the opposition as postmaster of Albany since he had fought well at Fallen Timbers and Queenstown and according to Jackson carried "more than a pound of British lead in his body." Nathan Reid, Jr., whom he recommended for postmaster of Lynchburg, Virginia, satisfied two of Jackson's requirements since he was the son of an officer in the Revolution and the brother of Jackson's old aide-de-camp John Reid. Suspicious of people he did not know, Jackson sought to retain control by appointing his friends. After naming James A. Hamilton as United States attorney for southern New York, Jackson told him, "Go to the duties of your office, and make as much money as you can; but remember, you are to be always at my command."[57]

He could also on occasion be deceptive and irritable. When James Monroe's son-in-law Judge George Hay came to inquire about the rumored dismissal of his son Charles, Jackson told the judge not to worry but then removed the son anyway. One man on hearing the story snapped his fingers three times and said that that was what Jackson's promises were worth. Joseph M. White of Florida, who protested the removal of twelve officers, swore never to deal with Jackson after the Old General "bristled into a passion" and treated him "rudely." At that particular time the president was already upset by the treatment of Peggy Eaton.[58]

Sometimes, however, he was surprisingly tactful. In the Hay case, for example, he was shrewd enough to write Judge Hay soon after the removal to explain his decision, and he showed great tact when the vindictive Isaac Hill tried to discharge John Quincy Adams's nephew William S. Smith from the Treasury Department. In a carefully worded letter to Secretary Ingham, Jackson suggested ever so gently that they retain Smith "from delicacy" but shift him out from under Hill, who had treated him discourteously.[59]

Jackson did not plan a spoils system, but he could not control the leaders in his coalition, who were already squabbling over patronage when he first took office. On 21 March Jesse Hoyt spoke "the universal sentiments" of the Albany Regency when he told Van Buren that the members expected "every man to take sides one way or the other, either for or against removals" and reminded him of "the old maxim of 'those not for us are against us.'" Hoyt was annoyed that Van Buren's late arrival in Washington had temporarily deprived the Regency of a strong spokesman, forcing Hoyt to apply to Secretary of the Treasury Ingham, a Pennsylvanian, for the post of attorney for southern New York. Hoyt later complained that Van Buren's friends were "falling off" in Albany because they doubted that he had any influence with Jackson.[60]

With that kind of pressure Van Buren had a difficult time dealing with the inconsistent Jackson. Soon after arriving in Washington he was alarmed to learn that Jackson planned to appoint Samuel Swartwout of New York City as collector of the Port of New York. Although the New York customhouse was not yet as dominant as it became in midcentury, when it collected three-fourths of all federal receipts, it was already a great source of revenue and easily the most important patronage position outside of Washington. Through its complicated system of fees and commissions the collector could expect to make almost as much as the $25,000 a year earned by the president and more if he was not overly scrupulous. A notorious speculator, Swartwout found the collectorship tempting.

Swartwout was a poor party appointment in New York because he was a Calhoun man and did not have the backing of the Regency. But, unfortunately for the Regency, Swartwout had won the president's unquestioning friendship in 1807 by testifying in his favor when Jackson was linked with the conspiracy of Aaron Burr in the West. Despite a last-minute flurry of letters organized by Van Buren against the nomination, Jackson put friendship over party and stuck by Swartwout. He lived to regret the appointment; in 1839 Swartwout absconded with over $1 million. The president also ignored party considerations when he failed to give Hoyt the attorney's office and bypassed another Regency man, Jonathan I. Coddington, for surveyor of the port. Even when Jackson named Van Buren's friend James A. Hamilton as United States attorney, Van Buren and the Regency disapproved, for the memory of Alexander Hamilton and Federalism made it a bad party appointment. An angry Coddington warned that Jackson would ruin the party by appointing his personal friends to office. Van Buren was so distraught that he "walked the streets . . . until a late hour" one evening and thought briefly of resigning.[61]

Realizing that he could not transfer his state system of patronage to Washington all at once, Van Buren moved with his usual caution. For example, he was so disgusted by the mad crush of jobseekers that he tried to clear supplicants off the streets before the administration awarded any more jobs. If it seemed expedient, he was ready to leave incumbents in office. In the State Department he kept Chief Clerk Daniel Brent and Superintendent Thomas P. Jones of the Patent Office because the former was capable and the latter was highly recommended by science scholars. "The literati of Philadelphia & Virginia," Van Buren quipped, "would regard the removal of the Dr. J. as an act of Vandalism." Still, Van Buren remained a party politician. He strengthened his ties with two groups of Jacksonians by arranging the appointments of Louis McLane as minister to Great Britain and William C. Rives of Virginia as minister to France. He quickly removed six of the fourteen lesser clerks in the State Department, and before long both Brent and Jones had been replaced.[62]

In spring and summer 1829 the Tennesseans Eaton, Lewis, and Donelson, not Van Buren, had the president's ear. Eaton was particularly influential. Calhoun's friend Virgil Maxcy of Maryland complained in April that Eaton was keeping him from being first comptroller of the Treasury, and another friend, nullifier James Hamilton, Jr., remarked a month later that Eaton had "back stair influence" over Jackson. Although James Parton believed that Lewis was opposed to the "fatal removal policy," Parton cannot be relied upon, for he based his conclusion on one letter written in 1839 and on Lewis's memories as an old man. In 1829 Maxcy believed that Lewis was influential with Jackson, and Moses Dawson, the Ohio spoilsman, was corresponding with Lewis about appointments. Donelson was never as important as Eaton and Lewis, but even he had a letter from Van Buren's own state of New York asking about a job in the New York customhouse.[63]

Calhoun, who rivaled both Van Buren and Eaton, criticized Jackson for using patronage "as an instrument to perpetuate power," but he was not above trying to use it himself. He wrote directly to Jackson to help make George M. Dallas United States district attorney in Pennsylvania. He also tried to secure a position for Maxcy but was twice blocked by Eaton. Calhoun's spokesman Duff Green was having difficulty getting his share of appointments. Instead of giving the Treasury printing contract to Green, Samuel D. Ingham chose a printer from Pennsylvania. When Green also lost the contract for the Post Office, Barry put the blame on Ingham. In June 1829 Kendall reported that Green was quarreling with almost everyone in the cabinet.[64]

The Jackson patronage system grew slowly in the states, and even where it was practiced, it was hampered by intraparty rivalry. In New Hampshire Isaac Hill's Concord machine presided over wholesale removals, fifty-one in the post offices alone, but an old rivalry between Hill, who favored Van Buren, and Sen. Levi Woodbury, who leaned toward Calhoun, got in the way of party unity. When Hill's nomination as second comptroller was rejected by the Senate in April 1830, Jackson blamed it on Woodbury and Calhoun and cooperated in having Hill elected to Woodbury's Senate seat in June. Although Calhoun had an advantage over Van Buren in Massachusetts when federal patronage was put in the hands of David Henshaw of the *Boston Statesman,* Van Buren was on good enough terms with Henshaw to give him the contract to print the federal laws. Van Buren's Regency distributed the spoils so systematically in New York that more postmasters were removed there than in any other state, but the Regency, run from Albany, had difficulty competing with a collection of Calhounites, Clintonians, former Federalists, and personal friends of Jackson in New York City. The appointment of Swartwout as port collector and the retention of James Monroe's son-in-law Samuel L. Gouverneur as postmaster were victories for this group. Congressman Churchill C. Cambreleng, a Van Buren man, wailed that a party had been formed in the city "in favor of Mr. Calhoun," which would use the patronage of the customhouse and the post office against the Regency. Van Buren's organ, the *New York Courier and Enquirer,* attacked Swartwout at the end of the year for not removing any of the Adams men from the customhouse.[65]

Rivalry continued farther south. In Maryland a former Crawford man—Sen. Samuel Smith—was pitted against a former Federalist—Calhoun's friend Virgil Maxcy. The frustrated Maxcy reported to Calhoun that when Van Buren came through Baltimore in March he was "closeted two or three hours with old Smith & saw no one else." Since that meeting Smith and Van Buren had been in control of patronage in Maryland. Calhoun retained some influence, however, since in May Maxcy was finally rewarded with the post of solicitor of the Treasury, a new position especially created by Congress. Virginia became a persistent source of conflict between Jackson, who was hostile toward the Old Dominion, and Van Buren, who had close ties with many of the Old Republicans in the state. To placate the Virginians, who felt slighted by being shut out of the cabinet, Van Buren arranged for a series of appointments. In addition to Rives as minister to France, he secured positions for John Randolph as minister to Russia and John Campbell as treasurer of the United States. He was not able to win over, however, the state's senators, Littleton W. Tazewell and John Tyler, whose states'-rights views were almost as extreme as Calhoun's.[66]

Patronage in Kentucky was in the hands of Kendall and Barry, but even here Van Buren exerted some influence. On the local scene Kendall's former assistant editor, Francis P. Blair, assumed command, taking full advantage of the Post Office, the United States marshal's office, and the state militia. Kendall boasted that with Barry as postmaster general the patronage in the Post Office would exceed any that could be dispensed by the National Republican governor. The Jacksonians also expected to have a number of jobs at their disposal when the marshal took the census in 1830. To spread the word Kendall urged Blair to send copies of his newspaper, the *Argus of Western America,* to every militia company. Although Kendall was confident that "a general clearing out" of Kentucky would take place, he was somewhat disappointed when Barry failed to act boldly and Van Buren began to interfere in appointments.[67]

No one had much power in the faction-ridden state of Tennessee. Here politics was complicated by the emergence of a third faction to compete with the Overton and the Erwin-Carroll groups. Led by White, Donelson, young congressman James K. Polk, and senatorial candidate Felix Grundy, the new faction held an antipathy toward the Eatons and was sympathetic with Calhoun. The Overton faction, on the other hand, defended the Eatons and backed Van Buren. In the race for governor in 1829 between Carroll and incumbent Sam Houston of the Overton faction, Carroll was suddenly handed the victory when Houston inexplicably abandoned his wife, resigned the governor's seat, and went to live with the western Cherokees. The new governor then confused the political scene even more by joining Overton and backing Van Buren. Even though all three factions supported Jackson, the president did not have much influence in his own state.[68]

At the end of his first year in office Jackson still clung to his democratic ideal of rotation in office. His reluctance to act as party leader and the fierce competition among his subordinates prevented the growth of an effective patronage system under presidential and party control. But the basis had been laid in a number of states, and a patronage system would grow with the party.

During this first year Jackson's choice of advisers, his inaugural address, his handling of the Peggy Eaton affair, and his removals policy reveal a president who had made little progress in carrying out the tasks confronting him. Few presidential administrations have started as badly as his. He had failed to use his inaugural to reduce the people's uncertainty about his position. Still an outsider, his behavior in the Eaton affair had increased rather than reduced the bitterness in Washington. In selecting his advisers and in dealing with appointments he had listened too much to the Tennesseans and had been unable to bring his sprawling coalition under control. With its conflicting ideologies, interests, and leaders, it was still far from being a political party.

There were hints, however, of the direction in which the coalition was heading. The Tennessee clique had been weakened by the Peggy Eaton affair. Calhoun's nullifier wing had lost ground in the choice of advisers, had split with Jackson over the Eaton affair, and had fallen behind in controlling patronage. The opening of Congress would test Jackson and the coalition even more. It might even show Webster and the public how the wind really blew.

3

FACING CONGRESS

The convening of the Twenty-first Congress on 7 December 1829 brought Jackson another challenge. After nine months of dealing with the entrenched society and bureaucracy of Washington, he was finally facing Congress. The confrontation offered yet another opportunity to assume control and to take a stand on the inroads of the market revolution. It also posed a threat, for Congress was not accustomed to cooperating with presidents.

Cooperation was difficult for several reasons. The swamp created by Tiber Creek at the foot of Capitol Hill made travel from the President's House along Pennsylvania Avenue to the Capitol hazardous at best and divided Washington into two camps. Although members of Congress had begun to move down from Capitol Hill to the boardinghouses on Pennsylvania Avenue, executive officials, who clustered about the President's House, mixed with them infrequently. And the high rate of congressional turnover, which averaged over 40 percent every two years, made it even harder for relationships to develop between the two branches of government. Etiquette ruled that the president come to the Capitol only for his inauguration and a few other ceremonial events and to sign bills at the end of a session of Congress. He was essentially a prisoner in the President's House.[1]

Rules and customs inhospitable to leadership of any kind, especially presidential, had grown up in the House of Representatives, the dominant legislative body during the first forty years of the Republic. The Speaker, the clerk, and the printer of the House were all chosen by secret ballot, making party discipline hard to enforce. There were no party whips or other extralegal officials to ensure party voting. The rise of the committee system, which was in its glory in 1829, also impeded efforts to control the House. Since 1789 the number of major standing committees had climbed from one to nineteen, each of which had grown into a "little legislature" responsible for legislation in a certain area and capable of blocking action by the whole House. The practice of residing in almost sixty boardinghouses and hotels broke the congressmen—and the senators too—into dozens of small cliques that rarely came together. Efforts to overcome these obstacles and to develop a coherent program in the House—even by a president as strong as Jefferson and by a Speaker as popular as Clay—had largely failed.[2]

In the Senate, where members were often more loyal to the institution than to any political party or president, a fragile understanding had grown up with the executive, in which each branch would rule in its own sphere and clashes would be kept to a minimum. This was especially true in confirming presidential appointments. Aside from Jefferson, presidents had removed officials infrequently, and when they did the Senate had rarely questioned their motives. The number of senatorial rejections of presidential civil appointments had been correspondingly small—averaging only six for each four-year term. Each side prized this independence and the cherished separation of powers on which it was based.[3]

Jackson's reputation and campaign promises only reduced the prospects of cooperation. His impetuous nature and arrogant behavior as a general augured similar behavior as president. When he arrived in Washington threatening to clean out corruption, he alarmed and antagonized Congress. Although his inaugural address was milder than expected, his reminder that he had come to reform the government set more teeth on edge. During the summer his intransigence in the Peggy Eaton affair and his hundreds of removals had served to confirm the expectations on Capitol Hill.

Jackson had been elected by such a broad coalition of conflicting groups that he could not be sure of a majority in Congress. Although on paper his party outnumbered its opposition 136 to 77 in the House and 26 to 22 in the Senate, the figures were deceiving because many members listed with the party were only nominally for Jackson. Hezekiah Niles pointed out that the Old Republicans, now led by Van Buren, and the nullifier friends of Calhoun competed with the friends of Jackson in Congress. He also could have mentioned the former Federalists who were in the coalition. The opposition was made up of National Republicans and a few Anti-Masons. The realistic Van Buren distrusted the administration's majority in the House, saying that many of the Jacksonians were new and not "very deeply imbued in the principles" of the party. In the Senate, where Jackson's appointees would have to be confirmed, every vote would be in doubt because two Jacksonians were absent and the president could not count on the two Virginia senators or, in the case of a tie, on Vice-President Calhoun.[4]

Jackson's precarious position in this unstable Congress was immediately reflected in the selection of key officers. Instead of installing his own men, he had to accept holdovers as printer for each house and as Speaker and clerk of the House. Since the Jackson party had controlled the previous Congress, these men were supposedly all Jacksonians, but in the case of printer and clerk there were doubts. Duff Green, printer for both houses, was more loyal to Calhoun than to Jackson. Clerk of the House Matthew St. Clair Clarke was reelected only after unsuccessful efforts by Van Buren and Calhoun to replace him. Jackson's most reliable officer was Speaker Andrew Stevenson, an Old Republican from Virginia.

Stevenson ran into difficulty when he tried to select committees on a partisan basis, a policy he had initiated in 1827. On the surface sixteen of the nineteen major standing committees, each with seven members, had a Jacksonian majority. The Ways and Means Committee, which would deal with the tariff and the Bank, had five Jacksonians. Anticipating a drive to remove Indians to the West, Stevenson put six Jackson men on the Indian Affairs Committee. The Post Office and Post Roads Committee, the center of controversy over patronage, also had six, the Public Lands Committee five. But the strength of these majorities was in doubt. One recent scholar has estimated that only seven—not sixteen— of the committees had safe administration majorities. Three of the Jacksonian chairmen were also less than reliable. George McDuffie of South Carolina, Ways and Means chairman, was a nullifier. Jacob C. Isacks of Tennessee, chairman of the Public Lands Committee, showed his independence during the session when he said defiantly that he "differed from the President—and what of it?" William Drayton of South Carolina, chairman of Military Affairs, did not share Jackson's hostility toward the Bank.[5]

The situation was similar in the Senate, where a Jackson man, President pro-tempore Samuel Smith of Maryland, chose the committees because President of the Senate Calhoun did not take his seat until 14 December. This arrangement of allowing the president pro-tempore to appoint committees continued throughout Jackson's first term. Fourteen out of twenty committees supposedly had a Jacksonian majority, but on close scrutiny the number could be reduced to nine. Some of the key chairmen were also in doubt. Smith himself, chairman of the Finance

Committee, favored the Bank. Mahlon Dickerson of New Jersey, the chairman of Manufactures, held protectionist views that made him unpopular with many people in the Jackson party. Kentuckian George Bibb, chairman of the Post Office and Post Roads Committee, was only nominally a Jacksonian, and South Carolinian Robert Y. Hayne of Naval Affairs was a nullifier.[6]

Making Jackson's task even more difficult was the turnover rate. As in previous Congresses few members had been there long enough to achieve seniority or to assume leadership roles. Almost half of the members of the House were new, including forty out of sixty from New York and Pennsylvania. After forty years of being overshadowed by the House, where Madison, Clay, Calhoun, and Webster had served with distinction, the Senate was now coming into its own. Webster had become a senator in 1827, and Clay would join him in 1831. Only four of the forty-eight senators had ten years of seniority. Thomas Hart Benton, who had eight, was Jackson's most trustworthy man in the upper house.[7]

The Capitol, in which Congress would meet, reflected the instability of its occupants. The building had been so badly burned and damaged by the British during the War of 1812 that Congress had not been able to return to it for eleven years. When Congress convened in 1829, work on the rotunda and the west façade was still going on. At that time the Capitol consisted only of the central portion of the twentieth-century building, with a small dome and with small wings to the north and south. The extension of the wings to accommodate the present Senate and House chambers would not be carried out until the 1850s, and the great dome would not be erected until 1863, during the Civil War. The House met in what is now Statuary Hall in the south wing and the Senate in what is now called the Old Senate Chamber in the north wing.

Jackson had compounded his troubles by failing to lay the groundwork for a program before Congress convened. Nothing he had said or done since taking office had given any solid clues about his stand or his party's on public lands, the tariff, federal internal improvements, Indian removal, and the Bank. Broad policy was needed because the issues were interrelated. A high tariff and a high price for public land meant more money for Jackson's one announced goal, that of paying off the debt—unless the money went into federal internal improvements. Costly Indian removal might require higher tariffs or fewer internal improvements. Tariff protection, the Bank, and federal internal improvements violated the states'-rights tradition of a weak central government. Indian removal also violated this tradition by requiring the use of federal funds, but it was also consistent with states' rights because it would give the states sovereignty over Indian lands.

Vital sectional interests were at stake. Although there was disagreement within sections, each locality had discernible interests. The Northeast (New England and the Middle Atlantic states) called for tariff protection, both on manufactured goods and on raw materials such as iron and wool. It strongly supported the Bank, aid to commerce, and less strongly, internal improvements and a high price for land. It resisted moving the Indians west. The Northwest (Missouri and states north of the Ohio River) generally agreed with the Northeast, except that it wanted a low price for land. The Southeast (Virginia, the Carolinas, and Georgia), on the other hand, opposed tariff protection, the Bank, and internal improvements but favored Indian removal. With much of its wealth tied up in land, the Southeast also preferred to keep land prices high. The Southwest (states south of the Ohio) was divided over the tariff, the Bank, and internal improvements but wanted Indian removal and a low price for land.

To deal with these sectional interests the administration had to counter Clay's American System, which appealed to the Northeast and the Northwest by combining the protective tariff and the Bank with internal improvements. As an alternative, Van Buren sought to recreate the old alliance of the Northeast and the Southeast by opposing internal improvements and compromising on the Bank and the tariff. Calhoun and Benton, on the other hand, though they differed on states' rights, were making gestures toward an alliance of the South and the West in which the former would accept cheap lands if the West would oppose the protective tariff. To create a program for his coalition Jackson would have to convince his followers to put sectionalism aside.

In preparing for these issues, Jackson had been receiving encouragement to remain loyal to the agrarian ideals of the Revolution and to reject the lures of the market. One supporter reminded him rather vaguely that he had been elected to perpetuate *"Republican Institutions,"* another that the people expected "retrenchment and reform of abuses," but Old Republican Alfred Balch of Nashville was more direct, warning Jackson of the "many evils" that accompanied the new capitalism. "Of all the evils," wrote Balch, "the greatest and most devouring" was the "great splendid national Government," which claimed the power to "make internal improvements." Almost as bad was "the spirit of avarice and commerce," which was "converting the Bank of the United States into a Mammoth Broker." Other than promising to serve virtuously, Jackson said little in reply, but the opening of Congress would allow him to be more specific.[8]

In his annual message to Congress on 8 December Jackson finally offered indications of his policies. At the beginning of his message he showed more concern for American merchants than might have been expected from a president portrayed as an old-fashioned farmer. He made it plain that his administration would try to increase foreign trade and to collect the large claims of American merchants against foreign nations. He spoke specifically of commerce and claims a dozen times, showing even more concern than the business-minded John Quincy Adams had four years earlier. Although increased trade would help farmers as well as merchants by expanding their export markets, Jackson's comments seemed to contradict the views of Balch and other Old Republicans, who considered the spirit of commerce an evil. During the next few years the administration would make great efforts on behalf of American merchants.

Jackson reclaimed his Old Republican credentials a few pages later by reiterating his goal of abolishing the national debt and by hinting that the tariff could be lowered once the federal books were balanced. He also suggested that many Americans considered John Quincy Adams's program of federal internal improvements unconstitutional, "inexpedient," and dangerous to "harmony." To prevent a surplus from piling up after the debt was abolished, he proposed a constitutional amendment for distributing the surplus revenues to the states, which could then build their own roads and canals. This balanced program, with commerce for the Northeast, restrictions on the tariff and federal internal improvements for the Southeast, and still some room for internal improvements for the West, seemed to be an effort to blend the views of Van Buren, Calhoun, and Benton.

Jackson's own hand appeared later in the message when he commented on the nation's contradictory policy toward the Indians. While "professing," he wrote, "a desire to civilize and settle them, we have at the same time lost no opportunity to purchase their lands and thrust them farther into the wilderness." He proposed instead that the government move the Indians to "an ample district west of the Mississippi." The removal would be voluntary, but those Indians who remained east of the river would lose their independence and be subject to the laws of the states. Perhaps Jackson could unite the coalition against the Indians.

At the end of the message two short paragraphs on the Bank stood out. Since Jackson expected the Bank to apply for a renewed charter well before the present one expired in 1836, he was calling the issue to the attention of the people. "Both the constitutionality," he intoned, "and the expediency of the law creating this bank are well questioned by a large portion of our fellow-citizens, and it must be admitted that it has failed in the great end of establishing a uniform and sound currency." With this sharp statement against the Bank, Jackson was raising an issue that might divide his coalition between men like Kendall and others like Eaton.[9]

The attack on the Bank shocked its president, Nicholas Biddle, who, at forty-three, had been running the Bank since 1822. With his sensitive features and literary interests, Biddle seemed more like a scholar than a banker. He had graduated from two colleges by the age of fifteen and had later published a volume of poetry as well as the history of the Lewis and Clark expedition. He was also an astute, power-seeking, arrogant banker.

Biddle's Bank, as it was often called, was a successor to the original Bank of the United States, the charter of which had expired in 1811. After the experiences of the War of 1812, when the absence of the Bank had made it difficult to finance the fighting, a new and larger Bank was chartered in 1816. The Bank was to store and transfer government funds, help collect taxes, provide credit, and issue bank notes, which would be an important part of the national currency. It was predominantly a private bank, with only one-fifth of the stock owned by the government. In 1830, with its twenty-five branches spread throughout the country, it had become such a powerful economic establishment that it defies modern comparison. The Bank's $13 million in notes made up 20 percent of the money in circulation in the United States. Its capital of $35 million was more than double the annual expenditures of the United States government. No corporation in America comes close to that today. Its deposits had reached $16 million, over a quarter of all deposits in the United States. In the course of daily business the Bank and its branches received the notes of the state banks and held them for unspecified periods of time. This gave the Bank great power because at any time it could present the notes to the state banks and demand repayment. The state banks were thus forced to keep specie on hand and follow sound banking policies. Biddle unwisely stated on one occasion that the Bank had the power to destroy any of the state banks. Unusually high annual profits of 8 to 10 percent of the par value of the stock went to an elite group of some 4,000 stockholders, almost 500 of whom were foreigners. At its best the Bank served the public well, providing a reliable currency and regulating the state banks. At its worst it was a privileged institution that benefited a small number of stockholders and that used its influence for selfish political purposes. Although the constitutionality of the Bank had been reaffirmed in the case of *McCulloch* v. *Maryland* in 1819, the Panic of 1819 had left it with many enemies.[10]

There were Jacksonians for and against the Bank. The Tennessee Jackson men, Overton, Eaton, and Lewis, approved of Biddle's bank; Overton served on the board of the Nashville branch. It was difficult for

Pennsylvania Jacksonians to oppose a bank that had its central office in Philadelphia. Along the Atlantic coast Samuel Smith of Maryland, George McDuffie of South Carolina, and former Federalists James A. Hamilton and Louis McLane recognized the usefulness of the Bank. On the other hand, Benton, Kendall, and other western agrarians, remembering the Panic of 1819, continued to be hostile. So did Old Republicans such as Thomas Ritchie of Virginia. Most important, nothing had happened to change Jackson's opposition to banks. During the election of 1828 he had become convinced that Biddle had used corrupt means to oppose him.

To win over the administration Biddle had to deal with complaints of partisanship coming from Louisville, New Orleans, and Portsmouth, New Hampshire. The Portsmouth complaint went back to August 1828, during the election campaign, when the head of the branch in that city cut back loans, mostly in Jackson towns. The next summer the Jacksonian members of the legislature and the citizens of Portsmouth sent Biddle petitions protesting the cutbacks. Sen. Levi Woodbury also protested directly to Secretary of the Treasury Samuel D. Ingham. Biddle first tried to mend fences by changing the Portsmouth board of directors and by increasing loans in the Jackson towns. But on receiving a sarcastic letter from Ingham, questioning "the universal purity of the bank," he lost his temper. The Bank, he said, was responsible to Congress alone, not to any "executive officer . . . from the President . . . downwards."[11]

Afraid that he had antagonized the president, Biddle hurried to Washington in November for a face-to-face talk. Jackson started diplomatically, thanking Biddle for his help in reducing the federal debt. The president then blurted out that he had disliked all banks ever since he read about the British South Sea Company, which had ruined thousands of investors through land speculation. Furthermore, he did not believe that the government had the power to establish a bank outside the District of Columbia. Biddle came away shaken but hopeful that the president would say something good about the Bank in his annual message.[12]

In preparing for the message Jackson received conflicting advice. Kendall and Sen. Felix Grundy of Tennessee offered plans for a reorganized bank with more state and federal controls, but Ingham and Attorney General John M. Berrien recommended that he say nothing about the Bank in his message. Though no supporter of the Bank, Van Buren also believed that there was no need to stir up trouble six years before the charter expired. Fearful that the president would plunge ahead anyway, Van Buren and Lewis brought in James A. Hamilton from New York to help with the message. After staying up almost all night trying to compose a moderate statement on the Bank, Hamilton finally drew up the paragraph that eventually appeared in the message. The next day, however, having second thoughts, he joined the others in urging Jackson to say nothing about the Bank, but the president insisted on including the fateful passage.

The congressional response to the passage favored Biddle. Early in April 1830 the Senate Finance Committee, chaired by Samuel Smith, issued a report written by Biddle himself that supported the Bank. Then on 13 April, the day of the Jefferson Day dinner, the House Ways and Means Committee, chaired by McDuffie, returned a report expressing the members' "respectful but decided dissent" from Jackson's criticism of the Bank. According to the majority not only was the Bank constitutional, but it had established a paper currency that was both uniform and sound. Biddle published both reports in the *Daily National Intelligencer* and other opposition newspapers. Jackson was disappointed by the lack of a strong response from the Jacksonian press, especially Green's *United States Telegraph*. If a vote had been taken on recharter during this session of Congress, Biddle would have won.[13]

Although Jackson kept talking about a new bank, he could not decide what he wanted. After Biddle's intemperate letter to Ingham in 1829, the president was preoccupied with asserting his authority over the Bank. Then in June 1830 he described a bank with branches in each state and with the "emoluments" of the bank going to the people, not just to "a few moneyed capitalists." By July he was telling Moses Dawson of Ohio that he wanted a bank for deposit only, with the right to issue bills of credit restricted to wartime. Uncertain in his own mind, he appeared resigned to several years of discussions about a new bank.[14]

While Jackson fumed about the Bank, cheap land was the major concern of western supporters. Because of the western-land cessions of the original states and the purchase of Florida and Louisiana, the federal government held title to almost all the unsold land in the western states. During the 1820s the West began to demand incentives to encourage the purchase of this land. Benton proposed a graduation plan that would slash the price of surveyed land if it remained unsold. Others urged preemption, which would allow squatters on certain lands preference in buying their property. With his stirring phrase "the lands belong to the people," Benton helped make land as powerful an issue in the West as the tariff was in the South.[15]

In late December 1829 westerners became angry when opposition senator Samuel A. Foot of Connecticut proposed restricting the sale of public lands to the acres already surveyed but not yet sold. Further, he suggested that the office of surveyor general be abolished. Westerners suspected that northeastern manufacturers were backing the proposal in order to slow down the flow of cheap labor to the West.

Foot's proposal set in motion a debate over the public lands and the nature of the Union. An obscure congressman from New York, who watched the debate, has left a colorful description of the three major participants. Benton, who spoke for the West, had a "fine portly figure . . . large whiskers—a narrow, retiring forehead—a grey eye, that can glance like lightning." The southerner Hayne, whose "regular" features were not as "manly" as Benton's, wore his "light brown hair . . . in *exquisite* style." Most memorable about Webster, who represented the Northeast, were his "large head, . . . prominent forehead . . . black, scowling brows—wide mouth—pale face." He had not "a particle of Mr. Benton's fiery indignation."[16]

Benton opened the debate on 18 January with a militant speech against the resolution, saying that its purpose was to turn the West into "the dominion of wild beasts." Suggesting his South-West alliance, he called for southern help in rejecting this northeastern plot. The next day Hayne accepted the overture. The West, he said, suffered from the Northeast's land policy as much as the South did from the Northeast's protective tariff. Then, coming to Foot's rescue, Webster changed the focus of the debate by calling the land policy of the Northeast a national rather than a sectional policy. He reminded his listeners that the western lands had been used for years as a national domain to provide a common fund for the common benefit. Northeasterners, furthermore, had brought benefits to the West by putting through the Northwest Ordinance with its ban on slavery. He contrasted the high Unionist ideals of the Northeast with the selfish sectional approach of Hayne and the South. Webster had turned the question away from the West and the public lands to the South and the nature of the Union.

Hayne took the bait. Admitting that he was "rankled" by Webster's attack, he defended slavery and South Carolina's doctrine of nullification. The way was then open for Webster to deliver his famous reply, in which he outlined the new concept of a perpetual Union. With soaring phrases he condemned nullification and concluded with the peroration "Liberty *and* Union, now and forever, one and inseparable."[17]

The debate was embarrassing for Jackson because it threatened to split his coalition further between Hayne and Benton, on the one hand, with their South-West alliance, and Van Buren, on the other, who had long favored cooperation beween the Northeast and the South. The fluidity of political parties was shown when Jackson appeared to side with neither but instead applauded Webster of the opposition for his defense of the Union. Legend has it that when told that Webster was "demolishing our friend Hayne" in the debate, Jackson replied calmly, "I expected it." For the next few years there was always the possibility that Webster would join the other former Federalists who were backing Jackson.[18]

The president was particularly embarrassed by the land question because of his recommendation in his annual message to distribute all surplus revenues, including those from land, to the states once the national debt was paid. Most westerners disliked the proposal because the heavily populated eastern states would receive proportionately more of the funds; most southerners disliked it because it would require the continuation of the high tariff. When Jonathan Hunt, an anti-Jackson congressman from Vermont, proposed setting up a select committee to inquire into distributing the proceeds from the sale of public lands, the South and the West provided almost all the opposition. Even so, the motion passed; and the difficulty of uniting the South and West in a common cause was demonstrated when western congressmen from Ohio and Kentucky, who wanted internal improvements, voted for the bill against the wishes of the South. Jackson did not have to face the issue of distribution again that year, however, for there was no further action during the rest of the session.[19]

The administration sided with the West on the issue of preemption. On 23 December 1829 a bill was proposed in the Senate granting preemption rights to all current settlers on public lands. It passed the Senate on 13 January, 29 to 12, the House on 29 May, 100 to 58, and was signed by the president on the same day. In voting on this bill the Jacksonians presented a reasonably solid front, supporting the measure 21 to 2 in the Senate and 74 to 25 in the House. Most of the Jacksonians opposing the measure came from Middle Atlantic states, which would not benefit from cheap land.[20]

The same patterns appeared when the question of graduation reached the floor of each house. In the Senate a combination of southern and western Jackson votes enabled a graduation bill to pass by a vote of 24 to 22. But it would not have passed without the additional vote of staunch Jacksonian Levi Woodbury of New Hampshire, who went against the general interests of his section to vote with his party. The bill failed in the House, however, 82 to 68, when the Jackson party could muster only a vote of 62 for the bill and 31 against. On both preemption and graduation the South-West alliance failed to materialize, as first fourteen and then eleven congressmen from the South voted against bills that the West dearly wanted.[21]

Another indication that the alliance was in danger had already appeared in February, when the House tabled George McDuffie's bill to lower the rates in the Tariff of 1828. A few weeks later the crippled, grim-looking McDuffie, who rarely smiled after being badly wounded in a duel, protested this rebuff. According to McDuffie, the high rates on imported manufactured goods reduced the market for European goods in America and thus forced European manufacturers to buy less cotton. The reduced demand, said McDuffie, lowered the price of cotton in direct proportion to the import tariff rates. With tariff rates averaging 40 percent, McDuffie claimed that the planters lost the equivalent of 40 bales out of every 100 produced. Although the argument was unsound—the Europeans did not simply exchange manufactures for cotton—the forty-bale theory became a popular rallying cry for the nullifiers.

The views of the nullifiers were the center of attention at the Jefferson Day dinner on 13 April. Southern and western Jacksonians had organized this dinner ostensibly to cement their sectional alliance. Egged on by Van Buren, however, Jackson began to suspect that the nullifiers had planned the dinner in order to trap him and other Jacksonians into supporting their doctrine. His fears seemed confirmed when nationalistic Jacksonians from Pennsylvania walked out before the dinner, saying that they suspected a plot aimed at them. Just in case, the president had prepared a toast—"Our federal Union: It must be preserved"—that would support states' rights but rebuke nullification.

Anticipation was high that evening as the time approached for Jackson to give his toast. Van Buren even climbed up on his chair in order not to miss anything. Glaring at Calhoun, the Old Hero made his toast more nationalistic he had planned by unintentionally omitting the word "federal," thus proclaiming, "Our Union: It must be preserved." He restored the word "federal" in the published version the next day. Calhoun was so shaken by Jackson's words and demeanor that his hand "trembled" and a "little of the amber fluid trickled down the side" of his wine glass, but he pulled himself together and replied: "The Union—next to our liberty most dear." It seems unlikely that any plot was involved—too many northerners had joined in planning the dinner—but Jackson could not be convinced. Plot or no plot, the dinner further strained the coalition as Jackson persisted in viewing the episode as a Calhoun conspiracy.[22]

The conflict between nationalism and states' rights was most evident in the issue of internal improvements. With the rapid movement west, there was never any question that roads, canals, and railroads would be built, but great debate arose over whether the federal government should take the major responsibility for a systematic program. Support for such a program had grown steadily, starting in 1806 with the passage of the bill for the Cumberland Road linking the Potomac River with the Ohio River and points west. Although James Madison and James Monroe each vetoed an important internal-improvements bill on constitutional grounds, the pressure for a vigorous national role continued. In his annual message in December 1825 John Quincy Adams called internal improvements "the most important means" of bettering the condition of the American people. Adams persuaded Congress to spend more money for internal improvements than it had done under any previous president, but he was unable to secure the federal program that he wanted. Instead, individual states and private companies resorted to congressional logrolling and pork-barrel tactics to win federal grants.

The corruption led many Old Republicans to oppose further federal internal improvements, believing that they would have the same evil consequences as the rest of the market revolution. In the Senate Van Buren proposed a constitutional amendment that would have prevented federal internal improvements unless the states involved granted permission. He also led the Jacksonians in voting against a series of bills for roads and canals. While senator, Jackson too had questioned the constitutionality of internal improvements, but he had also voted for several bills on the grounds of military necessity. It was not clear what position Jackson and Van Buren would take now that they were in power.[23]

Once in office Van Buren was besieged by letters from his Old Republican friends in the South urging the administration to follow the Jeffersonian states'-rights tradition by lowering the tariff and stopping federal internal improvements. Van Buren had already weakened his southern base by supporting tariff protection in 1828 and did not want to do it again. Jackson too wanted to restrain internal improvements because he was pledged to wipe out the national debt by the end of his term. Their coolness toward roads and canals encountered opposition from National Republicans and Anti-Masons, who supported Clay's American System, and from western Jacksonians such as Benton and Richard M. Johnson of Kentucky, who wanted internal improvements almost as much as they wanted cheap land.

In the Congress the advocates of internal improvements proposed seven bills. Four were federal projects: a survey of possible new undertakings, an appropriation for lighthouses, an extension of the Cumberland Road (now called the National Road) west of Zanesville, Ohio, and a second national road, running from Buffalo southwest to New Orleans. They also called for federal funds for three private projects—the Louisville and Portland Canal around the falls of the Ohio, a thirty-mile stretch of the Washington Turnpike from Rockville to Frederick, Maryland, and a sixty-mile road from Maysville to Lexington, Kentucky. The last two were particularly important because the first would link the National Road with Washington and the second was planned as part of a road from Zanesville extending south through Kentucky into Alabama. When all the bills passed except the road from Buffalo, Adams's dreams appeared fulfilled.

The voting on the bills revealed that the Jackson party was more divided over internal improvements than it was over land policy. Even though the administration opposed the bills, thirty-seven Jacksonian congressmen and seven Jacksonian senators voted consistently for them while fifty-five congressmen and thirteen senators from the Jackson party voted consistently against them. Many of the Jacksonian votes for the bills came from Middle Atlantic and northwestern states, which favored internal improvements. The opposition, on the other hand, hung together in favor of the program, with only four congressmen and one senator consistently opposing it. The results disappointed the supporters of a South-West alliance, who had expected a number of southerners to join the West in voting for internal improvements. Instead only three members of Congress from the Southeast voted consistently for the bills, and forty were opposed.[24]

Of all the projects under consideration the Maysville Road has drawn more attention than any of the others. Although the road was entirely in Kentucky, its proponents argued that some day it would become an important link in the national road system. The bill passed the House on 29 April, 102 to 86, and after passing the Senate was sent to the president. Jackson faced a dilemma. Although Old Republicans from the South were urging him to veto the bill, there was strong Jacksonian support for the road in the West. Benton had voted for it; Barry and Johnson, with their allegiance to Kentucky, urged Jackson to accept it because the road would go through a Jackson stronghold. According to Johnson, a veto would "crush" Jackson's friends in Kentucky as a sledgehammer would crush a fly upon an anvil. When Jackson discussed the problem with Van Buren during one of their horseback rides, the Little Magician offered to prepare a brief against internal improvements. The president accepted, and the brief became the basis for the president's message. During the next fortnight the two men kept their plans to themselves, fearing that their opponents would pass a more national bill including the Maysville Road if they knew that a veto was coming. There was also concern that if word of a veto got out it would endanger the passage of the Indian removal bill.[25]

The veto, delivered on 27 May, the day after the Indian bill passed the House, had the balance needed to satisfy the coalition. Using the strict-construction arguments of Van Buren and his southern supporters, Jackson adopted "the general principle" that the federal government could grant funds only to projects that were "general, not local, national, not State." Since the Maysville Road was "purely local," it could not receive funds. In words calculated to please the Old Republicans he went on to say that ridding the nation of its debt was more important than building roads. "How gratifying" it would be, he said, to show the world "the sublime spectacle of a Republic . . . free from debt."[26]

Had Jackson been content with these constitutional arguments, the veto would have stamped him as a confirmed believer in states' rights. But anxious not to antagonize his western wing, Jackson surrounded his core argument with a number of remarks defending the importance of internal improvements. He did not suppose that there was "an intelligent citizen who [did] not wish to see them flourish." Many states "with laudable zeal" were already engaged in "works of this character." If more federal aid was needed, he suggested that advocates push through an amendment to the Constitution, a task that he considered far less difficult than commonly thought. He reminded his readers that he was attacking a federal "system" of roads and canals, not all internal improvements. It was impossible, he said, to go back to the strict republican principles of 1798.[27]

The House debate over the Maysville veto followed party lines more than the voting on the internal-improvement bills themselves. Jacksonian Henry Daniel of Kentucky lauded the president for carrying out his promises of "reform," but William Stanbery of Ohio, who had left the Jackson ranks during the session, said the veto was "artfully contrived" by "the great magician" Van Buren as part of a general attack on internal improvements. James K. Polk retorted that Jackson was simply returning to the Old Republican position on internal improvements that Adams had dangerously undermined. The veto would prevent the growth of corruption and executive patronage. John Bell of Tennessee became so personal, calling Stanbery a "blackguard," that he had to be called to order. In the end few votes changed. Many Jacksonians continued to oppose the president and voted for the road, but the veto was upheld when supporters of the bill failed to muster the necessary two-thirds vote.[28]

Jackson's vetoes continued. On 31 May, the day Congress adjourned, the president vetoed the Washington Turnpike bill, citing the Maysville veto in his message. The Senate sustained his veto the same day. Jackson also took advantage of adjournment by pocket vetoing the Louisville Canal bill and the lighthouse bill. Only the general survey and the extension of the Cumberland Road slid by. Although the pocket vetoes were not unprecedented—there had been two previously by James Madison—they were sufficiently unorthodox to alarm those observers already critical of the new president. In his annual message the following December Jackson said that he was returning the bills to Congress unsigned because he believed them extravagant and local.[29]

By vetoing these internal-improvement bills Jackson reassured the Old Republicans in his coalition, thus enabling him to oppose the more extreme states'-rights position of the nullifiers. The popularity of the vetoes in the South was obvious though the *Richmond Enquirer* wished that he had expressed the Maysville veto in more sweeping terms. After the vetoes he received many messages congratulating him for what several writers called his "noble stand." On his way to the Hermitage he was greeted with praise when his boat docked at Cincinnati. A satisfied Jackson wrote to a number of his followers the identical remarks: "The veto works well." But not everyone in the coalition was pleased. Aware of the division among the Jacksonians, Felix Grundy reported that the Maysville veto helped the administration in Maine, New Hampshire, and New York, where federal internal improvements were unpopular, but he could claim only feebly that it did no harm in Pennsylvania, Kentucky, Ohio, and Maryland, where internal improvements were much more acceptable.[30]

Over the years interpretations of Jackson's policy toward internal improvements have shifted. In the 1960s historians who saw little difference between parties in America concluded that the Old Hero was both pragmatic and inconsistent. They attributed Jackson's Maysville veto to his "personal grudge" against Clay, in whose state the road was located, and pointed to the many projects that Jackson did accept. In recent years students more sympathetic to ideological considerations have argued differently. Jackson, they say, was seriously committed to the Old Republican ideals of states' rights and strict construction of the Constitution. He therefore ordinarily signed only bills that were clearly constitutional, such as internal improvements in the territories and the District of Columbia and improvements of rivers and harbors used in interstate or international commerce.[31]

It must be admitted that Jackson did have serious doubts about the constitutionality of certain federal internal improvements. Shortly after the Maysville veto, for example, he stated that he would not support surveys of any rivers except "navigable streams from the ocean" that passed through two states. His vetoes, furthermore—coming on the heels of Adams's open avowal of broad national policies—provided a dramatic rebuke to the concept of an integrated system of federal projects, checking the momentum of a drive that had started with Jefferson. There would be no further national program of federal improvements until the Civil War.[32]

But the conflicting demands of his coalition prevented Jackson from taking a purely ideological stand on the issue in any of his major papers. In the Maysville veto he was forced to balance constitutionality with practical matters such as location and expense. Americans could not, he conceded, go back to the principles of 1798. After the Maysville veto the president expressed delight at the political results but claimed no ideological triumph.[33]

Jackson had said no to a comprehensive national program—not to internal improvements in general. In 1830 he vetoed four of the six major internal-improvement bills, but he accepted the two most important ones, the survey bill and the bill for extending the National Road. He also accepted minor bills for constructing a road in the Michigan Territory and for dredging a tiny creek that ran from a corner of Pennsylvania into Ohio, both of which were far less national than the Maysville Road. By the time he had left office his administration had spent $10 million on internal improvements, twice as much as all previous administrations combined, even when adjusted for inflation. His annual expenditures for internal improvements almost doubled those of John Quincy Adams, who had already spent far more annually than any previous president. The amount spent by Jackson on the National Road alone after the Maysville veto was $3,728,000, compared with $1,668,000 spent on the road before the veto. And the road marched on, crossing Ohio by the end of his first administration and reaching Vandalia, Illinois, seventy miles short of the Mississippi River, the year after Jackson left office.[34]

The increase in state outlays during Jackson's presidency was even more spectacular. In the 1820s, state bond issues, two-thirds of which were for internal improvements, maintained a steady average of $2.65 million a year; during the period 1830–35 the annual average was $8 million; between 1835 and 1838 the average was $36 million. The figures show that Jackson's position on internal improvements was far less important than actions at the state and local level. During his years in office both his administration and the American people accepted traditional states'-rights arguments to oppose a comprehensive federal program of internal improvements, but at the same time they refused or were unable to stand in the way of the internal improvements that accompanied the market revolution.[35]

The liberal self-interest that lay behind the internal improvements was also present in the removal of the Indians. At the start of Jackson's administration the population of the United States totaled almost 13 million, and the frontier line had reached or crossed the Mississippi River along most of its course. Behind the frontier all suitable land had substantial white settlement except for approximately 100 million acres occupied by over 100,000 Indians in the states of Indiana, Illinois, Mississippi, Alabama, and Georgia and in the territories of Michigan, Wisconsin, and Florida. As the westward movement continued, white Americans in search of farmland looked eagerly at these Indian possessions.[36]

As Jackson had pointed out in his annual message, the United States government had long struggled with a contradictory Indian policy. Although committed to assimilating the Indians into the white American culture, successive administrations had also negotiated dozens of treaties in which the Indians ceded land and retreated west. From the days of Jefferson, pressure began to mount to replace this piecemeal policy with a new program in which all the eastern Indians would exchange their lands for tracts west of the Mississippi River. In his annual message of 1817 James Monroe called for removal, arguing that the hunter should give way to the farmer. Although Monroe negotiated a series of individual treaties, he was unable to implement an overall policy.

In the South the five so-called Civilized Tribes—the Cherokees, Creeks, Choctaws, Chickasaws, and Seminoles—had made great strides toward the sedentary farming culture practiced by the whites. The Cherokees, who were the most advanced, spoke a highly developed language, published their own newspaper, and owned slaves; in 1827 they had drawn up a written constitution similar to that of the United States. These tribes also occupied tracts of land much prized by white settlers. The situation was particularly acute in Georgia, which had large settlements of both Creeks and Cherokees. When Georgia ceded its western lands to the United States in 1802, the federal government had promised to remove the Indians from the state as soon as it could be done peacefully. In 1826 a dispute arose between the Adams administration and Georgia over the terms of a Creek treaty of cession. After Adams sent United States troops to protect the Indian boundaries, Gov. George M. Troup called out the state militia, forcing a settlement in favor of the state.

There was no doubt about where Jackson stood on the Indian question. Victor over the Creeks in 1814 and the Seminoles in 1818, he had an enviable reputation as an Indian fighter. The Old General did not hate Indians as some scholars have suggested; he had Indian allies in the Battle of New Orleans and he had adopted an Indian child after the battle of Tallushatchee. Yet like many white Americans at the time he considered the Indians inferior and treated them paternalistically. As governor of Florida he had spoken sternly to the Seminoles as their "father" and had demanded that his "children" abandon any claim to the coastal areas. In a letter to Calhoun in 1821 Jackson had ridiculed the "absurdity" of the concept of Indian sovereignty over land within the states. Southern elements in Jackson's coalition expected the new president to take steps to rid their land of Indians.[37]

They were not disappointed. After appointing two strong supporters of Indian removal—Eaton and Berrien—to his cabinet, the president publicly pressed both the Creeks and Cherokees to move west. On 23 March 1829 he chastised the Creeks for the murder of a white man on their land, saying that the Indians and the whites lived "too close together." It was typical of Jackson's first year in office that he relied on his Tennessee friends in dealing with the Indians. Eaton, speaking for the president, wrote to the chiefs of the Cherokees telling them they could either "yield" to the laws of Georgia or "remove . . . beyond the Mississippi." In endorsing a copy of this letter, Jackson praised Eaton for basing his policy on constitutional grounds. Jackson also called on Gen. John Coffee and Gov. William Carroll, who had served under him against the Creeks and the British, to pressure the Creeks and Cherokees to move.[38]

Since the question of Indian removal coincided with the Peggy Eaton affair and the debate over Sabbatarianism, Jackson was drawn into conflict with the evangelical Christian movement on several fronts. Frightened by the violent, materialistic behavior that they associated with the new politics and the market economy, the evangelicals, mostly Congregationalists and Presbyterians, sought to spread Christianity and to preserve the old Christian ways. They had long supported the efforts to civilize and Christianize the Indians; then in 1828 they had launched the Sabbatarian drive to protect the Sabbath. In the process they became the first group to exploit the technique of sending memorials to Congress. For a short time Ezra Stiles Ely, one of the spokesmen of the evangelical Christian movement, fostered the idea that Andrew Jackson, a good Presbyterian and a staunch republican, could serve as a sort of Christian leader. Van Buren had in fact taken advantage of this proposal in the election of 1828 by advertising Jackson's devotion to the church.[39]

Ely was quickly disillusioned. Even though Jackson had avoided traveling on Sunday, he showed no inclination to support Sabbatarianism. Many of his followers, Baptists and Methodists, resented the overbearing ways of the traditional Calvinists in the Christian movement. Even before Jackson took office, two of his strongest supporters had appealed to this sentiment with a stinging report against the proposal to close the Post Office on Sundays. In the report, for the Senate Committee on the Post Office and the Post Roads, Obadiah Brown of Washington, the author, and Richard M. Johnson, who was then in the

Senate and chairman of the committee, had called the proposal a violation of the tradition of the separation of church and state. They outraged the evangelical Christian leaders by comparing them with the "modern priesthood of Europe." Jackson's cabinet disappointed Ely because it included no New England Congregationalists and was dominated by southerners. Jackson's loyalty to Peggy Eaton, after Ely's warnings, and his plan to remove the most civilized Indians of all—the Cherokees—ensured the clergyman's estrangement from the new administration.[40]

The American Board of Commissioners for Foreign Missions, made up primarily of Congregationalists and Presbyterians and based in Boston, led the evangelical Christian fight against Jackson's plans for the Indians. This organization, which had developed an extensive program for civilizing the Indians, received widespread support in the North as it mustered moral and humanitarian arguments against removal. Its most effective spokesman was its corresponding secretary, the Reverend Jeremiah Evarts, whose simple, forceful writing style had already made him a strong advocate of temperance and Sabbatarianism. Starting in August 1829, Evarts published a series of twenty-four essays against removal in the *Daily National Intelligencer*, using the pseudonym "William Penn" in deference to the long-standing Quaker support for the Indians. At the opening of Congress Evarts started a campaign of forwarding northern memorials in support of the Cherokees.

To counteract this opposition Jackson sought to demonstrate the humanitarianism of his own program. "Humanity and national honor demand," he wrote in his first annual message, that the government save the Indians from "weakness and decay" by separating them from white men. He found a useful ally in Thomas L. McKenney, head of the Bureau of Indian Affairs since 1824, who had called for removal in 1827 after visiting the southern tribes. McKenney organized the New York Board for the Emigration, Preservation, and Improvement of the Aborigines of America, which received federal funds and was composed mostly of Episcopalians and members of the Dutch Reformed church. The board lobbied for removal, sending a memorial to Congress when it opened in 1829. At the same time Jacksonian Gov. Lewis Cass of the Michigan Territory published a learned article in favor of removal in the *North American Review*. Jackson also received valuable support from southern and western Baptists, led by clergyman Isaac McCoy of Indiana, who toured the East in 1829 to promote Indian removal.[41]

The president's political friends blended idealism and realism in supporting his Indian policy. Carroll said that the administration would have no difficulty carrying out Jackson's "correct and humane intentions," for the undisciplined Indians wanted no part of white rule. They did not, Carroll explained, like the whipping post and the other "laws of civilized society." Willie Blount, also of Tennessee, praised removal as an example of states' rights. The *Richmond Enquirer* denied piously that it wished "to wrest from the poor Indians their lands" but confessed it was even more opposed to allowing them to set up independent governments.[42]

After the discovery of gold on Cherokee land in the summer of 1829 the situation in Georgia worsened. White settlers clamored to move in, drawn by the assumption that the state would distribute the land by lottery in small parcels at a low price. The Cherokees, however, remained firm in their resolve to stay. Responding to white pressure, the state legislature on 19 December 1829 passed a statute declaring the laws and constitution of the Cherokee Nation null and void. Since the new statute would go into effect 1 June 1830, the president and Congress had about five months to resolve the question.[43]

In preparing for the expected congressional battle, Jackson saw to it that the two Indian Affairs committees were filled with supporters of removal. The committees—much more loyal than any of the others—were chaired by two Tennessee friends, Congressman John Bell and Sen. Hugh Lawson White, both strong supporters of removal. Six of the seven members of the House committee were Jackson men, four of them from the states of Tennessee, Georgia, Alabama, and Mississippi, which would benefit from removal. In the Senate White was backed by Benton and George M. Troup, the former Georgia governor who had stood up to John Quincy Adams in the dispute over Indian land in 1826.[44]

Under administrative guidance, the two committees worked in concert, reporting similar bills to the Senate and the House on 22 and 24 February. The bills gave the president power to set aside lands west of the Mississippi that Indian tribes or nations could "choose" to receive in exchange for their holdings in the East. Indians who had made improvements on their property would receive allotments of land, which they could use to remain in the East or could sell to help cover the expense of resettling in the West. In theory the Indians were protected since nothing in either bill was to be construed to authorize the violation of existing treaties, and the word "choose" was used to make sure that the Indians migrated voluntarily. The lack of specific details, however, gave the administration room to maneuver, and the allotment system destroyed tribal unity and opened the way for fraud and exploitation. It would not be difficult for speculators to find ways to buy the allotments from the unsuspecting Indians.[45]

When the debate in the Senate began on 6 April, opposition senator

Theodore Frelinghuysen was more than ready to lead the defense of the Indians. Six weeks earlier, when the Senate bill was reported, he had complained to Jeremiah Evarts about the tendency of other humanitarians to sit back and "slumber on." He had wanted to call up the bill at once and protest the "high-handed injustice of removing these people." Now in a six-hour speech, delivered over three days, he was so eloquent and spiritual that he became known as the "Christian statesman." Following Evarts's arguments, Frelinghuysen accused the Georgians of racial prejudice in refusing to grant the Cherokees their civil and political rights. Former Jacksonian governor John Forsyth of Georgia responded with a regional, paternalistic argument. He called the northerners hypocritical for trying to "arrest the progress" of Georgia by opposing Indian removal when they had previously disposed of their own Indians. Migration, he said, was the only humane solution possible for a people not "equal to the rest of the community." Forsyth mocked Frelinghuysen for having been "deceived" by the missionaries. After almost two weeks of debate and unsuccessful efforts to amend the removal bill, it passed by a party vote, 28 to 19.[46]

The administration was far less sure of success in the House, where debate on the Senate bill began on 13 May. The Jacksonians were less well organized in this rough-and-tumble body, in which half of the members were new, than they had been in the Senate. The twenty-four congressmen from Pennsylvania were particularly unreliable because they feared offending the Quakers, who had been stirred up against removal by Jeremiah Evarts's "William Penn" essays. Van Buren later called it a "Quaker panic." Elsewhere a number of congressmen who favored removal were uneasy about giving such a ruthless Indian fighter as Jackson the power to carry it out. The opposition sensed a chance to attack both Jackson and his party and looked to the House as "the theatre of triumph."[47]

As in the Senate, the House debate opened with a long speech defending the Indians, followed by a defensive reply. Henry R. Storrs of New York called the bill unconstitutional and compared Jackson with Napoleon Bonaparte for taking away the sovereignty of the Cherokees. He ridiculed the idea that the Indians would move voluntarily and bluntly predicted that Jackson would use federal funds to bribe the Indian chiefs. In his highly charged reply, Wilson Lumpkin of Georgia denounced churches for introducing a "religious party in politics" and for mounting harsh attacks on the whites in Georgia. "These canting fanatics," he shouted, had hidden behind religion in calling the Georgians "atheists, deists, infidels, and sabbath-breakers laboring under the curse of slavery." His emotional words suggested that Lumpkin feared that support for the Indians was only a first step toward abolitionism.[48]

The potentially high cost of Indian removal did not go unnoticed. The Indian removal bill contained an appropriation of $500,000 to help cover the expenditures, but the administration had acknowledged that total costs would be much higher—perhaps as high as $4 million. In one of the last speeches, opposition congressman Edward Everett of Massachusetts retorted that it was more likely to be "five times five millions." Congressman William Stanbery of Ohio said he opposed the bill because its costs would "strike a death-knell to the whole system of internal improvements."[49]

As the time to vote approached, the outcome was so uncertain that both sides resorted to parliamentary maneuvering. At a long afternoon and evening session on 24 May George McDuffie, siding with the administration on this issue, moved the previous question in order to bring the removal bill to a vote. When the motion failed, 98 to 97, Joseph Hemphill, one of the Pennsylvania Jacksonians caught up in the "Quaker panic," offered a substitute bill calling for a commission to study Indian removal and report back to the next session of Congress. To block the substitute, Wiley Thompson of Georgia again moved the previous question. This time the motion passed, 99 to 98, when Speaker Andrew Stevenson cast the tie-breaking vote, one of three times he cast such a vote on the Indian bill. Then efforts to lay the bill on the table and to adjourn failed. The administration finally managed to have the key motion passed to read the bill for the third time, 102 to 98, but only by getting three Pennsylvania Jacksonians to change sides and vote for it. Fearful of the Quakers, James Ford, William Ramsey, and John Scott had all voted against Thompson's motion for the previous question because they favored Hemphill's bill. The way was apparently clear for passage of the bill.

But victory did not come easily. The next day opponents of the bill, eager to stave off a vote until Jackson had sent in his veto of the Maysville Road, succeeded in having the bill postponed for another twenty-four hours. They hoped that westerners, angry at the veto, would vote against the Indian bill. On 26 May more trouble loomed when Ford, Ramsey, and Scott lost heart and considered voting against the bill. But the administration prevailed. Jackson held back his veto one more day, the wayward Pennsylvanians were kept in line, and the bill passed, 102 to 97. If the three Pennsylvanians had voted nay, the bill would have failed.[50]

An analysis of the House vote reveals that the opposition was more united than the administration. Only three of the opposition voted for the bill while twenty-four Jacksonians, including fourteen from Pennsylvania and four from Ohio, who were angry at Jackson because of the expected Maysville veto, voted against it. In addition twelve Jacksonians decided to "shoot the pit," as Van Buren put it, by not voting, compared with only one from the opposition. Three of those men not voting were from Pennsylvania, including James Buchanan; one was from Ohio. The bill managed to pass only because the administration coerced the three wavering Pennsylvanians. The sectional pattern was striking. The Southeast and Southwest voted 61 to 16 for removing the Indians, the rest of the country 82 to 41 against.[51]

Jackson had expected Congress to be difficult on economic issues and Indian removal, and he had also anticipated hard going on his nominations in the Senate. Although he had made hundreds of new appointments, only a few came early enough to be confirmed by the special session of the Senate immediately after his inauguration. With their uncertain majority the Jacksonians would be in trouble if the Senate fought back in the regular session. Jackson was concerned enough about the situation to go out of his way to defend his appointment policies in his annual message, especially his appointment of so many former members of Congress. He also delayed in bringing the names of his recess appointments to the Senate, nominating no replacements for any removed officials until 4 January and holding back controversial names such as Hill, Kendall, and Lewis until 10 February. By that time, when the Senate began to vote on the nominations, the administration was stronger, having regained the two votes that were missing due to absences at the opening of Congress.

On first glance it appears that the Senate failed to fight back; many of the appointments were confirmed quickly, with little opposition. The nomination of Henry Baldwin to the Supreme Court was confirmed almost unanimously two days after it was presented, the only nay votes coming from the South Carolina senators, who opposed his protectionism. During the session the Senate confirmed all but 7 of Jackson's 319 civil appointments. But the resistance was far greater than the number of rejections might suggest. First, Amos Kendall was confirmed only when Vice-President Calhoun broke a tie vote. In addition, four others were rejected but sneaked through because their names were resubmitted late in the session when absences created a safe majority for the administration. Even then, Calhoun had to break a tie vote on behalf of Mordecai Noah. According to Webster the number of rejections would have been much higher if the opposition had not feared Jackson's "outdoor popularity." Jackson in turn did what he could to avoid further trouble. He decided against dropping John Branch of North Carolina from his cabinet over the Peggy Eaton affair, fearing that if he did the Jacksonian senators from North Carolina would join the opposition and place many of the nominations in jeopardy. And a long battle was just beginning. By the time Jackson's two terms were up, forty-nine of his civil appointments had been rejected. His average of twenty-five rejections per term was four times as great as the average of all previous presidents.[52]

The principal targets were newspaper editors, several of whom were tarnished in other ways. Jackson's speech writer Henry Lee, half-brother of Robert E. Lee, suffered the ultimate humiliation of being rejected as consul-general to Algiers by unanimous vote—46 to 0. Not only was Lee hated by the opposition because of his editorial excesses, but he was also notorious for having seduced his wife's sister. James B. Gardiner, editor of the Ohio *People's Press*, with the reputation of being a drunkard, was rejected for another post, 46 to 0. Isaac Hill went down, 33 to 15, largely because of publishing libelous stories about John Quincy Adams in the election campaign. He dragged down with him Samuel Cushman and John P. Decatur, for whom he had arranged patronage positions in New Hampshire. Moses Dawson of the *Cincinnati Advertiser* suffered the same fate by a vote of 42 to 5. Mordecai Noah of the *New York Courier and Enquirer* also lost before being later confirmed. With many, if not all, of the Jacksonians voting against these nominations, the administration clearly had not coordinated a unified system of party patronage. The zest and seriousness with which the Senate turned down the editors can be seen in John Tyler's statement, "On Monday we took the printers in hand" and in his later lament that Jackson's appointments had been as bad as the Sedition Act.[53]

During the harsh confirmation battles Jackson failed to reduce the bitterness that had grown up during the election campaign and the Peggy Eaton affair. The struggle left a residue of ill will that persisted throughout his administration, causing the rejection later of other more important officials. The bitterness soured members of his own party as well as his opponents. Jacksonian senators Littleton W. Tazewell, John Tyler, and William Smith of South Carolina turned against the president because they believed he had compromised his republican ideals with his partisan appointments. Jackson was particularly infuriated when Hill was not confirmed and was pleased when the irascible New Hampshire-man was soon elected to the Senate, joining most of the same men who had turned him down. The bitterness prevented the proper airing of constitutional issues about the confirmation process. Opposition senators David Barton of Missouri and John M. Clayton of Delaware raised such issues by declaring that the president had no right to remove an officer without the approval of the Senate and by asking repeatedly for the reasons for removals, but they got nowhere. The issue seemed to be whether Jackson would ride "roughshod" over the Senate, as Congressman John Bailey believed, or whether the Senate would "govern the country," as the president feared.[54]

During the session Jackson had made a vigorous effort to overcome the obstacles to presidential power but found it difficult to have his own way. Lacking a reliable base in Congress, he became frustrated and acted imperiously, behavior that only increased his difficulties. As the session wore on, he won his fight for Indian removal, lost a battle but not the war in his attack on the Bank, and had mixed results in other areas.

At the end he was still an outsider, suspicious of what he regarded as congressional obstructionism. In one possibly apocryphal but revealing conversation with Duff Green in spring 1830 he accused Congress of being involved in "President making" instead of supporting his measures. When Green suggested that Jackson had not made his policies clear, the Old Hero flew into a rage and shouted, "Let Congress go home and the people will teach them the consequence of neglecting my measures." When Congress presented him with the internal-improvement bills at the end of the session, he denounced the members for their extravagance.[55]

The session of Congress, which adjourned on 31 May 1830, reduced the uncertainty surrounding the presidency as Jackson began to establish his position on the market revolution and the new politics. Although he accepted the expansion of commerce more than dedicated Old Republicans liked, he pleased the traditionalists by attacking the Bank and by vetoing internal-improvement bills. Southern farmers were enthusiastic about his determination to remove the Indians, but western farmers were less sure about his commitment to cheap land. As his toast at the Jefferson Day dinner made clear, he was a states' righter but not a nullifier. Despite his many removals from office and his aggressive assertion of presidential leadership, Jackson had yet to adopt Van Buren's concept of party patronage. When he pressed Congress for action he was exerting personal, rather than party, leadership.

The session brought changes to Jackson's coalition. Van Buren and the Old Republicans, who had gained ground in the Peggy Eaton affair, continued to move forward with the Maysville veto and Jackson's toast at the Jefferson Day dinner. Correspondingly Calhoun's nullifier wing continued to lose strength. Benton's western agrarians had failed to solidify a South-West alliance, but they were still a strong element in the coalition, waiting for Jackson to resume his war on the Bank. The Middle Atlantic nationalists, who had different goals, were also waiting their turn but with different expectations. During the session the Jacksonians had taken steps toward becoming a political party, but they were still a loose coalition torn by internal conflicts. To bring the coalition under some sort of control Jackson would have to harmonize his administration, and to do that he would have to settle the Peggy Eaton affair and decide what to do about Calhoun.

4

★ ★ ★ ★ ★

SEEKING HARMONY

As the session of Congress entered its final weeks in May 1830, Jackson was no closer to harmony and control of his coalition than he had been when he first arrived in Washington. Van Buren and Calhoun were jousting for power; the Eatons detested the Donelsons and half of the cabinet; the Donelsons disliked Lewis; and Green felt threatened by Van Buren and Kendall. The president lacked confidence in Green, whose *Telegraph* spoke more for Calhoun than for the administration. He was also agitated by repeated rumors that Calhoun had plotted against him in Monroe's cabinet in 1818 when Jackson had invaded Florida. Constant backbiting within the coalition made it almost impossible to build a party and to adjust to the changing economy.

The political infighting had surfaced in December 1829 when James Watson Webb of the *New York Courier and Enquirer* suggested Van Buren as the party's nominee in 1832. This was the same month that an ailing Jackson had written John Overton secretly designating Van Buren as his successor. Although Van Buren remained characteristically silent about the next election, his rise in Jackson's favor did not go unnoticed. In January, for example, Daniel Webster observed slyly: "Van Buren has . . . the lead in influence and importance. He controls all the pages on the back stairs" at the President's House. When the Old Hero's health improved in the spring, Van Buren decided that he was not ready for the front stairs. At his bidding the *Courier and Enquirer* and the *Albany Argus* declared that the president should run again. William B. Lewis and Van Buren also saw to it that early party caucuses in Pennsylvania and

New York nominated Jackson for a second term. Duff Green, hostile but correct, told a friend that the secretary of state could not do without Jackson's popularity.[1]

Political discord took a more serious turn in May when Jackson decided to bring the Florida controversy into the open. In December 1817 Secretary of War Calhoun had ordered Jackson to take charge of the guerrilla war with the Seminole Indians on the border of Spanish Florida. Jackson, as might have been expected, moved his forces quickly, crossed the border, seized St. Mark's and Pensacola, and by June 1818 had taken control of the Spanish provinces of East and West Florida. When word of his actions filtered back to Washington, protests were immediately raised. Not only had Jackson fought a war on foreign soil without a congressional declaration, but he had also executed two British subjects for allegedly helping the Seminoles.

By the time Congress convened in November 1818 criticism of Jackson had become so intense that the House appointed two select committees to investigate the war—one of the first of many American congressional investigations. When the first report reached the floor of the House on 12 January 1819, it was immediately referred to the Committee of the Whole, thus allowing open discussion. The month-long debate that followed was at the time the longest debate on one subject ever held in Congress. The climax came in a harsh speech by Henry Clay depicting Jackson as a dangerous man on horseback. From that moment on, Jackson, who had hurried to Washington to take part in his own defense, harbored a deep hatred for Clay. By the time Jackson left Washington in March, he had been completely vindicated. The House had cleared him with four resolutions, and the Senate, where he had been defended by Eaton, had consented to the Adams-Onís Treaty, which delivered Florida to the United States. Nonetheless, Jackson was forever bitter about the lack of support from the administration. Neither Monroe nor Calhoun had accepted any responsibility for the invasion, and within the cabinet several members had recommended taking action against Jackson for exceeding his orders. Although informed that Calhoun belonged to this group, Jackson was convinced at the time that the real culprit was an old enemy, Secretary of the Treasury William Harris Crawford.[2]

During the 1820s Jackson continued to hear stories of Calhoun's betrayal. In 1826 Sam Houston managed to obtain a letter from Monroe to Calhoun, written in September 1818, clearly showing that both men had disapproved of Jackson's invasion of Florida. By the time Jackson saw the letter, however, he did nothing, for he was already united with Calhoun against John Quincy Adams. Early in 1828 Van Buren's close friend James A. Hamilton traveled to Georgia to discuss the Florida controversy with

Crawford. He failed to see Crawford but arranged to have Gov. John Forsyth pursue the matter. In the spring Hamilton received a letter from Forsyth quoting Crawford to the effect that Calhoun had been Jackson's enemy in the 1818 cabinet meetings. Eager to promote harmony in the campaign, Hamilton and Lewis decided not to show the letter to Jackson, who learned of it only in November 1829 during the Peggy Eaton affair. Still he did nothing until a letter from Crawford arrived in May 1830 directly blaming Calhoun. Jackson then wrote Calhoun a curt letter on 13 May asking whether the South Carolinian had tried to injure him in the cabinet discussions. When Calhoun replied that Jackson had no right to question his behavior, the president wrote a second letter on 30 May accusing him of "endeavoring to destroy [his] reputation." Never, continued Jackson, had he "expected to have occasion to say . . . in the language of Caesar, *Et tu Brute.* . . . No further communication," Jackson stormed, was "necessary."[3]

Although Jackson pretended surprise that Calhoun had betrayed him, it is far more likely that he had suspected him all along but was not ready to take any action until May 1830. By then he was convinced that Calhoun was responsible for the Peggy Eaton affair, and he had decided on Van Buren as his successor. He had also taken a public position against Calhoun and nullification in April at the Jefferson Day dinner. When Jackson finally cut off communication with Calhoun on 30 May, Congress was on the eve of adjournment. It was no longer necessary to accommodate Calhoun, who had served his purpose by casting the votes that confirmed Amos Kendall and Mordecai Noah. Now Jackson could put pretense aside.

Jackson, however, not yet strong enough to break openly with Calhoun, vacillated for the next half year. At the same time, Calhoun, still hopeful of becoming president, tried to downplay the conflict. He insisted that in the exchange of letters he had not lost his temper and that the president had not been "bitter." Meanwhile, Samuel Swartwout, Felix Grundy, and Richard M. Johnson, friends of both Calhoun and Jackson, worked for a reconciliation. At one point they appeared to have succeeded, when, after a visit from Swartwout, Jackson remarked that the "whole affair was settled." Adams and Lewis both believed that the controversy was over, and Roswell Colt of Baltimore advised Nicholas Biddle that the president and vice-president had "kissed & made up." In early February 1831 Calhoun had enough strength in Congress to have Green voted printer by both houses of Congress.[4]

But Calhoun and Jackson were both biding their time—Calhoun until Green was elected printer and Jackson until he had enough evidence to prove that he had behaved properly in invading Florida. As sensitive as ever, Jackson was eager to build his case. The key lay with John Rhea, who had been congressman from Tennessee at the time of the Florida War. Before attacking the Seminoles, Jackson had sent President Monroe a letter asking permission to take Florida and suggesting that authorization be sent secretly through Rhea. According to Jackson, while on his march to the Florida border he had received a letter from Rhea conveying Monroe's approval. Jackson also insisted that a year later he had burned the letter at the president's request, also delivered by Rhea. Monroe, however, said that he had barely glanced at Jackson's letter before passing it on to Calhoun and that in any event he had sent no authorization through Rhea.

Neither side of the story seems credible. When Jackson asked Rhea to corroborate his version, the Tennessean, by then seventy-eight, could not recall anything but did agree obligingly to endorse any story if Jackson would provide the facts. Monroe, for his part, would hardly have dismissed with a glance a letter as important as the one from Jackson. After Jackson gave Rhea the necessary information, Rhea in June 1831 sent Monroe a narrative of the events, which the former president, then on his deathbed, denied.[5]

On 17 February, a few months before Rhea wrote Monroe, Calhoun presented his own lengthy version of the controversy together with supporting documents in the *United States Telegraph*. Jackson was not caught by surprise; he had warned John Overton of the possibility five days earlier. Before the account appeared, Grundy brought a copy to Eaton in order to make certain that nothing in it would cause trouble with the president. When Eaton made several suggestions, Grundy asked him to clear them with Jackson and said that he would do the same with Calhoun. After Grundy wrote back that Calhoun approved, Eaton deceived Grundy into thinking everything was satisfactory by making no reply. Eaton, who knew very well that the publication would enrage the president, wanted to let Calhoun hang himself.

Calhoun's motive for reopening the controversy was to shift the blame to Van Buren. In his introduction, the vice-president stated that he was publishing the documents to defend himself against a person who was trying to use the Florida affair to ruin his career. Everyone recognized this person as Van Buren, who was suspected because his friend Hamilton had revived the affair with his trip to Georgia. Anticipating the charge, Van Buren had done his best to stay out of the controversy. The previous May when Lewis brought him Calhoun's first letter to Jackson, Van Buren refused to read it so that he could later say that he was unaware of its contents. Jackson had laughed at this and said, "I reckon Van is right. I dare say they will attempt to throw the whole blame upon him."[6]

Van Buren, who knew that he was on trial as much as Calhoun, published his own brief defense in the *Telegraph* on 25 February. Other articles defending him appeared in many of the Jacksonian newspapers around the country, but he was also the subject of bitter attacks. Gov. John Floyd, a Calhoun man, reported that Virginians were "disgusted" with Van Buren, and James K. Polk's friend Archibald Yell wrote that many Tennesseans had doubts about the Little Magician. National Republican Henry R. Storrs of New York predicted hopefully that Van Buren's career was over.[7]

Even though he stood first with Jackson at the moment, Van Buren was uncertain about his future. The president had wavered for years in his relationship with Calhoun; he might change again. Van Buren had served Jackson well in the Peggy Eaton affair and with the Maysville veto, but like Calhoun he was no longer indispensable. His presence in the cabinet along with Eaton on one side and Ingham, Branch, and Berrien on the other made harmony impossible and was damaging Jackson's presidency. Many people were blaming Van Buren for the situation.

Unfortunately the Eaton affair had not been resolved. Although the affair had been overshadowed by the controversy over the Florida War, it still continued to plague the Jackson household. In summer 1830 the scene had shifted to Tennessee as Jackson, the Eatons, and the Donelsons returned home. The Donelsons expected to remain there, for they were unwilling to follow Jackson's instructions to exchange visits with the Eatons. Determined to "govern [his] household, or . . . have *none*," Jackson told Lewis to start looking for a new secretary to replace Donelson. The Eatons' persecution continued in Nashville when some of Jackson's friends refused to associate with them, but later John Overton entertained them, and Eaton's neighbors near his home in Franklin welcomed them at a barbecue. At the end of the summer Mrs. Eaton decided to stay in Tennessee for several more months, much to the relief of Jackson, who was beginning to tire of the affair. Donelson relented sufficiently to go back to Washington in September, but without his wife.[8]

The affair continued to fester throughout the fall, as the president and his secretary spent over five weeks exchanging petty, stubborn letters. When Donelson complained about an old squabble between his wife and Mrs. Eaton over a bottle of cologne, Jackson replied too hastily that the letter showed Donelson's "prejudice," after which he sent two notes of apology, saying that he had written late at night while suffering a headache. Donelson finally told his uncle to find another secretary and wrote Emily that he would soon be home. In tears over the family fight, Jackson pleaded with Donelson to stay until Congress adjourned in March 1831. Although Donelson agreed, the letters continued, four of them hinging on whether he was a "guest" in Jackson's home. After the session Donelson returned to Tennessee, with the Eaton affair still unsettled.

Van Buren knew that harmony in the cabinet could not be restored until Branch, Ingham, and Berrien resigned; he also knew that Jackson could not ask them to do so without admitting that the Peggy Eaton affair was the reason. Yet if Van Buren and Eaton resigned first, then the president could force the others out without mentioning the affair. By now Van Buren was so distraught that he took the unusual course of asking the advice of his eldest son Abraham. When his son urged him to resign, Van Buren decided to talk it over with Jackson.

The events that followed suggest that the president was just as distressed as his secretary of state. During one of their horseback rides Van Buren was about to bring up the subject of resignation when suddenly Jackson's horse slipped and would have thrown him had not Van Buren seized the reins. After thanking him for possibly saving his life, Jackson went on to mumble morosely that perhaps he would be better off dead. Van Buren, who had noted how "depressed" Jackson was that day, decided to postpone the talk.

On a later ride, Van Buren finally managed to broach his plan to resign, and Jackson listened patiently for four hours. By the time they finally reached home, much later than usual, Jackson seemed receptive to the idea. The next morning, however, after a sleepless night, the sensitive president blurted out that if Van Buren no longer wanted to serve under him he would not stand in his way. It took an effusive outburst from Van Buren to convince Jackson that he was devoted to the president and felt great pain at the thought of leaving him. Only then would Jackson agree to reorganize the cabinet. Like the old tribal chieftains of the British borderlands of his ancestors, Jackson had to be satisfied that his subject was loyal.[9]

Jackson's willingness to accept Van Buren's proposal the day after it was brought up indicates that he had been thinking about it for some time and was ready to act. His eagerness to keep Peggy Eaton in Tennessee the previous August had shown that he was weary of defending her. Now that the Indian removal bill had been passed, Eaton's presence in the cabinet was no longer so important. If he resigned along with Van Buren, their departure would allow the president to drive out the others.

The dismantling of the cabinet did not go smoothly or quickly. Van Buren had to hold back his own letter of resignation until Eaton had agreed to resign. When Eaton did resign on 7 April, an angry Ingham refused to follow suit until directed to do so by the president almost two weeks later. Ingham did not finally leave office until 20 June. Branch and Berrien also made it public that they were resigning under pressure, and the latter remained in the cabinet until 22 June, after he had returned from negotiating with the Cherokees. When the breakup was over, Jackson still had to explain why the incompetent postmaster general William T. Barry was the only member retained. The president intimated that it was because the Post Office was being investigated by the Senate. It is more likely that he was retained because Jackson wanted to keep a loyal confidant in the cabinet.[10]

In the history of the presidency Jackson's bold shake-up of his cabinet is unique. Disharmony in the cabinet was not unusual before the Civil War; it had already existed under Washington, John Adams, Madison, and Monroe and would be noticeable under John Tyler and James Buchanan. But dismissing almost an entire cabinet at one time was another matter; John Adams came the closest when he ousted Hamilton's spokesmen James McHenry and Timothy Pickering. Tyler and Buchanan lost half their cabinets, but in each case the initiative came from the secretaries themselves, not from the president. Jackson's step was all the more dramatic because cabinet officers at the time had become accustomed to considerable independence and because no other formal body of advisers existed to rival them. Furthermore, this was only the first of two cabinet reorganizations under Jackson. By the time he left office twenty different men had served in his cabinet, a figure approached only by Madison and Tyler before the Civil War.[11]

The crisis, which had started a year earlier with Jackson's letter to Calhoun, took its toll on the president. Rumors were circulating that the Calhoun forces were using the cabinet changes as a "pulse feeler." If western elections in the summer and fall went against the Jacksonians, Calhoun and Clay supposedly planned to organize a coalition in the Senate that would reject Jackson's new cabinet. In April and early May, as the controversy wore on, Jackson grew exhausted and depressed. At one dinner he was noticed "napping constantly & finally sinking his eyes on the plate for an hour." Some observers said that the Old Hero was "the most unhappy man in the city."[12]

The main antagonists in the old cabinet—Eaton and Ingham—brought the crisis to a comic-opera conclusion in May and June. After forcing Jackson to fire him, Ingham published his correspondence with the president in the *United States Telegraph*, making it clear that he had been forced out because he would not entertain Mrs. Eaton. Outraged by what he considered an attack on his wife's good name, Eaton accused

Ingham of "abusive slanders" and demanded a "disavowal." When Ingham ridiculed this "blustering," Eaton challenged him to a duel and, accompanied by his cronies, walked the streets of Washington daring Ingham to face him. After first organizing his own guard, Ingham finally left the city. Apparently relieved by this denouement, Jackson told Van Buren that Ingham and his guards had made "another Parthian flight from this city." The departure of Ingham, followed by that of the Eatons, and the return of the Donelsons in September, brought an end both to the cabinet shake-up and to the Eaton affair.[13]

Rebuilding the cabinet was a difficult operation, because it involved taking care of Van Buren and Eaton as well as finding new secretaries. The decision to name Van Buren minister to Great Britain made it necessary to reassign the current minister, Louis McLane. Jackson also wanted to find a place for Eaton, preferably in the Senate, but when that failed, he appointed Eaton as governor of Florida and later as minister to Spain. The reorganization went so slowly that the cabinet offices were not all filled until 8 August, half a year after Calhoun published his side of the Florida story.

Jackson's anxiety was evident in the way he went about replacing Eaton as secretary of war. Eager to have the matter settled, he offered the post to Sen. Hugh Lawson White within forty-eight hours of Eaton's resignation. He chose White not only because his appointment would open a place in the Senate but because someone of his stature was needed in the cabinet. Furthermore, with the Donelsons still away, Jackson craved having another friend from Tennessee in whom to confide. In a letter to White, whose wife had recently died, Jackson invited him to stay at the President's House. "I have a large room for you," he wrote. "I . . . can sympathise for your sufferings, and you can keep your little son and daughter with you." Saying that White's acceptance would be "a great act of friendship" to him, Jackson admitted that he awaited his answer "with much anxiety." Jackson's agitation is reminiscent of his feelings two years earlier when he awaited word that Van Buren would join the cabinet.[14]

White, however, who remembered how he had been passed over in 1829, disappointed Jackson by rejecting his offer. The president then turned to Gov. Lewis Cass of the Michigan Territory, whose early years resembled Jackson's. Legend had it that he had walked from New Hampshire to Ohio as a boy and at the surrender of Detroit in 1812 had snapped his sword across his knee rather than hand it over to the British. To make way for Van Buren in England, Jackson appointed McLane as secretary of the Treasury. McLane had served with distinction in both houses of Congress and had won important trade concessions in the

British West Indies while minister to Great Britain. Levi Woodbury, the intelligent and noncommittal Yankee from New Hampshire who had stepped down from the Senate in favor of Isaac Hill, was now rewarded with the Navy Department. For attorney general the president chose Roger B. Taney, the attorney general of Maryland. A prominent Roman Catholic with an aristocratic background, Taney had once impressed John Marshall with his arguments before the Supreme Court. At sixty-six the new secretary of state, Sen. Edward Livingston, was older than the others. A member of the prominent New York clan but more recently of New Orleans, he had been Jackson's aide-de-camp during the War of 1812. During the Webster-Hayne debate he had given an important speech on the nature of the government, taking a traditional states'-rights position but granting the national government important powers.

The reorganization of the cabinet reflected changes in the needs of the president and in the shape of his coalition. As a group the new members were far different from the "Millennium of Minnows" that Jackson had put together in 1829. Needing help in fighting the Congress and the social leaders of Washington, Jackson appointed men who were recognized for their ability and their respectability. Two of the new members—Taney and Woodbury—later served on the Supreme Court; another—Cass—ran for president. Only one member of the cabinet—Livingston—came from the Congress. Furthermore, the cabinet better represented the changing Jackson coalition. Woodbury and Cass could speak for the growing number of rural Jacksonians in New England and the Northwest; Livingston for those in the new Southwest. The departure of Eaton, Branch, and Berrien reflected the declining strength of Tennessee and the Southeast in the coalition. Most important, the entire cabinet was united against Calhoun and nullification. With two former Federalists—McLane and Taney—from the Middle Atlantic states and two moderates from the West—Livingston and Cass—receptive to nationalist measures, leadership in the coalition veered from the states'-rights ideology toward a more nationalistic position. Livingston had been enough of a nationalist to vote to override Jackson's veto of the Washington Turnpike bill in 1830. Moreover, the new cabinet was more favorable toward the Bank, which numbered McLane, Livingston, and Cass among its supporters.[15]

Perhaps the most important change in the cabinet was the departure of Van Buren, who would leave for England in August. Van Buren had mortally wounded Calhoun with the cabinet breakup, but he had also hurt himself. Even though Van Buren professed pleasure at the prospect of serving abroad, it was obvious that he was losing power—at least temporarily—for other Jacksonians would now be in a position to influence the president. Stephen Van Rensselaer of New York remarked slyly to Clay that in England Van Buren would be "out of sight, out of mind." Gov. William Carroll of Tennessee, who supported Van Buren, reported reluctantly that a majority of the Tennessee delegation had sided with Calhoun. Van Buren later recalled that these months were "clouded by doubt and anxiety." One observer described him complaining of "dyspepsia" at a dinner. To another he appeared "pale and spiritless" and kept himself "much secluded."[16]

While the cabinet changes were under way, Amos Kendall made a brief attempt to take advantage of Van Buren's weakness. Although never enemies, Kendall and Van Buren had kept a wary eye on each other as they jockeyed to influence the president. Kendall had joined Van Buren in backing the Eatons and in opposing Calhoun, but he had never supported Van Buren as Jackson's successor. In April 1830, for example, as the New Yorker emerged as Jackson's favorite, Kendall wrote somewhat enviously that Van Buren "glide[d] along as smoothly as oil and as silently as a cat." Soon after the cabinet breakup was announced, Kendall showed his colors by trying to stifle Van Buren's aspirations to become Jackson's running mate in 1832. Writing to William B. Lewis from Concord, New Hampshire, on 17 May 1831, he warned Lewis that Calhoun hoped to continue as vice-president and suggested that they take steps to secure the nomination for someone else. In running down a list of potential candidates, he said of Van Buren: "I take it for granted that he does not wish to be run for Vice President—I am sure that he ought not to." Kendall then suggested another candidate, and although nothing came of his advice, he had raised doubts about Van Buren within the administration.[17]

Kendall had already strengthened his own position by bringing in Francis P. Blair to start a new administration newspaper, the *Globe*. In April 1830 when Green failed to fight back after the congressional reports supporting the Bank, Jackson had had enough of Green as his party spokesman. Writing on board a steamboat at Wheeling, Virginia, on his way to Tennessee in June, the president complained to Lewis that although Green had "professed" to be "heart and soul, against the Bank," actually Calhoun controlled him just as a puppeteer did his puppets. "We must," wrote Jackson, "get another organ to announce the policy, and defend the administration." Lewis was not surprised by the complaint because it came close on the heels of Jackson's sharp letters to Calhoun that had reopened the Florida controversy.[18]

Kendall was pleased with the complaint because he had been eager to establish a new party press for some time but had turned down a proposal from Eaton to set one up himself in combination with Green.

Now Kendall, Lewis, and Barry began casting about for an editor. Barry and Kendall thought at once of Blair, who had assisted Kendall on the *Argus of Western America* in Frankfort. At thirty-nine a sickly consumptive weighing barely 100 pounds, Blair had already lived longer than he had expected. He had fought side by side with Kendall and Barry during the Relief War in Kentucky, and his slashing attacks on nullification and the Bank had already come to Jackson's notice. In August, without Jackson's authorization, Kendall sounded out Blair about setting up a press in Washington. Since he was at least $20,000 in debt, Blair listened attentively as Kendall promised $15,000 in executive printing and much more following Blair's expected election as congressional printer.

During the fall of 1830 Jackson moved slowly because he was still uncertain about the Peggy Eaton affair and his relationship with Calhoun and Green. Concerned about the growing disaffection in Virginia, the president first considered Van Buren's friends Thomas Ritchie and Claiborne W. Gooch of Richmond for the job. Had either been appointed, Van Buren would have retained much more influence than he did while he was in England. By mid-October, however, while in the midst of his painful dealings with the Donelsons, Jackson finally settled on Blair. Some measure of Jackson's insecurity can be gauged by the efforts that were made to placate Green, as Kendall and Blair went out of their way to give him assurances that the new newspaper would be simply an "auxiliary" press not in competition with the *Telegraph*. Many observers held Van Buren responsible for the change in the party press, but he had had nothing to do with it and even believed until the following February that Blair was a Calhoun man. Kendall, the mastermind, now had a strong agrarian anti-Bank ally in Washington.[19]

Blair's first few months as editor of the *Globe* in the winter and spring of 1830–31 were as unsettled as the political situation surrounding the cabinet reorganization. On his arrival in Washington in late November his stagecoach overturned, leaving him with a nasty scalp wound. The skeleton-like Blair with a plaster on his head was not an impressive sight when he first met the president, prompting Lewis to remark sarcastically that they needed "sound heads" in Washington. Furthermore, Kendall's promises of strong financial support proved exaggerated, and Blair did not reach $15,000 in executive printing until 1834 and was not elected printer for either house until 1835. Only Barry in the Post Office was generous with executive patronage; in the State Department Van Buren remained neutral. Blair was so short of funds at first that he was not able to pay his press foreman standard wages for over a year. In contrast, the *Telegraph* received an average of over $70,000 a year from Congress between 1831 and 1835.

Fortunately for Blair, Jackson insisted that the executive offices increase their patronage of the *Globe*, and the State Department gave the *Globe* a contract to print the United States diplomatic correspondence for the years 1783–89. Between 1831 and 1837 the Globe received $241,000 for printing from all government sources, most of it toward the end of that period. This was a tidy sum but far less than the $345,000 that went to the *Daily National Intelligencer* and the $301,000 awarded to the *Telegraph* over the same six years. The *Globe*'s profits from its contracts between 1831 and 1837 amounted to $96,000, or $16,000 a year, which Blair divided with his partner John Rives. The circulation of the *Globe*, which became a daily in May 1831, grew rapidly. Blair claimed 2,000 subscribers in July 1831 and 3,700 in November; the rival *Intelligencer* boasted of 5,000 subscribers. By 1835 the circulation of the *Globe* had reached close to 10,000, making it one of the most-read newspapers in America.[20]

Blair at first was somewhat overawed by Washington society. In a revealing letter to his sister-in-law Maria Gratz he admitted sheepishly that he had arrived exactly on time, 7:00 P.M., at a stylish party only to find that the rest of the guests came at a later hour, depending on their social rank. Senators and congressmen arrived at 9:00, Barry and Eaton at 10:00, and the urbane Van Buren and British Minister Charles R. Vaughan at a fashionable 11:00. Blair, however, learned quickly and was soon playing euchre with Van Buren at Vaughan's residence and enjoying sociable evenings with Eaton, Barry, Kendall, Van Buren, and Jackson at the President's House. Once, he told his sister-in-law, they spent the evening teasing Jackson about a woman named Love, who had sent him a letter asking him for money.

Blair got along remarkably well with Jackson. He found the president kind, even affectionate, and a man of good judgment, with whom he quickly developed a close friendship. Still a Kentucky farmer at heart, Blair, or "Blaar" as Jackson pronounced his name, began to leave pails of milk at the President's House as soon as he had moved into his own home and was able to keep cows. On one occasion the president took the Blairs on vacation to the Virginia seaside. Jackson appreciated Blair's simple ways, his writing skills, and above all, his loyalty. Blair's devotion to Jackson never wavered. In March 1831, while the cabinet breakup was getting under way, he told Maria Gratz that his own prospects depended entirely on the president. He would be "a *great man* some day," he said, if Jackson lived. After dealing with politicians whose first loyalty was to themselves, the president was drawn to someone who was first and only a Jackson man.[21]

Within a week of his arrival, Blair, writing from his boardinghouse, had published his first issue of the *Globe*, and soon all pretense that his paper was an "auxiliary" press was put aside. Using sharp digs and sly innuendo, he began to attack Calhoun, nullification, and the Bank while vigorously defending Indian removal and rotation in office. The Bank, he wrote, made hidden profits in handling government funds, New Englanders were hypocrites about the Indians, and removals from office were necessary in order to rid the government of defaulters of the likes of Tobias Watkins. The *Globe* proved indispensable during the crisis over Calhoun's publication of the Florida documents and the resulting reorganization of the cabinet. During these and other crises Blair was able to multiply his effectiveness by exchanging stories and editorials with scores of other Jackson newspapers. The image of the fatherly Old Hero defending the rights of the states and the common people against the Bank and other agencies of the "monied aristocracy" is largely the work of Blair.[22]

The shift of the Jackson press and the breakup of the cabinet not only changed the Jacksonian power structure but also gave the opposition a weapon to use against it. Starting in 1831 the *Telegraph* and other anti-Jackson newspapers began to accuse the president of relying on the influence of informal advisers, who became known as the "kitchen cabinet." According to the opposition these advisers had been exercising a "malign influence" on a presumably easily led president ever since he took office. In this vein Green blamed the reorganization of the cabinet not on Jackson but on "Eaton, Kendall, Lewis, Van Buren, & Co." Donelson, Isaac Hill, and a few other Jacksonians were also named from time to time. References to the kitchen cabinet began to show up in private correspondence in summer 1831. In August a defensive Blair felt obliged to tell his sister-in-law that when the country's *"paramount interests"* were at stake Jackson was influenced by "neither *kitchen* nor *parlor* cabinets." Nicholas Biddle in December wrote that he feared that the "kitchen . . . predominate[d] over the Parlor."[23]

The term first appeared in public print in March 1832, when Sen. George Poindexter of Mississippi used it in the *Telegraph*. The "sinister"-looking Poindexter, a states'-rights Jacksonian who had gone over to Calhoun, was notorious for his drinking and gambling and for falsely accusing his wife of infidelity while divorcing her. He had been charged with killing an opponent in a duel by firing before the command. In his article in the *Telegraph* Poindexter accused the *Globe* of "petty slanders" and said it was edited by a few politicians called the "Kitchen Cabinet." From then on Blair gave the expression wide circulation by defending the administration against the charge on numerous occasions. Ordinarily intrepid, Blair began carrying a pistol in his umbrella after denouncing "Old Poins" in the *Globe*.[24]

According to several recent scholars the kitchen cabinet has modern counterparts. Politically it has been compared with the national political party committee and administratively with the White House staff. One scholar has described the kitchen cabinet as "a series of interlocking circles" made up of "cabinet members, government officials, members of Congress, friends, and on occasion, acquaintances mov[ing] in complex patterns around the President." Though instructive, these modern comparisons are not entirely valid since the established political party structure and the governmental bureaucracy of today did not exist in the Jackson years. The kitchen cabinet, furthermore, had no real structure; it met so irregularly and its membership changed so often that in only one instance did the same three advisers work together more than once on a presidential message.[25]

Jackson did of course have a number of unofficial advisers, especially during his first two years in office. Intent on becoming an active president challenging entrenched interests, he needed close personal advisers to help him deal with problems that went beyond the duties of the regular cabinet. More than any president before him he needed men who could offer ideas, writing skills, organizational ability, and political contacts—in addition to loyalty. Since he could count on such help from only Eaton, Barry, and Van Buren in his first cabinet, he turned to informal advisers, and the concept of a kitchen cabinet grew.

But this concept has been exaggerated. A majority of the members were such well-known public figures that they can hardly be regarded as men operating secretly in the president's private quarters. One active member at first was Duff Green, who later split with the administration and spread the concept of a kitchen cabinet. The unofficial advisers certainly did not replace the official cabinet. Despite its lack of harmony, Jackson's first cabinet carried on the business of the government in much the same way that cabinets had operated from the beginning, and its members had a great deal of influence. Even much-criticized Secretary of the Treasury Ingham exercised power in sensitive areas, dispensing patronage, carrying on a fight with the Bank, and advising Jackson on his first annual message. Attorney General Berrien also gave advice on the Bank and could not be immediately replaced since he was involved in Indian removal, and Secretary of the Navy Branch's correspondence with Jackson was second only to that of Van Buren among the members of the cabinet.

After the cabinet breakup Jackson had much less need for personal advisers because he had more confidence in his new cabinet. By the start of his second term he was relying mostly upon well-established, official advisers: Van Buren, who became vice-president; Kendall, who became postmaster general; Secretary of the Treasury (later Chief Justice) Taney; other members of the cabinet; and in the Congress, Thomas Hart Benton and James K. Polk, who became Speaker. The most significant unofficial adviser was Blair.

Until recently it had been assumed that Jackson's cabinet had met rarely, one scholar putting the number of meetings as low as sixteen, but the discovery of the diary of Mahlon Dickerson, who was secretary of the navy, 1834–38, changed that assumption. By extrapolating from the data in this diary, James C. Curtis has concluded that Jackson's cabinet met regularly, ordinarily on Tuesdays, from late 1831 to 1837. He counted ninety-two meetings between 1834 and 1837 alone.[26]

The personal statements of Levi Woodbury and Roger B. Taney support the case that Jackson began to use his cabinet after the reorganization in 1831 but only after some pressure. In his terse Yankee prose Woodbury wrote that Jackson did not use the cabinet "for advice till broke up first Cabinet & public opinion fav[or]ed Cabinet meetings & urged on him by us." In his so-called Bank War Manuscript, written between 1849 and 1854, Taney described several meetings in fall 1831 in which the cabinet debated the phraseology of a statement on the Bank for the president's annual message. Taney's wording suggests that such sessions continued to take place and demonstrates that the discussions were substantial.[27]

Yet the Old General never became comfortable with his cabinet. According to Levi Woodbury in 1834, Jackson "shuns consulting all, as he is so military & dislikes councils of War & Cabinets." Taney wrote that Jackson called no cabinet meeting to discuss the veto of the bill to recharter the Bank. And Kendall recalled that Jackson "never took a vote in his Cabinet. Questions were submitted and discussed; but when it came to decision, 'He took the responsibility.'"[28]

As soon as Jackson had completed his cabinet breakup, he left for the Rip Raps, an island owned by the government in Hampton Roads in Chesapeake Bay. He had already fallen into the habit—that he would follow for eight years—of vacationing in alternate summers at the Rip Raps and at the Hermitage. In July 1831 he needed the vacation since he had spent a difficult nine months after returning from Tennessee the previous fall. He had had a long, drawn-out test of wills with the Donelsons over Peggy Eaton. His fight with Calhoun, culminating in the establishment of the *Globe* and the reorganization of his cabinet, had left him morose and depressed all spring. Although the Eaton affair was now over and harmony had apparently been restored in the cabinet, other more serious battles loomed—the Bank War and the election of 1832.

5

THE BANK VETO AND
INDIAN REMOVAL

With his new cabinet finally organized Jackson returned to dealing with Congress. After the busy session of 1829–30, Congress had accomplished little during the short session the following winter. Now with Congress ready to convene again in December 1831 the president would have another try at influencing economic legislation. As he had learned in the previous sessions, it would not be easy, for the chief executive, especially one such as Jackson, faced many obstacles in Congress. In addition his Bank opponents were already coming to the support of Nicholas Biddle, his political opponents were rallying around Henry Clay for the coming presidential election, and his own coalition was still divided. Concern was growing about whether the Jackson party could carry Pennsylvania and other states where the Bank was popular. Furthermore, the president had still not shaken the doubts that had gripped him during the cabinet breakup. Though confident of his own popularity, he was uncertain about how to proceed.

Jackson's indecision coincided with the rise of Secretary of the Treasury Louis McLane in the new cabinet. With Van Buren in England, Secretary of State Edward Livingston getting old, and Attorney General Roger B. Taney unfamiliar with Washington, McLane was able to assume leadership from the start. His sharp mind, his long experience in Congress, and his success in opening the British West Indies had brought him the respect of Washingtonians and especially of Jackson. In writing Van Buren in September 1831 the president remarked, "Mr. McLane's mind is a host to me." Worn down by ill health and more than two years of political battles, the president seemed willing to let this ambitious and capable insider take the initiative. McLane, who had his sights set on the vice-presidency, was more than willing. With his base of power in the Treasury Department, he could play Hamilton to Jackson's Washington.[1]

With his Federalist background McLane brought a nationalistic perspective on issues that had not had much expression heretofore in the Jackson administration. Up to 1831 the major battle within the coalition had been between the nullifiers and the more moderate states' righters, the Old Republicans and the western agrarians. During the next two years the moderate states' righters would vie with nationalists such as McLane and Livingston. Sensing the change when he received Jackson's letter praising McLane in October, Van Buren wrote back warning the president that "a great portion" of his new cabinet did not believe in "strict construction of the Constitution [as] the only true and saving ground."[2]

McLane's support of the Bank also brought him into conflict with Taney and with the westerners Blair, Benton, and Kendall. While Jackson was ridding himself of Calhoun, he was also continuing his attack on the Bank. In his annual message in December 1830, he had proposed replacing the Bank with a government institution with no private stockholders, which would make no loans and would issue bills of exchange only to cover expenses. Blair, who had just arrived in Washington, followed suit with a series of articles in the *Globe* against the Bank, accusing it of political bribery in Pennsylvania, New Hampshire, and Kentucky. According to Blair, the states had every right to tax the Bank; it was merely a "convenient," not a "necessary," government agent. Jackson received further support in January when George Bancroft, already at work on his *History of the United States,* published an article opposing the Bank in the *North American Review.*[3]

Benton continued the assault by introducing a Senate resolution in February 1831 against the renewal of the Bank's charter. In a long speech he offered clues about the course that many Jacksonians would follow. He ignored the question of constitutionality and attacked the Bank for "having too much power over the people." Not content with simply overturning the Bank, he demanded an entirely new monetary system based on gold and silver and concluded with his formula for a new two-party system: "a hard money party against a paper party." In the first of many roll calls on the Bank issue that would be held over the next few years, the Senate rejected Benton's resolution, 23 to 20, but the vote was closer and the coalition stuck together better than expected. All the Jacksonians but three voted for the resolution; the entire opposition voted against it.[4]

The Bank was also becoming an issue in New York. Although Van Buren and the Albany Regency have been blamed for starting the Bank War, the charge is not convincing. As an Old Republican, Van Buren had occasionally attacked the Bank for its "constitutional encroachments" on states' rights, but he had also sought to get the Bank to establish branches in Albany and Oswego, where he owned property, and he had tried to tone down the criticism of the Bank in Jackson's first annual message. His political friends were also of two minds. Thomas Olcott and Benjamin Knower of Albany, for example, opposed the Bank, but Gulian C. Verplanck of New York City and Rudolph Bunner of Oswego favored it. Churchill C. Cambreleng, later an outspoken critic of the Bank, had served as a director of the New York City branch.[5]

Late in 1830 the New York Jacksonians took their cue from Washington and began to unite against the Bank. Van Buren and James A. Hamilton had a hand in preparing Jackson's statement against the Bank in his annual message, and Bunner was complaining that no one in favor of recharter could be reelected. Cambreleng, he said, was now speaking out against the Bank. When Jacksonians in the state legislature offered resolutions in March 1831 against rechartering the Bank, Biddle organized a lobby to defend it, and Jacksonians were forced to take a position. The *Albany Argus* came out against the Bank, but the *New York Courier and Enquirer* shifted ground and began to support it. In both the state senate and the assembly the Jacksonians voted as a bloc against the Bank, and the resolutions passed by substantial margins. The Bank War had tightened party lines in New York.[6]

Not all Jacksonians were interested in fighting the Bank. A congressional poll taken by Congressman Robert P. Letcher in December 1830 showed that six Jacksonian senators and over fifty Jacksonian congressmen favored the institution. As might be expected, the list included a sizable number from the Bank's home state of Pennsylvania. A resolution in favor of recharter passed both houses of the Pennsylvania legislature almost unanimously in March 1831. In the following August another pro-Bank Jacksonian complained that the attacks of Jackson and Blair on the Bank had backfired against the party in the Kentucky state election.[7]

Soon after taking office that August, McLane showed his own sympathy for the Bank by inviting Nicholas Biddle to come to Washington. Biddle agreed but first met with his stockholders and was given the power to apply for recharter at any time even though the charter still had over four years to run. When he arrived in Washington in September, he was delighted to learn that McLane and Secretary of State Livingston were already trying to get Jackson to take a less hostile approach toward the Bank. Livingston, who was preparing the president's annual message, had agreed with McLane to put nothing in the message about the Bank. Biddle now wondered if McLane and Livingston could go further and persuade Jackson to say that he was leaving the matter up to Congress. He also hoped that McLane would propose recharter in his Treasury report.[8]

During the next month McLane discussed his plans for the coming session of Congress with the president. One of his proposals called for selling the government's stock in the Bank back to the Bank itself and using the funds to complete paying off the national debt. With the debt extinguished it would be possible to reduce government revenues drastically. He would eliminate the income from land by selling the public lands to the states in which they lay and distributing the proceeds to all the states. Tariffs could be reduced too, but he favored retaining protection for wool, hemp, and iron as well as woolen and cotton cloth. Boldly taking issue with Jackson, McLane recommended rechartering the Bank, provided that certain "judicious checks and limitations" were included in the bill.[9]

Still uncertain about his own program, Jackson was impressed by McLane's ambitious proposals. For the first time the president was party to what he called a "full and lucid" master plan. McLane had a position on everything except Indian removal, and Jackson had his mind made up on that. Jackson found the suggestions for paying off the debt and reducing government revenues especially appealing. He was also surprisingly willing to entertain the idea of revising the Bank's charter rather than insisting on the destruction of the institution.

Jackson therefore gave McLane permission to support recharter in his annual Treasury report and agreed to say in his own message that he would leave recharter up to Congress. He was not, however, making an agreement with the Bank; he still insisted that its charter be modified, and he opposed any recharter before the presidential election. While visiting Philadelphia on 19 October McLane told Biddle the good news but warned that it would be "inexpedient" to apply for recharter in 1832.[10]

At a cabinet meeting held to discuss Jackson's message to Congress, McLane learned that one member strongly opposed the Bank. Taney later recalled that as he listened to the message being read he was "startled" to learn that the president was leaving the matter to Congress. He promptly remonstrated, arguing that the public would infer from the wording that the president had given up his opposition to the Bank and would acquiesce in whatever Congress decided. A debate followed in which McLane and Livingston defended the statement, although the other members had little to say. Somewhat embarrassed, Jackson appeared to side with McLane and Livingston, and the meeting ended on that note. The next day, however, the president showed Taney a slightly changed version, which put more emphasis on Jackson's previously expressed views. Still, despite the change, the president had apparently backed off from his attack on the Bank.[11]

Having agreed to let McLane publish his comprehensive program in his Treasury report, the president did not devote much space to his own policies in his annual message. His most important statement came when he announced that he wanted a lower tariff that would serve "all our national interests" and "relieve the people from unnecessary taxation." Faced with obstacles to his Indian removal policy, Jackson could only remark that "with perseverance" they would attain their goal of clearing all Indians out of the states. As previously arranged, the president said that he was leaving the Bank question up to Congress. He ignored internal improvements, public lands, and distribution.[12]

McLane filled in the details the next day in his report, with his plans for distribution, the recharter of the Bank, and a reduced but still protective tariff. His report was greeted with a chorus of protests from Old Republicans and westerners. Cambreleng called it "as bad as it possibly can be—a new version of Alexander Hamilton's two reports." Blair refused to endorse the plans for modifying and rechartering the Bank, saying that McLane spoke for himself, not for the administration, and insisting that Jackson had not changed his position on the Bank. Thomas Ritchie also disagreed on the Bank. McLane, however, was undaunted, boasting that he had cut the ground out from under Clay and his American System and had put the administration in the position of harmonizing sectional differences.[13]

The next two months were particularly difficult for Jackson, who suddenly found his new administration almost as unharmonious as his first. McLane, furious at Blair for not supporting him on the Bank, launched an effort to get rid of him as editor of the *Globe* and was joined by Van Buren supporters, who felt that Blair was cool toward the Little Magician. It was an odd alliance because McLane and Van Buren were rivals for the vice-presidency. The conspirators settled on Amos Kendall to replace Blair, also an odd development because Kendall himself was against the Bank and not noticeably friendly toward Van Buren. The mess was further complicated by Van Buren's absence in England and the battle over confirming his nomination that was going on in the Senate. Ill health made the situation even worse for the president, who was weakened by influenza and suffered persistent pain from the bullet in his left arm. As the winter wore on, Jackson seemed almost as morose and irritable as he had been during the cabinet breakup.[14]

Meanwhile the Twenty-second Congress, which would deal with Van Buren and the Bank, was getting started, with the Jackson party no stronger than it had been for the past two years. In the Senate 23 Jacksonians were balanced by 21 National Republicans and 4 Calhoun men. Although the 126 Jacksonians greatly outnumbered the 66 National Republicans, 17 Anti-Masons, and 4 nullifiers in the House, the margin was nowhere near as great as it appeared; many of the Jacksonians were undependable. Andrew Stevenson was elected Speaker by only one vote, and Duff Green, not Blair, was to serve as printer for both houses. The new Congress was notable, for John Quincy Adams was sitting in the House and Henry Clay had been elected to the Senate. With Clay and Webster as senators and Vice-President Calhoun presiding over the Senate, the great triumvirate sat in the same house for the first time.[15]

With the setting so muddled Biddle was uncertain whether to apply for the recharter of the Bank. In mid-December, however, he was forced to make a decision when he received a letter from Clay urging him to go ahead. Clay, who had just been nominated for president by the National Republicans and was in need of a campaign issue, thought that "if *now* called upon," Jackson would not veto a recharter bill but would probably do so if reelected. Webster as well as Clay's running mate, John Sergeant, who was one of Biddle's chief advisers, also wanted Biddle to apply.[16]

To determine his congressional support, especially among Jacksonians, Biddle sent his most influential adviser, Thomas Cadwalader, to Washington. After consulting with McLane and Samuel Smith, Cadwalader found that the Bank would command small majorities in both houses. The support included four Jacksonians in the Senate and about forty in the House, somewhat down from the year before. McLane and Smith both urged Biddle to wait until after the election when more Jacksonians could vote for the Bank without embarrassing their president while he ran for reelection. They feared that an early application would force a confrontation with Jackson, who could be expected to react angrily by vetoing. Despite these arguments, Cadwalader recommended that Biddle apply at once.

Pulled in both directions, Biddle listened to Clay and Cadwalader rather than to McLane and Smith. His closest advisers, including Cadwalader, believed that Jackson would not dare alienate voters in states such as Pennsylvania by vetoing. They also believed that McLane and Livingston would be able to restrain the president. Cadwalader's advice was apparently decisive, for shortly after receiving it Biddle took steps to apply for recharter.[17]

The half-year debate in Congress that ensued was painful for both the Jackson party and the Bank. Sen. George M. Dallas of Pennsylvania, whom Biddle picked to present the Bank's memorial for recharter, typified dozens of Jackson supporters who wanted to vote for the Bank but feared antagonizing the president. Dallas showed his reluctance in his presentation speech on 9 January 1832, remarking that the memorial was *"dangerously timed."* With their party divided, administration leaders were resigned to having the bill pass, but after holding a congressional caucus they decided to fight a delaying action. They hoped to postpone the bill until after the election, but if not, they would put the Bank on the defensive and prepare the ground for a veto. As Benton later recalled in the military metaphors that characterized the Bank War, they would engage the Bank "in a general combat, and lay it open to side-blow, as well as direct attacks."[18]

The campaign began in the House when William S. Archer of Virginia proposed sending the memorial to a select committee, which could be counted on to take its time. George McDuffie, however, fought off the motion, and the memorial went to his Ways and Means Committee, on which he and the majority supported the Bank. In the Senate the next day Benton stalled by asking for the names of all Bank stockholders, including foreigners, and of all those who owed money to the Bank. He followed with other diversionary motions, one that dealt with the notes issued by the Bank and a second that put a ten-year limit on the recharter.[19]

To counteract these tactics, Biddle started a campaign to have memorials in favor of recharter sent to Congress. While he was rounding up over a hundred of these memorials, the Jackson party, hampered by McLane's reluctance to oppose the Bank, could muster less than a dozen opposing memorials. Realizing the importance of the votes of Pennsylvania's congressional delegation, Biddle succeeded in getting another resolution from the Pennsylvania legislature supporting the Bank. He also sent two of his leading attorneys, John Sergeant and the renowned constitutional lawyer, Horace Binney, to Washington to lobby for the Bank.

In the first week of February, Biddle sought to come to some understanding with the administration. He tried to get Dallas to take the Pennsylvania resolutions to the president, warn him of the danger of losing such an important state, and offer to serve as a liaison between Jackson and Biddle. Dallas, tired of being caught between the Bank and the president, hesitated and finally refused. Meanwhile Livingston and former Pennsylvania congressman Charles J. Ingersoll drew up modifications for the Bank charter that they believed Jackson would accept. By these terms the government would own no stock in the Bank, but the president of the United States would appoint one director at each branch. The Bank would hold no real estate, and the states would have the power to tax the property of the Bank.[20]

But no arrangement was possible, for Biddle's initiatives and the Senate's rejection of Van Buren's nomination as minister to Great Britain had resolved any indecision Jackson might have had. After a surgeon removed the bullet from his arm his health rapidly improved, and he threw himself fully into the Bank War. In addition Jackson had found out about McLane's efforts to get rid of Blair and had come to the editor's rescue. Cambreleng reported happily that McLane had "ruined himself" with the president. "Do not fear," the New Yorker exulted, "we shall take care of the Mammoth [the Bank] in some way or other." According to Cambreleng, the president was keeping a *"confidential"* aide busy monitoring the struggle in Congress. Although McLane continued to have the president's ear on some issues, he had lost his influence in the battle over recharter of the Bank.[21]

In the House, after McDuffie's Ways and Means Committee had reported back a recharter bill on 9 February 1832, Augustin Clayton of Georgia sought to slow the process by calling for a select committee to investigate the Bank. The Jacksonians were confident that the Bank could not win on the committee question. "If the investigation was denied," said Benton, "it would be guilt shrinking from detection; if admitted, it was well known that misconduct would be found." To press the attack Clayton read a long list of Bank abuses to the House, keeping the text covered so that no one would recognize Benton's handwriting. McDuffie, surprisingly, did not fight the proposal for a select committee even though he knew that a majority of its members would be hostile to the Bank.[22]

Discouraged by this development, Binney soon returned to Philadelphia, and the Bank men heaped scorn on McDuffie. Ingersoll called his performance a "capitulation"; John Quincy Adams said McDuffie was "either a coward or a traitor." It is more likely that the South Carolinian, loyal to the planters in his state, wanted the Ways and Means Committee to spend the next few weeks on the tariff instead of on the Bank.

The report of the investigating committee on 30 April brought up many of the old charges against the Bank—that it had had political motives in appointing directors, that its money had influenced elections, and that it had subsidized journalists and politicians. There was some truth in each charge. When Jackson took office, the Bank had tried to curry favor by appointing Jacksonians to the board in Nashville. The Bank had sided with Adams in New Hampshire. Loans and retainers went to influential journalists, such as Green, and members of Congress, such as Webster. Little of this was illegal, flagrant, or even out of the ordinary for the era—except perhaps Biddle's unwise loan to James Watson Webb of the *New York Courier and Enquirer,* after which the publisher shifted his support to the Bank, and even this episode has been convincingly explained. But the Bank was kept on the defensive. The issue was joined, and the way was being prepared for a veto.[23]

On 23 May Biddle came to Washington to take personal command of the operation. After consulting McLane and Livingston of the administration and McDuffie and Webster in Congress, he agreed to accept certain modifications in the Bank charter. The bill that Dallas presented to the Senate on 23 May placed limits on the power of the Bank to hold real estate and to establish branches. It also gave the president of the United States the power to appoint a director at each branch and reserved to Congress the right to keep the Bank from issuing small notes. Branch drafts were limited, and it was implied that the states could tax shares of Bank stock held by their citizens. The first three changes answered Jackson's criticisms, and the last two were designed to please local banks and the states.[24]

The bill passed both houses—28 to 20 in the Senate and 107 to 85 in the House—and was sent to the president on 3 July. The Jacksonians failed to unite against the Bank. In the Senate six Jacksonians, including the two from Pennsylvania, went against Jackson by voting for the Bank; perhaps a dozen might have done so if the bill had been presented after the election. The National Republicans, on the other hand, voted unanimously for the Bank. The influence of sectionalism was apparent: Twenty-four of thirty northern senators voted yea; fourteen of eighteen southern senators voted nay. Three of the five Jacksonians who voted for party over section by opposing the Bank—Isaac Hill, William L. Marcy, and Nathan Sanford—represented the banner Jackson states of New Hampshire and New York. A similar pattern appeared in the House, where twenty-nine Jacksonians voted for the Bank and only two members of the opposition—an Anti-Mason and a nullifier—voted against it.[25]

As expected, Jackson vetoed the bill. On returning from England, Van Buren hurried to the President's House on the evening of 7 July, before the veto message had been completed, to find the Old Hero pale as a "spectre" and full of fight. "The bank," he said, "is trying to kill me, *but I will kill it!*" With only Taney in the cabinet actively opposing the Bank, Jackson held no cabinet meetings to discuss whether to veto the bill but did ask individual members for their opinions about the content of the veto message. Kendall, Taney, Woodbury, Donelson, and Jackson himself did the writing. Although Taney, who submitted a draft, later claimed most of the credit, the veto was mostly the work of Kendall, whose bold style is evident in much of the document. Completed and signed on 10 July 1832, it was sent at once to the Senate.[26]

Jackson's veto message has been called "a ringing statement of . . . the rights of the common man," which "struck the nation like a manifesto for social revolution," characterizations that fail to take into account the entire document. At the beginning, to be sure, and again at the end, Jackson attacked the Bank in words that bordered on class warfare. In evocative language rich with words such as "monopoly," "gratuity," and "opulent," he denounced the "favors" enjoyed by the Bank's stockholders. In no uncertain terms he repudiated the "exclusive privileges" that made "the rich richer and the potent more powerful." He added an appeal to nationalism by noting that many foreigners owned stock in the Bank.[27]

But in the middle passages of the veto Jackson adopted a more sober voice, questioning the constitutionality of the Bank. Claiming equal right with the Congress and the Supreme Court to interpret the Constitution, the president pointed out a number of provisions in the proposed charter that he considered unconstitutional. Perhaps, he said, the necessary and proper clause could be used to justify a financial agent for the federal government but not a banking monopoly or the privileges proposed for this bank. The bill, he insisted, violated states' rights by giving the Bank too much power over the state banks and by denying the states the power to tax it.

In this middle portion of the text Jackson was also practical and conciliatory. It was only fair, he said, to veto the bill at this time, for the population changes of the 1820s had left a number of states underrepresented in the House. The following fall the new federal ratio based on the census of 1830 would go into effect, bringing representation back in line. Since the Bank still had four years to run on its present charter, the next two Congresses would have ample time to bring up a new recharter bill.

Jackson also showed restraint in other ways. In his attack on privilege, he disavowed any interest in leveling social classes. He insisted that government could not produce "equality of . . . wealth," that "distinctions in society" would "always exist." He did not fully express his resentment toward banking or make any reference to his long-held conviction that all banks, especially the Bank, were corrupt. At one point he even seemed to support a group of rival bankers—probably one headed by Jacksonian David Henshaw of Massachusetts—who had sought to "take a charter" for a new national bank "on terms much more favorable" than those offered by the Bank.

Some of the moderation can be attributed to Taney. Kendall was surely the major contributor, especially in the more emotional passages at the beginning and end, but Taney deserves credit for a number of the ideas in the message. In a fifty-page memorandum to the president on 27 June the attorney general had laid out many of the arguments against the constitutionality of the Bank, especially those based on the necessary and proper clause. Taney's memorandum is the source of Jackson's contention that the Constitution might justify a financial agent but not one as powerful as the Bank. Jackson also drew on Taney for his criticism that the recharter bill did not allow two national banks.

Jackson's message was in many ways a product of his coalition. The strident attack on the privileged rich at the start and finish reflected the bitterness of Kendall, Benton, and other westerners toward the Bank after the Panic of 1819. The careful constitutional analysis in the middle carried the imprint of the Old Republicans. There was even the nod toward up-and-coming bankers in the coalition in the reference to Henshaw's efforts to form another national bank. Mainly lacking was the respect for the Bank as a valuable national institution that McLane would have added. The message combined Jackson's antibank feelings with the mixed ideologies and interests of the coalition.

It has been argued that Jackson dangerously expanded executive power in the veto message by claiming an equal right with Congress and the Supreme Court to determine the constitutionality of congressional legislation. Perhaps, but in claiming that right Jackson was simply stating the standard republican belief in the independence of the three branches of the government. Like other republicans he was more interested in restricting the Supreme Court than he was in increasing the power of the executive. As he made clear in the veto, he was defending Congress as much as the presidency from the Court. "The authority of the Supreme Court," he wrote, "must not, therefore, be permitted to control the Congress or the Executive."[28]

Most important, the veto was a potent political message aimed at the people in an election year. As soon as Jackson's veto was taken up in the Senate on 11 July, the political leaders of the opposition party, who had been strangely quiet during the debate over the Bank, sprang into action. Webster took issue with Jackson's "inflamed statement" about privilege. The Bank, he said, had no more powers than those "usually conferred on similar institutions"; the stockholders received economic benefits, not "gratuitously" but in return for "a valuable consideration in money." Repeating one of his favorite themes, Webster insisted that the bill was passed not to benefit the stockholders but to "promote great public interests, for great public objects." He condemned Jackson for "extend[ing] the grasp of executive pretension over every power of the government" and for "seek[ing] to inflame the poor against the rich."[29]

The next day presidential candidate Clay attacked along the same lines but even more harshly. He was particularly critical of Jackson for saying that if asked he would "cheerfully" have drawn up a plan for a new bank. Clay wondered sarcastically if Jackson wished to emulate the king of France, who had had the power of legislative initiative. He reacted with "deep alarm" at Jackson's statement that he would support the Constitution only as he understood it. Clay accused Jackson of "an electioneering motive" in his veto. The same charge, of course, could also have been made against Webster and Clay since both were thinking of the coming election. Otherwise their speeches had little effect, for the supporters of the recharter bill could not find the votes to override the veto. On 13 July the bill passed again by a vote of 22 to 19, far short of the required two-thirds majority.[30]

On the very next day, only two days before Congress adjourned, Jackson signed into law a new tariff bill. The president, who had called for tariff reduction in his annual message, had never shown the same passion over the tariff that he had over the Bank. Ever since taking office, he had approached the issue primarily as it related to the national debt, which he was determined to eliminate. As long as the debt existed, he wanted tariff revenues to bring it down. Once the debt was eliminated, tariffs could be lowered as a means of avoiding a surplus, a potential source of sectional disputes. As one scholar has put it, Jackson "opposed only excess revenue, not the principle of protection." He had temporized on the tariff, therefore, calling for "modification" in 1829 but a year later suggesting protection for important raw materials and manufactures that were "essential to national defense." Now with the debt dropping, the presidential election approaching, and nullification looming, Jackson was ready to lower the tariff.[31]

Members of Congress, responsive to sectional interests, took the tariff question more seriously than the president. As in the previous Congress, southerners were clamoring for tariff reduction while northern manufacturers were fighting to retain tariff protection. In the House the question was sent both to McDuffie's low-tariff Ways and Means Committee, which had four southern members, and to the protectionist Committee on Manufactures, with Adams as chairman and five members from the Northeast. In the Senate it was sent both to the Manufactures Committee, which included Clay, and to the Finance Committee, whose chairman, Samuel Smith, was a close friend of McLane. Proposals ranged broadly. Clay recommended immediately cutting the duties on items that did not compete with American goods in order to save tariff protection for the rest. McLane, who had Jackson's backing on this issue even though they had parted over the Bank, proposed moving more slowly but lowering the average rate from 45 percent to 27 percent over a period of years. McDuffie demanded a slash in rates to 12.5 percent.

The administration worked hard for McLane's bill, the *Globe* insisting that it was a moderate plan, midway between Clay's protectionism and McDuffie's free-trade approach. In support, Ritchie wrote that he favored this "liberal adjustment" of the tariff. New York Jacksonians, however, were split between merchants, who favored low tariffs, and farmers and manufacturers, who wanted various forms of protection. In 1828 the Albany Regency had sided with the protectionists by supporting the Tariff of Abominations. McLane wrote angrily to Jackson in May of the difficulty of convincing many New Yorkers that the demands of the South were "just." If New York persisted in asking for more protection, he said, the Union would be threatened. The secretary went so far as to write articles supporting the tariff bill for the *Globe* and *Niles' Register*.[32]

In an unexpected development, the decision on which course to take lay with Adams, who chose to back his political opponents McLane and Jackson rather than his political ally Clay. After consulting with McLane, Adams presented the secretary's tariff bill to the House Committee on Manufactures, which raised the rates in the bill before endorsing it. The committee bill, calling for overall rates of about 33 percent, passed the House on 28 June. The Senate then passed the House bill with protectionist amendments but was forced to give up the amendments when the bill went to conference committee.

The McLane-Adams tariff bill, which the president signed on 14 July, eliminated the worst of the "abominations" of the 1828 act. Gone was the intricate system of valuation, which had masked high rates. The bill reduced revenues by cutting the average rates from 45 percent to 33 percent but kept the protective system intact. Textile manufacturers were willing to accept this reduction because the bill decreased duties on raw materials while keeping the duties on most woolen and cotton goods high. To please the South, however, the bill lowered the duty on coarse woolen cloth, used for slaves' clothing. Jackson commented cheerfully that the "modified Tariff [had] killed the ultras" and that "the people [would] see that all their grievances [had been] removed."[33]

The voting on the tariff showed that Jackson was overly optimistic. Even on the final bill, with average rates lowered to 33 percent, southern congressmen, who considered the reductions inadequate, voted nay, 45 to 30, northern congressmen yea, 87 to 35. Sectionalism was even more pronounced in the voting on the more protectionist Senate version, before the conference committee removed the amendments. Southern senators voted nay on that bill, 15 to 3, northerners yea, 32 to 8. Although the Jacksonians, including the New Yorkers, showed a strong majority for the final bill in the House, they were badly divided in the Senate. The bill could not have passed without solid backing from the opposition. The tariff remained a sectional instead of a party issue.[34]

Distribution, however, became a more partisan matter. McLane's plan to sell the public lands on credit to the western states and to distribute the proceeds to all the states found little support in either the West or the South. The western states could not afford to buy the land, and westerners preferred to have the government reduce the price of land through a graduation plan. Southerners continued to fear that distribution would be used only to justify a high tariff. As a result, Jackson refused to endorse McLane's plan, and after three years of supporting some form of distribution, gave it up altogether.

When Clay offered his own distribution plan in April, the National Republicans rallied to support it. Like McLane, Clay proposed distributing the proceeds from the sale of lands to all the states, but he abandoned the impractical idea of selling the land first to the western states. To appeal to his National Republican constituency, he proposed using the proceeds for internal improvements, education, and the colonization of free blacks. With the Northeast in favor of the bill and the Southeast unalterably opposed, Clay needed to pry votes from the West. To do so, he offered a direct rebate of 12.5 percent of the land proceeds to the states from which they came, plus grants of land for internal improvements. He also argued that the more settled western states, such as Louisiana, Kentucky, and Ohio, would benefit more from these internal improvements than they would from the cheap land being offered by the Jacksonians, which would mainly help the frontier. In an election year it was an artful political package.

When the bill passed the Senate, 26 to 18, partisanship prevailed, as all twenty-one National Republicans voted for distribution while sixteen out of twenty-three Jacksonians, as well as two of the four Calhoun senators, opposed it. The only Jacksonians voting yea were four from Middle Atlantic states, where internal improvements were popular, but three others, from the West and perhaps interested in roads, failed to vote. Clay's maneuvers paid off, for the western senators divided, seven voting yea, seven nay, and four not voting. Five of those voting yea were from the settled West. When the bill reached the House too late for serious discussion, Jacksonians succeeded in postponing it by another party vote.[35]

On internal improvements Jackson continued the policy he had established in 1830. As Congress drew to a close in July, he signed a bill for one special project but pocket vetoed a rivers-and-harbors bill. Chiding him for these decisions, the *Richmond Enquirer* argued that on the basis of constitutionality, he should have reversed his positions. The *Enquirer* explained that it opposed most internal-improvement bills but was willing to accept those for certain rivers and harbors, where the federal government traditionally had jurisdiction. In defending his decisions in his annual message five months later Jackson reminded Congress of his opposition to bills that were not "national in their character" and warned in Old Republican language that excessive federal expenditures would "promote a mischievous and corrupting influence upon elections" and would only "add to the splendor, the patronage, and the power of the General Government." As in his Maysville veto Jackson pointed out that those who disagreed with his position could try to amend the Constitution.[36]

Party lines were more clearly drawn on Jackson's Indian policy. Ever since the passage of the Indian removal bill in 1830 the president and his opponents had waged a running battle over the way in which the administration was carrying out removal. The issue was so important to Jackson that he kept as much control over it as possible by asking friends such as John Coffee and William Carroll to negotiate with the Indians or even occasionally dealing directly with them himself. Since the Indian Bureau was in the War Department, he appointed secretaries of war—Eaton and Cass—whose views on removal corresponded with his own.

In addition the president kept his eye on the head of the bureau— Thomas L. McKenney—who was a holdover from the Adams administration. McKenney had been useful in helping to secure passage of the removal bill, but as an Adams man he was unpopular with the Jacksonians, who began to replace his agents with members of their own party. McKenney also annoyed Eaton and Jackson by refusing to cooperate in a dubious scheme involving their friend Sam Houston. After living almost a year with the Cherokees, Houston had returned in February 1830 to lobby for a lucrative contract to provide rations for the Indians on their way west. The scheme hinged on giving western competitors insufficient time to make bids. When McKenney refused to go along and news of the plan leaked out, the administration broke off the negotiations. McKenney stayed on at the bureau until August 1830, when he protested too loudly about cuts in funds for the Cherokees, and Jackson dismissed him.[37]

In removing the Indians Jackson had decided to concentrate on the 60,000 who remained in the South. In 1831 Houston told Alexis de Tocqueville that the situation in the South was much more critical than that in the North, where the Indians who were left could easily be "pushed back." The Choctaws, who lived in Mississippi, were the first choice because they appeared to be the most willing to move. In April 1830, during the debate on Indian removal, a group of them had voluntarily drawn up their own removal treaty. Although nothing came of the offer, it had encouraged Jackson to think that they would not be hard to move.[38]

But in summer 1830 the Choctaws disappointed him by failing to send representatives when Jackson invited the chiefs of the southern tribes to meet him in Tennessee. Speaking to the leaders of the Chickasaws, the only chiefs who came, the president delivered a stern warning. If they spurned his offer of land in the West, he said, they could not call upon their "great father" to "relieve" them of their "troubles." They would remain in the East under white rule and would soon be assimilated. After negotiating with Eaton and Coffee in August, the Chickasaws signed a provisional treaty for moving west, with the condition that they first approve the designated territory.[39]

The president then sent Eaton and Coffee to Dancing Rabbit Creek in Mississippi to deal with the Choctaws. Suspecting that missionaries might advise the Choctaws to reject his proposals, Eaton ordered them off the Indians' lands before he would start negotiating. He then distributed gifts among the Indians and soon won their cooperation. The treaty, signed on 27 September and ratified the following March, carried out the terms of the Indian Removal Act. The Choctaws agreed to exchange their lands for territory in the West and to move in three groups between 1831 and 1833. The treaty provided for land allotments, taken from tribal land, to be given to the chiefs, to heads of families who wished to remain behind, and to Indians who had been cultivating the soil. It was presumed that the great majority of these Indians would sell their allotments and move west. Those who did remain would become citizens of Mississippi. On hearing the news, Jackson was greatly elated. "Providence appears to smile," he wrote, on their efforts to "preserve these people from *annihilation as tribes,* and the machinations of ours and their worst enemies."[40]

The way in which the Choctaws were removed exposed the bitter reality of Jacksonian Indian removal. Commissary General of Subsistence George Gibson was given contradictory instructions to act humanely, move swiftly, and save money. Jackson, who was determined to eliminate the federal deficit and who had promised that removal would cost no more than $4 million, often badgered his officials to cut costs. In order to save money the government sought extremely low bids from contractors, who sometimes provided substandard pork and other inferior foodstuffs. The prospects for fraudulent profit were so great that politicians fought for even low-level jobs in the removal operation. When some of the Choctaws threatened not to move, Eaton warned them that they would end up in jail and sent in a cavalry company.[41]

The emphasis on economy and the unusually cold winter of 1831–32 combined to bring the Choctaws great hardship. Tocqueville, who was en route to New Orleans, described their suffering as they crossed the Mississippi River at Memphis:

> It was then the middle of winter, and the cold unusually severe; the snow had frozen hard upon the ground, and the river was drifting huge masses of ice. The Indians had their families with them, and they brought in their train the wounded and the sick, with children newly born and old men upon the verge of death. They possessed neither tents nor wagons, but only their arms and some provisions. I saw them embark to pass the mighty river, and never will that solemn spectacle fade from my remembrance. No cry, no sob, was heard among the assembled crowd; all were silent.[42]

After taking notice of such distress, the government revised its plans for the two remaining Choctaw removals, but the suffering on the trail and in Mississippi continued. In 1832 cholera was especially hard on the Choctaws, and a shortage of funds made proper care impossible. Determined more than ever to save money, the administration required officials to justify all expenditures. Jackson even approved of a commutation plan whereby Indians would be given a small sum of money and told to move on their own. On hearing that a similar plan had been adopted later for the Chickasaws, Jackson told Coffee that "the stipulation that they remove at their own expence and on their own means, is an excellent feature" and insisted contentiously, "Surely the religious enthusiasts, or those who have been weeping over the oppression of the Indians, will not find fault" with the treaty "for want of liberality or justice to the Indians."[43]

The experiences of the Choctaws revealed serious flaws in the removal system. The allotment plan, designed ostensibly to help the Indians, only opened the door to widespread fraud and exploitation. White businessmen set up shop near the Choctaws, lent them money, and then took the allotments at drastically reduced rates when they failed to pay their debts. The administration did little to protect the Indians. When more Choctaws than expected asked for allotments in order to remain in Mississippi, officials did everything possible to force them to sell out and move. After white squatters moved illegally onto Choctaw land, the government made only half-hearted attempts to remove them.

Jackson did manage to move 12,000 Choctaws west, but at a cost of $5 million, more than he had estimated for the removal of all the Indians.[44]

The Creeks in Alabama and the Chickasaws in Mississippi underwent similar misfortunes. On 24 March 1832 the Creeks signed an allotment treaty in which they gave up their land in return for allotments for chiefs and heads of households. Once again speculators moved in, bought up the allotments at a fraction of their worth, and drove the Creeks off their lands. When the uprooted Creeks began to wander about, occasionally stealing and sometimes even committing murder, Cass sent in United States troops to force the Indians to emigrate. Before Jackson left office, 15,000 Creeks had been moved west. The Chickasaws, meanwhile, who had signed the first removal treaty in 1830, spent two years waiting for the government to find satisfactory land for them across the Mississippi. When that failed, an allotment treaty was negotiated in October 1832. Five years later, 5,000 Chickasaws were moved west.[45]

The removal of another southern tribe led to war. Like the Chickasaws, the Seminoles of Florida signed a provisional treaty in 1832 to move west if suitable land could be found. The Seminole party sent to examine the land that had been set aside was intimidated into signing a removal treaty in 1833, but the main body of the tribe refused to endorse it. When a band of Seminoles ambushed a group of whites in 1835, a war broke out that lasted seven years, at a cost of $10 million and the lives of 1,500 white soldiers. The Seminoles also suffered heavy losses; out of an estimated population of 5,000, less than 3,000 could be rounded up in 1842 to move west.

War had also broken out in the North in 1832 when Chief Black Hawk led a band of 2,000 Sac and Fox Indians across the Mississippi River into northern Illinois to reoccupy their old tribal lands. A combined force of regular United States troops and Illinois militia drove Black Hawk north into Wisconsin, where he turned and defeated the militia. The war, in which twenty-three-year-old Abraham Lincoln briefly participated, continued well into August before Black Hawk was captured as he tried to flee back across the Mississippi, and many of the Indians were massacred.[46]

Of all the Indian tribes that were removed none commanded more attention than the Cherokees. The 18,000 civilized Cherokees, most of whom lived in northern Georgia and Alabama, attracted broad support from humanitarians and from Jackson's political opponents. On 1 June 1830, six days after the passage of the Indian removal bill, the Georgia statute declaring the laws of the Cherokees null and void went into effect. As a result petitions began to arrive in Congress demanding the protection of the Cherokees. The most prominent was the "Memorial of the Cherokee Nation," written by Jeremiah Evarts, the author of the William Penn essays against Indian removal, which accused the administration of "abandoning" the Cherokees to "the oppressive and cruel measures" of the state of Georgia. In addition the Cherokees and their white supporters hired John Sergeant and former attorney general William Wirt, who filed for an injunction from the Supreme Court to restrain the state of Georgia from executing its laws in the Cherokee Territory.[47]

Before the injunction case could get under way, a Georgia court in December sentenced an Indian named Corn Tassel to be hanged for murdering another Indian within the Cherokee Territory. Although the United States Supreme Court issued a writ of error to the state court and ordered the state to appear before the Supreme Court in January, the Georgians would not give in. Both Gov. George Gilmer and the legislature denounced the Supreme Court, and Corn Tassel was hanged on 24 December. Gilmer was equally contemptuous in ignoring a subpoena served on 27 December in the injunction suit. The missionaries living among the Cherokees heightened the tension by issuing a statement on 29 December "invit[ing] the prayers of all our fellow Christians" in support of the Cherokees.[48]

The excitement surrounding the Cherokee case was intensified by a debate in Congress that winter concerning the power of the Supreme Court over the states. Supporters of states' rights brought a bill to the floor of the House in December calling for repeal of section 25 of the Judiciary Act of 1789, which empowered the Supreme Court to hear appeals from state courts. Although defeated decisively on 29 January 1831, the bill demonstrated the extent of southern and western hostility toward the Court. Jackson had taken a similar stand in his annual message of 1830, saying that the states were "not responsible" to the central government for the "justice" of their laws. He underlined his position in a special message to the Senate on 22 February 1831, defending his administration for not protecting Choctaw land from intruders. The federal government, he asserted, could not prevent the states from extending their jurisdiction over Indian territory. Jackson later showed the same feeling against the Court in his message vetoing the recharter of the Bank.[49]

The case of *Cherokee Nation v. Georgia* proved to be a disappointment for the Indians' cause. Chief Justice John Marshall, speaking for the majority on 18 March, declared that the Cherokees could not sue in the Supreme Court because they were a "domestic dependent nation" rather than a "foreign state." Van Buren was delighted and later wrote that the Cherokees' case was both "fictitious" and "factious." The opposition press, however, believed that the decision failed to do moral "justice" to the Cherokees.[50]

A second Cherokee case developed a year later from a new Georgia law requiring all white persons living in the Cherokee Territory to have a state license. When two missionaries, Samuel A. Worcester and Elizur Butler, refused to get licenses, they were convicted and sentenced to four years at hard labor. Enlisting the aid of Wirt and Sergeant, they appealed to the Supreme Court. By this time Wirt was running for president on the Anti-Masonic ticket, and Sergeant was the National Republican candidate for vice-president and was involved in trying to recharter the Bank. Interest in the case of *Worcester* v. *Georgia* ran high; over fifty members of the House left their seats to hear Sergeant and Wirt present the case before the Court on 20 February 1832.

On 3 March Marshall ruled that the Cherokee Nation was "a distinct community, occupying its own territory," within which the federal government had exclusive jurisdiction. Since "the laws of Georgia [could] have no force" within the Cherokee boundaries, Marshall overturned the judgment of the Georgia Superior Court, which had convicted the missionaries. He also issued a special mandate to that court, ordering it to reverse its decision. In an open letter to the *Georgia Journal* Sen. George M. Troup told his fellow Georgians that the decision "flagrantly violat[ed] . . . their sovereign rights."[51]

Almost as soon as the verdict was handed down, rumors circulated about whether Jackson would enforce the court order. He did nothing. Over thirty years later Horace Greeley recalled being told that Jackson had said, "Well, John Marshall has made his decision, now let him enforce it." The story reinforced the image of an arrogant Jackson, refusing, in this instance, to obey the order of the Supreme Court. It is unlikely, however, that Jackson ever made such a remark, and even if he did, it was meaningless because the court issue had not yet been settled. The Supreme Court could not issue a final judgment until the Georgia court had refused in writing to comply with the mandate. The Georgia court did refuse to grant the missionaries a writ of habeas corpus but put no official record in the court minutes. Since the Supreme Court would not meet again until January 1833, its hands (and Jackson's as well) were tied until then. Jackson was correct when he wrote, "The decision of the supreme court has fell still born, and they find they cannot coerce Georgia to yield to its mandate."[52]

Jackson had to walk a fine line in the Georgia missionary crisis. Anxious to keep pressure on the Cherokees to move, he would do nothing to help them retain their land. In addition the start of the South Carolina

Nullification Crisis in November 1832 gave him a statesmanlike reason for not backing the Supreme Court. The president did not dare to do or say anything that would antagonize Georgia into joining hands with its neighbor. But leaving the missionaries in jail would only make them martyrs, so he and Van Buren worked behind the scenes to get both sides to draw back. In mid-December Secretary of War Cass and several members of the Albany Regency urged Gov. Wilson Lumpkin of Georgia to pardon the missionaries. In addition Van Buren's friend Sen. John Forsyth of Georgia gained assurances from Wirt that he would present no motions on behalf of the missionaries to the Supreme Court in January. On 14 January 1833, at the height of the Nullification Crisis, Lumpkin ordered the two prisoners released, and the matter was closed.[53]

Jackson deserves credit for settling the Cherokee matter in the midst of the Nullification Crisis, but he also deserves blame for contributing to the problem by encouraging Georgia's actions from the start. By rebuffing the Cherokees in 1829 and repeating the rebuff in his 1830 annual message, he had stiffened Georgia's determination to take over the Cherokees' land. Congressman Lewis Williams of North Carolina noted correctly that "Gen Jackson could by a nod of the head or a crook of the finger induce Georgia to submit to the law." Instead he sided with the state.[54]

The question of removing the Cherokees went on for several more years. The tribe was divided into two rival factions, a small "Treaty party" favoring removal, led by Major Ridge, who had fought with Jackson against the Creeks in 1814, and the majority "National party," opposing removal, led by John Ross, who had also fought beside Jackson. To encourage migration, Cass had adopted a program of individual removal in 1831 and appointed Benjamin Currey superintendent of Cherokee removal. Despite his hard work and his kindness toward the Indians, Currey managed to transport fewer than 200 Cherokees in the next two years. The Cherokees became skeptical of Currey when the government failed to live up to an agreement to reimburse them for their abandoned property. The Indians received part of the money on their departure, but the government failed to pay the rest when they arrived in the West.

Encouraged by the *Worcester* decision and hopeful that Jackson would be defeated in the fall, Ross used delaying tactics throughout 1832. Even after Jackson's election victory he remained stubborn, especially when the government refused to send troops to protect the Cherokees in Georgia from intrusion by white settlers. These intruders were claiming Cherokee land that they had won in a state land lottery but which they were not entitled to occupy until the Indians had abandoned it. Hoping that the intrusion would force the Cherokees to capitulate, the administration had been unwilling to make any concessions.

Cass finally negotiated a removal treaty in spring 1834 with a small group of Cherokee chiefs, but the treaty found little support among the main body of the tribe. One band of Cherokees became so angry at the negotiators that they ambushed one of them, a chief named John Walker, and murdered him. Although Ross was not directly involved in the murder, the government sought to undermine him by holding him responsible. With Ross's National party now on the defensive, the government turned to the Treaty party, which represented only a small portion of the tribe. In February 1835 this group signed a treaty ceding all Cherokee land to the United States for $4.5 million. Later that summer, however, at a mass meeting, with John Ross present, the Cherokees turned down the treaty by a vote of 2,225 to 114.

At this point Governor Lumpkin sent in the Georgia Guard, a military force that terrorized the antitreaty Indians and finally in November imprisoned Ross. Following his release in December, Ross went to Washington, and the Treaty party took advantage of his absence to call a council of less than 500 Cherokees. This rump group then signed a removal treaty on 29 December at their capital of New Echota. Despite vigorous protests against the "Christmas Trick of New Echota," the treaty was ratified in the Senate by the margin of one vote in May 1836. The government agreed to pay the Cherokees $5 million for their land and would also cover the costs of removal and provide allotments for Indians who preferred to stay in the East.[55]

Although the Cherokees were given until 1838 to leave, the whites around them would not wait. In June 1836, one month after the treaty had been ratified, Major Ridge and his son John asked Jackson for military protection. Whites, they wrote, were taking their plantations and suing them for back rent. "The lowest classes of the white people [were] flogging the Cherokees with cow hides, hickories, and clubs." Finally forced to move west in November 1838, 16,000 Cherokees embarked upon a march that became known as the "Trail of Tears." Four thousand died along the way.[56]

During his presidency Andrew Jackson moved almost 46,000 Indians across the Mississippi and made arrangements to move a similar number in the future. In the process he acquired over 100 million acres of Indian land at a cost of about $70 million and over 30 million acres in the West. In the South such an acquisition of good farm land helped increase the cotton crop, which formed an important basis for the American economy, but at a high price for a president who had promised strict republican economy. In 1828, Adams's last full year in office, annual federal expenditures other than interest on the debt totaled about $13.3 million; by 1836, Jackson's last full year, they had risen to $30.7 million, an increase of 130 percent. Some of the increase was due to internal improvements and some to an increase in prices, but much of it was for Indian removal. And the expenditures, especially those for the army in Florida, continued for years after Jackson left office.[57]

Indian removal cost the nation more than mere federal outlays, for it encouraged the white majority to exploit a nonwhite minority. The administration used bribery and intimidation, it took advantage of tribal divisions to divide and conquer, and it withheld military protection. White entrepreneurs practiced fraud and deceit in acquiring Indian land. And, aside from an early sharp outcry, the American people accepted it all. Not only were the Jacksonians returned to office, but when they were finally replaced by Whigs, the new government continued the Indian policy it had inherited. White Americans based their acceptance on the self-serving premise that removal was humane and good for the Indians, the only way in which they could be saved from white men. It was costly for Americans to endorse both the cruelty and the specious reasoning that justified it.

Twentieth-century Americans have divided over Indian removal. One recent critic has argued that Jackson adopted a policy of "paternalism," "infantilization," and "genocide" toward the Indians as a means of compensating for the early loss of his parents. Another has called it "a blending of hypocrisy, cant, and rapaciousness," with "a frightening consistency"—a determination to drive the Indians across the Mississippi.[58]

Jackson's leading biographer has answered these critics, arguing that the policy was based on good intentions and was far from genocide. Jackson, furthermore, was paternalistic toward everyone, not just Indians. The most complete apologia for Jackson's Indian policy can be found in the works of Francis Paul Prucha, who accepts the Jacksonian argument that the Indians had to be separated from white men. According to Prucha, Jackson was "genuinely concerned for the well-being of the Indians and for their civilization," while the "less-than-disinterested" missionaries with their "bombast" were politically motivated. Prucha believes that Jackson had little choice, considering the alternatives facing him. He could have let the Indians be destroyed, he could have tried to assimilate them, he could have defended them in enclaves in the East, or he could have moved them west. Only the last, Prucha claims, was feasible.[59]

It is difficult to find evidence of a conscious desire for genocide or infantilization in Jackson's policies, but to say that the president was

117

"genuinely concerned for the well-being of the Indians" is to exaggerate. Prucha, for example, documents Jackson's supposed generosity toward the Indians by quoting from the president's letter to John Coffee about the Chickasaw removal in which he referred to the "liberality" and "justice" of his policies. Prucha neglects, however, to include the part in which Jackson congratulated Coffee for getting the Indians to move at their own expense—not a good example of generosity. And the missionaries' "bombast," like the Jacksonians' "cant," is largely a matter of opinion.[60]

As for alternatives, Jackson might have tried to defend those Indians who wished to stay in small settlements and move the others. Such a situation occurred in upstate New York where some 5,000 Indians from the Iroquois Confederacy still remained in a half-dozen enclaves at the end of the nineteenth century. There were also a small number of Cherokees left in western North Carolina. Faced with living within narrow boundaries, many Indians, especially those not yet converted to farming, would eventually have consented to move. Even if Jackson had to move most of the Indians west, he could have done it in a more humanitarian way. Absorbed in the constitutional and policy issues, Prucha spends too little time describing the sorry tale of how removal was carried out.[61]

Jackson's Indian removal policy was based on the predominant white American assumption that white farmers were superior to Indian hunters or even to Indian farmers. Jackson, who routinely called the Indians his "children," summed it up in his 1830 annual message. "What good man," he asked, "would prefer a country covered with forests and ranged by a few thousand savages to our extensive Republic, studded with cities, towns, and prosperous farms?" He defended his policy as humanitarian and virtuous, consistent with his agrarian republican ideals. Actually it was carried out according to the individualistic doctrines of the market revolution. Individual Indians sold their allotments at the only price they could get—the market price—often at a fraction of their true value. In the process land speculators acquired 80 to 90 percent of the allotments. Jackson's Indian policy was based on agrarian republican ideals, but it opened the door to the realities of the new economy.[62]

At the end of Jackson's first term, Indian removal was only one of several policies that looked back on old agrarian ideals and ahead to free-enterprise capitalism. The president's fight to ward off the evils of the market revolution continued to be inconsistent. His tolerance of McLane's support of the Bank was a good example. Even when he asserted himself and fought the recharter of the Bank, often on constitutional grounds, he presented no clear vision of a new banking system. In lowering the tariff Jackson deprived the manufacturers of some of their privileges, but he did not take away their basic protection. Although he continued to veto internal-improvement bills, his administration persisted in spending large sums of money for roads and canals. Instead of saving the old America he appeared to be compromising with the new.

In dealing with the economic changes Jackson still lacked the support of a united party. On the issues before Congress his administration and his party had been even more ambivalent than he had been. Only on the question of distribution had Jackson's beliefs formed anything like party policy, and even then he had to change his position. The fight between McLane and Blair in the early winter weakened party unity. Even so, the Jackson coalition was becoming more of a party. The debates in Congress had grown more partisan, each successive battle widening the distinction between the Jacksonians and their opponents. Clay had been referring to the growing partisanship when he spoke of the "electioneering objective" in the Bank veto. John Sergeant had shown the same party spirit in opposing Jackson's Indian and Bank policies. Heading the National Republican ticket against Jackson in the election of 1832, Clay and Sergeant would have further opportunities to display this partisanship.

6

★ ★ ★ ★ ★

FOREIGN POLICY

While Jackson had been struggling with Congress, he had also been keeping one eye on foreign affairs. When he took office in 1829, the same uncertainty and anxiety over his policies at home existed for those abroad as well. Even Jackson's friends feared that he would act impetuously and would be quick to resort to force against foreign nations. His record as a general, especially his invasion of Florida, led many observers to assume that he would use military power to extend the frontiers and to threaten foreign powers. The new president's lack of experience concerned European diplomats, who had become accustomed to American presidents with impressive backgrounds in foreign affairs. Every president since Washington had served first as secretary of state, except John Adams, and he had helped negotiate the Peace of Paris and had been minister to Great Britain. British officials were particularly alarmed because Jackson, who had fought Britain in two wars and carried a scar on his head from a British sword, had a reputation as a confirmed Anglophobe.

In foreign affairs as well as in domestic the market revolution set the agenda. The rapid growth of surpluses of cotton, tobacco, grain, and fish put pressure on the administration to find markets and to ease trade restrictions abroad. Between 1806 and 1825 trading opportunities had opened up in South and Central America, as the fall of the Spanish and Portuguese empires led to the rise of new republics. The British, however, with their strong navy and merchant fleet, had gained the upper hand both diplomatically and economically. Overall, American exports, which had reached a peak of $108 million in 1807, had never recovered from the embargoes and blockades during the Napoleonic wars and stood at only $69 million in 1824. The decline in exports threatened to restrict the growth of American agriculture, commerce, and manufacturing.[1]

Despite their allegiance to the republican ideals of the Revolution, the early Jacksonians had shown a surprising lack of enthusiasm for revolutions. John Randolph, for one, had led the opposition against recognizing the Greek revolution in 1824, and Van Buren had organized a powerful resistance in 1826 against Adams's proposal to send delegates to the Panama Conference, which had been called by the new republics of South and Central America. Some of the opposition was based on the doctrine of nonintervention, which had been formalized by the Monroe Doctrine in 1823, and some on a defense of slavery. Randolph made an angry speech denouncing the Panama Conference on the grounds that it would require the United States to deal with countries that had abolished slavery and that might send black delegates. The fight over sending delegates from the United States served to unite the Jacksonians against Adams.

Adams had his way on this issue but was far less successful in his efforts to expand American trade and to collect payment of the $14 million in spoliation claims of American merchants against European governments. These claims had grown out of the seizures of American ships during the Napoleonic wars. Even though the administration negotiated nine commercial treaties, American exports continued to decline, dropping to $64 million in 1828, and no claims were settled. The Jacksonians in the Congress persistently attacked Adams for these failures.[2]

As soon as Van Buren wound up his duties as governor of New York and took over the State Department, he sought to relieve the anxiety of the foreign diplomatic corps about the new president. As a former senator Van Buren was already on good terms with a number of the diplomats, especially his "brother Dutchman," the Chevalier Huygens of the Netherlands and his fellow party-goer, Charles R. Vaughan of England, and was able to reassure them informally that Jackson had nothing but peaceful intentions. With their help he held a reception on 5 April, only a week after his arrival, at which the president removed any "unjust impressions" with a friendly speech and charming behavior. Vaughan, for one, was so impressed that he wrote back to London that Adams could not have done as well.[3]

Jackson and Van Buren then went to work to improve American commerce. In making diplomatic appointments they gave first priority to the posts in Great Britain, France, and Spain, not only because of their obvious political importance but also because the countries were the three leading export markets. A number of issues remained unresolved. The United States wanted relief from oppressive trade restrictions in the British and Spanish West Indies and also sought payment for the large claims of American merchants against the governments of France and Spain.[4]

Owing to the importance of these issues, Jackson appointed ministers to Great Britain and France before Van Buren's arrival in Washington, selecting Littleton W. Tazewell and Edward Livingston. Van Buren felt threatened by both men, Livingston because he was a friend of the president and Tazewell because he was the highly-regarded chairman of the Senate Committee on Foreign Relations. When the two men, who were getting on in years, hesitated at departing as promptly as the administration wanted, Van Buren used that as an excuse to replace them with two younger men, who were also his friends. Louis McLane was sent to England and William C. Rives to France. Jackson also followed Van Buren's advice in selecting Levi Woodbury as minister to Spain, but when Woodbury too balked at leaving immediately, the post went to a lesser figure, Gov. Cornelius P. Van Ness of Vermont. The three new ministers were aboard ship and on their way to Europe by early fall 1829. Their mission was to improve American trade, a goal that Jackson underscored by his many references to commerce in his annual message in December.

Soon after his arrival in London, McLane brought up the question of reopening trade between the United States and the British West Indies. The islands of the West Indies had long been a major export market for continental North America. Before the American Revolution, about one-fourth of the value of exports from the American colonies came from the farm products, flour, fish, and lumber sent to the West Indies in exchange for sugar, molasses, coin, and slaves. The islands continued to be a valuable outlet for American produce in the early years of the republic, absorbing about one-eighth of all exports. In 1811 the British West Indies alone, which included Jamaica, the Bahamas, and islands in the Lesser Antilles, took $4.6 million of a total of $61 million in American exports.[5]

After the War of 1812, British navigation acts and American retaliation reduced exports to the British West Indies to a trickle; even after mutual concessions they rose only to $2 million a year. When the United States refused to grant British ships from the West Indies most favored nation status in 1826, the British completely closed their West Indies ports to direct trade by American ships, and the United States responded in kind. The loss in trade was not as great as was feared, for increased American exports to the rest of the West Indies made up much of the deficit, but politically the loss was a blow to the Adams administration.[6]

Although Jackson generally kept a close eye on foreign affairs, he left the West Indies question in the hands of his secretary of state. Before dispatching McLane to England, Van Buren had worked out a plan with him and with their friend, Congressman Churchill C. Cambreleng, who represented the commercial interests of New York City. McLane was to tell the British that in order to reverse the errors of the Adams administration the new government was willing to lower duties for cargoes on British ships. When McLane made little progress during the fall, Jackson was disappointed since he had hoped to announce some good news in his first annual message. Nonetheless, the supposedly Anglophobic president remained calm and included soothing remarks in the message. Great Britain and the United States, he was sure, held "sentiments of mutual respect" and were determined "to preserve the most cordial relations." With Great Britain, so "distinguished in peace and war," the United States "looked forward to years of peaceful, honorable, and elevated competition." By springtime, however, an impatient Jackson told Van Buren that "in case of a failure" they should ask Congress for a nonintercourse act for trade with Canada and should plan to enforce it with "a sufficient number of cutters." Sounding more like the legendary Old Hero, he said that they should "be prepared to act . . . with that promptness and energy due to our national character."[7]

Within a few weeks, fortunately, McLane reported an agreement and asked Van Buren and Cambreleng to have Congress pass enabling legislation. Congress quickly passed two bills, one authorizing the president to reopen American ports to British ships from the West Indies as soon as the British reciprocated and another giving the British ships most favored nation status. On 5 October 1830 Jackson issued a proclamation reopening the trade, and the British did the same a month later.

Sensing that the agreement would be well received, Jackson hurried back to Washington from the Hermitage so that he could issue the proclamation in time for the fall congressional elections. The news came too late to sway the elections, but it did much for the popularity of the Jackson party, especially in Maine, whose merchants could now compete for trade in the British West Indies on an equal basis with their Canadian rivals. In New York City James A. Hamilton reported that the news pleased "all ranks and parties, except the factious cavilers."[8]

The economic and political results of the agreement were not quite as favorable as the administration had hoped. Even though the United States exported $1.4 million worth of produce to the British islands during the next year, the increase was offset by reductions elsewhere in the

West Indies. In addition, Van Buren's tactics gave the opposition an argument that they could use against his confirmation as minister to Great Britain. They would be able to say that he had played politics and truckled to the British by accusing Adams of "errors" and by offering to lower duties.[9]

In balance, however, Jackson deserves great credit for regaining an export market that Adams had lost. In so doing, he had confounded his critics by delegating authority, suppressing his anti-British feelings, and acting temperately. Even more important from a party standpoint was the administration's ability to coordinate the work of party members, such as McLane and Cambreleng, in the diplomatic service and Congress. Coming on the heels of the Indian removal act and the Maysville veto, which had pleased the South, the West Indies trade agreement strengthened the Jackson party in the North.

In France, Van Buren's other friend, William C. Rives, faced difficult negotiations over American spoliation claims of $7 million and much smaller French claims. He expected commercial disagreements over American duties on wine and French duties on cotton to be more manageable. In July 1830, while McLane was wrapping up the West Indies agreement, Rives was encouraged when the liberal "Citizen King," Louis Philippe, came to power and was expected to be sympathetic toward the United States. But no agreement followed; the French people were still reluctant to take responsibility for the seizures of Napoleon, and the French government could ill afford to pay the large American claims. Jackson, however, remained unusually restrained. Although he had warned a year earlier that "a possible collision" with France loomed, he had nothing but praise for the new government in his annual message in December 1830.[10]

Rives kept up the pressure and was rewarded by a treaty, signed on the Fourth of July 1831, that was fair to both sides. American concessions on French wines were balanced by French adjustments on American cotton. France agreed to pay $4.6 million for American claims, and the United States was to pay only $270,000 to settle the Revolutionary War claims of the Beaumarchais family of France. A delighted Jackson reported to Van Buren that the treaty was popular with the merchants; in New York City even the opposition press was applauding it. When the treaty was brought to the Senate in December, it was unanimously approved, and on 2 February 1832 the two nations exchanged ratifications.[11]

The euphoria of the administration over Rives's Fourth of July settlement gradually faded as the French Chamber of Deputies let almost three years go by without appropriating any money to settle the claims.

When the Chamber voted down an appropriation bill in April 1834, Jackson's administration split over how to proceed. McLane, who had become secretary of state, and Secretary of War Cass wanted to make reprisals, but the new secretary of the Treasury, Taney, and Van Buren, who had become vice-president, preferred to await further word from France. The moderates prevailed.[12]

The victory was temporary, for after the French Chamber once again failed to act favorably, Jackson would no longer sit back. In his annual message of 1834 he asked Congress for a law "authorizing reprisals upon French property," even if they led to "hostilities." After the House passed a defense bill to support the president, a conflict flared up when the bill was sent to the Senate. Intent on embarrassing Jackson, the opposition repeatedly made the point that he was trying to increase his executive power. The *Daily National Intelligencer* declared that the United States "was not yet ready for a dictatorship," and Clay and Webster both warned that the right of Congress to make war was at stake. After much bitterness the bill failed in early March 1835.[13]

Jackson's message nonetheless made an impact on the Chamber of Deputies, which in April voted to appropriate the money but only if the president first explained his warlike words. Jackson was so outraged at what he considered a demand for an apology that he refused to reply when the French foreign minister inquired about his intentions. He became even more angry in September when an American living in France warned that the French planned to procrastinate until Jackson's "firm" policy was "sacrificed" by a less militant successor. The president said that it was "high time that this arrogance of France should be put down." European nations should be taught that they could not interfere in American "domestic policy." To apologize, he thundered, would be "disgraceful."[14]

When the United States broke all ties with France in November, war seemed imminent. In preparing for his annual message in December Jackson drafted a warlike statement. He wrote that he could not understand why the French had taken "offence" at his previous message, which only "detailed the truth." The French Chamber had "insult[ed]" the United States "by demanding apology for pretended insult." He called on Congress to pass "energetic measures" that would "enforce a peaceful complience [sic]."[15]

Once again Jackson's advisers urged him to show moderation, and to the surprise of many, his words in the actual message were far more gentle than those in his original draft. Though insisting that "the honor" of his country should "never be stained by an apology," Jackson explained that he had not intended to "menace or insult" the French government. Nor did he intend to make any "charge of ill faith" against the king of France. But before the king had a chance to respond, a crisis developed when word arrived in the United States that the French had mobilized their fleet. To resolve the crisis Jackson accepted a British offer to mediate. He also sent a special message to Congress on 15 January, however, asking for a ban on French goods and for immediate appropriations for the navy and coastal defenses. At last in February, after receiving Jackson's moderate annual message, the French government sent word that it would pay the claims. On 10 May 1836 Jackson announced that the United States had received the four installments that were due.[16]

During much of the long struggle with France the administration was also forced to wait for news from Spain, where Cornelius P. Van Ness was dealing with a complex situation. Unlike McLane in England, who could concentrate on the West Indies, and Rives in France, who could focus on the claims, Van Ness had to deal equally with American claims of $2.5 million and with severe Spanish trading restrictions in both Spain and the Spanish West Indies. The Spanish islands, primarily Cuba and Puerto Rico, demanded attention because they provided an even greater market for American produce than the British West Indies. In 1826 American exports to Cuba alone totaled $3.75 million compared with $2.1 million to all the British West Indies. Next to Spain, the United States was Cuba's largest trading partner. Americans also exported $1 million worth of goods annually to Spain and received back some $400,000 in imports.[17]

Even though Van Ness had nothing to report after two years, Jackson appeared unruffled, insisting in December 1831 that it was his "earnest endeavor" to "preserve friendly relations." In 1832 Van Ness did succeed in getting the Spanish to lower tonnage duties in Spain itself but was unable to get similar reductions in the Spanish West Indies. On the matter of the claims, Jackson continued to show restraint by conceding that they had been exaggerated. In 1834 the United States accepted $600,000, a fraction of the original amount. When the Spanish that same year stubbornly refused to lower what the president called "discriminating" duties in the West Indies, Jackson finally displayed his annoyance and convinced Congress to pass retaliatory tariff measures. But the Spanish would still not give in.[18]

In addition to the agreements reached with France and Spain, the Jackson administration made four other settlements of American spoliation claims. Most of the credit, however, should go to holdovers from the Adams administration, not to Jackson appointees. In Denmark the distinguished American lawyer Henry Wheaton, who served as chargé d'affaires between 1827 and 1835, proved to be a shrewd negotiator. After demanding $1.7 million to settle several American claims, he signed a treaty on 28 March 1830 for $650,000, which was more than the claimants had anticipated. At about the same time, another holdover, Chargé William Tudor in Brazil, won a payment of $250,000 for claims arising from the Argentine-Brazilian War. Two years later, in January 1832, the third Adams man, Thomas L. L. Brent of Virginia, settled American claims against Portugal for $150,000.[19]

Still, of the four settlements the only one arranged by a Jackson man proved to be larger than the other three combined. In 1809 King Joachim Murat of Naples, who had been installed by Napoleon Bonaparte, had seized almost fifty American ships, leading to large claims. After France agreed to settle its claims with the United States in 1831, the administration assumed that Naples would follow suit. Jackson appointed former congressman John Nelson of Maryland as chargé to settle the claims and sent him off in October with a convoy of four warships. But the government of Naples was slow to act during the winter, and Nelson asked for additional help. The arrival of several more warships in July so frightened the Neapolitans that they settled the claims in October 1832 for $1.7 million—a sum that more than satisfied the American merchants. With that settlement and the Spanish settlement in 1834, Jackson had made agreements to collect some $8 million of the $14 million in claims. After years of frustration it was a solid accomplishment.[20]

As they searched for trade, the Jacksonians reached out in all directions. In the Near East, American merchants were losing money because there was no commercial treaty with the Ottoman Empire, and they had to deal through the British Levant Company. To rectify the situation Jackson sent a special commission to Constantinople soon after he took office. On 7 May 1830 one of the members, Charles Rhind, who had arrived early, signed a treaty by which the Turks granted the United States most favored nation status. The fruits of the treaty were not realized for another year and a half, however, because the United States Senate would not accept a secret clause providing for American help in rebuilding the Turkish navy. Negotiations continued until 5 October 1831, when both sides agreed on a treaty.[21]

The administration hoped for similar success in increasing trade with Russia. Exporters of sugar and other raw materials were particularly anxious to have better access to the ports of the Black Sea. A major obstacle was finding a minister. The eccentric John Randolph was prevailed upon to take the mission, but when he finally arrived at St. Petersburg in August 1830 he found the weather so cold and unpleasant, even in the summer, that he turned around and came home. After further delay Jackson appointed James Buchanan, who reached the Russian capital in summer 1832 with instructions to press for a commercial treaty. Buchanan, who barely tolerated the weather himself, secured both the principle of reciprocity and the most favored nation status in a treaty signed in December 1832. The treaty included trade concessions in the Black Sea.[22]

Meanwhile, efforts were also being made to expand American trade in Asia and the East Indies, where the United States had a flourishing pepper trade on the island of Sumatra. On 7 February 1831, at Quallah Battoo, Sumatra, a force of Malays seized the merchant ship *Friendship,* out of Salem, Massachusetts, and killed three Americans. By the time the ship was recovered, the assailants had removed everything of value except the pepper. Responding to cries of outrage from American merchants, Jackson sent out the fifty-gun frigate *Potomac* with orders to investigate and to seek restitution. When the *Potomac* arrived off Quallah Battoo almost exactly a year after the incident, sailors and marines quickly leveled the town, killing a hundred Malays. The attack may have salvaged American honor, but it did little to enhance American trade. Jackson also had to weather a storm of criticism for his use of force when news from the *Potomac* reached Washington.[23]

In March 1832, only a month after the attack on Quallah Battoo, a less aggressive mission departed for Asia under the leadership of Capt. Edmund Roberts of Portsmouth, New Hampshire. Through the influence of Levi Woodbury, to whom he was related, Roberts had been named special agent to arrange treaties with the Sultan of Muscat, near the Persian Gulf, as well as with the rulers of Siam and Cochin China. He was subsequently authorized to negotiate with one of the kings of North Sumatra and with the emperor of Japan, whose country had been closed to the outside world for two centuries. Sailing west around Cape Horn and across the Pacific, Roberts reached Sumatra, where the strong Dutch influence made a treaty impossible. After staying for several months in Canton, China, he decided not to visit Japan and set off for Cochin China, in what is now southern Vietnam. Although a dispute over diplomatic etiquette prevented any agreement there, he was able to conclude a treaty with Siam in March 1833 that allowed American trade almost duty free. In September he made an even more favorable treaty with the Sultan of Muscat, with whom he was already acquainted, granting the American consul extraterritorial rights and setting duties at only 5 percent. He continued to sail west by way of the Cape of Good Hope, reaching home in April 1834.

The success of the voyage so impressed the administration that it provided even greater support for a second mission in 1835. This time

Roberts was to sail east around the Cape of Good Hope, exchange treaty ratifications at Muscat and Siam, try again at Cochin China, and then go on to negotiate a commercial treaty with Japan. Despite running aground near Muscat, he carried out his two ratifications but was again unable to secure a treaty with Cochin China. Having contracted cholera, he stopped off at Canton to recover his health, but before he could set sail for Japan he died of the disease in June 1836. It would be another eighteen years before Commodore Matthew C. Perry would succeed in opening the island kingdom.[24]

Although the Jackson administration made several commercial treaties in Central and South America, it did not materially expand United States trade in the region. Only in Mexico, where a most favored nation treaty was signed in 1831, did American exports increase. A similar treaty in Chile a year later did not prevent the Chileans from continuing to discriminate against the United States. A treaty with Venezuela in 1836 came too late to produce any results during Jackson's presidency, and no treaty was necessary in Brazil because William Tudor had already negotiated one for President Adams. By the end of Jackson's two terms, American exports to Brazil were no greater than they had been in Adams's last year.[25]

The administration was also unsuccessful in advancing American boundaries. In 1827 Adams had signed a treaty with the British, giving the king of the Netherlands the power to arbitrate the Maine boundary, which had remained unsettled since the Revolution. Soon after taking office, Jackson sent William Pitt Preble of Maine to the Netherlands to keep an eye on developments. Preble protested angrily in 1831 when the king drew the line along the St. John River instead of along the highlands to the north, which the United States claimed as the boundary. Jackson, however, was willing to accept the line because the land given up was of little value and because it gave the United States more than half the disputed area. After intensive meetings with the agents from Maine in May 1832, Livingston, McLane, and Woodbury won them over. In June, however, the Senate declared the Dutch king's boundary not binding and later recommended reopening negotiations with Great Britain. The dispute was not settled until the Webster-Ashburton Treaty in 1842, which gave the United States less than Jackson could have secured.[26]

Jackson was much more emotionally involved in acquiring Texas from Mexico. To help carry out this project, he had selected Anthony Butler of Mississippi as chargé, not because of his tact or integrity but because he had been a comrade in arms, was well informed about Mexico, and shared the Old Hero's enthusiasm for extending the frontier.

Butler carried secret instructions for Minister Joel Poinsett, ordering him to open negotiations for the purchase of Texas as far south and west as the Rio Grande and the great desert. Texas, said Jackson, "was necessary for the security of the great emporium of the west, Neworleans [sic], and that god of the universe had intended the great valley [of the Mississippi] to belong to one nation." Jackson was not too fastidious about how the land was to be secured. As he told Van Buren, if the Mexicans raised constitutional issues, $3 million could "amend the Mexican Constitution," and Jackson was prepared to "go as far as five millions."[27]

Arriving in December 1829, Butler found himself in charge of the United States legation in Mexico because Poinsett had been asked to leave for interfering in Mexican politics. The new chargé faced a thorny situation, for after fighting off a Spanish invasion from Cuba in the summer, the liberal government, which had been somewhat friendly toward the United States, had been overthrown by anti-American conservatives. Jackson instructed Butler to "cultivate the most friendly relations" with the Mexican government but also to proceed with plans to purchase Texas. These orders were no secret, and Mexican newspapers were openly speculating that Butler would offer $5 million for Texas. Butler instead got involved in tortuous and unsuccessful negotiations over claims of American citizens against the Mexican government and temporarily put aside the Texas question.[28]

As Butler continued to have difficulty, Jackson grew concerned when he heard that his friend Sam Houston was organizing a Texan independence movement. Soon after leaving to live with the Indians in spring 1829, Houston began to brag that he planned to conquer Mexico or Texas; he told Dr. Robert Mayo, a persistent office seeker, the same story a year later. When Mayo reported the story to Jackson in November 1830, the president did nothing other than instruct Secretary William Fulton of the Arkansas Territory to be on the lookout. Jackson's minimal response has convinced at least one historian that the president was in league with his old comrade, but this conclusion is dubious. Jackson knew that if Texas became independent, any attempt to annex it would lead to a long, divisive debate in Congress in which antislavery spokesmen might block any agreement. The president much preferred to buy Texas from Mexico and present a completed deal to the Senate.[29]

In 1831 Jackson was fed up with Butler's excuses about his inability to buy Texas. He was also distressed by news that Butler had signed a boundary treaty that had been completed by Poinsett three years earlier and had drifted unsigned ever since. Since the treaty confirmed the boundaries of the Adams-Onís Treaty, which kept Texas as part of Mexico, Jackson preferred to let it die, but after a long delay he reluctantly sent it to the Senate in February 1832, and it was soon ratified.[30]

After signing the treaty, Butler returned to his primary task of buying Texas. In 1832 he held two promising sessions with Foreign Minister Lucas Alamán on the subject, only to have Alamán's conservative government overthrown by the liberals, who were utterly opposed to the sale of Texas. In fall 1833, as General Antonio Lopez de Santa Anna marched toward Mexico City to take over the government, Butler decided to try bribery. On 28 October he reported that he had been asked to bribe certain officials with $200,000 or more and had replied that the money was available. He reminded Jackson that he had been authorized to use his own "discretion" in spending United States funds in order to "effect our purpose." Jackson was alarmed because Butler had sent the letter by mail without encoding it and angry because Butler had suggested that the president had authorized "corruption." "Nothing," said Jackson, "could be farther from my intention." He warned Butler not to give the appearance that he was "attempting to bribe" Mexican officials. To this Butler replied impudently that Jackson's advice proved "how little" he knew of "character" in Mexico, where "bribery" was "common."[31]

Jackson was conveniently overlooking his 1829 instructions in which he had stated: "I scarcely ever knew a Spaniard who was not the slave of avarice, and it is not improbable that this weakness may be worth a great deal to us, in this case." Jackson had also told Butler that it did not matter whether Butler spent the allotted $5 million for the "purchase of men or to pay their national debt," provided he acquired Texas in a hurry. Jackson did not care how the money was used but did not want to be linked with bribery.[32]

At the same time Butler recommended that the United States seize the land in eastern Texas between the Sabine and Neches rivers, arguing that it was cheaper to fight than to negotiate. When he repeated the proposal in March 1834 and asked Jackson to put him at the head of the occupied territory, Jackson was annoyed. On the back of Butler's bold request he wrote: "A. Butler: What a scamp. . . . The Secretary of State will reiterate his instructions to ask an extension of the treaty for running boundary line, and then recall him." Jackson, who continued to have difficulties dealing with Congress, could not afford to be accused of planning to invade Mexico.[33]

The president, however, let a year and a half pass before finally cutting Butler loose. On learning that he was to be recalled, Butler whined that unnamed people were against him and asked permission to stay another six months, a request that was reluctantly granted. In April 1835, well after the deadline, Butler managed to get an agreement for a new joint commission to survey the boundary, after which he returned to Washington to meet with Jackson. When Butler in June again advised the use of bribery, Jackson rejected the idea but still let Butler return to Mexico for another six months. He was finally replaced by Judge Powhatan Ellis of Mississippi in January 1836, about the same time that the French were deciding to pay the spoliation claims.[34]

Butler's diplomacy represented one of Jackson's greatest failures. The president had sent him to Mexico to acquire Texas and to improve relations that had been damaged by Joel Poinsett's intrigues. With Mexico in turmoil and public opinion running against the United States, any diplomat would have had difficulty, but Butler was so crude and corrupt that he made the situation worse and helped sow the seeds for war. Jackson, however, deserves a share of the blame. First he hinted that Butler could use bribery, next he showed outrage when Butler decided to try it, and then he let him stay on for two more years.

Jackson deserves less blame for the Texan revolt, but once again his indecisive diplomacy played a role in what happened. After doing little to prevent a revolution in Texas, the president did his best to be neutral when it finally broke out in fall 1835. Even after Santa Anna killed hundreds of Americans at the Alamo and at Goliad, the president remained strictly neutral. He showed his firmness in April 1836 when he received a provocative letter from Stephen F. Austin, who was in New York drumming up support for Texas. Austin urged Jackson to end the butchery by going to war against Mexico, but Jackson wrote on the back of the letter, "Our neutrality must be faithfully maintained."[35]

The victory of Sam Houston over the Mexicans at San Jacinto on 21 April 1836 made Texas independent and also made it harder for Jackson to continue American neutrality. When Santa Anna, who had been captured, promised to give Texas its independence if he was released, Austin asked Jackson to guarantee that Santa Anna would carry out the agreement. Jackson, however, refused to do so, saying that once captured, Santa Anna lacked the authority to grant independence.[36]

Jackson was also under pressure from warhawks in the Southwest, who were enthusiastic about the Texan revolt and were alarmed by the threat of violence from Indians who still remained east of the Mississippi. In Alabama the Creeks who had been forced off their lands and were wandering at large succeeded for a while in cutting off the mail between New Orleans and the North. In Florida, where the Seminole War had begun, all land south of St. Augustine lay in Indian hands. The warhawks asked Jackson to send troops to suppress the Creeks and the Seminoles as well as other Indians farther west. Gen. Richard G. Dunlap of Tennessee, who was on his way to raise troops in East Texas, wanted Jackson to use the slightest excuse to teach Santa Anna to respect the "rights of humanity." In July Dunlap asked the president to order a Tennessee militia brigade into Texas.[37]

The situation worsened when Jackson sent Gen. Edmund P. Gaines across the Texas border at the Sabine River, supposedly to protect Louisiana from the Indians. Yet when the president was attacked by the opposition press and by members of his own administration, he reconsidered his policy. Amos Kendall wrote that the world was already blaming the United States for the Texan revolt and would not approve of Gaines's advance. If war came with Mexico, Kendall would support it, but he wanted it to be for reasons that the world would consider "right," not simply to conquer other people "for their own good." Jackson promptly replied that he agreed with Kendall's view and on 4 September told Gaines to protect American neutrality and to attack only those Indians who were disturbing the peace and who were protected by the Mexicans. Jackson also rejected Gaines's request for militiamen from Tennessee.[38]

In dealing with the Texas question and the other foreign policy issues during his administration Jackson received strong support from four capable secretaries of state. Van Buren was responsible for the West Indies treaty and the settlement of many of the claims. Livingston, who was secretary between 1831 and 1833, deserves credit for the treaty with Russia and the first Roberts mission, and he handled the Maine boundary dispute as well as possible. During his brief tenure in the office McLane tried to persuade Jackson to take a firmer stand against the delinquent French government but lost out to more moderate voices. John Forsyth, the fourth secretary, dealt with the French and Texan negotiations with great caution and skill. Under a weaker president any one of these men might have won greater fame as secretary of state.

But Jackson retained control of foreign policy in most instances. At times he was more militant than his secretaries of state. In dealing with Mexico and Texas in particular he had shown some of the nationalism that had been expected in 1829. He had been willing to use bribery to acquire Texas, and he had done little to prevent the start of the Texan revolution or the surge of volunteers to the Texan army. The same nationalism was also demonstrated in the promptness with which he responded to the Malay attack at Quallah Battoo and in his aggressiveness toward France in his 1834 annual message. It was impossible for Jackson to suppress his nationalism on all occasions.

But in general the supposedly warlike, anti-British president had surprised his observers with his moderation. He had displayed admirable restraint in dealing with Great Britain, with Spain, and for several years, with France. Only when the French refused to live up to their agreement did Jackson show flashes of the warlike stereotype. Even though he was intent on purchasing Texas, he officially adhered to established American policies of neutrality and nonintervention.

Throughout his foreign policy Jackson demonstrated a steady concern for trade and commerce. By helping American farmers find export markets for their surplus cotton, tobacco, and foodstuffs, this policy was well within the tradition of an agrarian economy. But the Old Hero was so aggressive in his support for commerce that he was also in tune with the rising capitalism. With his efforts to expand trade and the western frontier, he well represented the agrarian interests of his western supporters. At the same time he advanced the commercial interests of northeastern Jacksonians such as McLane and Cambreleng. John M. Belohlavek, the leading authority on Jacksonian foreign policy, describes it as "a meld of republican virtue and self-righteousness with entrepreneurial spirit and practical diplomacy." In his final message Jackson boasted that American commerce with many of the nations of Europe was still "expanding."[39]

He showed the same concern for free-enterprise capitalism in his appointments to diplomatic posts, many of which went to businessmen or men with close ties to business. Thomas P. Moore, minister to Colombia, worked on behalf of the merchant Elisha Riggs of Washington. Cornelius P. Van Ness, minister to Spain, was brother of John P. Van Ness, president of the Bank of Metropolis in Washington. Levi Woodbury, who had influence over appointments, was related by marriage to the Portland merchant Asa Clapp. Edmund Roberts, who was related to Woodbury, had married into the mercantile Langdon family of Portsmouth. It was not unusual, of course, for such people to be named to diplomatic posts, but Jackson appointed more from this class than might have been expected in 1829 when his administration was first getting under way.[40]

More often than not these diplomats were successful. The opening of the British West Indies, the Ottoman Empire, and the Black Sea was a major accomplishment. Had he not been struck down by cholera, Edmund Roberts might have added to these achievements by opening Japan. All told, the Jackson administration successfully negotiated at least ten commercial treaties and agreements in addition to the six claims settlements. Between 1828 and 1836 American exports and imports both doubled, the best record of any president before Woodrow Wilson.

Jackson, however, should not get too much credit, for considerable groundwork had been laid by John Quincy Adams, and impersonal market forces had much to do with the growth. The unfavorable balance of trade, which Jackson inherited, continued, regardless of his efforts. Furthermore, the Jacksonian boom in foreign trade did not carry over into the next few administrations but instead fell prey to the Panic of 1837. In addition, there was often little correlation between the growth of trade and Jacksonian treaties. Under Jackson, the greatest expansion in American exports was to Great Britain but without the benefit of a new trade treaty. Despite unusual efforts in Central and South America, exports there barely kept even, as the British continued to dominate trade. There was a great surge in imports from the Americas, mostly sugar from Cuba, where Van Ness was unable to get a treaty, and coffee from Brazil, where the treaty had been negotiated by the Adams administration. Imports from Asia doubled, but much of the increase was from China, where the Jacksonians had not negotiated any treaty.[41]

Jackson did not overlook the connection between foreign affairs and politics. Working in tandem with Van Buren and his successors, the president extended the party's patronage system to the State Department in Washington and to diplomatic and consular posts abroad. Because of such political considerations, some of his appointees were not always distinguished; a few were even outright failures. The unstable Randolph stayed only a short time after being dispatched to Russia. The emotional William Pitt Preble was less than satisfactory at The Hague. The chargés at Mexico City and Bogota—Butler and Moore—proved corrupt and uncontrollable. At the same time some of his other appointments were exceptionally talented, notably McLane and Rives, and they held the most important posts.

In his handling of diplomacy Jackson was, on the whole, more restrained than nationalistic, more inclined toward increasing commerce than in holding back the market revolution. These policies were in many ways similar to those of Adams. Jackson's eagerness to settle American claims, for example, benefited the merchant capitalists of the eastern seaports, men whose political allegiance was generally to Adams and Clay. With his concern for both the agrarian and the commercial interests in his coalition, he showed a keen political awareness. In the election of 1832 his foreign policy would be a political issue.

7

★ ★ ★ ★ ★

A JACKSON VICTORY

In antebellum studies the election of 1832 has been overshadowed by the more colorful and influential elections of 1800, 1828, and 1860. Even students of the Jackson administration, preoccupied by the Bank War and the Nullification Crisis, have not given the election the attention it deserves. This is unfortunate, for Jackson's reelection left an indelible mark on the history of the presidency. It was one of the few elections that served as a referendum on a dominant issue and was the only one that emulated British elections by pitting the chief executive against the leader of the opposition in the legislature. It was also unusual, though not unique, in that both major candidates were slaveholders, and it was the first election with a third party. Most significantly, it accelerated the rise of the second American party system by introducing national nominating conventions and party platforms and by strengthening the identity of the two major parties.

After three years of the Jackson presidency the second American party system had still not come into full flower. No well-established parties existed at the national level. Even at the state level there were only a few highly developed organizations, such as the Jackson parties in New York and New Hampshire. Instead of two parties Calhoun saw three: his own a free-trade party of "principle," Clay's protectionist party of "interests," and a party in the middle led by Jackson. This political fluidity led many observers to consider change inevitable. Clay thought that Americans "live[d] in an age of revolution," and Webster believed that it was time for parties to be "sorted out, anew."[1]

The election of 1832 fostered the growth of the two-party system by establishing party names, which would become indispensable elements of a national system; without them candidates would have continued to outweigh parties. By 1830 the majority of Jackson's opponents had settled on the term "National Republicans." Even the *Globe* began to call them that, though occasionally Blair would belittle them by referring to them as "Federalists." Jackson's supporters, less consistent, called themselves "Democratic Republicans," "Republicans," or "Jacksonians," but in states with strong Jackson parties the word "Democrats" began to appear. Jackson used the term in 1832, and the *Globe* gave impetus to it by calling for a "Democratic party" convention. Even though the party still clung to the old names at the convention, more and more Americans adopted the name "Democratic party" during the campaign—enough so to justify using the name later in this chapter and throughout the rest of the book.[2]

Until the rise of the West in the 1820s American parties largely reflected the interests of New England, New York, and Virginia, but as the West became strong enough to balance the Northeast and the Southeast, a more truly national political system began to develop. The census of 1830 gave the western states almost a third of the electoral votes in the election of 1832, compared to only one-sixth in the election of 1816. Meanwhile New England's share of the votes had dropped from 22 percent to 17 percent and the Southeast's from 26 percent to 21 percent. The effect of the change on the presidential candidates was startling. Before 1824 no westerner had run for president, but between 1824 and 1860 every election had at least one western candidate, and over half, including the election of 1832, had two. In this new America, politicians would have to consider the interests of the West.[3]

Just as it had four years earlier, political maneuvering began again almost as soon as the election of 1828 had ended. Although the renomination of Jackson by several state legislatures in 1830 removed Van Buren as a Jacksonian candidate, it did not discourage others from getting into the race. Jackson's health was so precarious that neither John McLean nor Calhoun's spokesman Duff Green thought that the Old Hero would run again. Whether he would or not, the assumption grew that there would be enough candidates in the field to send the election to the House of Representatives, a common belief in election campaigns in the antebellum years.[4]

In April 1830, before Calhoun had split with Jackson, Green was confident that the South Carolinian could carry the Southwest and New England, but New York, Pennsylvania, and Ohio were especially "doubtful." Calhoun had many connections, including Samuel Swartwout in

New York, Virgil Maxcy in Maryland, Felix Grundy in Tennessee, and Ninian Edwards in Illinois. He had also asked Edward J. Mallett of Providence, Rhode Island, to keep him informed of "public sentiments" in New England. When the Jacksonian legislators in Pennsylvania voted for a resolution calling for the reelection of Jackson, friends of Calhoun almost kept it from passing. Calhoun fully expected that either he or McLean would get the nomination if Jackson did not run.[5]

But Calhoun's split with Jackson, his preoccupation with nullification, and his unwillingness to commit himself weakened his presidential prospects. Even after the cabinet breakup in April 1831 he refused to come out openly against the administration, saying instead that he would remain independent. Green became annoyed at Calhoun's diffidence, chided him for "waiting so long" to declare himself, and warned that McLean would steal his votes unless he acted. Although Calhoun was nominated in New York City in late summer, he turned his attention more and more to nullification, and his hopes for the presidency died.[6]

The fluidity of American politics, which had encouraged Calhoun and McLean to run, also assisted the Anti-Masons. The movement erupted in upper New York State in 1827 after the supposed abduction and murder of William Morgan, a Mason, who had talked of exposing the order. When influential members of the Masons blocked efforts to investigate Morgan's disappearance, grassroots conventions were called to take political action. Anti-Masonry had a broad appeal, flourishing among prosperous city dwellers as well as among less affluent farmers along the Erie Canal. Its members attacked Masonry as a corrupt, privileged, machinelike organization, depriving the people of their rights— the same way that Jacksonians attacked the Bank.

Anti-Masonry spread rapidly in the Northeast and played a major role in the politics of New York and Pennsylvania. Not only did it appeal to a strong Anti-Masonic sentiment, but it also offered an alternative to National Republicanism for attacking the Jackson party. The egalitarian message of the movement enabled the Anti-Masons to win twenty-one seats in the New York legislature in 1828 even though they lost the governorship to Van Buren in a three-man race. Two years later most of the New York National Republicans supported the Anti-Masonic candidate for governor, but enough of them defected to the Jackson party to give it the election. In Pennsylvania, the Anti-Masons pushed the National Republicans aside and came close to defeating the Jacksonian George Wolf for governor in 1829 and 1832. Encouraged by their showing, the Anti-Masons decided to mount a campaign against Jackson, a prominent Mason. At a meeting in Philadelphia in September 1830 they called for a national nominating convention to be held at Baltimore the following year.[7]

In casting about for a candidate, the Anti-Masons turned first to Henry Clay, who was temporarily retired on his plantation in Lexington, Kentucky. Shortly after Jackson's inauguration Clay had made several defiant speeches encouraging opposition to the new regime. Jackson's challenge to Clay's American System with his Maysville veto in spring 1830 offered the Kentuckian a natural and timely opportunity to come out of retirement. Accordingly, he toured the Northwest that summer and was nominated by National Republican meetings in Connecticut, Delaware, and Kentucky. Even though Clay was a Mason, Anti-Masonic leaders looked to him as a candidate who could unite National Republicans and Anti-Masons against Jackson. The overtures ended, however, after Clay stubbornly refused to make any statements against the Masonic order. When the Anti-Masons approached Calhoun, who was not a Mason, in spring 1831, he appeared to be fishing for an invitation by calling the doctrines of the order "pernicious." But when he refused to run openly against the order, the Anti-Masons turned instead to John McLean.[8]

The rudimentary quality of party politics in 1831 can be seen in the frequent suggestions that Clay and Calhoun were conspiring to run together against Jackson. Just before Calhoun cut his ties with Jackson in February by publishing his Florida correspondence, Nicholas Biddle was told that Calhoun still might run again with the Old Hero but that Clay was doing all he could to get Calhoun on his ticket. In the spring Van Buren heard that Anti-Masons were planning to join Clay and Calhoun in a convention in Pennsylvania, whereupon Blair announced that Calhoun and Clay were plotting against Jackson.[9]

Talk of such an alliance diminished in fall 1831 as Calhoun came out openly for nullification and the Anti-Masons and National Republicans held national conventions. On 26 September the Anti-Masons assembled in Baltimore for the first national nominating convention in American history. Having failed to convince McLean to run, they nominated former attorney general William Wirt, who was active at the time defending the Cherokees. The nomination of Wirt, a former Mason, and the sentiments expressed at the convention show how far Anti-Masonry had changed from a moral crusade to a pragmatic political party. In his acceptance letter Wirt declared that he had no strong feelings against the Masons, and in their address the Anti-Masons said that the goals of Masonry were "laudable" but that it had fallen on evil days. The fervor had gone out of Anti-Masonry largely because it had been so successful. In New York the number of Masonic lodges had dropped from 480 in 1825 to 77 in 1830.[10]

On 12 December 1831 the National Republicans convened in Baltimore, where they nominated Clay for president and John Sergeant, who like Wirt was also defending the Cherokees, for vice-president. At the close of the convention they published an address accusing Jackson of "vindictive party spirit" in his "scandalous" dissolution of the cabinet. The address condemned the president for instituting "universal proscription," for following "vacillating" policies on the tariff and internal improvements, and for planning the "destruction" of the Bank. "Most important," he had approved of "inhumane and unconstitutional outrages" against the Indians. Because of its stridency the address was more a personal attack on Jackson than a political party platform. The first true platform was adopted by the National Republicans the following May when delegates to the Young Men's National Republican Convention in Washington published a less personal, more straightforward statement endorsing the American System except for the Bank.[11]

Long before these conventions took place, the *Globe* ended speculation by announcing that Jackson would run again. The announcement, which came on 22 January 1831, triggered a struggle within the coalition over the vice-presidency. Van Buren was the early favorite because of Jackson's support, but the cabinet turmoil weakened his chances. Old Republicans in Virginia, who normally would have backed Van Buren, were beginning to rally around Judge Philip P. Barbour. Among the pro-Bank, Middle Atlantic nationalists, Louis McLane and Sen. William Wilkins of Pennsylvania were talking about running. Candidates representing other wings of the coalition were Unionist senator John Forsyth of Georgia and western agrarian congressman Richard M. Johnson of Kentucky. Other members were suggesting John McLean, and a few even wanted to keep Calhoun as vice-president. With the coalition already divided over the cabinet, the scramble for the vice-presidency posed a serious threat to harmony.[12]

At this point, on 17 May, Kendall tried to take advantage of the situation by sending his letter to Lewis opposing the nomination of either Calhoun or Van Buren. Kendall, who was visiting Isaac Hill in Concord, New Hampshire, at the time, went over the list of those men in the running for vice-president and concluded that Barbour was the best bet. He recommended that they ask the strongly Jacksonian New Hampshire legislature to nominate Barbour. If the others in the administration had accepted this advice, they would have been following the long-established tradition of nominating candidates in state legislatures as well as mending the breach between Jackson and Virginia. They would also have been undercutting Van Buren.[13]

But Lewis, who was still for Van Buren, stood in the way. After consulting "several . . . friends," undoubtedly including Jackson, Blair, and the much-interested Van Buren, Lewis wrote Kendall on 25 May, offering a different plan. He first reviewed Kendall's list of candidates and concluded that none would be "satisfactory to the different local interests." The only way to "harmonize" the party, he decided, was to wait a year and hold a national nominating convention in the middle of the following May. He then proposed that the New Hampshire Jacksonians call for the convention. On Kendall's suggestion the state organization promptly complied, and on 6 July the *Globe* published and soon thereafter endorsed the New Hampshire proposal. By putting off the choice of a vice-presidential candidate for a year, Lewis and Kendall helped to restore party harmony and also helped Van Buren, who would be in a stronger position to win the nomination a year later.[14]

The idea of holding a convention was not in itself new. Conventions had been used in local elections as early as the eighteenth century, usually in well-populated areas with competing political parties. By the election of 1832 a full-fledged convention system was in force in the Middle Atlantic states and existed to a lesser extent everywhere else but the Southeast. Van Buren had pointed out the advantages of a national convention in 1827 in his letter to Thomas Ritchie calling for a Jackson party. Such a convention, he had argued, "would draw anew the old Party lines" and "would greatly improve the condition of the Republicans of the North and Middle States by substituting *party principle* for *personal preference.*" Ritchie, Benton, and a few other Jacksonians did not support the idea of a convention in 1832, fearing that political concerns would outweigh the old ideals, but they were won over later.[15]

With their emphasis on the Anti-Masonic and National Republican conventions, students have not always given the Jacksonian Democrats enough credit for calling their convention. Party conventions serve several important functions: They provide a democratic way for the people to be represented, they nominate candidates, and they inculcate party spirit. With 334 delegates representing 23 states, the Democratic Convention of 1832 was far more representative than the others, neither of which had more than 168 delegates from more than 18 states. The Democratic party also accomplished more at its convention than did either of the other parties. The National Republicans had generally agreed on their ticket before their convention, and both the Anti-Masonic and National Republican parties soon disappeared. When the Democrats nominated a vice-president at their convention, they helped unify their party, making it the first truly national American political party. As it turned out, their choice, Van Buren, ultimately became their presidential candidate in the next election. The Democrats also continued to hold conventions after 1832, but the others did not.[16]

As plans for the convention were falling into place in summer 1831, Van Buren left for England still enjoying Jackson's support. Not only did Jackson want Van Buren as vice-president, but he also reminded him during the fall of an incredible plan they had concocted in which Jackson would turn the presidency over to him. *"You will understand me,"* he wrote conspiratorially. By December, however, as McLane gained power in Van Buren's absence, Jackson's commitment waned. He told Van Buren that if he was "not called to the vice Presidency," he should return to become secretary of state again.[17]

Van Buren had steadily denied being a candidate for vice-president, fearing that any show of interest would confirm the widely held view that he was merely a selfish politician. But in late fall and early winter Jackson's letter and several others made him think twice about his subterfuge. Minister to France William C. Rives confided that he was interested in the vice-presidency himself. Then came the disturbing news that McLane, another possible vice-president, had gained the president's confidence and was proposing the rechartering of the Bank. Although Van Buren did not know it, McLane was also at this time starting his plot to remove Blair from the *Globe*. Van Buren wrote one letter to Rives, urging him not to run, and another to Jackson, trying to determine where the president stood. To offset McLane's influence, he told Churchill C. Cambreleng to show the president the errors in McLane's position on the Bank.[18]

While this manuevering was going on and as the Bank bill began to make its way through Congress, the Senate took up Van Buren's nomination as minister to Great Britain. Hoping to defeat and humiliate the New Yorker, the opposition brought out a parade of well-prepared speakers. Webster began by accusing Van Buren of having put "party above the country" in 1829 when he instructed McLane to repudiate Adams's policy in the West Indies. Clay continued on the partisan theme by blaming Van Buren for bringing the spoils system with him from New York to Washington. The Jacksonians in reply defended partisan politics, Samuel Smith of Maryland pointing out that the spoils system was flourishing in other states besides New York. William L. Marcy of the Albany Regency went further when he uttered his famous statement that American politicians followed "the rule, that to the victor belong the spoils of the enemy."[19]

On 25 January 1832 the Senate vote on confirmation—twenty-three for Van Buren and twenty-three against—was as partisan as the debate.

All the National Republicans and Calhoun men opposed the nomination, and all the Jacksonians voted for him. The tie vote was arranged when George Bibb of Kentucky, nominally a Jacksonian but sliding toward Calhoun, agreed to absent himself. With this opportunity the vice-president cast, with great "alacrity," the deciding ballot against his rival. In one of the rare instances in which Calhoun abandoned his self-control, the so-called "cast-iron man" crowed triumphantly: "It will kill him, sir, kill him dead. He will never kick, sir, never kick."[20]

But Van Buren lived to kick again. The rejection so angered Jackson that he reacted, according to Henry Wikoff, "like a lion goaded to fury" or a "volcano in eruption." Beginning to sound like a party man, the president blamed the "factious opposition" in the Senate and swore that he would see to it that Van Buren was elected vice-president and returned to the Senate as its presiding officer. About the same time Jackson rescued Blair from McLane's plot and came out unequivocally against the Bank. This general clearing of the air set the course of the Jackson party for the remainder of the election year.[21]

In New York the rejection gave Van Buren the popular support that he had previously lacked. At least fifty towns and counties held meetings of protest, and the *Albany Argus* was filled with letters. The Regency was delighted at the response. Marcy, always pragmatic, said that Van Buren should run for vice-president because the president was "rapped [sic] up" in him and would not live long enough to complete a second term. When several members of the Regency suggested that Van Buren be content to run for the Senate, Marcy retorted, "Don't be fastidious. When party feeling is strong almost any thing that is done is right."[22]

The rejection also helped make Democrats out of Jacksonians. Blair, who had been cool toward Van Buren, now implored him to come home and "save the Republic" from Clay and Calhoun by running for vice-president. Andrew J. Donelson, long suspicious of the Little Magician, predicted that he would become vice-president. The *Globe* carried articles supporting Van Buren from such widely separated states as Rhode Island, Georgia, and Ohio. Speaker Andrew Stevenson, a good party man, told the more idealistic Ritchie that he must give up his "scruples" about Van Buren's nomination. Although serious intraparty divisions still existed, especially over the Bank and nullification, the Democratic party was more a reality after Van Buren's rejection than before.[23]

Even so, Van Buren's road to the vice-presidency was not entirely clear, for McLane made two attempts to derail the nomination. Three days after Van Buren's rejection and a few days before the plot against Blair was uncovered, McLane tried to convince Jackson that Van Buren's nomination would endanger the president's "success and the safety of the whole party." When Van Buren learned of this in England, he wrote Jackson, reminding him that in the past, scheming Federalists had hurt Republicans such as Aaron Burr, DeWitt Clinton, and Henry Clay. He was obviously implying that a former Federalist, McLane, could hurt another Republican, Andrew Jackson. The letter was of course unnecessary, since long before Van Buren learned of McLane's remarks, Jackson had committed himself to Van Buren.[24]

McLane nonetheless tried again. On the eve of the convention Lewis learned that McLane, Eaton, Overton, and Barry were engaged in a last-minute conspiracy to nominate McLane's close friend Samuel Smith for vice-president. Only by warning Eaton that they would have to *"quarrel with the General"* if they persisted did Lewis manage to abort the plot. When the convention got under way, Van Buren's friends helped him further by establishing a rule requiring a two-thirds vote for nominating a vice-president. The rule, which remained in effect until 1936, destroyed the chances of Johnson, Barbour, and Wilkins, none of whom would be capable of reaching the two-thirds level. Van Buren was nominated with 260 of 326 votes. The Democrats did not officially nominate Jackson for president; instead they passed a resolution in which they "concur[red] in the repeated nominations" for president that Jackson had already received in a number of states. Van Buren was unaware of these developments, remaining in Europe after his rejection and thereby avoiding the convention and the fighting over the tariff and the Bank.[25]

While the Democrats were quarreling over the vice-presidency, the issues being debated in Congress began to play an important role in the election. The question of rechartering the Bank became such a hot issue that Samuel Smith predicted in June that the election would be "contested on the principle of Bank or no Bank." John Tyler's son Lyon later wrote that Clay made the Bank one of the keynotes of his campaign. Having served as legal advisers to Biddle, both Clay and his running mate John Sergeant were closely identified with the Bank. In August Biddle told Clay that Jackson would "pay the penalty" for "making the Bank a party question." To make this prediction come true he spent $100,000 on the election and distributed 30,000 copies of the veto message in the belief that Jackson's own words would hurt him. When the practical Clay suggested that they also circulate criticisms of the veto, Biddle sent out 20,000 copies of Webster's Senate speech.[26]

Democrats, too, used the Bank issue. In the *Globe* Blair devoted most of his editorials to the Bank and also mailed a special supplement with the veto message to thousands of party members. In words that mirrored the veto message, he compared it to the Declaration of Independence and contrasted the "virtuous" Jackson to the "insidious enemy." To prove that the Bank was corrupt, he listed the sums of money that it had paid to Webster and other opposition politicians. If this *"Gambler's Bank"* had been rechartered, he added, the price of its stock would have shot up. Blair warned that the large number of British stockholders in the Bank raised the possibility that the United States might return to "British thraldom."[27]

Jackson, Van Buren, and Barry believed that their party would benefit from the Bank issue, Barry even predicting gains in Pennsylvania, where Bank strength in Philadelphia would be offset by weaknesses in the outlying counties. Clay admitted scornfully that Democratic propaganda against the Bank, especially Benton's "rodomontade," was hurting his campaign. After a close Democratic victory in the Kentucky state election in August, Jackson insisted that the margin would have been greater if the party had had more time to circulate copies of his veto message. Democratic governor John Breathitt, however, reported that the veto had been a liability until he produced lists of foreign stockholders.[28]

The close fight over the removal bill and the role of Wirt and Sergeant in the Cherokee cases made Indian policy another important issue in the campaign. Opposition leaders played up the dismissal of Thomas L. McKenney as head of the Indian Bureau and persuaded Jeremiah Evarts to publish a book with the major congressional speeches against removal. Webster was urged to find proof of Jackson's alleged statement that he would not enforce Marshall's decision. When Wirt used the story in his campaign, Jackson angrily retorted that Wirt's course was "truly wicked." In April 1832 Clay denounced Jackson's treaty with the Creeks. Interest in the Indian question became so intense that even in faraway New Hampshire it temporarily overshadowed the Bank War as a political issue.[29]

The Democrats responded vehemently, calling their program humane and their critics fanatical. Blair pointed out that Jackson had never been asked to enforce Marshall's decision and said that Clay was hiding behind the Indians just as the British had done in the War of 1812. If Clay won the election, he warned, the Cherokees would become an independent state. When the war against Black Hawk went badly in summer 1832, Jackson sent more troops than were needed to put it down. They only served to embarrass him when they were quarantined in Chicago during an outbreak of cholera. To further deflect criticism Jackson appointed a commission to make certain that Indians in the western territory were being treated properly. Some idea of Jackson's concern can be seen in his agitated letters to his subordinates asking them about the removal of the Chickasaws.[30]

Jackson also tried to use foreign policy to his advantage and encountered predictable partisan opposition. He won an early victory in 1832 when the Senate unanimously ratified the French treaty despite several obstructionist moves by Clay. The president was so eager to settle the Neapolitan claims before the election that he sharply criticized Secretary of State Livingston for wasting ten days in making preparations and ordered Chargé John Nelson to have a settlement by 1 March 1832. Nelson disappointed him by not signing the treaty until 14 October. News of the Quallah Battoo affair reached Washington just after the Bank veto in July and well before the election. On hearing the story of the American assault on the town, the *Daily National Intelligencer* denounced Jackson for ordering the attack without negotiating first. During the next few days a spirited war of words took place between the *Intelligencer* and the *Globe*, which called the attack a justifiable defense against piracy. The furor subsided as soon as it became evident that the captain of the *Potomac* had exceeded the president's orders.

Boundary disputes also had a partisan overtone. When Jackson submitted the Mexican treaty, which left Texas as part of Mexico, to the Senate in spring 1832, he tried to have it postponed so that he would have more time to extend the boundary. But Chairman Littleton W. Tazewell of the Foreign Relations Committee refused, and the treaty was ratified in April. Soon afterward Clay and Webster blocked Jackson's efforts to settle the Maine boundary by tying amendments to a favorable report from the Foreign Relations Committee.[31]

The parties also reacted to other issues that were less important in the campaign. The National Republicans tried to use the tariff issue both ways against Van Buren. In North Carolina, where protection was unpopular, he was called the "father of the tariff," and in the North Webster said that New York congressmen were supporting low tariffs in order to improve Van Buren's standing among southerners. Blair made it clear all summer that Jackson was unalterably opposed to nullification, which was threatening in South Carolina. The spoils system was turned against both Jackson and Van Buren, and the *Globe* accused Clay of selling out the West with his distribution bill. Issues were more important in this election than they had been in the election of 1828.[32]

Nonetheless, the election of 1832 turned more on Jackson and Clay than on issues and parties. The Bank and Indian policies outweighed the other issues precisely because they were more closely related to Jackson than were nullification, the tariff, distribution, or the spoils system. With

147

their party structures still not well developed, the Democrats and the National Republicans had to rely on their candidates rather than on their parties or the issues to galvanize local interest. Not until 1836 did the Democrats reach the point that their party outweighed their candidate. The Whigs did not reach such a point until 1840, and even then they based much of their campaign on "Old Tippecanoe," William Henry Harrison.

If an issue was ever going to overshadow the candidates, it would have been in the Senate on the Bank veto, but the debate quickly dissolved into a personal battle between Jackson and Clay. In his speech against the veto, Clay warned that the next step would be to give Jackson the power of legislative initiative. If so, he said, Congress would become unnecessary and the government could be "economically conducted by ukases and decrees." When Benton defended the president and accused Clay of discourtesy, the two senators got into a row, not over the Bank but over Benton's frontier brawl with Jackson. Personalities continued to dominate the campaign, with Wirt fearing "despotism" if Jackson was elected and the Democrats attacking Clay as a rake. In his scurrilous "Twenty-Three Reasons Why Clay Should Not Be Elected President," Isaac Hill accused Clay of spending "his days at the gaming table and his nights in a brothel."[33]

Amid the charges, Blair's image of Jackson as a man of "spotless honor," "protecting our rights abroad, fostering our interests at home" towered above the campaign. "A fearless leader," he had seized Alabama from the Indians, saved Louisiana from the British, and now "head[ed] the bold array against the Bank Monster." To take advantage of his republican image of honor and virtue, Jackson ran a traditional campaign, remaining silent and out of sight while the people decided. When Clay attended rallies, the *Globe* called him a "demagogue" who had "humiliated" himself by stooping to such measures.[34]

While Jackson retreated to the Hermitage, his party ran a new-style campaign, using card files, passing out buttons, and carrying illuminated transparencies at night in their parades. Kendall and Blair coordinated the activities of hundreds of local organizations, with the *Globe* serving as a clearinghouse for Democratic newspapers. Democratic members of Congress saved money for the party by franking the copies of the *Globe* sent out to the faithful. The opposition tried to keep up by running articles in the *Daily National Intelligencer*, circulating pamphlets, and staging their own celebrations. Their success, however, was limited because the National Republicans and Anti-Masons were not fully reconciled to the new techniques and could not work together. Only in cartooning were the Jackson forces outdone. One particularly effective cartoon showed "King Andrew the First," with a crown and scepter, holding a "veto" in his left hand and stamping the Constitution and the Bank underfoot. Despite the cartoons, the young Anti-Mason Thurlow Weed of New York had to admit ruefully that the "huzza strength" of Andrew Jackson was difficult to beat.[35]

The Democrats also gained an advantage by establishing a "Central Hickory Club" in Washington and by circulating an address drawn up by Kendall and printed in the *Globe*. The address reviewed the party's philosophy and achievements, defended the administration against political charges, and wholeheartedly attacked the opposition. The statement read like an Old Republican litany as the Democrats pledged to preserve a federal Union that was limited to only those powers delegated by the states. Government, they said, existed solely to maintain republican institutions and to *"keep off evil."* Kendall cited statistics to demonstrate that no proscription of Adams men had occurred and gave examples of defaulters among those persons who had been removed. He took great pains to show that the administration had not wasted federal funds and denounced the Bank for corrupting the press and for combining with the nullifiers.[36]

A devastating cholera epidemic cast a pall over the campaign in some areas during the summer. Van Buren, who had lived through a similar epidemic in London, found the disease raging in New York City when he arrived home on 5 July. By mid-August there had been 5,175 cases and 1,986 deaths in the city. Unwilling to risk his life again, he turned down a public reception and went to Washington. Since cholera had spread there as well, both he and Jackson left the capital later in July, Van Buren for Lebanon Springs, New York, and Jackson for the Hermitage. The president did not return until late October, Van Buren not until late the following February.[37]

As the campaign entered the fall neither side was fully confident. Clay thought he would win but only if Wirt carried enough states to send the election to the House. Although encouraged by the Democratic victory in Kentucky in August, Jackson was still worried about Clay's home state. He was so concerned that he broke his rule about campaigning by stopping off at Lexington in September on his way back to Washington. An anxious Blair even wondered if the Democrats would win in New York. It was a measure of the Democrats' uncertainty that they were not sure of carrying Van Buren's home state.

The election was held on different dates throughout November, starting on the second in Ohio and Pennsylvania and ending in Rhode Island on the twenty-first. When Jackson carried Pennsylvania, which had been in doubt, it was apparent that he would be reelected. The final popular vote was 688,242 for Jackson, 473,462 for Clay, and 101,051 for Wirt. Jackson carried the electoral college with 219 votes to 49 for Clay and 7 for Wirt. The pattern of the popular returns, especially the vote for Jackson, was similar to that in the elections in 1824 and 1828. With 114,000 more votes than the combined total of his opponents, Jackson had won a remarkable victory.[38]

The victory, however, was not as great as it might have been. Jackson carried New York, the state that Blair was worried about, but lost Kentucky, the state in which he had campaigned. His share of the popular vote dropped slightly between 1828 and 1832, from 56 percent to 55 percent, the only time this has happened to a president reelected to a second term. In addition, Jackson's majority in the House of Representatives fell from fifty-nine to forty-six between the year he took office and 1833 and in the Senate from a majority of four to a minority of eight. Neither the presidential nor the congressional figures are conclusive. Methods of tally-keeping changed in several states between the two elections. In Alabama, for example, where Jackson won an easy victory in 1832, no votes were recorded, costing him a net of at least 10,000 votes. Furthermore, the congressional elections in the twenty-four states were held over such a drawn-out span of time that the issues had changed somewhat between the first election and the last. The voting for members of the Congress that convened in December 1833 extended from July 1832 in Louisiana to November 1833 in Mississippi.[39]

It does not appear that the issues had much effect on the outcome of the election. Jackson's Bank veto, to be sure, cost him some votes in a few states. In Pennsylvania, for example, the party suffered losses in Philadelphia after some encouraging gains there in city elections between 1828 and 1832. Jackson lost western New York, partly because of the Bank. In addition, the Bank was surprisingly popular in North Carolina and Missouri, but Jackson carried all four states, three of them with wider margins than in 1828. In Massachusetts he benefited from the Bank issue because the veto won over members of the Workingmen's party.[40]

Jackson's Indian policy also hurt a bit but was hardly decisive. Van Buren later recalled that Indian removal had cost the Democrats 8,000 to 10,000 votes in New York. He remembered receiving "a spirited denunciation" from his niece in western New York, "where the pro-Cherokee feeling had been lashed to a great height." The same feeling proved costly in Pennsylvania and Ohio as well. Still, Jackson won the three states. In Georgia, Alabama, and Mississippi, which Jackson would have carried anyway, his removal policy endeared him to settlers, who were eager to take over the vacated lands. He lost some of that support in

Alabama when he sent troops to remove white squatters intruding on Creek land.[41]

Nor was the election the start of the modern American two-party system. There were, after all, three parties, not two, in the election, and Wirt's 8 percent of the popular vote was a respectable performance for a third-party candidate. Historians have tended to oversimplify the election and to assume that Anti-Masonic votes were just more Clay votes, forgetting that there were Democratic as well as National Republican Anti-Masons. Although the Baltimore convention strengthened the Democratic party, it still remained a coalition. Old Republicans in both Virginia and North Carolina nominated a ticket of Jackson and Philip P. Barbour, which ran unsuccessfully in place of the regular ticket in seven southern states. In Pennsylvania nationalist Democrats offered a ticket of Jackson and William Wilkins, which carried the state, leaving Van Buren with 30 fewer electoral votes than Jackson. The legislature of South Carolina, in the throes of nullification, deserted Jackson altogether and gave the state's electoral votes to extreme states'-rights governor John Floyd of Virginia and free-trader Henry Lee of Massachusetts. Two-party politics had not yet arrived.[42]

Yet the election of 1832 did help the development of the major parties. Partly because of the excitement over the issues, voter participation, which had risen from about one-quarter of the eligible voters in 1824 to over one-half in 1828, remained high at about 55 percent. The fight over Van Buren's nomination as minister to Great Britain and his subsequent nomination for vice-president made the partisanship greater. In many ways their convention of 1832 marked the birth of the Democratic party. Both major parties responded to the election with new party techniques and stronger party organizations.[43]

The election results—both presidential and congressional—also revealed a great change in the regional makeup of the parties. The Democrats improved their position in New England, carrying two states in 1832 after winning none in 1828 and adding one seat in the Senate and three in the House. In the Middle Atlantic states they carried one more state and improved their majority in the House. Their majority of congressmen and senators from the Northwest also increased noticeably. In the South the Democrats lost two states in the popular vote and suffered serious losses in the House and Senate.

The changes in some of the states were striking. The number of Democratic congressmen from New York climbed from ten to thirty-two, and in New Jersey, where the election was by a general ticket instead of by districts, six opposition congressmen in 1829 converted to six Democrats in 1833. Indiana and Illinois became new Democratic strongholds with a combined total of nine Democratic congressmen in 1833 compared with only two in 1829. In Pennsylvania, where Jackson's policies cost votes, Democratic congressmen dropped from twenty-four to fourteen. There were also serious losses in North Carolina, where the Bank had supporters and where Indian removal was not as popular as elsewhere in the South. Eight of South Carolina's nine House seats went from the Democrats to the nullifiers, and Democratic congressmen from Clay's Kentucky dropped from ten to four. Despite the influence of Benton, who hated the Bank, Missouri sent two pro-Bank congressmen to Washington in 1833.[44]

As a result there was greater regional balance after the election. In 1828 the Jackson party carried every state south of the Potomac and Ohio rivers. To the north it won only six states, and even at that the victories were perilously close in New York and Ohio. In 1832 the Democratic party lost two states in the South and carried nine northern states.

But neither the decline of regionalism, nor the rise of issues, nor the growth of political parties was the important story in the election of 1832. The victory in 1832 was more than anything else a personal one for Jackson. Throwing off the indecision that had beset him throughout 1831, Jackson squashed McLane's bid for power, vetoed Biddle's Bank bill, and turned back Clay and Wirt in the election. Where issues were important in the campaign, they had more effect on congressional races than on the presidential election. In Pennsylvania, for example, Jackson's policies on Indian removal, the Bank, the tariff, distribution, and internal improvements were so unpopular that many Democratic congressmen were replaced by their opponents, and Van Buren was no help either; but Jackson won 58 percent of the presidential vote. Although Jackson believed that he had received a popular mandate for his policies, that mandate was not as strong as he imagined. If anything, Jackson's policies kept him from winning an even greater victory. Jackson did, however, receive an impressive personal mandate. The people liked Old Hickory.

8

DEFENDING THE UNION

In the words of Democrats Louis McLane and Alfred Balch, nullification "continue[d] to rumble, like distant thunder" during the election campaign, darkening the skies with its "portentous clouds." The center of the storm was in South Carolina, where a special set of circumstances created a situation different from anywhere else in the nation. Geographically, South Carolina consisted of two sections, a small lowcountry of malarial swamps along the coast and a larger upcountry reaching west into the Piedmont. In the lowcountry, absentee landlords, many of whom lived in Charleston, derived a comfortable living from rice and indigo, produced by black slaves who tolerated the swamps better than whites did. The density of blacks in the lowcountry—frequently over 85 percent of the population—far exceeded that in any other part of the Union. The upcountry, where cotton was the principal crop, also had a high proportion of slaves—well over 50 percent of the population. South Carolina was almost totally dependent on its crops of rice, indigo, and cotton.

The heavy dependence on agriculture deprived the state of the competing interests that prevented extremism in other states. Little of the conflict between lowcountry and upcountry that divided Virginia and other states of the Southeast existed in South Carolina. Planters from the interior had strong ties with the planters and merchants of the seacoast and often spent several months a year in Charleston. Nor did conflict arise from outside influences, for there were few immigrants, and 96 percent of the population—black and white—were native to the state.

As a result of the white homogeneity, democracy and political parties had not developed. South Carolina, where the governor was elected by the state legislature, held no statewide elections before 1860, and in 1832 it was the only state that still chose its presidential electors in the state legislature.

As their Exposition and Protest had indicated in 1828, South Carolinians faced difficult times when Jackson took office. After thirty years of intensive farming, much of the cotton land in the upcountry was worn out and low yielding. A drop in the price of cotton compounded the planters' difficulties. Cotton that sold for eighteen cents a pound after the War of 1812 brought only twelve cents in the late 1820s, and only nine cents in 1830—a decline that greatly outstripped the drop in consumer prices. Alarmed by the situation, upcountry planters were beginning to move to the more fertile soils of Alabama and Mississippi. In the low-country the planters had no comparable escape. Indigo growers had been in trouble ever since losing the English bounties during the Revolution. Profits from rice had also plunged because of the gross inefficiency of the absentee plantations. Here the unusually high density of the black population made whites fearful of a slave insurrection. Only a few years before, in 1822, the Denmark Vesey slave conspiracy had been uncovered in Charleston just in the nick of time.[1]

Out of this setting emerged a group of South Carolinians who considered themselves culturally special. They believed themselves more aristocratic, more paternalistic, and in general superior to planters and merchants in other parts of the South. More sensitive than most southerners, they reacted aggressively to the hard times and to the tariff and antislavery policies of the North. To defend themselves they evolved the doctrine of nullification, and a generation later they would lead the way to secession.

Nullification was an extreme form of the traditional American belief in states' rights that had come out of the Revolution. Thomas Jefferson and James Madison had drafted a classic expression of the traditional point of view in the Kentucky and Virginia Resolutions of 1798–99 in order to protest the Alien and Sedition acts. They based their resolutions on the compact theory of government, in which the states had undivided sovereignty and had delegated only a limited number of powers to the central government. The remaining powers were retained by the states—including the right to declare acts of the central government void. Jefferson and Madison, however, had never endorsed individual state nullification, and their resolutions never clarified the action a state could take if the central government refused to bend to its wishes. Many people believed that the state would have to secede. The matter soon became moot when the Alien and Sedition acts expired or were re-pealed.

Under the economic pressure of the 1820s South Carolinians revived and expanded on the Kentucky and Virginia resolutions. The first outright support for state resistance appeared in summer 1827 in a series of essays entitled "The Crisis," written by the lowcountry planter Robert J. Turnbull. At the same time President Thomas Cooper of South Carolina College in upcountry Columbia delivered a frightening oration in which he questioned "the value of the Union." The hunched-over Cooper, then sixty-seven, was a radical agitator who had grown up in England and had visited Paris during the French Revolution. Devoted to liberty and to states' rights, he made his college a hotbed of nullifier ideology.

The constitutional theory of nullification was elaborated by John C. Calhoun in his Exposition of 1828 and later in an address written at his Fort Hill estate. Since individual state conventions had created the Constitution, he argued, such bodies had the power to declare acts of Congress unconstitutional and to nullify them. There would be no reason for a state nullifying an act to secede; once nullified the law would then be inoperative within the state. Calhoun believed that nullification was the only way in which the interests of the individual states could be protected from the tyranny of the central government. The theory encountered fierce opposition from nationalists and from traditional states' righters, who argued that it would lead to anarchy and would thwart the will of the majority.[2]

South Carolina leaders were divided among radical nullifiers, who wanted to act at once, moderate nullifiers, who preferred to wait, and Unionists who rejected nullification completely. For the next three years the moderates—Calhoun, Sen. Robert Y. Hayne, and young editor James Hammond—held back the radicals—Turnbull, Cooper, and congressmen James Hamilton, Jr., and George McDuffie—by arguing that Jackson should be given the chance to show what he could do for the South. Hayne wrote Van Buren in 1830 that the danger of nullification had been exaggerated and that Jackson could stop it by attacking the American System. During these years Calhoun kept his support of nullification secret, partly because he hoped to succeed Jackson as president and partly because he believed that he could do more to save the Union and help the South within the Jackson administration than he could as a radical nullifier.[3]

By spring 1831 Calhoun's break with Jackson made his position less tenable, but he still hoped that if South Carolina remained quiet he could be elected president. He explained these ideas to Hammond in March, only to be rebuffed. From that point on the radicals intensified

155

their campaign. In May McDuffie attacked the tariff once again, asking his listeners not to be "terrified by mere phantoms of blood." He and Hamilton then organized the States' Rights and Free Trade Association, hoping to win the state over to nullification before the presidential election. With his state becoming more violent by the day, Calhoun finally decided that he must come out openly for nullification in order to restrain the hotheads. In August he retired to his plantation and composed his Fort Hill address, defending nullification as a moderate way to save the Union.[4]

Fears of a slave uprising that summer destroyed any hope of moderation. On New Year's Day 1831 William Lloyd Garrison had published the first issue of the *Liberator* in Boston, promising that he would be "as harsh as truth, and as uncompromising as justice" in attacking slavery. As if in response, a series of slave outbreaks took place in the South, including one incident in South Carolina in which a slave cook poisoned several hundred people at one dinner. Most terrifying of all, on 21 August the young slave preacher Nat Turner led a rebellion in Southampton County, Virginia, in which fifty-seven whites were butchered. Alarmed by the prospect of a slave rebellion in his hometown of Georgetown, South Carolina, Congressman Thomas R. Mitchell asked Jackson to send troops. The anger and fear helped the radical nullifiers win control of the state legislature in November, but they still lacked the two-thirds majority needed to call a convention to nullify the tariff.[5]

Despite his belief in states' rights, Jackson had no sympathy with nullification. He had made this clear at the Jefferson Day dinner in 1830, and he did so again to Hayne in February 1831. "For the rights of the states," he wrote, "no one has a higher regard and respect than myself." But he could not agree "that a state ha[d] the power to nulify [*sic*] the Legislative enactments of the General Government" or that Jefferson ever held "such an opinion." Our government, he concluded, "depends on a will of the majority," and "in all Republics the voice of a Majority must prevail." By thus putting democracy ahead of nullification, Jackson agreed with most Jeffersonian Republicans at the time, including many in South Carolina. Congressman Mitchell, who despite his fears was not a nullifier, wrote that "the doctrine of State Rights" was adopted by "patriots" who "revered State Sovereignty. . . . Yet who among them ever imagined [that] a State had a right to put her veto on the proceedings of the Central Government?"[6]

Although Jackson was concerned about the danger of an uprising in South Carolina, he did not believe that serious economic or constitutional grievances lay at the root of the controversy. As a planter from the expanding Southwest, he could not understand why the South Carolinians were so upset about the tariff. He was confident that his tariff reduction bill would take the steam out of the nullifiers. Since he considered the constitutional theories of nullification ridiculous, he was uninterested in debating the question of states' rights. He instructed Blair to treat the doctrine as "absurd" and said that he planned to "pass" it off "as a mere buble [sic]" in his 1832 annual message.[7]

Instead of discussing the issues, therefore, Jackson personalized the movement and kept insisting that Calhoun was organizing a conspiracy against him and the Union. In the wake of the Jefferson Day dinner, he accused Calhoun of leading Hayne and Hamilton astray when the reverse was closer to the truth. On reading Calhoun's Fort Hill address, Jackson told a Tennessee friend that it was part of Calhoun's conspiracy in the cabinet. Jackson's confidants agreed. Blair attacked Calhoun regularly in the *Globe*. John Randolph called Calhoun "a thrice doubleass," who would have more trouble than Benedict Arnold getting votes in Virginia. According to McLane, Calhoun had "produced the whirlwind & the storm," which in the end would destroy him.[8]

Alarmed about the prospects of a revolt, Jackson began to make preparations well before the South Carolinians took any action. In February 1831 he refused to appoint a nullifier as district attorney in South Carolina, saying he could not trust such a person to collect the bonds that merchants often used instead of cash in paying tariff duties. During the election campaign in the fall of 1832 he made military plans. Afraid that the nullifiers had "corrupted" the forces in Charleston, he ordered Secretary of War Lewis Cass to relieve them with "a faithful detachment." He also instructed Cass to warn his officers against a surprise attack by the state militia. In early November the president sent two companies to man the federal forts on islands in the harbor. In addition he put Gen. Winfield Scott in command of the army there and assigned Jesse Duncan Elliott to the naval command at Norfolk, whence he could quickly dispatch ships to Charleston.[9]

To keep track of events in South Carolina Jackson built a small network of informers. On 7 November he sent George Breathitt, brother of Kentucky governor John Breathitt, to Charleston in the guise of a post office inspector to uncover nullifiers who had infiltrated the post office, the armed forces, and the revenue service. Breathitt was also to check on the condition of the forts and to discover the "real intentions of the nullifyers." Jackson reminded Breathitt of "the highly delicate and confidential character" of his mission and urged him to use proper "caution." In addition Jackson entrusted Breathitt with a letter to Joel R. Poinsett, who began to supply the president with more information.[10]

Poinsett was the most prominent of a number of South Carolinians who had begun to resist the nullifiers. After being withdrawn from Mexico in 1829, he had returned to Charleston, where he joined a group of Unionists including former president of the Bank Langdon Cheves, Congressman William Drayton, and Judge Daniel Huger. Although the Unionist movement was strongest among upcountry planters and Charleston merchants, its leaders were not substantially different from those of the nullifiers. Each side boasted representatives from the aristocratic lawyers and planters of the lowcountry; many members of each group lived in Charleston; they were similar in age; and each side included several good friends of Jackson and Van Buren.

Once Calhoun had openly avowed nullification in 1831, he, McDuffie, Hayne, and Hamilton turned a protest movement into a strong political organization. Since the first three men spent much of their time in Washington, the local burden fell on Governor Hamilton, who proved to be a superb organizer. Pamphlets were circulated and statewide conventions were held in Charleston and the state capital in Columbia in winter 1831–32. He won over the mechanics of Charleston by promising that lower tariffs would help reduce their poverty. The Unionists, who were taunted as "submissionists," lacked the leadership to match this performance. As the state election approached in fall 1832, violence became common in Charleston. Armed nullifiers and Unionists took to the streets nightly; bricks were thrown when the Unionists marched a night or two before the election. The elections, held on 8–9 October, were close in many districts, but the nullifiers won a two-thirds majority in the legislature with a total state vote of 25,000 to 17,000.

As soon as the results were announced, Governor Hamilton issued a proclamation calling for a special session of the legislature. When it met on 22 October, the members received a message from Hamilton demanding a convention. The governor was following Calhoun's theory of nullification, according to which only a state convention could nullify an act of the federal government. The legislature promptly enacted a law calling for a convention to meet at Columbia on 19 November. Five days after the convention opened, on 24 November, the delegates passed an ordinance declaring the tariffs of 1828 and 1832 null and void in South Carolina. The ordinance declared that after 1 February 1833 it would be illegal for the state or the federal government to enforce the payment of duties established by the tariffs. No one could appeal state cases that might arise under the ordinance to the United States Supreme Court. State officials and jurors were required to take a test oath to uphold the ordinance and all laws supporting it, but legislators were exempted; other officials elected before the ordinance was passed did not have to take the oath unless specifically required to do so by the legislature. The ordinance called upon the legislature to pass laws to enforce these provi-sions. According to Poinsett, the "violent measures" of the nullifiers so "intimidated" many of the Unionists that they were thinking of leaving the state.[11]

When Jackson learned of the ordinance, he first tried to isolate South Carolina by seeking support from a wide variety of political lead-ers and by making concessions to the South. At Jackson's bidding, Amos Kendall wrote several editorials for the *Globe* in late November calling on National Republicans to unite with Democrats to preserve the Union. Other articles appeared in the *Globe* urging a further reduction of the tariff. On 4 December Jackson used his annual message to offer a peace-ful solution to the crisis. Bowing to the economic grievances of the South, he asked for an end to the protective system. He called upon "the moderation and good sense" of all concerned to "overcome" the "ob-structions" in South Carolina that "endanger[ed] the integrity of the Union." If such a course failed, he promised to use existing laws to sup-press the revolt, and if the laws were inadequate he would ask Congress to take any necessary steps. Aiming his remarks directly at South Caro-lina, he concluded with a strong defense of states' rights. The Founding Fathers had been wise, he said, "to withhold from the General Govern-ment the power to regulate the great mass of the business and concerns of the people."[12]

Even without its passages on the Nullification Crisis, this annual message would stand as one of Jackson's most important papers because it also contained his most coherent statement of political and economic policy. Since 1829 the president had gradually developed a program. During the Twenty-first Congress he had introduced Indian removal and limitation of internal improvements; during the first session of the Twenty-second Congress he had brought in modest tariff reduction and the war on the Bank. In this message he added cheap land and the end of protection and hinted that he might remove the government deposits from the Bank. For the first time he wove all the threads into one fabric, embroidered with agrarian and egalitarian language reminiscent of the Bank veto. Jackson declared democratically that "the wealth and strength of a country" were its people, that it was the "labor alone" of the "hardy population of the West" that gave "real value" to the lands. He defended a further reduction of the tariff on the grounds that protection tended to promote "monopolies" and "concentrate wealth into a few hands."[13]

With this message Jackson accentuated his agrarian, states'-rights position, turning toward Benton, Blair, and Kendall among his advisers and away from the more nationalistic, commercial-minded McLane and Livingston. Believing he had a mandate from the people in the election of 1832, Jackson might have pursued this agrarian program vigorously in the ensuing session of Congress had it not been for the Nullification Crisis, which pushed him back toward the nationalists. When the crisis was over, he did take up such agrarian policies as deposit removal and reliance on gold and silver rather than on paper money, but he was never able to unite his party behind an agrarian program. Only once again—in his Farewell Address—did he make such a clear agrarian statement.[14]

Six days after his annual message Jackson swung abruptly toward the nationalists by issuing his Nullification Proclamation. The president wanted a forceful, moral statement against nullification because he strongly opposed it and because Poinsett had warned that the Unionists needed support. When Kendall's draft proved too legalistic, the president called on Blair, Cass, and especially Livingston, who had delivered an effective speech defending both states' rights and the concept of the Union during the Webster-Hayne debate. The president also took the unusual step of writing a draft himself. He wrote so furiously with a large steel pen that when he had finished fifteen or twenty pages, an observer noted that the last three still glistened with wet ink. Jackson turned the draft and related notes and documents over to Livingston, but even he failed to satisfy, and the president asked him to make revisions after reading his version. Jackson sat up until almost midnight on the evening of 4 December writing a conclusion, which he sent to Livingston with a note. Let the proclamation, he said, "receive your best flight of eloquence." Livingston rewrote the president's conclusion, but the thrust and feeling of the entire document was unmistakably Jackson's.[15]

Still contemptuous of nullification, Jackson opened the proclamation by ridiculing the nullifiers' "strange position," calling it absurd in three places. He warned of establishing a dangerous precedent; if tariff collection could be stopped in Charleston, it could be stopped in every other port. Taking sharp issue with states' righters, even with his own position in his annual message, he attacked the nullifiers' premises. The Union, he wrote, had existed in late colonial America before the states were formed. Not the states but the people of the United States, "acting through the State legislatures . . . and in separate conventions," had drawn up and ratified the Constitution. The people, not the states, were represented in the presidency and in the House of Representatives. The Constitution formed "a *government*, not a league." He refuted the nullifiers' doctrine of undivided state sovereignty, declaring that the states had "surrendered many of their essential parts of sovereignty" to the central government. Jackson's description of a perpetual Union was so compelling that Abraham Lincoln used it as the model for his first inaugural address.[16]

Jackson's turn toward such a nationalistic interpretation of the Union shocked observers and has perplexed students of the era. The reaction to the proclamation was so intense that most of the state legislatures passed resolutions establishing their position on the constitutional issues involved. John Quincy Adams was particularly dismayed by "the glaring inconsistencies of principle" between the annual message and the proclamation. According to Adams, Jackson advocated states' rights and low tariffs in his annual message because of pressure from the slaveholding South but then issued the proclamation because of his hatred of Calhoun. Some students of the Nullification Crisis, however, have argued that Jackson was not inconsistent and that he designed the proclamation in order to distinguish his own traditional states'-rights views from the more extreme views of the nullifiers.[17]

There is some merit to this view. Theoretically the doctrine of the supremacy of the Union did not necessarily contradict the states'-rights belief in a restricted central government. In his republicanism Jackson believed that the best way to maintain a strong nation was to keep the central government weak. But he did not make that argument in his proclamation, and he did a poor job of defending the traditional states'-rights position. He refused to accept the compact theory of government on which the doctrine of states' rights was based and failed to explain the concept of reserved state powers. Just as in his toast at the Jefferson Day dinner when he omitted the word "federal" in the phrase "our federal Union," he went too far in his nationalism. Only this time he did it deliberately. Intent on winning over the people and suppressing nullification, he overstated his case. He left too strong an impression that sovereignty rested with the people, not with the states, and that nullification meant secession and treason. The patriotic fervor of his nationalism rang out at the end of the proclamation when he called on the people of South Carolina to turn away from "treason" and "show that the descendants of the Pinckneys, the Sumpters, the Rutledges . . . will not abandon that Union to support which so many of them fought and bled and died."[18]

To back up his proclamation Jackson prepared to use force. On 9 December he asked Poinsett to organize Unionist volunteers in South Carolina into a civilian posse, which would stand ready to back up the federal marshal. If the South Carolina assembly passed a law to raise an army, the president intended to ask Congress for the power to call up volunteers to put down the "rebellion" and to arrest the leaders for "treason." He promised Poinsett that he would have 50,000 soldiers and militiamen in South Carolina forty days after the nullifiers committed such "acts of treason." On 17 December he ordered Cass to stand ready to provide swords, pistols, muskets, and artillery to "crush the monster in its cradle before it mature[d] to manhood." Jackson's letters throughout December are peppered with terms such as "treason," "rebellion," and "war."[19]

Jackson's proclamation was enthusiastically received by nationalists in and out of the Democratic party. The New York Democrat James A. Hamilton considered the proclamation "masterly." Among the opposition, Philip Hone said that it ranked with the Farewell Address of George Washington, and John Quincy Adams's son Charles Francis considered the style like his father's. At the first meeting to acclaim the proclamation, held in Boston, former Federalists Daniel Webster and Harrison Gray Otis gave orations.[20]

But the Old Republicans in the Democratic party responded in horror, one member even predicting that the "madness" in South Carolina would destroy the party. Although still loyal to the party, Cambreleng could not agree with Jackson's uncompromisingly nationalistic interpretation of the origins of the Constitution. The Old Republican sentiment was most intense in Virginia. When John Randolph, who was now dying, learned about the meeting in Boston, he wrote acidly that Jackson had delivered his friends, "bound hand and foot, to . . . the ultra federalists, ultra tariffites, ultra internal improvement and Hartford Convention men." Congressman William F. Gordon considered the proclamation completely contrary to his belief in state power.

Blair was hard-pressed to convince these critics that the proclamation did not contradict the annual message and that Jackson was still devoted to the rights of the states. In Virginia Jackson's strongest supporter, Thomas Ritchie, was forced to argue unconvincingly that he agreed with the president on all but *doctrinal points.* Gordon and Sen. John Tyler— both at odds with Jackson—were so delighted at the discomfiture of the administration that they were once seen dancing "around the room like children in a delirium of joy."[21]

Although diametrically opposed on the proclamation, both the nationalists and the states'-rights Democrats agreed that force ought not to be used. On 12 October during the election campaign Webster had warned that Jackson was likely to blockade Charleston if nullification occurred. "For one, Sir," said Webster, "I raise my voice beforehand against the unauthorized employment of military power." Once nullification began, Democrats, many of whom feared the worst from Jackson, began to cry out against resorting to force. Silas Wright, just elected to the Senate from New York, was alarmed by rumors that Jackson would be disappointed if blood was not shed in South Carolina. Another New Yorker wanted to avoid "blood and suffering" by lowering the tariff but feared that manufacturers were too greedy to support a compromise. Congressman Thomas H. Hall of North Carolina represented many voices in the party when he told Van Buren that he wanted "calm" and peace.[22]

No one was more concerned about Jackson's strong stand than Van Buren, who corresponded with the president from New York during the crisis. Having based his career on the doctrine of states' rights and on an alliance of North and South, Van Buren was afraid that the proclamation would endanger his party and his chances of becoming president. When Jackson asked him for his views on the proclamation, Van Buren answered with his usual caution. Although he believed privately that the proclamation violated true republicanism, he simply wrote on 22 December that he was having difficulty answering claims that the document infringed on states' rights. The times, he added, required "great discretion & good temper." The Little Magician was even more concerned a day or two later when he received a letter, dated 15 December but delayed, in which the president expressed his view that the nullifiers would be committing treason if they raised troops. Van Buren wrote back tactfully that there should be no "faltering" but questioned whether passing laws to raise troops constituted treason. He also suggested that it might have been better if certain "doctrinal points" had been "omitted" from the proclamation. Worried that Jackson might further antagonize the Virginians, Van Buren hoped that the president would allow them "*honest* differences of opinion." Aware that he was addressing the president more boldly than usual, he conceded in a conciliatory way that Jackson would say that he "was on his old track—caution—caution."

Before receiving either of these letters, Jackson fired off two more to Van Buren on 23 and 25 December. The president was particularly angry at the news from Virginia that a committee of the House of Delegates had endorsed the Virginia Resolutions of 1798, though disapproving of nullification. In words that must have frightened Van Buren, who had many friends in the Old Dominion, Jackson twice referred to the "absurdity of the virginia doctrine." He also threatened once again to send troops into South Carolina. Unsure of how to rein in the president, Van Buren put off replying for over a week.[23]

While the Democrats were reacting to Jackson's warlike behavior, the South Carolina legislature, which had convened on 27 November, was framing the legislation to carry out the ordinance of nullification. The legislature started out aggressively, casting the state's electoral votes for John Floyd instead of Jackson and electing Hayne governor to replace

James Hamilton, Jr., who in turn was to command the state's armed forces. Calhoun was returned to the United States Senate as Hayne's successor, resigning as vice-president on 28 December. Governor Hayne set a bold tone with a resounding inaugural address, announcing that he intended to enforce the "SOVEREIGN WILL" of South Carolina against the "USURPATION" of the federal government.[24]

After a week or two, however, the legislators began to back off in the face of Jackson's threats of force and the disinclination of neighboring states to support South Carolina. The nullifiers were concerned also when the Unionists, who were holding their own convention, suddenly seemed willing to fight. Impressed by the Unionist protest against the arbitrary test oath, the legislature ruled that officials elected before the ordinance need not take the oath unless they were enforcing nullification. Instead of punishing those importers who paid tariff duties, the legislature provided a way to protect those who refused to pay. The latter could get tariff bonds instead of paying cash and could then refuse to pay their bonds. In any court case that might follow they could plead that the duties were null and void, and jurors in South Carolina, sworn to obey the ordinance, would have to acquit them. In case the collector refused to accept tariff bonds or seized imported goods, the importer could get a writ of replevin to recover his goods, forcing the collector to go to court to defend his position. Once again the jurors would have to rule for the importers. This roundabout system of enforcement was designed to make the federal government defy a court decision in order to enforce the tariff laws. But it was far short of complete nullification since it left Unionist merchants free to pay the duties without any penalty.

Governor Hayne also behaved with restraint when the legislature gave him the authority to accept volunteers and to call out the state militia. Hayne asked for volunteers on 26 December, and within a month 25,000 had stepped forward. Although many observers expected him to order the troops to Charleston, the governor decided that they should train at home because in Charleston they would appear to threaten the United States forts. The neighboring states would then consider South Carolina the aggressor and would be more likely to support the president. As a result of Hayne's decision, Jackson had less reason to worry about the safety of the forts.[25]

Congress was showing the same sort of moderation. In an effort to save the Union and to mend the rift in the party, the Democrats turned to the House Ways and Means Committee for a tariff-reduction bill. Chaired by Van Buren's friend Gulian C. Verplanck and consisting of five Democrats and two members of the opposition, the committee was loyal to the Democratic party. Van Buren men Cambreleng and William S.

Archer of Virginia worked with the committee in drawing up a bill that would win over the nullifiers. The bill, which was taken up in the House on 8 January 1833, cut duties in half, returning them to the levels of 1816.

Responding to the protests against the use of force, Jackson, too, began to act more peacefully than his enflamed language had promised. On receiving another letter of caution from Van Buren in early January, the president replied: "I beg of you not to be disturbed by any thing you hear from the alarmists. . . . Be assured that I have and will act with . . . forbearence [sic]." Above all, he promised that he would not let himself "be branded with the epithet, *tyrant.*" Conscious of criticism, Jackson was saying less about sending troops and arresting the chief nullifiers, even after the South Carolina legislature authorized Hayne to raise an army. Instead, the president was putting his faith in his plan for a civilian posse of Unionist volunteers that he had asked Poinsett to organize. Jackson also reduced the possibility of a clash by moving the federal troops from the citadel in Charleston to the island forts. In addition he and Secretary of the Treasury McLane devised a plan whereby tariffs in Charleston would be collected by officials on revenue cutters instead of on shore, thus preventing the nullifiers from interfering.[26]

It was at this point that Jackson and Van Buren further isolated South Carolina by defusing the Indian crisis in Georgia. The key letters asking Governor Lumpkin of Georgia to release the missionaries were orchestrated on 17 and 18 December by Van Buren's former law partner and later United States attorney general Benjamin F. Butler of the Albany Regency. Lewis Cass and Sen. John Forsyth of Georgia helped win Lumpkin over by giving him assurances that there would be no further efforts to block the removal of the Cherokees.

Jackson also avoided a similar embarrassing situation on 2 January when another Regency man, Gov. William L. Marcy, announced that New York would settle its long-standing boundary controversy with New Jersey out of court. Since 1829 the state of New York had aligned itself with Georgia against the Supreme Court by taking the same states'-rights position on the boundary dispute that Georgia was taking in the Indian affair. When New Jersey sued New York before the Supreme Court in 1829, New York first refused to appear, declaring that the Supreme Court had no jurisdiction, and then in March 1832 sent Butler to defend the state's position. Chief Justice John Marshall had become so alarmed at this attack on the jurisdiction of the Supreme Court, coming just nine days after his ruling on *Worcester* v. *Georgia,* that he postponed the boundary case until January 1833. By helping to keep two explosive states'-rights cases off the Supreme Court docket, Jackson's political allies were making it easier for the president to deal with nullification with forbearance.[27]

But a forbearing president was not a happy president. As "the fatal first" of February approached, the day that nullification would go into effect, Jackson grew increasingly frustrated and irritable. Even though the nullifiers had shown restraint, they had raised troops, and Jackson lacked the backing to do anything about it. Many of the strongest figures in his party, even in his own administration, had turned against him. The president was particularly galled by the absence of support from the South. The states of North Carolina, Georgia, Alabama, and Mississippi had refused to endorse his proclamation, supporting instead the Virginia Resolutions of 1798. All of these states, to be sure, had disappointed the nullifiers as well by rejecting nullification, but that gave the Old Hero little solace. He complained of ill health and "very oppressive labor" to his son Andrew and told Van Buren that he was "surrounded with the nullifiers of the south." Silas Wright reported that the president had become "very sensitive" and "even abuses" Thomas Ritchie.[28]

Jackson found little encouragement on Capitol Hill, where the Verplanck tariff bill was running into trouble. Led by Webster, manufacturers in both parties opposed the bill, saying it cut tariffs too much and too abruptly. Van Buren's own New York delegation was badly divided. The bill also lost ground with some individuals because it was linked with Van Buren. Samuel Swartwout remarked archly that he was relieved that the bill was proposed by Verplanck rather than by "a certain little gentleman politician." Jackson himself was not much help. Even though he had supported tariff reform in his annual message, he had never had confidence that lowering the tariff would end the crisis. He continued to believe that Calhoun and the nullifiers were not serious about the tariff but were engaged in a conspiracy to undermine the administration. Taking his cue from Jackson, Blair did not push for passage of the bill, and without united party backing it seemed unlikely to pass.[29]

But Jackson had many supporters. Word of noisy, enthusiastic meetings endorsing the proclamation came from New York City, Nashville, and New Orleans. Gov. William Carroll of Tennessee offered to lead 10,000 volunteers to South Carolina. James W. Wyly of Unionist eastern Tennessee wrote that the "old chief" could raise so many troops in two weeks that they could stand on the Saluda Mountains and "piss enough . . . to float the whole nullifying crew of South Carolina into the Atlantic." And in the northern states of Pennsylvania, Indiana, and Illinois the legislatures passed resolutions endorsing the proclamation.[30]

Spurred on by such support but frustrated by the politicians in his party, Jackson sought some way to confront the nullifiers, force them to surrender, and thus uphold the authority of the federal government. With the help of McLane, he began to draw up a message to Congress asking for additional authority. When Van Buren heard of the message, he warned Jackson that many moderates were worried that it would be a "firebrand" and urged him not to make any move unless he had to. Now listening to the peacemakers, Jackson reassured him but insisted that he could not "sit with arms folded."[31]

Jackson's message to Congress on 16 January was much milder than expected. In it the president was content to ask for a few specific powers that would help the government thwart the process that the nullifiers had designed to prevent the collection of the tariffs. At the ports of Georgetown and Beaufort, where there were no island forts, Jackson asked for authority to set up "floating custom houses" on board United States warships. To prevent the use of tariff bonds, on which the replevin process depended, he requested the right to collect the duties in cash only. Jackson sought authority to transfer customs cases from state courts to federal courts. In case the nullifiers used force to confiscate property, he wanted permission to use federal troops and to call up the state militia without a proclamation. These were modest proposals, designed to keep the peace rather than to make war. Jackson did not accuse the nullifiers of treason, and he asked for the right to use force only if the nullifiers struck first.[32]

But Jackson's reputation and the gravity of the crisis led Congress, the public, and students of nullification to call the document the "Force Bill Message" and to treat it as though Jackson had asked for the power to crush South Carolina. As soon as the message was read in the Senate, Calhoun demanded the floor and let loose a bitter tirade accusing the administration of "despotism." Jackson complained wryly that evening that Calhoun had let off a great deal of "ire" against him. Privately Calhoun believed that the proposed bill would help the nullifiers, but in public he fought it to the end.[33]

The Senate then sent the message to the five-man Judiciary Committee, which seemed likely to support Jackson. The two National Republicans on the committee, Webster and Theodore Frelinghuysen, were strong nationalists. Of the three Democrats, the chairman, William Wilkins of Pennsylvania, was also a nationalist, and Felix Grundy of Tennessee, a traditional states' righter, was solidly against nullification. Only one, Willie Mangum of North Carolina, had any sympathy with the nullifiers.

Five days later on 21 January, Chairman Wilkins was back with a bill that included almost all of the proposals in Jackson's message. Officially titled a bill to "enforce the collection of the revenue," the measure has ever since been known as the "Force Bill," and at the time nullifiers called it the "Bloody Bill." The day after it was introduced, Calhoun spoke at length, not directly on the bill but on the constitutional issues surrounding it. No longer angry and emotional, he coldly and calmly defended the compact theory of government and the right of state nullification. After Grundy replied in defense of the Union, debate on the bill was postponed until 28 January.[34]

Aside from the terms of the Force Bill, Jackson had little but bad news during the last ten days in January. He learned from Poinsett that the Unionists, frightened by the nullifiers' troops, were not coming forward to form the civilian posse on which he had been counting. He also heard rumors that North Carolina and Virginia had offered troops to South Carolina and that the nullifiers were considering secession. The legislatures in the two most important states—Virginia and New York—had still not passed their resolutions on the proclamation. Then on 23 January McLane reported that the Verplanck tariff bill was doomed. Even though Jackson had not held out much hope for the bill, he knew that its failure would make his job more difficult. Van Buren's friends sent word back to Albany that things were "horrible" in Washington.[35]

Some idea of Jackson's continuing frustration can be gauged from the unusually harsh letter he sent to Van Buren on 25 January. "Why," he roared, "is your Legislature silent at this eventful crisis?" The silence, he continued, gave "rise to dark inuendoes [sic] of your enemies, that . . . you are awaiting the results of the virginia Legislature." He then moved on to the tariff, blaming its likely defeat on a speech by nullifier congressman Richard Wilde of Georgia. Wilde, he said, "threw a firebrand into the House. . . . He is *wielded by Calhoun.*"[36]

There was no relief the next day when the Virginia legislature finally passed its resolutions on the proclamation. Jacksonians had held control of Virginia until December 1832, but the proclamation put Ritchie and the Jackson organization on the defensive. The state was divided between those people sympathizing with the nullifiers and those, like jurist Dabney Carr, who feared that Calhoun would "destroy the Union." As a result the resolutions satisfied neither the nullifiers nor Jackson. In a carefully worded statement the legislators entreated South Carolina to rescind its ordinance of nullification but refused to endorse the proclamation. They wrote that they "regard[ed] the doctrines of State Sovereignty and State Rights, as set forth in the Resolutions of 1798 . . . as a true interpretation of the Constitution." They also voted to send a commissioner to South Carolina to deliver the resolutions and express their "good will." On 16 February the reelection of Sen. John Tyler, a strong critic of both the proclamation and the Force Bill, further demonstrated the administration's loss of strength in the Old Dominion.[37]

When the Force Bill returned to the floor of the Senate on 28 January, Willie Mangum compounded Jackson's difficulties by moving another postponement. Although the motion was defeated, 30 to 15, it revealed that the administration had lost most of its southern support. All fifteen senators voting to postpone were from slave states, including otherwise reliable administration men such as William R. King of Alabama and Bedford Brown of North Carolina. The only southern Democrats holding firm were Felix Grundy and John Forsyth. With the evidence mounting that he could not count on his party to defeat nullification, Jackson now had to look ahead to a long senatorial debate over the Force Bill.

While the debate was getting under way, the Force Bill was running into trouble in the House. On 8 February a strongly Democratic Judiciary Committee brought in a bill that failed to give Jackson the military powers he had requested. With three southern Democrats on the committee voting against the administration, the only Democrats supporting Jackson were John Bell of Tennessee and Samuel Beardsley of the Albany Regency. It was another indication that the Democratic party was badly split.[38]

On 12 February Henry Clay delivered the party a further blow by introducing a new tariff bill in the Senate. In an effort to maintain Democratic control, Grundy, who represented the administration, succeeded in having a motion passed for a select committee to deal with the bill. Jackson then intervened by asking President pro-tempore Hugh Lawson White, who would select the committee, not to appoint opposition senator John M. Clayton. When White refused, leaving the committee stacked four to three against the administration, Jackson was "mortified," considering it a "direct insult." Even though White was no longer close to the administration, he was still a Democrat and from Tennessee to boot.[39]

Jackson was further upset because that same day there had been several unsuccessful motions to postpone the Force Bill, and rumors were flying that the Senate would soon kill it by laying it on the table. Just as in his letter to Van Buren only two weeks earlier, he showed his frustration in another angry letter, this time to Grundy. He ordered the senator to "lay *all* delicacy . . . aside" and see to it that their "friends" in the Senate push the bill through. If there was a vote to table, Grundy was to have the names of those senators voting recorded in the Senate Journal so that Jackson would know who had backed the nullifiers.[40]

During the next few days Jackson's disposition grew worse. First

James K. Polk in the House brought up a bill, recommended in the president's annual message, for the government to sell its stock in the Bank. Despite the importance of the bill, it was given only a first reading, debated for only a few hours, and then voted down, all in one day. It was an embarrassing defeat for Jackson, who had viewed the bill as the start of a renewed attack on the Bank. Then a coalition of nullifiers and National Republicans in the House rejected administration efforts to have Blair elected printer in an election that went on for fourteen ballots. The Senate did the same a short time later. After the House decision Benton complained about the "strange state" of affairs. Jackson had been "reelected by four to one," but the Democrats were in a "minority in both houses" and had just been "defeated in two mortifying instances—the election of a printer and the rejection . . . of the bill to sell bank stock." Benton was critical of Jackson, believing that the militia provisions of the Force Bill went too far. With only two weeks to go before Congress adjourned on 2 March, Jackson had lost whatever control he had had over the situation. There hardly seemed time to resolve the crisis.[41]

Yet already a broad compromise was under way, with Jackson playing a lesser role than Webster, Clay, Calhoun, and the leaders of the nullifiers, and with party affiliation being subordinated to other considerations. The nullifiers had taken the first step on 21 January when they held a mass meeting in Charleston and voted to postpone the beginning of nullification from 1 February until the present Congress resolved the question of the tariff. If Congress was unable to do so or if it passed the Force Bill, nullification would in all likelihood be put into operation. The arrival of Commissioner Benjamin Watkins Leigh of Virginia in Columbia on 4 February, bearing the state resolutions, also proved helpful. The Virginians offered to mediate and urged both sides to "abstain from any and all acts" that might "endanger the existence of the Union."[42]

Webster had been on the president's side in the Nullification Crisis from the start. He had spoken in favor of the proclamation, had praised Jackson's Force Bill Message, and had played a part in drawing up the bill. In one of his efforts on the floor of the Senate, he had chided Democrats for not supporting their own administration's bill. Needing help and unsure of his own party, Jackson had sent Livingston to discuss the crisis with Webster. When the observant John Tyler saw Webster at the President's House "in all his glory," he concluded that the Godlike Daniel would become "the great champion of the administration." The journalist Matthew Davis reported that without the help of old Federalists such as Webster, Jackson would "stand almost alone, in both Houses of Congress." Such help was not new, for Jackson had several former Federalists in his cabinet, one of whom, McLane, had helped write the Force Bill Message. Temporarily at least, party lines were being shredded.[43]

Until he offered his tariff bill on 12 February, Clay had contributed little to the debate over nullification. As a nationalist he supported the principles of the Force Bill and had voted on each occasion against postponement, but as a southerner he had taken each step "reluctantly" and had maintained his ties with the South. Now with the Verplanck bill going nowhere and the administration in disarray, he saw an opportunity to take credit away from Jackson for saving the Union. To get the necessary votes he had to come to some understanding with the administration similar to Webster's or ally himself with the nullifiers. The hostility between himself and Jackson prevented the first; so "Harry of the West" made a "great leap across the Potomac," as some observers described it, to unite with Calhoun.[44]

Although Calhoun, with his image as a man of principle, was not eager to deal with Clay, he too realized that compromise with Jackson was impossible and that only an arrangement with Clay could bring the tariff reduction that would enable the nullifiers to back down and still save face. So Calhoun accepted the overtures coming from Clay's friends Congressman Robert P. Letcher of Kentucky and Sen. Josiah S. Johnston of Louisiana. As soon as Clay offered his tariff bill, Calhoun announced that he would support it, in the "spirit of mutual compromise."[45]

With their reputations as the Great Nullifier and the Great Unionist, Calhoun and Webster commanded more attention than Clay in the Senate debate on the Force Bill. Although the debate has never received the attention given to the Webster-Hayne debate, it was in many ways superior. The issues of states' rights and the Union had had several years in which to mature, more was now at stake, the debate went on over a longer period of time, and Calhoun was a far stronger opponent for Webster than Hayne. Calhoun had already defined the parameters of the debate in his speech the day after the Force Bill was introduced. He had concluded with three resolutions stating that the American system of government was a "constitutional compact" of the states, that each state had an equal right to judge for itself any alleged violation of the Constitution, and that any "assertion" that the American people were "formed into one nation" was false. From then on speakers took positions on his resolutions as well as on the Force Bill.

Calhoun and Webster had both held back in the debate, each hoping to speak last, but after William C. Rives delivered a strong defense of the bill on 14 February, Calhoun felt he could wait no longer. In a long speech over the course of two days, 15–16 February, he stuck narrowly to the Force Bill, refusing to amplify his own resolutions. By thus limiting himself, Calhoun did not make an especially profound speech, but he was content because he anticipated that Webster would speak on the resolutions as well as on the bill, thus giving Calhoun the right to answer him later.

After riding to the Senate in the president's carriage on 16 February to hear the end of Calhoun's speech, Webster was ready when it was over. He spoke for an hour in the early afternoon and then rested while the Senate took a short recess. When he resumed his speech at 5:00 P.M., word had spread and the chamber was filled with a splendid audience including justices of the Supreme Court, congressmen, cabinet members, and other prominent figures. Cass and William B. Lewis were there, as they often were, to report back to the president. Addressing the subject of the Union as well as the Force Bill, as Calhoun had expected, Webster contended that Calhoun's doctrine would result in the dismemberment of the Union. Sounding much like Jackson, he maintained that the Constitution was "a government proper, founded on the adoption of the people, and creating direct relations between itself and individuals [and] that no State authority [had the] power to dissolve these relations." He concluded after three hours with a stirring peroration: "I shall exert every faculty I possess in aiding to prevent the Constitution from being nullified, destroyed, or impaired; and even should I see it fall, I will still, with a voice feeble, perhaps, . . . call on the *People* to come to its rescue." The crowd broke into spontaneous applause.[46]

Jackson told Poinsett the next day that Webster had "handled [Calhoun] as a child." The president, however, had spoken too soon, for ten days later Calhoun finally defended his resolutions and exposed a number of flaws in Webster's argument. John Randolph was on hand to witness Calhoun's triumph. When a large hat blocked the Old Republican's view, he demanded, "Take away that hat. I want to see Webster die, muscle by muscle."[47]

Calhoun won the debate but lost the vote. The Force Bill had already passed the Senate on 20 February by a vote of 32 to 1, the single dissenting vote coming from John Tyler of Virginia. In a show of defiance, fifteen others failed to vote, thirteen of them Democrats or nullifiers, ten from the South, and the other three—Samuel Smith of Maryland, and Benton and Alexander Buckner of Missouri—from border slave states. Of the twelve Democrats who voted for the bill only four were from the South: White and Grundy of Tennessee, Rives of Virginia, and Forsyth of Georgia.[48]

The passing of the Force Bill in the Senate, even though the South detested it, was another important step in the emerging compromise. The bill was needed to resolve the crisis because it meant so much to

Jackson. Even though the bill would be superfluous if a compromise went through, Jackson wanted it because it was his bill; it had become a symbol for him. The way in which the southern senators dealt with the bill indicated how the crisis would be solved. Although the southern senators lacked the votes to defeat the bill, they could have delayed it, perhaps even until Congress adjourned, but instead they contented themselves with refusing to vote. An agreement had apparently been made whereby the southerners would let the bill slide by without any further delay in exchange for a promise of tariff reduction. Four days later the Democrats caucused and agreed to follow this arrangement in the House.[49]

In his new tariff bill Clay proposed lowering rates, which averaged 33 percent at the time, with only small annual reductions until 1842, when they would finally be dropped sharply to 20 percent. The result would be about the same as in the Verplanck bill, but much of the reduction would be put off for nine years. Even though manufacturers opposed any tariff reduction, many were willing to accept the new bill because it maintained protection for almost another decade. Some hoped—Clay even privately suggested—that the act would be amended upward before 1842. Manufacturers were also won over by a committee amendment that duties would be based on the value of imports at the port of entry in the United States. Since the price of goods would be higher there than in Europe, the home-valuation clause increased the actual rate of tariff protection well above 20 percent. Although the nullifiers in Congress would have preferred the Verplanck bill, they had no hope of getting it. Anxious to find a way out of the crisis when they saw that the rest of the South would not endorse nullification, they accepted Clay's proposal.[50]

Since the Constitution requires revenue bills to originate in the lower house, it was necessary to introduce the Clay bill in the House of Representatives, which had not yet voted on the Verplanck bill. On 25 February, Clay's agent Robert P. Letcher suddenly asked the House to "amend" the Verplanck bill with Clay's bill. This unusual proposal to replace one bill with another passed immediately by a vote of 105 to 71. A day later the Clay tariff bill passed the House by the same majority, 119 to 85.[51]

The speed and irregular manner in which Clay's tariff bill was pushed through the House strongly suggests prearrangement. So does the fact that the bills were supported by a high percentage of Democrats. Benton recalled later that the plan to substitute the Clay bill had been "agreed upon." According to Congressman Nathan Appleton of Massachusetts, the Democrats made their decision at the same caucus at which they had agreed to back the Force Bill. "It was arranged," said Appleton, who was privy to what was going on even though a member of the opposition, "that [the bills] should go through side by side."[52]

There is no evidence of an agreement between Clay and Jackson, but it is likely that the president was willing to have Democrats vote for the bill. Jackson at the time was being urged by many elements in the party—including the *New-Hampshire Patriot* and the *Richmond Enquirer*—to compromise and accept a lower tariff. A day or two before the vote he had received a letter from Van Buren suggesting that he back Clay's tariff. After losing interest in the Verplanck bill, the *Globe* had resumed its support of tariff reduction as soon as Clay announced his compromise bill. The president himself gave Silas Wright the impression that it was best to support the bill. It was not surprising that Jackson would go along with an opposition tariff bill, for he had never thought that tariffs were worth fighting about. All along he had believed that the Force Bill was far more important than tariff reform in defeating nullification. He was willing to tolerate Clay's tariff bill in return for his own Force Bill.[53]

Meanwhile, a similar compromise was being worked out in New York, where Van Buren was trying to fashion resolutions that would support the president but also uphold the traditional doctrine of states' rights. His work was made more difficult by a split in the Regency between protectionists led by Governor Marcy and free traders headed by Benjamin F. Butler. On 24 January a tariff meeting in Albany broke up with no agreement, after a noisy fight over whether to recommend lowering duties. While Van Buren temporized, Jackson fumed, finally sending him the bitter letter of 25 January asking why the New York legislature was "silent."

In his report on the proclamation, written for the legislature, Van Buren tried to find common ground between Jackson's statement that the people had formed the Constitution and the states'-rights view that it had been done by the states. He argued that the people of the individual states had established the Constitution, not the people of the nation as a whole and not the state governments. He insisted that neither the states nor the central government had the sole right to determine the constitutionality of a given act. The report endorsed "the sovereignty of the States" but denied that the states retained the right of secession.

Although Van Buren did not back the proclamation, he did praise Jackson for his efforts to "preserve our republican system." The report pointed to Jackson's success in "arrest[ing] the increase of monopolies" and in "promot[ing] economy." Aware of the political implications, the opposition *New York American* commented that the report was designed to promote Van Buren's "future prospects in the South." Democratic congressman Mark Alexander of Virginia put it more gently by saying that Van Buren had taken "his cue from Ritchie, by denouncing nullification while . . . professing great devotion to the principles of —98."

When the report and the accompanying resolutions were brought to the legislature, members of the opposition tried to embarrass Van Buren by introducing a resolution stating that Jackson's proclamation contained the only "true principles" upon which the Constitution could be "maintained and defended." After successfully tabling this dangerous statement, the Democrats tried in vain to include a resolution supporting the Kentucky and Virginia resolutions. The result was a series of compromise resolutions, adopted on 23 February, which denounced nullification and the right of secession and approved of the president's efforts "to sustain the authority and execute the laws of the United States." Otherwise the resolutions merely approved of "the general views and conclusions" of Van Buren's report. Van Buren did secure one victory when the legislature called for a "modification of the tariff." Although everyone knew that Van Buren did not speak for Jackson, the strong statement of the Old Republican doctrine in his report—which Jackson had not made in his proclamation—helped reestablish the traditional states'-rights position of the party.[54]

In Washington, the compromise still faced major hurdles before Congress adjourned on 2 March. The Force Bill still had to pass the House, the tariff bill had to pass the Senate, and a distribution bill, which Clay considered an integral part of the compromise, was pending in the House. Jackson was propitiated by changes in the House Force Bill that made it much stronger than the bill that had come out of committee. As in the Senate version, he was given all the military powers he had requested except the power to call out the militia without a proclamation. McDuffie and other extremists, who hated the bill, then threatened to kill it by stalling until Congress adjourned. Clay's bill to distribute to the states the proceeds from the sale of public lands had already passed the Senate, but its future in the House, where it had died the year before, was in doubt.

The climax came during three long sessions of both houses, from Thursday 28 February through Saturday 2 March, each running far into the evening. The managers of the compromise fought off McDuffie's rebellion in the House by threatening not to bring up the tariff bill in the Senate. As a result, the Force Bill had its third reading in the House at 1:00 A.M., 1 March, and passed, 149 to 47, when the House reconvened later in the day. The Senate then passed the tariff at 5:45 P.M. by a vote of 29 to 16. The distribution bill passed the House by a vote of 96 to 40 at 11:00 P.M., still on 1 March.[55]

The voting in the House of Representatives on the tariff, the Force

Bill, and distribution shows the extent of Clay's compromise. The three bills all passed the House with substantial support from both parties and all sections of the country. By lowering the tariff, but not in essence until 1842, Clay won votes from both the North and the South and satisfied the nullifiers in South Carolina. Southerners responded by letting distribution and the Force Bill pass without any further struggle. The inclusion of the Force Bill in the compromise won over many Democrats, who knew that Jackson considered the bill essential.[56]

A comparison of Jackson's position with the Democratic voting record on two of these bills in the House reveals the president's lack of control. Jackson demanded the Force Bill and vigorously opposed distribution. Only 60 percent of the House Democrats voted for the Force Bill and barely 30 percent went on record against distribution. Many Democrats simply did not vote on distribution; those who supported it were northern Democrats whose constituents favored it or southerners who did so in return for lower tariffs. Even the voting of a selected list of fifteen strongly partisan Democratic congressmen showed that Jackson was not in command. Eleven of them did vote for the Force Bill, but only five voted against the distribution bill.[57]

In the Senate both parties split badly on the tariff. The alliance voting for it consisted of four southern National Republicans, ten northern National Republicans, twelve southern Democrats and nullifiers, and three northern Democrats; eight northern National Republicans and eight northern Democrats opposed the bill. Voting for the bill was the unlikely combination of the antiprotectionist nullifier Calhoun, the protectionist National Republican Clay, and the administration men John Forsyth and Isaac Hill. They were opposed by the protectionist National Republican Webster and the protectionist administration senators George M. Dallas and William Wilkins. The New York senators, both Democrats, divided, Silas Wright supporting the bill and Charles E. Dudley opposing it. Their offsetting votes symbolized the rift in their state and national parties.[58]

Jackson went along with most of Clay's compromise. On receiving the three bills on 2 March, he signed the Force Bill and the tariff but not the distribution bill. He briefly considered vetoing the latter, but fearing an override he gave it a pocket veto instead. In a letter to Joel Poinsett on 6 March the Old Hero tried to make the best of the situation. Ignoring the absentees, Jackson noted approvingly that the Force Bill had passed the House "by the unparalled [sic] majority of 102." Still insisting on the primacy of the Force Bill, he pointed out that it was passed before the tariff bill. He went on to rationalize that he had "always thought" that the tariff should be reduced to "the wants of the Government," especially after the passing of the Force Bill had shown "the world" that Congress was not to be "deterred by a faction," which "she was prepared to crush in an instant" if "found in rebellion or treason." The tariff, he conceded, was "not of the exact character" he would have preferred, but he hoped it would have "a good effect in the South."[59]

On the final day of the session both the House and the Senate disposed of an additional piece of business, each of which should be considered in the context of the compromise. The House that day took up a resolution concerning the Bank. In his annual message Jackson had raised the question of whether the government deposits, which had remained in the Bank after Jackson's veto, were safe. After a rather perfunctory examination, the Ways and Means Committee brought in a resolution declaring the deposits entirely secure. For Jackson, who was looking for an excuse to remove the deposits, the ensuing vote, 109 to 46 in favor of the resolution, was a disappointment. With a chance to support Jackson against the Bank, only forty-six Democrats voted against the resolution, and the remaining eighty Democrats either voted for it or abstained. All of the opposition either voted for the bill or did not vote. It was one more defeat for Jackson during the Nullification Crisis.[60]

Jackson was more successful, however, when the Senate voted on the appointment of Samuel Gwin to a land office in Mississippi. Early in 1831 Jackson had appointed Rachel's nephew Stockley Donelson Hays of Tennessee as surveyor of public lands for the state of Mississippi. Miffed because he had not been consulted, Sen. George Poindexter of Mississippi succeeded in having a resolution adopted that a nonresident should not be appointed to a federal post in any state. As a result Jackson had to agree to a truce whereby a friend of Poindexter's became surveyor and Hays was made register of the land office at Clinton, Mississippi. The battle was revived in October when Hays suddenly died and Jackson appointed Gwin, also from Tennessee, to replace him. After Poindexter blocked the appointment, Jackson renominated Gwin in June 1832, only to have the nomination tabled.

The battle over patronage continued when Jackson gave Gwin a second recess appointment and Gwin began acting as the head of Democratic patronage in Mississippi. Gwin was rejected once again in February 1833, but the affair was finally compromised on 2 March. The Senate repealed its prohibition of out-of-state appointments and confirmed Gwin's nomination for a different Mississippi land office. For Jackson and the party-minded Democrats this marked an important victory because it strengthened party patronage in a growing southern state.[61]

While Jackson was weighing his gains and losses, Calhoun was hurrying to Columbia, South Carolina, in order to keep the radicals there from prolonging the crisis. He was not needed, however, because the nullifiers had no intention of going any further. Their convention, which reopened on 11 March, promptly repealed the ordinance of nullification. As a symbolic gesture of defiance the members then nullified the Force Act but acted more realistically in dealing with the tariff. When a committee proposed calling the new tariff "cause for congratulation and triumph," the convention struck out the two words "and triumph."[62]

Whether the outcome of the crisis was a triumph for Jackson or Clay, the Union or South Carolina, nationalism or states' rights has been a matter of some dispute. William W. Freehling has long supported the traditional view that Jackson, the Union, and nationalism were the winners. The last few days of Congress, he argues, "marked a great victory for Jackson—probably his greatest victory as President," pointing out that the president was the only leading political figure who supported both tariff reduction and the Force Bill, measures that Freehling says ended the crisis. For Freehling, Calhoun and the nullifiers were clearly the losers. Calhoun, he says, "compromised . . . swiftly and thoroughly. . . . At every stage of negotiations [he] caved in."[63]

It is difficult to accept the thesis that Jackson was the victor because it is based on the questionable premise that the tariff and the Force Bill solved the crisis. Actually the nullifiers gave up not only because of the tariff but also because no southern state came to their aid, and Jackson backed off because his proclamation and his threats to use force were so unpopular. There is also considerable question about whether Jackson really supported tariff reduction.

And Jackson hardly "triumphed." After an auspicious start with his well-conceived annual message, he suffered several defeats. His proclamation was rejected by much of his own party and most of the state legislatures, and the Verplanck bill failed partly because he himself did not support it. He had setbacks when Blair was not elected printer and when the bill to sell the government stock in the Bank was defeated. At the end of the session Jackson lost again as the distribution bill and the resolution supporting the deposits in the Bank both passed. His Force Bill did pass, but only because of help from Clay, and by that time it was merely a symbol. Freehling himself concedes that Jackson lost politically because the crisis put "some southern Democrats . . . in revolt" and because "the Calhoun-Clay alliance formed the nucleus of a potent opposition party."[64]

More recently Richard E. Ellis has taken the contrary position that the triumph, if there was one, went to South Carolina and the doctrine of states' rights. Ellis is much more critical than Freehling of Jackson's handling of the crisis. He paints a picture of a violent president threatening to hang John C. Calhoun and demanding a Force Bill that seemed all the more menacing because of Jackson's bellicose reputation. He is particularly hard on Jackson for splitting his party. Although Ellis exaggerates Jackson's violent behavior, he has made a major contribution to the study of the crisis by focusing on the dispute over states' rights between the traditionalists and the nullifiers rather than on the fight between nationalists and states' righters. He looks at the crisis as the participants did by relating it to the early history of the United States, which they knew well, rather than to the Civil War, which they could not foresee.[65]

On the whole the settlement of the Nullification Crisis marked a triumph for moderation on all sides. Far from being the unbending extremist that many critics have called him, Calhoun did not openly come out for nullification until he had given Jackson over two years to show what he could do for the South. Even then he continued to interpret nullification as a way in which states could protect themselves without seceding. To the end of the crisis he tried to hold back the radicals, and he participated willingly in the compromise. The other nullifiers in South Carolina, such as Hayne and Hamilton, also saw the need to compromise, first by devising the moderate process for nullifying the tariff, then by postponing nullification, and finally by accepting the compromise.

Jackson too deserves credit for learning as the crisis developed, for finally showing moderation, and for weathering the storm. He emerged from the crisis with his popularity intact and the Union saved. His approach to nullification went through four stages. Underestimating the depth of feeling in South Carolina, he first ridiculed the doctrine. Next, in 1832, he tried to undercut the nullifiers by pushing through lower tariffs in July and by offering to reduce tariffs even more in December. In this stage he consistently maintained a traditional states'-rights republican position. Then in a sudden swing he issued the overly nationalistic proclamation, began to talk about sending in more troops and arresting the nullifiers for treason, and disassociated himself from the Verplanck bill. As a result, the Force Bill seemed much more drastic than it really was. Throughout this stage Jackson weakened his reputation as an agrarian states' righter. Finally, he responded to the Old Republicans and the others opposing the use of force by saying less, changing his definition of treason, and by not sending in additional troops. Although never an open participant in the final compromise, he contributed to it by letting his followers vote for the tariff and distribution.

In the Nullification Crisis the major political figures, eventually including Jackson, behaved as Van Buren had said the new-style politicians would by working to heal sectional differences. But the crisis retarded the growth of the new political parties. By setting Jackson and nationalists such as McLane against the states' righters among the Democrats, the crisis threatened to splinter the party. Jackson got little support in the votes on the compromise. By bringing Jackson and Webster together on one side, Clay and Calhoun on another, the crisis upset the structure of the emerging two-party system. Whether these setbacks to the growth of parties would continue would depend on Jackson's behavior during the ensuing year, especially regarding his policy toward the Bank.

Part 2

THE DEMOCRATIC PARTY, 1833–37

9

RENEWING THE BANK WAR

Coming only thirty-six hours after the completion of the compromise, Jackson's second inauguration gave him the chance to recover from his setbacks of the past few months. The inauguration, which took place on 4 March 1833, offered the perfect setting in which to present his version of the crisis, proclaim his vision for the future, and take the stage away from Clay. After the wrenching struggle between the states' righters and the nationalists among the Democrats, Jackson needed to redefine his own states'-rights position and to establish himself as the leader of a united party. Only four months earlier he had received a mandate from the people, and the following month he had delivered his agrarian states'-rights annual message. Now he could recover the momentum lost during the conflict with South Carolina. Nine months stretched ahead in which he would have the stage to himself, without the distractions of Congress. He would never have a better chance, for the Union had been saved, and despite his difficulties, the Old Hero was at the height of his popularity with the people.

But as in his first inaugural Jackson failed to take advantage of his opportunity. Stating no claims of an electoral mandate, he offered no echoes of his annual message and made no attempt to rally the Democrats for the future. He preferred instead to look back on saving the Union. Although he did warn against encroachments on the rights of the states, he continued to emphasize nationalism at the expense of states' rights. "Without union," he said, "our independence and liberty would never have been achieved; without union they never can be maintained." He also made no attempt to heal party wounds through the agency of the *Globe*. On the day of the inaugural Blair attacked one Democrat, Gulian C. Verplanck, for supporting the Bank and four days later attacked another, Thomas Ritchie, for opposing the Force Bill.[1]

The northern opposition responded well to Jackson's emphasis on the Union. Philip Hone, not inclined to praise Jackson, called the message "well done." He later concluded that Jackson was the "most popular man we have ever known," more so even than George Washington. Charles Francis Adams, who seemed to agree, wrote that Jackson "conquer[ed] everything." The inaugural was a "prudent performance," with enough on each side to be "safe." The young Adams added loyally that his father was the superior man but lacked Jackson's popularity.[2]

Jackson, Hone, and Adams reflected the softening of party rancor and the loosening of party ties that had accompanied the Nullification Crisis. As states' righters in his own party deserted him, Jackson had been forced to fall back on northern nationalists such as McLane and Livingston in his own party and Webster in the opposition to deal with the crisis. Amos Kendall had published editorials in the *Globe* in support of Unionism. Rumors had spread of a Union party with Webster and Adams joining the cabinet and the latter succeeding Jackson as president in 1837. Now that the crisis was over the Old Hero was beginning to plan a triumphal tour to the Northeast similar to James Monroe's trip in 1817, which had ushered in the Era of Good Feelings.[3]

Although Van Buren hated Unionism as a threat to the Democratic party and Kendall lost interest in it once the Nullification Crisis had ended, the idea did not die easily among other Democrats. McLane, Cass, Livingston, and Grundy remained sympathetic to the new Unionism; even Barry and Taney showed interest. The Maine newspaperman Seba Smith, who had been poking fun at the Democrats with his fictional letters of the make-believe Major Jack Downing, noted the division. In one of the letters the major described a dispute between the party men Van Buren and Kendall and the Unionists McLane and Livingston over the way Democrats should treat Webster. The rumors of a Union party became so strong that two of Van Buren's most loyal newspapers—the *Albany Argus* and the *New-Hampshire Patriot*—felt obliged to deny that anything was afoot. Silas C. McClary of Ohio bluntly warned Van Buren in June that the old parties were virtually extinct.

McClary was especially conscious of the change because of the political tour that Webster had just taken to Ohio. After traveling through New York, Webster had stopped at Buffalo, Cleveland, and Columbus before reaching Cincinnati, where he was tendered a nonpartisan dinner on 19 June. At every stop he insisted that he represented no party and spoke only for the Union. He attacked the nullifiers and praised the strong Unionist stand of Andrew Jackson. Webster was "treated very kindly" by Benjamin Tappan and other Democrats, and—much to the dismay of Van Buren's adherents—was being mentioned for the presidency.[4]

But the bland inaugural and the prospects of a Union party were false harbingers. During Jackson's first term economic, social, and political changes had been paving the way for a second term socially more explosive and politically more partisan than expected. While Jackson had been fighting the political battles of his first term, the transportation and market revolutions had continued to expand the American economy. During these four years the first 300 miles of railroads were laid down and another 50,000 tons of steam vessels were launched, making it even easier to ship goods to market. The opening of almost 200 new banks multiplied the money available for investment. In response to these stimuli cotton planting and textile manufacturing grew apace, with annual cotton production climbing from about 750,000 bales to almost a million and the number of cotton spindles increasing by some 400,000. The lure of jobs brought 130,000 immigrants during the term, helping to swell the population of New York City by 100,000. And the expected removal of the Chickasaws and Choctaws helped attract 100,000 American planters and slaves to the lush cotton lands of Mississippi.[5]

This continued economic growth quickened the transformation of subsistence farmers and artisans into commercial farmers and wage laborers, vulnerable to fluctuations in the economy. Once business had recovered after the Panic of 1819 jobs had remained plentiful and prices steady as the nation enjoyed a period of slow, uninterrupted economic growth. But any sudden change in the economy would increase the likelihood of conflicts among workers or between workers and their employers. The arrival of Irish Catholics, Germans, and other non-English immigrants made similar conflicts likely between people of different ethnicity and religion. These changes had the greatest impact on the cities of the Northeast, aggravating stress, eating away at the old republican sense of community, and inviting confrontation.

The economic tension during Jackson's first term was compounded by the problems of slavery and race. The spread of slaves and cotton into the Southwest increased the value of slaves, making southerners more defensive about their "peculiar institution," a defensiveness that was heightened by the Nat Turner slave insurrection. Racial fears also intensified in the North, where most whites shared the southern belief in white supremacy. The expanding activity of the abolitionists added to the tension. Like the industrial changes, the friction engendered by race and slavery was greatest in the towns and cities, where escaped slaves and free blacks competed with whites for jobs and where abolitionists held their meetings and published their newspapers.

New political methods accelerated the move toward democracy. More and more candidates were nominated by conventions instead of by caucuses, and voters increasingly voted secretly with printed ballots. State party systems, which had appeared in the Middle Atlantic states by 1829, spread through much of New England during Jackson's first term and were beginning to emerge in the South and West. As Van Buren's view spread that political parties were legitimate agents for resolving conflict, antipartyism continued to decline. Although the two-party system had been somewhat set back by the Nullification Crisis, it was poised for rapid recovery. Because of the continuing upheaval Jackson's second term was destined to become a watershed in American history, with much of the impetus coming from outside Washington.[6]

Behind the façade of Unionism the Bank question was already threatening to destroy the political calm. Isaac Hill, for one, had never been fooled. "Wait till Jackson gets at the Bank again," he sneered, "and then the scalping-knives will glisten once more." Even while flirting with the administration, Webster warned that any further attack on the Bank would "create warm opposition in the North, & drive those, who would willingly support Genl. J. in all just measures, back to the arms" of Clay and Calhoun. Despite his preoccupation with nullification and his rapprochement with Webster, Jackson had not forgotten the Bank. He had raised the question of whether the federal deposits there were safe in his annual message in 1832 and a few days later had warned Tennessee congressman James K. Polk that the Bank, "the hydra of corruption," was "only *scotched, not dead*." Blair and Kendall were constantly goading him to complete the job by removing the federal deposits from the Bank. Blair convinced the president that Biddle was using the people's money against their will, and Kendall feared that the Bank would swing the next election and be rechartered unless "stripped" of its "power."[7]

The Bank issue heightened the tension between Kendall and Van Buren. When Van Buren returned to Washington from England, he had seen immediately how much Kendall's influence over the president had grown. During Jackson's first two years in office Van Buren and Kendall had played an equal role in speech writing, but for the next two-and-a-half years, while Van Buren was absent in England or in New York, Kendall had a hand in preparing at least five messages and Van Buren none. The first thing the Magician read on reaching the city in July 1832 was the Bank veto message, most of which was written by Kendall. Later, in the fall, Kendall also wrote the Address of the Central Hickory Club, which served as the Democratic platform in the election.[8]

Further evidence of Kendall's influence came in November when he published his editorials on Unionism at the start of the Nullification Crisis. To make matters worse Kendall wrote Van Buren at the same time recommending that the administration reach out toward "men of all parties" in the North and West. These sentiments alarmed Van Buren because they put his Old Republican alliance of North and South in jeopardy. When Van Buren wrote back opposing Unionism, Kendall widened the gap between them by attacking Van Buren's devotion to party politics. Americans, he wrote, had been "misled by misrepresentation and party excitement."Kendall warned that if Van Buren could not adapt to the new Unionism the party might have to turn away from him in 1836.[9]

The hostility between the two men flared again over the question of removing the deposits. A few days after the inauguration the new vice-president called Kendall to the President's House and "warmly remonstrated" him for his "continued agitation" for deposit removal when only a few days earlier the House of Representatives had declared the deposits safe in the Bank. Kendall shouted back, and after lecturing each other about the "financial and political" implications of removal, the two usually controlled men parted angrily. Learning afterward that Jackson sided with Kendall, the realistic Van Buren appeared to give in.[10]

Jackson then gathered his cabinet together on 19 March and asked each member to submit answers to a series of direct questions. Were the deposits safe? Could the government rely on the Bank? Should the Bank be rechartered? Should a new national bank be established? What should be done with the deposits in the Bank? Jackson's opinions, which he offered at the meeting, were just as direct. "Under no circumstances," he began, should the Bank be rechartered. He was willing to consider a new national bank but only one based in Washington and controlled by the central government. Before undertaking such a step, however, the government should try to get along without any national bank and place the deposits in state banks.[11] Jackson's use of the meeting suggests that he had become more comfortable in using his cabinet than in his first term. His support for state banks and his willingness to consider a national bank with federal controls showed that he was not unalterably opposed to banks or to a strong central government. He still had doubts about his war on the Bank, for he expected Biddle to retaliate and in a letter five days later wondered whether the state banks could "safely" handle the federal financial transactions.[12]

The response of the cabinet officers and the other members of the administration gave him further pause. After his exchange with Kendall, Van Buren did not directly oppose removal, but he preferred to wait until Congress could deal with the question. Although willing to go along, Woodbury and Barry were lukewarm about removal. McLane, Cass, Lewis, and James A. Hamilton opposed it. According to McLane the risks involved in using the state banks exceeded those from continuing to use the Bank. It was best to stay with the old system, "not for the sake of the bank, but that of the community." McLane also made the worrisome point that the power to remove the deposits rested with the secretary of the Treasury—not with the president. Jackson showed his uncertainty when he commented on McLane's statement that there were "strong points in this view—all ably discussed."[13]

The only member of the cabinet strongly supporting removal was Attorney General Taney, who was influenced by President Thomas Ellicott of the Union Bank of Maryland, for whom Taney had served as counsel. Like Kendall, the attorney general believed that the deposits should be removed as soon as possible because otherwise the Bank would use the deposits against the administration. He and Ellicott eased the president's fear that Biddle, in retaliation, might order his branch banks not to accept the notes of other branches, thus stifling the circulation of money. They pointed out that under its charter the Bank would still be obliged to transfer the public funds. State banks receiving notes drawn on different branch banks could simply present them as public funds to the nearest branch bank, which would then have to transfer them to the issuing branch for redemption.[14]

The views of William J. Duane were also important, for he was about to replace McLane as secretary of the Treasury. Well before deposit removal became an issue Jackson had decided to send Secretary of State Livingston to France, replace him with McLane, and appoint a new secretary of the Treasury. After discussions within the administration it was agreed to appoint someone from Pennsylvania. In a meeting between McLane and Jackson the name of William J. Duane was brought up, either by the president or perhaps, deviously, by McLane. It was later suggested that McLane expected to influence Duane and thus control two departments.

Since Duane had opposed the Bank and was the son of the old Jeffersonian newspaperman William Duane, who had been indicted under the Sedition Act, Jackson assumed that he could be relied upon to continue the Bank War. Unfortunately for Jackson, he sent McLane, who favored the Bank, to discuss the appointment with Duane instead of sending Taney or someone else who opposed it. Although McLane never admitted it, he must have learned that Duane would be far more sympathetic to the Bank than Jackson expected. By the beginning of 1833 all parties had agreed to the three-way shift. The way in which the cabinet was reshuffled suggests once again that Jackson lacked firm control over his appointments. Livingston's replacement on 29 May 1833 was the first in a series of cabinet shifts that were not completed until Kendall was appointed postmaster general two years later.[15]

Changes were also taking place in Jackson's personal life that spring. Within three months two of his oldest friends and most trusted advisers, John Overton and John Coffee, died, leaving him with almost no one from his own generation in whom he could confide. Early in April he lost his household manager Antoine Michel Guista. Jackson had not been on good terms with his housekeeper, who had served previously under Adams, but Guista had managed a staff of twenty-four servants efficiently and would be missed. A month later the president was aboard a steamboat on the Potomac when he was rudely assaulted by Robert Randolph, a former lieutenant in the navy. Randolph harbored a grudge against Jackson because the president had ordered him dismissed from the navy after being accused of theft. In a foolish attempt to salvage some honor, Randolph had tried to tweak the president's nose but succeeded only in scratching his face. No real harm was done, but the reaction of Jackson and other Democrats suggested that no Unionist Era of Good Feelings was at hand. Jackson accused Randolph of being part of a conspiracy to assassinate him, and a number of his supporters blamed the opposition party. The combination of events was upsetting to Jackson. On learning of Overton's death, he complained that his body was weak and his spirits low.[16]

They were little better in late June, when the aging Old Hero almost died himself while on his tour of the Northeast. The tour, which coincided with Webster's trip to the Northwest, encouraged more talk of a Union party. Isaac Hill's *New-Hampshire Patriot* expressed the fear that political amalgamation would result from the tour just as it had in 1817 when Monroe made his trip. The tour also drew attention to the new railroads, for on his way to Baltimore Jackson covered the last twelve miles by train. He moved on to Philadelphia and Trenton before arriving in New York City on 12 June. A series of disasters and Jackson's deteriorating health then turned the tour into an ordeal that almost cost the president his life. He narrowly escaped falling into the water off the Battery when a bridge that he had just crossed collapsed. He was almost thrown to the ground when his horse reared, and later he was nearly hit by a burning wad that flew out of a cannon. Already exhausted by the time he reached Boston, the president was bled and put to bed to escape the cold rains. He carried on, however, to Salem and Lowell, Massachusetts, and Concord, New Hampshire, before he was forced to cut the trip short on 1 July. After a headlong return trip, he was back in Washington on the Fourth of July. Although he gradually recovered, he was still so worn out in August that he took a four-week vacation at the Rip Raps.[17]

The question of removing the deposits followed Jackson on his tour. On 1 June, a few days before it began, the new secretary of the Treasury, William J. Duane, arrived in Washington. That evening he received a call from Reuben M. Whitney, a Philadelphia merchant who had worked for the Bank but had deserted to the Jackson administration early in the Bank War. Saying that he had been sent by the president, Whitney shocked Duane by announcing that Jackson had decided to remove the deposits. Kendall, he added, was already drawing up a letter instructing the new secretary on the procedure. The next evening Whitney was back, with Kendall in tow, to pursue the subject further, but Duane, "mortified" by the efforts to "reduce [him] to a mere cypher," refused to enter into any discussion. When Duane finally saw the president on 3 June, Jackson denied that he had sent Whitney and Kendall but admitted that he planned to remove the deposits. Jackson was surprised to learn that Duane did not agree and immediately "repelled" his suggestion that the matter be handled by Congress or the judiciary. The two talked again on 5 June, and then, promising to send Duane a letter with his views, Jackson left on his journey.[18]

Before writing Duane, Jackson first wanted to discuss deposit removal with Van Buren, who joined the party in New York City. Realizing that Jackson would listen to his vice-president, both McLane and Kendall had written Van Buren, trying to sway him. McLane asked him to urge the president to postpone his decision, and Kendall wanted him to use his "great influence" with the president to speed up removal. Van Buren apparently did neither, but Jackson heard nothing to deter him. On reaching Boston he wrote Duane a letter, enclosing a long statement explaining why he wanted to remove the deposits. Echoing the agrarian Kendall, who had prepared much of the statement, he described the corruption of the Bank and argued that "the purity of our Government and the liberties of the people" would be forever affected by banking policies. Drawing on the less-agrarian Taney and Ellicott, Jackson dismissed the idea that the Bank would be able to retaliate. He even used a phrase from an early Van Buren letter, in which the New Yorker, then in favor of removal, warned of "embarrassments" if they did not remove the deposits before the charter of the Bank expired in 1836. Jackson's policies were still being influenced by his coalition.[19]

In July while Jackson recovered from his exhausting tour, he and

Duane exchanged several letters and held two meetings. The new secretary opposed any drastic action, saying that if the state banks refused to cooperate and removal failed, the Bank would find it easier to secure recharter. To this Jackson replied that removal was not a drastic step. Since the government was not legally obliged to keep the deposits in the Bank, removal was simply a matter of expediency.[20]

Although a number of banks had shown interest in receiving federal deposits, Jackson was worried that when the terms were spelled out there would not be enough takers. He shared his worries with Kendall, who volunteered to visit the banks and find out. Since Duane, as secretary of the Treasury, had the sole power to remove the deposits, Jackson went through proper channels and asked him to draw up Kendall's instructions. In complying with the request Duane prepared a series of questions about the advisability of removal that Kendall was to put to the bankers; he also included a clause stating that he had not made up his own mind. When Kendall complained that the document would invite dozens of replies opposing removal and that Duane's hint of opposition would only raise doubts, Jackson abandoned protocol and allowed Kendall to write his own instructions. Under the new orders Kendall was simply to ask bankers if they were interested in receiving federal deposits and was to discuss terms only with those who said yes. Duane then reluctantly signed the new instructions, leaving Kendall free to deal with the banks.[21]

Much depended on Kendall's trip, for most members of the administration were still dead set against removal. Woodbury later revealed that even Taney had "flin[ch]ed and doubted" that summer because "the majority vs. him was so strong." Kendall took up his task with vigor, spending late July and most of August visiting banks in Baltimore, Philadelphia, New York, and Boston. He arrived in Baltimore on 28 July and was delighted to find that three of the five banks that he approached, including, not surprisingly, Ellicott's Union Bank of Maryland, were interested. In Philadelphia Kendall expected no offers except from the Girard Bank, where Whitney had paved the way, but four of nine banks proved willing to discuss terms. Seven banks were cooperative in New York, including three that had already been approached—the Bank of America, the Manhattan Bank, and the Mechanics Bank. In Boston four stepped forward, of which the Commonwealth and Merchants banks had the best Democratic credentials. While Kendall was in Boston, he also received offers from banks in Portsmouth, New Hampshire, and Portland, Maine. It was an encouraging start.[22]

In addition to lining up banks Kendall also sent Jackson news calculated to stiffen the Old Hero's resolve. From Philadelphia he reported that two pro-Bank Democrats, Henry Toland of that city and Edward Livingston, had recently received loans from the Bank. He also passed along the rumor that the Duane appointment had been orchestrated by McLane so that he could control two cabinet positions. In New York, Kendall had barely arrived when he encountered Van Buren and McLane, who tried to convince him to postpone removal until the end of the year. In a letter to Jackson from New York on 14 August, Kendall said that he would go along with the plan only if McLane and Duane would use their influence to get Congress to "sustain" removal. By hinting that Toland, Livingston, Van Buren, McLane, and Duane were engaged in some sort of Bank conspiracy, Kendall expected to arouse Jackson's fighting spirit.[23]

While Kendall was encouraging Jackson from afar, Blair was doing the same at the Rip Raps, where he was vacationing with the president. According to Blair, who probably exaggerated, Jackson was under pressure to give up his plans to remove the deposits, with "letters entreating a surrender" pouring in on him daily. During this "siege," as Blair called it, the editor helped the president deflect the entreaties and draw up the first draft of a statement defending removal.[24]

Jackson was now eager for Van Buren to commit himself. Happily ensconced at Saratoga Springs, New York, the vice-president first played for time, pleading that he wanted to consult Sen. Silas Wright. He then made the visit to New York in which he and McLane tried to convince Kendall to wait until January. Pleased by neither the delay nor the rumors about McLane, the president sent Van Buren a sharp letter on 16 August, similar to the one he had sent him during the Nullification Crisis. Because of the friendship between Van Buren and McLane, Jackson wrote, it was being hinted that the vice-president was opposed to removal and was "privately a friend to the Bank." "This must be removed," thundered the president, "or it will do us both much harm." Jackson concluded by asking Van Buren to send him comments at once on the paper that he and Blair were preparing.[25]

After meeting with Wright on 18 August, Van Buren delayed again, saying he had to wait until the Regency had been polled. Even when Wright reported back, Van Buren was still unable to give a firm opinion, for the Regency was as divided over deposit removal as it had been over the tariff. The agrarian Wright, who did not trust the new business ethics, suspected that speculators, including New York Democrats James A. Hamilton and Jesse Hoyt, were counting on "instantaneous removal" to make a killing "from some cursed Wall St. operations." In his letter to Jackson on 4 September Van Buren said that he and Wright preferred to wait until 1 January but would support immediate removal if the president insisted. This was hardly the firm commitment that the president wanted.[26]

Jackson was still somewhat uncertain. Most members of his cabinet were hostile, Van Buren and other advisers wanted to wait, and Biddle was already giving indications that he would retaliate. On 8 September Jackson wrote James A. Hamilton, only lately a convert to removal, asking for real "proof" that the state banks would be able to handle the federal funds. But a day later Kendall handed in his report, urging immediate removal. He assured the president that seven banks—the Union Bank of Maryland, the Girard Bank in Philadelphia, the Bank of America, the Manhattan Bank, and the Mechanics Bank in New York, and the Commonwealth and Merchants banks in Boston—were ready to receive the deposits. With this advice Jackson decided to go ahead.[27]

During the next two weeks Jackson followed a deliberate process, with three cabinet meetings and many conferences; but in keeping with his usual custom, no votes were taken, and it was obvious that he had made up his mind. At the regular cabinet meeting on 10 September he read a short paper outlining his plans. He said that he wished to set a date at which time the government would stop putting money in the Bank. Funds there would not be removed at once but would be gradually used for current expenses. He asked the cabinet members to read Kendall's report and other documents and decide whether the behavior of the Bank justified removal and whether the funds would be safe in the state banks. Saying that he wanted "harmony," he left no doubt about where he stood. The "corrupt" acts of the Bank, he said, left "no excuse for further delay." If they did not act, what reason could they give the country for their "apathy"? They would meet again in a week and come to an "understanding."[28]

After meeting each member individually during the week, Jackson brought the cabinet back together again on 17 September. He promptly informed the gathering that he intended to remove the deposits and would give them a statement of his views the following day. Only two cabinet officers—Barry and Taney—wholeheartedly supported him. Woodbury agreed to back him but argued that removal was not necessary to protect the deposits. McLane, the only one to give his objections in any detail, wanted to wait until Congress convened. Cass preferred to leave the decision up to Duane. Jackson already knew that Duane also preferred to wait for Congress; the two had had a long conference a few days earlier.[29]

In the draft for Jackson's statement, which he and Blair had worked on at the Rip Raps, the president had adopted an egalitarian tone reminiscent of his Bank veto and his 1832 annual message. Calling the Bank an "aristocracy of incorporated wealth," he twice declared that the "purity and simplicity" of republican institutions were at stake. He insisted that keeping the federal deposits at the Bank perpetuated the same "system of favoritism in behalf of the monied classes" as the protective tariff and internal improvements. The draft was first edited by Kendall and then passed on to Taney, who wrote the final, far less egalitarian, version. Since the Bank's charter would not be renewed, Taney began, Congress would have to deal with the question of the deposits by 1836, and it was "safer to begin too soon than to delay it too long." The precedent for removal had been set by Secretary of the Treasury William Harris Crawford in 1817, when he placed deposits in a number of state banks. Only briefly at the end did Taney adopt anything like the moral, ideological tone of the president. Removal, he said, was "necessary to preserve the morals of the people, the freedom of the press, and the purity of the elective franchise." Aside from this flourish, the language was sober and legalistic; Blair said later that Taney had turned a "combative Bulletin" into "a calm judicial" brief. As in Jackson's Bank veto, Taney had softened Jackson's rhetoric.[30]

After Andrew J. Donelson, who was still Jackson's secretary, read the statement to the cabinet the next day, Jackson and Taney moved swiftly. On 20 September Blair announced in the *Globe* that starting 1 October the government would stop depositing its funds in the Bank. As Jackson had told his cabinet, the deposits already at the Bank would not be removed at once but would be withdrawn bit by bit as the need arose. The next day, however, Jackson ran into a serious snag when Duane refused to issue the order. After a tense conversation and several letters, Jackson dismissed him on 23 September, replacing him immediately with Taney. Two days later Taney issued the order.[31]

Throughout the crisis Jackson's correspondence shows that he was far less independent, composed, and authoritative than tradition and the orderly succession of events have suggested. He was more disappointed than angry that he had to proceed without Van Buren's firm support. He was unusually grateful for Taney's loyalty. When Taney backed his decision to remove the deposits and reassured him that arrangements could be made quickly, Jackson wrote on Taney's note that this was evidence of his secretary's "virtue, energy and worth." The president even offered his hand to Duane when the secretary stayed to talk with him after Donelson had read the statement to the cabinet. Almost pleading, he said that if Duane "would stand by him it would be the happiest day of his life."[32]

Jackson was particularly anxious to maintain harmony in the cabinet even though the majority opposed immediate removal. After the cabinet breakup in 1831 and the musical chairs in the Treasury Department, he could ill afford to have anyone quit. It would damage his administration and lend credence to his reputation for having "a belligerent, unruly temper." He dealt with the problem by having Blair insert a sentence near the end of his statement on removal, saying that the president took sole responsibility and was asking no cabinet officer "to make a sacrifice of opinion or principle." When McLane and Cass talked of resigning, he told them "kindly and firmly" that it was not necessary. He was delighted to report on 25 September that the two had decided to "remain where they now are—harmoniously." Looking back he confided that he had "suffered more" over the cabinet question than at any time in his life. It had been "excruciating" to his "private friendships."[33]

The heavy flow of letters between Jackson and Van Buren—thirty altogether that summer and fall—leaves a picture of a rather unsure president craving friendship, needing someone to confide in, and seeking approval without asking for much in return. On receiving Van Buren's letter waffling on deposit removal, he wrote back, perhaps wistfully, that he had "counted on" Van Buren's support and hoped he could be in Washington by the first week in October, presumably to help with the banking crisis. Since the letter reached Van Buren just as he was preparing to accompany Washington Irving on a tour of the old Dutch settlements in New York, the vice-president agreed to support immediate removal but ignored the request to come to Washington. Three days later he sent another letter apologizing for "not notic[ing]" Jackson's request. He thought it best not to come at once, for it would encourage their enemies to blame removal on him and the "monied junto in N York." If the president really wanted him to, he would consider it an "honor to share any portion" of Jackson's responsibility. It is difficult to understand how Van Buren got away with this double talk, but he did. Jackson acquiesced, saying that he was "pleased" with Van Buren's "spirit" and would not need him until 20 October.

Then between 19 September and 5 October he wrote Van Buren eight more letters, giving an almost day-by-day account of the removal of the deposits, painting himself as a modern tribune, patiently and bravely protecting his people against evil enemies. Twice he described his letters to Duane as "calm and dignified" while Duane's were "indecorous." He had dealt with McLane in a "kindly and friendly" way and was prepared to deal firmly with the Bank, whose "corruption" had "filled every honest mind with indignation." Knowing that the "perpetuity of our republican government demanded it," he had done what God told him was "right."[34]

Van Buren replied promptly—five times—reassuring Jackson that he had acted correctly and was receiving public acclaim. Since Jackson had complained of suffering from fevers, Van Buren expressed his sympathy several times, blaming them on the "infernal hot coal fires" at the President's House. He spoke kindly of the children living with the president. Interspersed with the personal remarks were occasional political comments. He counseled Jackson to keep his cabinet intact and made suggestions about deposit banks in New York and the appointment of an attorney general to replace Taney. Some of his comments were self-serving, such as his suggestion that his rival McLane needed to mix more with common people. Van Buren said nothing about returning to Washington and did not reach the capital until early November. Even then he stayed only a short time before returning to Albany.[35]

The interaction of Van Buren, Kendall, and Jackson that summer and fall offers insight into the roles of the Old Hero's two chief advisers. Though sometimes adversaries, Kendall and Van Buren had much in common. With their undistinguished social backgrounds, they well represented the pragmatic organization men surrounding the president. Composed and thoughtful, they served as superb foils for the impulsive, intuitive Jackson. Although Kendall came to Washington from Kentucky and Van Buren from New York, they both brought the flavor of rural New England to the administration. Born in Massachusetts on the New Hampshire border, Kendall lived but fifteen of his eighty years in the West. With his industry, his conscience, his sense of moral superiority, and his "talent for silence," he was the quintessential Puritan. Van Buren was born in Kinderhook, New York, just a few miles from the Massachusetts border, sent one son to a New England school, another to a New England college, and was surrounded in the Albany Regency by transplanted Yankees.[36]

Kendall's behavior during the Nullification Crisis and the removal of the deposits shows him at his best—acting as Jackson's trusted aide who knew what the president wanted and carried it out. Once a protégé of Clay, Kendall had the same relationship with Jackson. When he arrived in Washington in 1829, he told Blair that he would side with neither Calhoun nor Van Buren but would "go with Old Hickory." From then on he rarely left Washington and was almost always at Jackson's side. Since their ideas were often alike, Kendall had no difficulty carrying out Jackson's early policies of reform and his war on the Bank. When Jackson turned in another direction to resist nullification, Kendall adjusted accordingly, writing the Unionist editorials and trying to convince Van Buren. He was in his element making arrangements for deposit removal and serving as Taney's agent in the months that followed. By thus sticking with the president Kendall bested both Van Buren and McLane throughout the Bank War.[37]

Van Buren had a different relationship with Jackson. When the two first served together in the Senate, Van Buren, who was then better known politically than Jackson, won the Old Hero's respect; the respect grew as Van Buren went about organizing the Jackson party. When they disagreed—as on party patronage, the role of Virginians in the party, the response to South Carolina, and deposit removal—Jackson respected Van Buren's opinion and even occasionally followed his advice. He knew that Van Buren saw political nuances that he often missed and would slow him down when he was too impulsive. Unlike Kendall, Van Buren was often away from Washington, sometimes because of his duties and other times to keep out of trouble. In one way or another he avoided the fighting over the selection of the cabinet, the tariff, the recharter of the Bank, his own nomination for vice-president, the Nullification Crisis, and the removal of the deposits. And yet he retained Jackson's confidence.

Van Buren was able to do so because he had Jackson's friendship as well as his respect. The friendship developed during Van Buren's two years as secretary of state when the two rode horseback together and worked as a team to defend the Eatons. Van Buren ate so often at the President's House that he seemed to be one of the family; he even played games such as blindman's buff with the children in Jackson's household. The letters back and forth during the removal crisis show that despite their disagreements their friendship was as strong as ever and that Van Buren could provide the approval and the sympathy—as well as the political advice—that Jackson needed. By 1833 he was one of the few persons left in whom Jackson could confide—if only by mail. Rachel Jackson, Coffee, and Overton were dead, Eaton had left the administration, and Jackson was no longer completely comfortable with Donelson. Jackson respected the views of Kendall and Taney, but he rarely confided in them. He could confide in Blair and Barry, but they did not carry Van Buren's political clout. As a result no one played the role of Jackson's friend and adviser as well as Van Buren.

As Taney and Kendall put deposit removal in operation, the United States government enjoyed an annual surplus of some $10 million, with receipts in excess of $30 million and expenses of about $20 million. For the first time since the founding of the Republic there was almost no federal debt. As a result the federal deposits at the Bank had risen to almost $10 million, about half the Bank's total deposits, both figures at or near all-time highs. With such resources the Bank dominated American banking; its $20 million in deposits made up 20 percent of all bank deposits in the United States; its loans and discounts, which were over $60 million in 1833, had a profound influence on the economy of the country. By easing or tightening its credit the Bank could control the state banks. Because of its size and its policy of maintaining large specie reserves of gold and silver coin, the Bank had a stabilizing effect on the nation's banking. In 1833 the Bank held a specie reserve equal to 24 percent of its current liabilities (deposits plus notes in circulation), compared with an average of only 8 percent at all Massachusetts banks and 9 percent at the banks participating in the New York Safety Fund. The removal of $10 million from the Bank, even if done gradually, would be felt in all the other banks across the land.[38]

The impact came almost at once as the Bank began to contract its loans, contributing to a financial panic. There was then and continues to be now disagreement over who was responsible for this panic. Advocates of the Bank pointed out that the administration broke its word by immediately withdrawing large sums from the Bank rather than letting the deposits dwindle gradually. This is partially true. Taney feared that Biddle might attack the deposit banks in Baltimore, Philadelphia, and New York by collecting the notes of one or more of them and suddenly presenting them for redemption. On 4 October, therefore, the secretary gave the five banks Treasury drafts totaling $2.3 million on the federal deposits at the Bank. If Biddle made a sudden demand on any one of the banks, it could use its drafts to withdraw the necessary amounts from the federal deposits at the Bank. The banks were not to use the drafts for their own investment purposes. Taney was embarrassed on 7 October when his friend Thomas Ellicott of the Union Bank of Maryland presented two drafts of $100,000 each to branches of the Bank, endorsing them over to another bank in which he was involved to cover unsuccessful speculation in stocks. Since the Treasury had been in the custom of giving warning before such withdrawals, the suddenness of Ellicott's withdrawals alarmed Biddle. He responded the next day by ordering the loans and discounts of the Bank reduced by $5.8 million. Biddle's worst fears seemed confirmed when the Girard Bank of Philadelphia and the Manhattan Bank of New York each presented drafts for $500,000 in November. These withdrawals were followed by a $350,000 run on the Savannah branch of the Bank later in the month.[39]

The Bank's case is weakened by evidence that Biddle had decided on a policy of contraction during the summer, long before removal began. He told the New York branch on 30 July that the Bank would soon have "many things to do [to] crush the Kitchen Cabinet," but in the meanwhile the branch should "keep within [its] income—and bring the State Banks in debt." On 13 August, while Kendall was visiting the prospective banks of deposit, Biddle ordered the branches to shorten the terms of their bills of exchange and to keep discounts "at their present level." James A. Hamilton had reported the harmful effects of this pressure on New York banks in letters to Jackson urging removal in mid-September. When removal went into effect on 1 October, the Bank decided to start cutting its discounts. All these steps were taken before Ellicott tendered his drafts on 7 October. Biddle went on to order a total of over $9 million in reductions by January 1834, far more than the $5 million in Treasury withdrawals during the same period.[40]

Regardless of who was at fault, the financial community was soon suffering a banking panic, much of it centered in New York City, where Samuel Swartwout described the situation as "dreadful." Philip Hone wrote in December that Jackson's "ill-advised measure of removing the public money" had caused "great distress" among New Yorkers who relied upon "their credit to pay their debts." For personal loans the borrower was "completely at the mercy of the lender." Stocks had fallen "prodigiously"; his own $50,000 in railroad stocks had declined to less than $12,000. He concluded: "A panic prevails." In late January Hone twice cited brokerage and banking failures.[41]

The panic spread throughout the United States. In Virginia a frightened John Tyler predicted "a crash of the local banks of the North." Later in the winter a traveler brought news of the panic in Pennsylvania, Ohio, and Kentucky. Conditions still seemed so bad in May 1834 that Hezekiah Niles complained that he had "never seen or felt anything like the present pressure."[42]

Neither Biddle nor Jackson helped matters with his rhetoric. Biddle told one of his branch presidents that the Bank must stick to its policy of "firm restriction." He said that if "the Bank permits itself to be frightened or coaxed into any relaxation of its present measures," because it fears "offending," it "will inevitably be prostrated." Later he said that "all the merchants may break, but the Bank of the United States shall not break." And still later he declared that the Bank would not be "cajoled from its duty by any small drivelling about relief to the country." Just because Jackson had "scalped Indians and imprisoned Judges" did not mean that he would "have his way with the Bank."[43]

Jackson was equally bellicose. In describing Taney's plan to make Treasury drafts available at the deposit banks, Jackson added, "I am ready with the screws to draw every tooth and then the stumps [sic]." After hearing the cries from New York he boasted to Van Buren, "I am not in any panic. Were all the worshippers of the golden Calf to memorialise me and request a restoration of the Deposits, I would cut my right hand from my body before I would do such an act."[44]

As Jackson began to slug it out with Biddle, the political weather had undergone a sea change from the calm Unionist March day when he had been inaugurated. Although the economic and political trends of his first term made some change likely, Jackson had started it by removing the deposits. Instead of wasting the nine-month recess between sessions of Congress as he had four years earlier when he had been preoccupied with the Peggy Eaton affair, Jackson had overcome heavy resistance and his own doubts to renew the Bank War. In doing so, he had aligned himself with Kendall's agrarianism and Taney's anti-Bank position rather than with the pro-Bank Federalist views of McLane or even the moderate Old Republican views of Van Buren.

10

★ ★ ★ ★ ★

TWO-PARTY POLITICS

As Congress convened in December 1833 the spreading financial panic and the intensity of feeling on both sides of the Bank question created a sense of urgency, leading many observers to dub the new session the "Panic session." Supporters of the Bank feared that Jackson would not back down. The Jackson forces were uneasy because they anticipated a strong effort to restore the deposits and perhaps even to push through a bill to renew the charter of the Bank.

Jackson was especially concerned because the Democrats still lacked control of Congress. In the Senate fewer than twenty of the forty-eight members were reliable Democrats; the party had a small majority in the House, perhaps thirty, but many Democrats were of marginal loyalty. As a result the Democrats still could not elect Blair printer for either house, and they expected a stiff fight for Speaker of the House. Having been told that he was to be named minister to Great Britain to replace Van Buren, Andrew Stevenson had already passed the word that he would not be a candidate.[1]

Since the Speaker would choose the committees that would deal with the Bank question, Jackson wanted the right man for the position. James K. Polk, who had served well during the Nullification Crisis, was interested, but at thirty-eight he seemed young and inexperienced compared to the fifty-eight-year-old Stevenson. Lacking the votes to have Stevenson confirmed as minister to Great Britain, the administration decided to delay the appointment and prevailed upon him to run again for Speaker. But as late as 30 November Jackson was far from sure of the outcome. The president told Blair that Stevenson should not be "brought forward" until "noses [had been] counted" and it was determined that he *"surely"* would be elected. Jackson himself had spoken to Democratic congressman James M. Wayne of Georgia, who had considered running. In a display of party loyalty Wayne backed out, saying that he would do nothing that might "split the party." With the party united behind him and the opposition divided, Stevenson won by a surprisingly large majority, with 142 votes to 75 for the combined opposition.[2]

Despite their uncertain position, Jackson and Treasury Secretary Taney took the offensive as soon as Congress convened. In his annual message the president announced that he had been forced to remove the deposits from the Bank because it had been "attempting to influence the elections of the public officers." He denounced the recent contraction policy of the Bank as an effort "to control public opinion, through the distresses of some and the fears of the others." The next day Taney carried on the attack with a detailed report defending removal and accusing Biddle of squeezing about $6.25 million from the financial community in the two months preceding the removal of the deposits. According to his reasoning, public deposits at the Bank had increased by some $2.25 million during that time, and the loans and discounts of the Bank had decreased by over $4 million. Biddle, he said, had started the panic.[3]

In the Senate the opposition countered by maneuvering to control the choice of committees. Throughout Jackson's first term the Senate had continued to entrust this power to its presiding officer, with the understanding that, by absenting himself from the chair, the vice-president would leave the power to the president pro-tempore. Unwilling to challenge this arrangement, Vice-President Van Buren had dallied in Albany tending to local politics and did not plan to arrive until 14 December. By this time, presumably, President pro-tempore Hugh Lawson White, still in sympathy with the Democrats, if not with Jackson, would have appointed the committees with the interests of the party in mind. To prevent this, the opposition forced through a measure on 10 December requiring the Senate to choose all committees by vote. It was an early indication of the weakness of the Democrats that they could muster only eighteen votes against this partisan maneuver.[4]

When Democratic floor leader Felix Grundy moved to postpone the selection of committees until 16 December, Daniel Webster revived thoughts of a Union party by supporting the motion. Grundy, also a Unionist, had already consulted with Jackson and wanted Van Buren available to help with any possible deal. With Webster and eight other

New England National Republicans joining the Democrats, the motion carried easily. Fearing a revived Webster-Jackson entente, Clay implored Sen. John M. Clayton, who was still in Delaware, to hurry to Washington. "If you are here," Clay wrote, "I believe we shall be safe, even if there be defections. For God's sake then come to us. And do not let anything keep you away."[5]

Clay's panicky letter and Webster's eagerness to deal with the administration show the fluidity of political parties at the time. Arriving in Washington on 14 December, Van Buren was summoned to the President's House, where Grundy quickly outlined plans for "an arrangement" with "Webster and his friends." With the Democratic party as he understood it at stake, Van Buren warned that "the people" would be confused and alarmed if they learned that Jackson, "the fearless opponent" of the Bank, had made a bargain with Webster, one of the Bank's "most unscrupulous supporters." Moved by Van Buren's unusual fervor, Jackson came down in favor of the party, telling Grundy to give up any thought of a deal with Webster. The idea of a Union party was dead. Jackson's quick support of Van Buren after their disagreement during the summer is another example of the closeness between the two. It is also likely that having removed the deposits Jackson realized that no lasting agreement with Webster was possible.[6]

Jackson's decision to scuttle the Union party sent Webster and the other New Englanders back to the opposition and further weakened the administration in the Senate. After the Senate had voted on committees, Democrats controlled only seven of the twenty standing committees and only two of the ten most important. Opposition stalwarts such as Nathaniel Silsbee, Theodore Frelinghuysen, George Poindexter, and John M. Clayton chaired the committees of Commerce, Manufactures, Public Lands, and Judiciary. As a reward for returning to the fold Webster was given chairmanship of the Finance Committee. Webster also remained in the employ of the Bank, for at this point he sent his notorious note to Biddle requesting that his "retainer" be "*refreshed* as usual."[7]

Meanwhile the Democrats were working to shore up their position in the House. Now becoming more and more involved in congressional politics, Jackson played an important role in choosing committees, working through Stevenson, Kendall, Lewis, and Whitney, and sending lists of potential committee members to his cabinet officers for approval. The Ways and Means Committee, which was expected to handle the question of the deposits, was so arranged that it had a solid Democratic majority of six to three. The administration selected the loyal if unspectacular Polk for chairman and loaded his committee with some of the best Democrats available—Henry Hubbard of New Hampshire, Churchill C. Cambreleng of New York, Isaac McKim of Maryland, George Loyall of Virginia, and John McKinley of Alabama.[8]

Designating Polk as party spokesman, Jackson's advisers made plans to attack and to keep the opposition on the defensive, just as they had done during the fight over rechartering the Bank. They planned to refer Taney's report to Polk's Ways and Means Committee, which would squelch debate by keeping it off the floor of the House. The committee would then start another investigation of the Bank, move a series of anti-Bank resolutions, and initiate legislation for regulating the deposit banks.

But the Democrats still lacked effective control of the House and were badly outmaneuvered on the floor throughout the month of December. As was customary, the president's annual message was referred to the House sitting as Committee of the Whole, which would refer specific sections to the appropriate standing committees. When McDuffie asked that Taney's report be treated the same way, Polk unsuspectingly acquiesced, expecting that the report would then be referred to his Ways and Means Committee. Instead, McDuffie moved to keep Taney's report and those sections of the president's message concerning the Bank in the Committee of the Whole. Polk protested, but Thomas Chilton of Kentucky retorted sharply that the Tennessean showed "vanity" in trying to get the report sent to his committee. Since debate in the Committee of the Whole was unlimited, the administration faced the situation it most feared, an interminable debate over the removal of the deposits.[9]

The Democrats tried desperately to squirm out of the hole. Polk moved twice to reconsider the vote that had sent Taney's report to the Committee of the Whole, only to have Chilton and then McDuffie move adjournment. Jackson, who followed the parliamentary maneuvers closely, suggested that Polk end debate by calling the previous question, but when the motion was made the Democrats lost by three votes. As the Democrats became frustrated, Whitney, an important link with Congress, complained that he had had to "work all last night and this forenoon with the Wire workers" to get enough Democratic votes to send another Bank question to Ways and Means.[10]

The plight of the Democrats was worsened by the hundreds of memorials pouring into Washington from groups protesting against the bad economic conditions brought on by the panic. Thomas Hart Benton vividly recalled these "hundred days," when

a phalanx of orators and speakers were daily fulminating against [Jackson]—while many hundred newspapers incessantly assailed him—while public meetings were held in all parts, and men of all sorts, even

beardless youths, harangued against him as if he had been a Nero—
while a stream of committees was pouring upon him.

The flood became so great that both houses set aside a special time every
day to deal with the memorials. Many groups attacked Biddle for his
contraction, but the majority put the blame on Jackson for removing the
deposits. Finding it difficult to respond convincingly, the Democrats
tried the strategy of ignoring the panic.[11]

Most of the attention focused on the Senate, where Clay was in
command. After Jackson's message vetoing Clay's distribution bill was
read on 5 December, the senator rose angrily to ask why the president
had said nothing about the subject during the nine months since it was
passed. On 10 December he criticized Van Buren for not being in the
chair and supported the proposal to have committees chosen by vote.
He continued his attack by offering an insulting resolution asking the
president to submit a copy of the "paper," if it was "genuine," which was
said to have been read to his cabinet concerning removal of the deposits.
After the resolution passed, 23 to 18, Jackson refused to comply, saying that the Senate had no right to demand such an executive communication.[12]

Clay's most powerful assault began on 26 December when he offered two resolutions, one censuring Jackson for assuming unconstitutional and "dangerous" powers in removing the deposits and the other
calling Taney's reasons for removal "unsatisfactory and insufficient." In
his speech, which began that day and was not concluded until 30 December, Clay brought the crowd to its feet more than once with an emo-
tion-charged philippic denouncing "the concentration of all power in
one man's hands," which was "approaching tyranny." He denounced
Jackson for dismissing Secretary of the Treasury Duane for the sole purpose of removing the deposits from the Bank. Van Buren in the chair
ignored the "trampling & clapping" of the crowd during the speech but
was finally forced to clear the gallery at the conclusion. When Jackson
was shown the speech, he roared, "Oh, if I live to get these robes of
office off me, I will bring the rascal to a dear account." The removal of the
deposits had become another personal battle between Jackson and Clay
as well as a party battle.[13]

In his reply to Clay, over three days, Benton accused him of asking
the Senate to usurp the House's power to impeach. If the Senate supported these resolutions, Benton warned, it was liable "to be tried by
the people, and to have its sentence reversed." Increasingly partisan
speeches followed by Wright and Forsyth of the Democrats, Poindexter,

Webster, and Tyler of the opposition. Clay changed the subject but not the target with another set of resolutions, aimed at the spoils system. He proposed stripping the president of his power to remove officials at pleasure and giving Congress the power to prescribe the terms of tenure.

The presence of Van Buren as presiding officer added to the drama. In defending the administration, Benton compared Van Buren's decorum now that he was in the minority with the lack of it displayed by Clay and the others when they had been in that position. The most exciting moment came on 7 March when Clay was delivering a flamboyant address blaming Jackson for the panic. Staring at the vice-president, Clay shouted that no one could better alter Jackson's course and relieve the distress than Van Buren:

> Go to [the president] and tell him . . . the actual condition of his bleeding country. Tell him it is nearly ruined and undone by the measures which he has been induced to put in operation. . . . Depict to him, . . . the heart-rending wretchedness of thousands of the working class.

While Clay was speaking, Van Buren looked on intently as if, as Benton described it, "treasuring up every word." Suddenly when the speech was over, he rose and marched deliberately, without his usual smile, toward Clay. There was a gasp as many spectators thought that he might strike the senator; instead, Van Buren merely walked up to him and asked him graciously if he could have a pinch of his fine maccoboy snuff. Clay was deflated for a moment, but the pressure on Jackson continued.[14]

As the time to vote on Clay's censure resolutions approached, Democratic strength in the Senate had reached its nadir. One of the party's strongest members, William C. Rives, had resigned on 22 February 1834 under pressure from the Virginia legislature. He had been replaced by a Jackson opponent, the clubfooted Benjamin Watkins Leigh, who had been the commissioner from Virginia to South Carolina in the Nullification Crisis. In the first of two roll calls on 28 March the Senate voted, 28 to 18, that Taney's explanation for the removal of the deposits was unsatisfactory. Then in a dramatic move the Senate voted, 26 to 20, to censure the president for assuming "authority and power not conferred by the Constitution and laws" in removing the deposits. It was an unprecedented attack on the power of the executive.[15]

By this time Jackson was faring better in the House, where Polk had finally taken the offensive with a strong speech attacking the Bank on 30 December 1833. Lacking the oratorical skills of his more famous colleagues, the intense, stiff Polk contented himself with a sober review of the many charges against the Bank. He did such an effective job that his speech was quickly circulated in pamphlet form to Democratic newspapers. Then when Secretary of War Cass removed the Bank as pension agent for Revolutionary War veterans, Biddle gave Polk an issue by refusing to give up the pension records. Jackson turned the matter over to Congress, and the House sent it to the Ways and Means Committee. Polk promptly brought in a majority report blaming the Bank for the interruption in pension payments.[16]

In February 1834 a series of political and economic events also began to favor the administration. Early in the month former governor Enos T. Throop of New York reported that the shortage of money in his state had been exaggerated. In Biddle's own Philadelphia an antirecharter meeting was held on 6 February, and ten days later the Girard Bank decided not to support recharter. Biddle was particularly nettled on 26 February when Democratic governor George Wolf of Pennsylvania harshly criticized the Bank's tight-money policy. The heaviest blow against the Bank occurred on 24 March when Governor Marcy of New York asked the legislature for a bond issue to authorize the state to lend as much as $5 million to the city banks if the need arose. The legislature made the authorization, but the loan never became necessary. As these events unfolded, Biddle was shaken by advice from Clay, Webster, and Horace Binney to ease credit and to abandon his efforts for recharter.[17]

The logjam in the House finally broke when Polk got a motion passed sending Taney's message on removal to the Ways and Means Committee. Having already consulted Taney, Polk was able to bring in a majority report before the end of the month. It read much like his December speech on the transgressions of the Bank, but this time Polk abandoned the Democratic pretense that there was no panic. He boldly accused Biddle of contracting credit in order to regain the deposits and to force the recharter of the Bank.[18]

After a month of debate and only a week after the Senate had censured the president, Polk on 4 April brought four resolutions on the Bank to a vote in the House. In a dramatic show of party strength the Democrats carried all four votes by solid margins. The first, against recharter, passed 134 to 82; the second, against restoring the deposits, was more controversial and was approved by a narrower margin, 118 to 103. The last two motions were mere formalities. One, to continue the deposits in the state banks, passed, 117 to 105; the other, to hold another investigation of the Bank, was carried, 175 to 42. On hearing the news Jackson exulted, "The overthrow of the opposition . . . was a triumphant one, and puts to death, that mammouth [sic] of corruption and power, the

Bank of the United States." The president was essentially correct. When joint resolutions came over from the Senate in June denouncing Taney's reasons for removal and proposing the restoration of the deposits, the House voted to lay them on the table. A month later the directors of the Bank began to abandon the policy of contraction.[19]

Encouraged by the news from the House, Jackson reacted swiftly and angrily against the censure of the Senate. He called on Taney, Kendall, and the new attorney general, Benjamin F. Butler, to prepare a "Protest," which would show that the Senate, not the president, had usurped power. He reminded Andrew Jackson, Jr., that it had been "a corrupt and venal senate that overturned the liberty of Rome before ever Cezar [sic] reached her gates."[20]

Jackson's Protest, which went to the Senate on 15 April, started with Benton's argument that the Senate had usurped the House's power of impeachment. "Without notice, unheard, and untried," the president said, "I find myself charged on the records of the Senate." He then made a strong case for the power of the president to remove public officers and to provide for the custody of public money. "Every species of property," he claimed, except that used to support Congress or the judiciary, was "in charge of officers appointed by the President, responsible to him, and removable at his will." The Protest was a bolder assertion of executive power than Jackson's statement in the Bank veto message.[21]

Jackson was taken aback by the angry reaction in the Senate. George Poindexter called the Protest a "miserable tirade," never to be placed in the Senate Journal. Fearful that he might have overstated his case, Jackson turned to Van Buren, and the master of caution advised him to take the unusual step of sending an explanatory note to the Senate. It was almost a retraction. Nothing in the Protest, the president explained, was intended to deny "the power and right of the legislative department to provide by law for the custody, safe-keeping, and disposition of the public money and property of the United States." The executive had no right to deal with the public money unless empowered to do so by an act of Congress. The president who wrote this conciliatory note was far from the self-confident dictator that his enemies were calling him. The note, however, failed to mollify the Senate, which voted 23 to 16 not to place the Protest in the Journal.[22]

Jackson's continued weakness in the Senate kept him from getting major appointments confirmed. Early in the session, the Senate rejected Jackson's nominations for government directors of the Bank—a key test because these directors had been feeding the administration damning information about the Bank. When Jackson stubbornly nominated the same men in May 1834, they were soundly rejected, 30 to 11, and Jackson had to make less controversial nominations. Worried by the prospect of further rejections, Jackson held back a number of other important nominations until late in the session. After the vote on censure on 28 March, Webster taunted the administration, pointing out that Secretary of State McLane, Secretary of the Treasury Taney, and Attorney General Butler had not been confirmed even though each had held office for many months. When Butler and Taney were finally nominated in June, Butler was confirmed but the controversial Taney was rejected, 28 to 18. Since McLane, who had again lost his influence with Jackson, had already resigned as secretary of state, Jackson either had to make several hasty appointments before Congress adjourned or run the risk of further alienating the Senate by making more recess appointments. He chose the conciliatory course, nominating John Forsyth as secretary of state, Levi Woodbury as secretary of the Treasury, and Mahlon Dickerson to replace Woodbury as secretary of the navy. Unlike the cabinet shake-up in 1831, this one had been forced on the president by the Senate. Having established its authority, the Senate quickly confirmed all three.

Jackson was also outmaneuvered in three other votes, the first being that for Speaker of the House, when Stevenson finally resigned on 2 June to be named minister to Great Britain. Throughout the winter James K. Polk and John Bell of Tennessee, both longtime supporters of Jackson, had engaged in complex maneuvers to win the position. Polk, who had the support of Van Buren, Kendall, and Blair, was the administration favorite, but Bell, who was moving away from Jackson, had strong support from the old Tennessee clique of Eaton and Lewis as well as from members of the opposition. Faced with a close fight, the president's advisers secretly decided to support Polk but coyly passed the word that the administration could not decide between him and Bell. The growing opposition party, made up of National Republicans, nullifiers, and recalcitrant Democrats, also used deception, putting forward the nullifier Richard Wilde of Georgia but being ready to shift to Bell or to Polk, once they knew which one was not the administration favorite.

By the seventh ballot Polk had 83 votes and Bell 76 of the 112 needed for election, and the opposition had to decide which of the two it preferred. Since Polk had had a record of sympathizing with states' rights, the nullifiers were prepared to abandon Wilde for him, provided he was not the administration candidate. When Bell began to move ahead on the eighth ballot and the word was relayed to the Senate floor, Sen. Willie Mangum, who had deserted the Democrats, noted a flicker of disappointment on the face of Van Buren. Mangum quickly warned the nullifiers in the House that Polk was the administration favorite, and they turned to Bell, putting him over the top. Jackson, who had prepared a big party to celebrate Polk's election, was dismayed. The next day Patrick, the president's doorkeeper, warned visitors to go away because the president was "in a miserable bad humor."[23]

Jackson was just as disappointed by two votes in the upper house. After having insisted that Stevenson resign as Speaker before he could be considered as minister to Great Britain, the Senate then rejected him, 23 to 22. Finally, two days before adjournment, the Senate selected George Poindexter president pro-tempore, an obvious insult to Jackson, who could not abide the Mississippian. The administration had never had much luck in the selection of presidents pro-tempore: Samuel Smith, 1829–31, had supported the Bank; Littleton W. Tazewell, 1831–32, had condemned rotation in office; Hugh Lawson White, 1832–33, had appointed an antiadministration select committee on the tariff; and now, "Old Poins." Jackson also had to face the fact that Blair had still not been elected printer by either house.

As Congress drew to a close at the end of June, it was obvious that the panic was over. Whether it had been brought on by Biddle or by Jackson still remains a question, but it now appears that it was far less severe than the alarmist letters, speeches, and memorials at the time proclaimed. There were, to be sure, good reasons for the gloomy protests. Interest rates and bankruptcies rose, and employment and real estate values fell. Yet the actual panic was relatively brief and mild. Few runs on banks occurred, and banks did not refuse to redeem their notes in specie. Despite the claims of the memorials Biddle's contraction and the removal of the deposits did not cause any decline in the supply of money. In many instances state banks took up the slack. The total of loans and deposits for banks in Massachusetts, Rhode Island, New York, and Pennsylvania, for example, increased during the panic, rising from $61 million in fall 1833 to $63 million a year later. Wholesale prices, furthermore, fell only 13 percent in the six months between October 1833 and April 1834 and then started up again. This drop was modest compared to the drop of 31 percent over the first six months in the Panic of 1837.[24]

A major reason for the mildness was a sudden net importation of about $16 million in gold and silver from abroad during the fiscal year 1834, an enormous amount compared to an annual average of only $1 million for the previous decade. Part of the influx was caused by the rise in interest rates during the panic, which encouraged foreign investment in the United States; but most of it would have occurred anyway because of a steady surplus of American imports over exports that began in Jackson's first term. Europeans reinvested so much of their profits in American internal improvements that large stocks of gold and silver flowed into the United States. About $5 million of this specie went into the Bank and $10 million into the state banks, offsetting the removal of the deposits and Biddle's contraction. If Biddle and Jackson had not sounded so warlike and unyielding, the panic might have been even milder. In all likelihood businessmen and bankers were so frightened by the rhetoric that they adopted a wait-and-see attitude and refused to commit funds until the smoke had cleared. To that extent Biddle and Jackson were responsible for the panic.[25]

Jackson had won the test of wills, for the failure of Congress to restore the deposits or to recharter the Bank during the Panic session marked the beginning of the end of the Bank as a powerful political and economic force. By September the Bank had ended its restrictions on credit. When its federal charter finally expired in 1836, it was rechartered with the title of the Bank of the United States of Pennsylvania, but it had none of the influence of the old Bank. No longer fearing the Bank and encouraged by the return of prosperity, state banks expanded their loans, setting off a boom that lasted until the end of Jackson's presidency.

The political results of the Bank War and the panic proved to be long lasting, for the bitter struggle had finally brought two-party politics to Congress. Democrats had been forced to support Jackson and to oppose the Bank; their opponents had become so angry at the president's "executive usurpation" that they began to unite and call themselves Whigs. A confused congressional party structure, which had found room for nullifiers and Anti-Masons as well as for National Republicans and Democrats, began to turn into a two-party system of Democrats and Whigs. Although the new labels were not immediately adopted by all participants, the party lineups were far more distinct than in the past.[26]

The many roll calls during the session reveal the steady stabilizing of party lines. This was particularly apparent in six votes in the Senate: two relating to the nomination of the government directors of the Bank, and one each on the censure resolution, the resolution condemning Taney's report, the resolution against Jackson's Protest, and Taney's nomination. In these six votes seventeen Democrats voted consistently for the party position, and twenty-seven members of the opposition voted consistently the other way. The only waverers were John P. King of Georgia, a Democrat, and William Hendricks of Indiana, John Black of Mississippi, and Gabriel Moore of Alabama, who had once been Democrats.[27]

The same regularity can be seen in the voting in the House. In one study of selected House roll calls, it was found that party voting shot up dramatically in the 1833–34 session. Before that time, during Jackson's first term, on the average only 34 percent of the Jacksonians voted as a bloc at least 80 percent of the time, and only 42 percent of the National Republicans. During the Panic session, however, party voting rose to 71 percent for the Democrats and 63 percent for the National Republicans. The high degree of regularity was particularly apparent in the votes on the Bank. Only 6 of 127 Democrats voted in favor of rechartering the Bank, and only 6 of 80 members of the opposition voted against it. Compare the Democratic regularity with the voting on rechartering the Bank in 1832 when twenty-nine Democrats had bolted from their party. In the Pennsylvania delegation, where it had been dangerous to vote against the Bank, only one Democrat bolted in 1834 compared with fourteen in 1832.

The voting revealed how well defined and how well organized the parties had become in Congress. The administration had such accurate lists of party affiliation that it was able to predict the outcome of each vote on the Bank with surprising accuracy. Blair predicted in the *Globe* that the margin against rechartering the Bank would be fifty (it was fifty-two) and against restoring the deposits between sixteen and twenty (it was fifteen). From this point on both Whigs and Democrats prepared systematically for each session of Congress.[28]

Contributing to this new party regularity was the doctrine of instructions. According to the doctrine, the state legislatures had the power to "instruct" United States senators, whom they had elected, to vote a certain way on key issues. They could also "request" congressmen to do the same but not "instruct," because the congressmen were elected by the people. Senators would be obliged to resign if they could not follow these instructions. Instructions from state legislatures concerning the Bank began to appear in Congress during the fight over recharter. The legislature of Pennsylvania, under Bank influence, instructed Sen. George M. Dallas to vote in favor of recharter, and the New York legislature, under the sway of the Albany Regency, instructed Sen. Charles E. Dudley to vote against recharter. Both men complied with the instructions. During the Panic session the legislatures of a number of states instructed their senators to support the president and to oppose the Bank. When many of them ignored the instructions and voted to censure Jackson for removing the deposits, he was outraged. Three days after the vote, the *Globe* attacked opposition senators Sprague of Maine, Frelinghuysen and Southard of New Jersey, Ewing of Ohio, Bell of New Hampshire, Mangum of North Carolina, Black of Alabama, and Poindexter of Mississippi for violating their instructions. Jackson himself cited the first four in his Protest. If the four senators had voted as instructed, he pointed out, the censure resolution would not have passed.[29]

The party spirit shown in congressional voting and legislative instructions was part of a nationwide increase in partisanship. At both the state and local level Jackson's enemies were beginning to consolidate into the Whig party. The term "Whig" was first used in 1833 by states'-rights advocates in South Carolina and Georgia, who attacked "King Andrew" just as the Whigs in Great Britain had fought King George III during the Revolutionary War era. The first well-organized state Whig parties sprang up in 1834 in New York, Massachusetts, and New Jersey in the North and in Virginia, North Carolina, and Kentucky in the South. At the core of the new party were the National Republicans, who stood behind Clay's American System. Large numbers of Anti-Masons such as William H. Seward of New York and Thaddeus Stevens of Pennsylvania also fell in line. They were joined by humanitarian reformers such as antislavery and temperance advocates.[30]

The Whigs also took advantage of defections from the Democratic coalition, generally from the South. The first to leave were the nullifiers of South Carolina and other Calhoun men such as George Poindexter who found their way into the Whig party. Calhoun himself later joined them. John M. Berrien and John Branch bolted after being forced out of the cabinet. Dissatisfied Old Republicans, mostly Virginians such as Littleton W. Tazewell, John Tyler, and John Floyd, followed as the gap between Jackson and the Old Dominion widened. The nomination of Van Buren for vice-president cost the allegiance of other southerners, and the battle over nullification forced out still more. The removal of the deposits drove out Willie Mangum and, in time, John H. Eaton.

Social and economic issues forced out numbers of northerners as well. Jackson's Indian and Sabbatarian policies alienated Quakers and other evangelical reformers in Pennsylvania, New Jersey, western New York, and Ohio. Twenty-eight of the Democrats who voted to recharter the Bank, mostly northerners, had left the party by 1836. Many other northerners, especially prosperous businessmen and bankers, deserted because of the Bank War or because of Jackson's hard-money policies. Congressman William Stanbery of Ohio was typical of Jacksonians from the Northwest who left because of the internal-improvement vetoes. A substantial number of Democrats from both North and South became Whigs because they could not stomach the president's autocratic ways.[31]

In the long run the Democrats benefited from these defections, for the coalition had been too broad to be effective. Isaac Hill's *New-Hampshire Patriot*, one of the earliest and most partisan Democratic newspapers, recognized this problem during the campaign of 1832 when "amalgamators" in the party began to support Clay. The *Patriot* recommended getting rid of such people, saying, "Our party is too large already." Within the broad coalition expectations had been too great: Carolinians expected lower tariffs, Pennsylvanians higher tariffs; westerners cheap land, slave owners protection for their peculiar institution; and so it went. The defections helped transform the coalition into a more sharply focused, more spirited political party. The change could be seen as the party pulled together during the Panic session. The chief beneficiaries were agrarians such as Kendall and Benton, but commercial-minded Democrats such as Marcy and Cass remained an important element in the leadership of the party.[32]

In the short run, however, the rise of the Whigs was damaging to the Democrats. In April 1834 they were put on the defensive in New York City when Whigs attacked Governor Marcy's proposal to lend $5 million to the city banks. On the eve of the election Van Buren, whose presidential hopes were threatened, admitted that he and other party members were all "on tiptoe." The New Yorker had offered to bet Clay a suit of clothes that the Democrats would carry the city and was fortunate that Clay turned him down, for the Whigs won the council and almost unseated Democratic mayor Cornelius Lawrence. After the election, Clay introduced the term "Whig" to the Senate by boasting that the "patriotic whigs" had triumphed in New York. At the same time the Democrats lost control of the Virginia legislature to a Whig combination of states' righters and supporters of Clay. James Love of the Whigs was able to write in May that New York and Virginia were deserting the Democrats. The rout continued in the spring and summer as the Democrats lost in Connecticut, Virginia, Louisiana, Indiana, and Illinois, states that they had carried in the previous election.[33]

With his party's future in doubt, Jackson kept close track of state and national politics as he traveled to Tennessee in the summer. After learning that the Whigs were buying up all available copies of the *Globe* in southwestern Virginia, he sent back orders for Blair to distribute more. On arriving at the Hermitage on 5 August, he was encouraged by letters from Van Buren and Lewis with hopeful reports from the key states of Ohio, Pennsylvania, and New York. Soon after settling in, he attended a session of the Tennessee constitutional convention at Nashville and discovered that John McLean was trying to set up a newspaper to promote his perennial presidential aspirations. Jackson also warned Van Buren of other efforts to head him off in 1836. The president was confident, however, that if the Democrats carried Ohio and New York in the fall, all the maneuvering would cease. By the time Jackson left the Hermitage in early September he could write optimistically, "Our political horizon is quite clear here, and auspicious omens all over the country to the north, and to the south." On the eve of the crucial fall elections, Jackson was much more involved in party politics than he had been during his first term.[34]

The fall results were gratifying, as Democrats, aided by the return of prosperity, won a number of important elections. Late in October Van Buren sent the cheering news that Pennsylvania, New Jersey, and Georgia had done "nobly." Then came the exciting report from Ohio that Democratic wheelhorse John Lucas had been reelected governor, though the legislature had gone to the Whigs. Most important, Governor Marcy won a great victory in New York, defeating the young William H. Seward by a wide margin. The outcome in New York City, which had been so disappointing in April, was "astonish[ing]." Large bets had been placed. The Whigs, who expected to win and appeared to be ahead on the second day, had cannon and refreshments ready. When the Democrats were declared victorious, there was great "gloom" at the Whig headquarters as the party members quietly put out the lights.[35]

With their victories in fall 1834 the Democrats brought to a successful conclusion a twelve-month odyssey in which they had fought their way through a series of potential disasters—the panic, the stalemate in the House, the censure of Jackson by the Senate, the rise of the Whig party, and the state defeats in the spring and summer. In the process they had once and for all defeated the Bank and had seen the economy recover from the panic. More important, they had emerged from it all with a stronger party.

11

★ ★ ★ ★ ★

A VIOLENT DEMOCRACY

In summer 1834 the nation emerged from the panic only to find itself in the midst of another crisis—an outbreak of rioting—brought on by the same economic and social changes that were already dividing America in 1829. During Jackson's first five years in office these changes had multiplied, causing divisions over jobs, religion, race, and slavery to widen and social disorders to grow.[1]

The year 1834 was particularly traumatic because it was marked by a sharp shift in the economy. The financial panic of that year brought about the first break in almost a decade of economic growth and put many people out of work. When the economy resumed its upward trend later in the year, a boom developed, causing a sudden inflation in prices and a corresponding reduction in real wages that made it difficult for workers to feed their families. Between 1834 and 1837 wholesale prices climbed 50 percent and retail prices even more, an increase unparalleled since the War of 1812.[2]

These sudden, highly charged developments only accelerated the breakdown of American institutions that had caused so much anxiety at the end of the 1820s. The power of the church, the bar, the family, and other long-established institutions had withered away under the pressure of the expansion, pluralism, and individualism that accompanied the market revolution. The decline in these old institutions led to a determined search for new ones to restore the lost sense of order. In 1834 several movements were well under way, including the new party system and the evangelical movement, both of which pioneered in organizing masses of people. The emergence of the Democratic and Whig parties and the increase in partisanship during the Panic session of Congress gave evidence of the rise of the new system of politics. The vigor of the Sabbatarian, temperance, and Christian missionary societies reflected the power of the evangelical revival. With its "benevolent empire" of voluntary groups the evangelical movement provided what one historian has called the institutional "equivalent of an established church."[3]

The battle over slavery provoked conflicting institutional responses in the South and the North. In the South the last serious debates on emancipation were held in the Maryland and Virginia legislatures in 1831 and 1832. When they had ended, the South began to move—though not as suddenly or completely as once thought—toward the closed society of the 1850s. Thomas R. Dew laid out some of the arguments in defense of slavery in his summary of the Virginia debates, which he published in 1832. Fearful of more Nat Turners, slave owners and local officials began to set up systems of patrols and passes that restricted the slaves' mobility.[4]

Northerners, meanwhile, were creating antislavery institutions. In 1832 William Lloyd Garrison published a pamphlet attacking the African Colonization movement and led seventy-two abolitionists in founding the New England Anti-Slavery Society. Encouraged by Garrison's success, abolitionists from New England and the Middle Atlantic states met in Philadelphia on 4 December 1833, two days after the opening of the Panic session of Congress, and founded the American Anti-Slavery Society. Within two years the new society boasted over a thousand chapters and was beginning to distribute abolitionist pamphlets in the South.[5]

The rise of a new laboring class also created problems that demanded new institutional responses. One such response arose from the evangelical revival when it came to manufacturing cities and towns such as Rochester, New York. In the 1820s flour-milling and trade along the Erie Canal had made Rochester the fastest growing city in the United States. They had also brought to the city a large crowd of unruly free workers, uncontrolled by the old institutions of family or the craft system. No longer living under the same roof with their families or their master craftsmen, the workers caroused, failed to observe the Sabbath, resisted discipline, and did shoddy work in the mills—behavior that alarmed the good citizens of Rochester, especially the employers. The swift evangelical response to the situation was not surprising, for Rochester lay in the heart of the Burned-Over District, which had given birth to so many reform movements in the past. When the local temperance and Sabbatarian societies were unable to tame the workers, the city leaders called in Charles G. Finney and his Second Great Awakening. On his arrival in winter 1830–31 businessmen, master craftsmen, professionals, and other upper- and middle-class citizens were the first to join his revival, but soon workers also began to take part. Through group prayer and public conversions Finney gradually turned the workers toward lives of godliness, sobriety, and thrift. As they became better Christians, they also became more tractable citizens and more reliable workers. In Rochester and other cities the Second Great Awakening helped ease the transition of workers from aspiring craftsmen to wage laborers.[6]

When Finney and the Second Great Awakening came to New York City in the early 1830s, they had to compete with other reformers and other institutions for the allegiance of workers in the city. A cold winter and a severe depression in early 1829 brought calls for change. The most radical demands came from Thomas Skidmore, who was about to publish his *Rights of Man to Property*. Skidmore, whose ideas were based upon the radical agrarianism of seventeenth-century England, denounced all private property and demanded an end to inheritance. The maldistribution of land, he reasoned, was responsible for the low wages, long hours, and other inequities of the new system of labor. Somewhat less radical were Robert Dale Owen's proposal for free public education and the demands of master artisans and small merchants for an end to the auction system that was flooding New York with cheap British imports.

The response was so great that the year 1829 has been called the "annus mirabilis" of radicalism in the city. On 19 October 5,000 artisans, journeymen, and ordinary workers met at Military Hall, New York, nominated candidates for the state legislature, and endorsed a platform. In the preamble, written by Skidmore, the workers set as their goal a world in which all persons would enjoy "an equal amount of property" when they reached "the age of maturity." In the list of demands that followed, the workers took a stand against the auction system, private commercial banks, and imprisonment for debt. Taken as a whole, it would be the most radical labor statement in America for years to come. The movement, however, was short-lived. Several workingmen were elected to the assembly in the November election, but a month later the movement was taken over by more moderate elements, who rejected the agrarian ideas of Skidmore. They formed a Workingmen's party, which ran badly in 1830 and soon fell apart.

In 1833 the workers mounted another effort when representatives from nine trades formed the General Trades' Union. Instead of pursuing the goals of reformers such as Skidmore and Owen, the trade unionists organized dozens of craft unions and carried out a series of strikes. Aided by the sudden drop in real wages, the General Trades' Union grew so rapidly that by 1836 it had enrolled two-thirds of all the workers in Manhattan. Between 1833 and 1836 trade unionists and other workers throughout the Northeast and as far west as Cincinnati took part in as many as 200 strikes.[7]

By 1834 this combination of new institutions and abrupt social and economic changes created an unstable situation, out of which flared at least a hundred riots over the next three years, the greatest wave of violence since the era of the American Revolution. As two generations of Adamses were quick to point out, the violence seemed to threaten old American institutions that were already under attack. Dismayed by the New York City election riot that April, Charles Francis Adams confessed that his "faith in a democratic government" was weakening. A few months later John Quincy Adams, frightened by the rioting that summer, declared flatly that his "hopes of the long continuance" of the Union were "extinct."[8]

The most common violence occurred in labor riots, often on canals and railroads. Although low wages and poor working conditions led to most of the outbreaks, ethnic animosities sometimes contributed, usually in clashes between Irish factions or between natives and Irish. The New York City election riot, for example, which began as a political and economic battle over the Bank, became an ethnic-religious struggle between Irish Catholic Democrats and their American-born Protestant opponents.

Starting in summer 1834, the spread of the American Anti-Slavery Society provoked antiabolitionist and antiblack riots in Pennsylvania, New York, and New England. New York was a particular target because so many of the antislavery chapters were located in the state. The riot in New York City in early July 1834 became so violent that six churches and sixty other buildings were destroyed. Philip Hone, who dubbed this the "riot year" in New York, mourned that "insubordination to the laws" was everywhere. When the English abolitionist George Thompson arrived in New York City in September, antiabolitionists, who resented the intrusion of a foreign agitator, drove him and his family out of their boardinghouse, and the next summer mobs in Lynn, Massachusetts, and Concord, New Hampshire, attacked him with stones and eggs. The antiabolitionist riots continued through 1835 and into 1836, the most prominent one occurring in Boston, where William Lloyd Garrison almost lost his life.[9]

Meanwhile dozens of other riots reflected a wide range of grievances and anxieties. Nativist fears, which had surfaced in the canal and railroad riots, led to other attacks against the Irish in Boston, New York, Philadelphia, and Buffalo. A mob of poor Protestant laborers burned the

Ursuline convent in Charlestown, Massachusetts, in August 1834, forcing the nuns into the streets at midnight. More bizarre were riots against prostitutes in Irville, New York, and gamblers in Vicksburg, Mississippi. The violence led many people to believe that the market revolution was destroying the old republican order.[10]

Some of the violence involved Jackson himself. With the panic at its worst and Jackson under censure from the Senate in 1834, the rumor spread of a conspiracy in Baltimore to raise 5,000 soldiers to *"destroy"* the president. When warned of the danger, Jackson increased the tension by threatening to hang all 5,000 "as high as Haman." The president also began to receive death threats. In February a curt note arrived that began, "Damn your old soul, remove them deposits back again, and recharter the Bank, or you will certainly be shot in less than two weeks, and that by myself!!!" Other threats came in April and October.[11]

Death drew closer on 30 January 1835 when Jackson walked out onto the east portico of the Capitol after attending the funeral of Congressman Warren R. Davis of Mississippi. As the president leaned on the arm of Levi Woodbury and received the cheers of the waiting crowds, an unemployed house painter named Richard Lawrence pushed up to within eight feet and drew a pistol. When the pistol misfired with an audible click, he drew a second one, which also misfired. The Old Hero, as combative as ever, raised his walking cane and started toward his assailant, only to be restrained by Woodbury. Jackson's life had been spared because the percussion caps exploded but failed to ignite the powder—perhaps because of dampness. Had the president been killed that day, in the midst of the many riots, more might now be made of the connection between Andrew Jackson and the wave of violence.

Jackson and his administration responded to this violence and the new institutions in ways that reveal much about the man and his presidency. The Jacksonians clearly deplored the uprisings and sought to control them, but in so doing they sometimes let partisanship get in the way and even at times resorted to force themselves. Jackson, who seemed to revel in combat, often responded in his own unbridled manner. Lunging after Lawrence, the president had shouted, "Let me alone! Let me alone! I know where this came from." Jackson was referring to his archenemy, George Poindexter, whom he charged with arranging the attempt on his life. The president's backers soon secured affidavits from two local laborers that they had seen Lawrence entering Poindexter's house a few days before the attempt. The *Globe* supported the accusation and even suggested that Poindexter had threatened the president. If Poindexter was not responsible, the *Globe* thought it highly likely that Lawrence had been stimulated by speeches "depict[ing] the president as a Caesar." Blair mentioned specifically a speech by Calhoun just two days before the event.

Equally partisan, opposition leaders accused the Democrats of staging the affair in order to elicit sympathy for the president. They claimed that Blair had published copies of death threats against the president for the same reason. One writer in the *United States Telegraph* even signed his letter "Pisistratus," after the Athenian tyrant who had blamed his enemies for self-inflicted wounds. When a Senate committee investigated, it found no evidence against Poindexter. After a brief trial a few weeks later, the court declared Lawrence not guilty by reason of insanity, a decision that effectively refuted the partisan charges on both sides. Nonetheless, Democratic newspapers continued to blame Poindexter and other senators. The entire affair was reminiscent of the incident two years earlier when Robert Randolph had assaulted Jackson, for in each episode Jackson and others had been quick to detect a conspiracy. Each episode also demonstrated the growing partisanship of the era and the widespread assumption that political parties would resort to violence.[12]

During this period of riots and other forms of violence the Jackson administration was drawn into contact with the growing American labor movement. In *The Age of Jackson* Arthur M. Schlesinger, Jr., introduces the concept that the ideas of Jacksonian Democracy emerged in response to the needs of urban workers. He cites the writings of eastern intellectuals such as Theodore Sedgwick of Massachusetts and the rhetoric of Jackson himself. In his Bank veto message Jackson appealed to the "humble members of society" and attacked the "exclusive privileges" of the commercial and financial aristocracy. During the panic he offered a similar message, assuring the "mechanics" of Philadelphia that he was "sensible" to "the sufferings and wants of all classes of his fellow citizens." The *Globe* announced that year that Jackson offered the "Mark of Reform" on behalf of the "working men" against the aristocracy and the "monied power."[13]

Jackson also appealed to labor with his ardent support of hard money, especially as prices began to rise in 1834. He believed that the increasing use of paper money hurt the laboring classes because they depended upon bank notes under twenty dollars, which could easily be manipulated by the bankers. Remembering the gold and silver coins that had predominated in the simpler economy of his boyhood, he began a campaign to ban the circulation of small notes. In summer 1834 he offered a toast in favor of hard money at a session of the Tennessee constitutional convention. "Gold and silver coinage," he proclaimed, "can cover and protect the labor of our country without the aid of a national bank." In his annual message in 1835 he warned that "fluctuations" in the value of paper money "render[ed] uncertain the rewards of labor." Jackson's crusade against the Bank and in favor of hard money enabled Democrats to do well in the poor wards of New York City in 1834.[14]

Jackson's statements in behalf of labor, however, should not be used to demonstrate that he and his party were the defenders of the working class. The word "labor," first of all, had a much broader meaning in the 1830s than it does today, embracing many occupations that would not now be considered labor. Jackson aimed his Bank veto broadly at "the farmers, mechanics, and laborers." Even the radical labor leader George Henry Evans included grocers, teachers, and farmers as "workers." When Jackson spoke of labor, he was not referring specifically to factory workers and day laborers but to the members of what he considered the American producing classes as contrasted to the nonproducing financial and commercial classes. In his mind the latter—not the producers—were reaping the rewards of the market revolution.[15]

In dealing directly with labor problems, the Democrats seldom sided with the workers. A good example is found in the Chesapeake and Ohio Canal riot in January 1834, a riot in which Jackson had a personal interest since John H. Eaton was president of the canal company. The riot was brought on by low pay and efforts by Irish laborers from Cork to keep out competing workers from Longford. Sharp fighting between the two groups left half-a-dozen men dead and work at a standstill. Alarmed at the fighting and the rise of vigilante groups, the Maryland legislature passed a resolution on 28 January asking the federal government for military support. Jackson immediately ordered the secretary of war to "put down the riotous assembly" by sending in "at least two companies of regulars." In so doing he became the first president to send troops to suppress a riot in a situation in which he was not enforcing a federal law. The troops not only stopped the fighting but strengthened the company's hand by staying on the scene for several months. Eaton admitted candidly that the presence of the troops made it easier to dismiss workers who had been involved in the riot. Jackson had appealed to labor by attacking the Bank, but in the Chesapeake and Ohio strike he showed that he "favored combinations of labor [no] more than combinations of capital." By thus siding with management, he demonstrated none of the sympathy for workers that some writers have attributed to him.[16]

The following year creditors in Baltimore who had lost money through the speculations of Thomas Ellicott at the start of the panic grew restless when they despaired of getting their money back. The protests of the creditors, many of whom were workers, soon led to mob violence in August 1835, which was eventually suppressed by troops called out by the mayor of the city. It might have been expected that Roger B.

Taney, who had been embarrassed by his friend's speculations, would have sympathized with the suffering workers. Instead, he was more concerned that "the tone of society" had so "sadly changed in the last two years" that there was a growing tendency toward "mobs and . . . violence in opposition to the civil authority." He wrote several letters applauding the use of force in putting down "the Mob cabal," calling the crowd a "parcel of ruffians." Like his chief, Taney favored law and order at the expense of workers.[17]

Democrats were given another opportunity to support the workers when a branch of the party in New York City broke with the regular Democrats at Tammany Hall over labor issues. By supporting the ten-hour workday, hard money, and the end of state banking monopolies, these so-called "radicals" enlisted the backing of many of the workers. After the radicals gained control of a party meeting on 29 October 1835, the conservatives left in a body and turned out the gaslights. The radicals promptly lit candles with matches, called locofocos, went on with the meeting, and were henceforth known as Locofocos. If Jackson had wished to show his support for workers, he could have backed the Locofocos. Instead, the Jackson administration denounced them for their "spirit of agrarianism" and took federal printing away from their organ, the *New York Post*.[18]

The next spring a general strike in New York City called by the General Trades' Union brought Democratic mayor Cornelius Lawrence face to face with the workers. Lawrence had owed his election in 1834 in part to the union, which had supported him with a workers' rally. Despite this debt, however, the Democratic mayor turned against the workers by calling out units of the state militia, which marched outside the city hall. Frightened by this show of force, many of the strikers went back to work.[19]

A government policy change at the Philadelphia Navy Yard that same year has been used to show that Jackson had the interests of the workers at heart. Amos Kendall reported in August 1836 that the head of the yard was unable to get workers—even immigrants—to work more than twelve hours a day, primarily because the other employers in the city had given in to that limit. Pointing out that public servants in Washington considered even ten hours a day "a hardship," Kendall urged Jackson to establish the twelve-hour day in the navy yard. Although Jackson carried out the suggestion, his acceptance of a twelve-hour day in order to keep workers when they were scarce is hardly evidence that the president was backing workers.[20]

After the appearance of *The Age of Jackson* a lively debate ensued over the question of whether urban workers voted for Jackson, the results of which were inconclusive. Although workers in New York City had maintained close ties with the Jackson organization for several years, they revolted against it in 1829 by forming the Workingmen's movement. After the movement collapsed, many of them returned to the fold and voted for Jackson but not with enough regularity to support the Jackson wage-earner thesis. In Boston the working-class wards voted steadily against the Old Hero, although his support was stronger in those wards than it was in the more affluent wards. Even when the vote for Jackson went up in 1832 in Boston, the gain in the workers' wards did not match the increase outside of Boston. The workers in Philadelphia also gave more votes to the opposition than to the Jacksonians.[21]

Perhaps the best example of Jackson's low level of concern for urban workers emerges from his visit to the textile mills at Lowell in 1833, just as the wave of riots and strikes was getting under way. After reviewing a procession of over 4,000 workers, most of them women, he toured one of the mills, showing great interest in the new technology. He said later that the mills "were perfect" and that "nothing in the world could exceed them." According to reports he asked many questions about the machinery but only one—concerning wages—about the condition of the workers.[22]

The Democrats showed equal unwillingness to support abolitionism. Jackson continued to own slaves both in Washington and at the Hermitage while he was president, and he was surrounded by past or present slaveholders such as Kendall, Blair, and Taney. Among the party rank and file not only southern Democrats but northerners as well were hostile to abolitionism, believing that it threatened to split their party and the Union. In New Hampshire, for example, the Democratic *Dover Gazette* dubbed abolitionists the "deluded fanatics of hypocritical philanthropy," and Democrats in Barnstead declared that the "pathetic appeals" of the abolitionists were "sapping the foundation" of American liberty. Many northern Democrats were openly racist, none more so than United States Attorney John Parker Hale of the Granite State. Hale, who later became an antislavery senator, heckled an abolitionist speaker in 1835 by calling slaves "Beasts in Human Shape." The antiabolitionist bias of the Democrats was so pronounced that many historians have accused the party of being consciously proslavery. Revisionists, however, have argued that northern Democrats opposed abolition "not because they liked slavery, but because they loved the Union more." A third interpretation seems more likely. During Jackson's second term the demands of party had grown so strong that Democrats would oppose almost any obstacle to party unity. With a difficult election expected in 1836 to elect Jackson's successor, northern Democrats opposed abolitionism in order to preserve their party, which would need southern votes. As Democrats became more and more proparty, they felt obliged to become more antiabolitionist and thus more proslavery.[23]

When the American Anti-Slavery Society began to mail abolitionist tracts into the South in 1835, southern Democrats pleaded that something had to be done. Secretary of State John Forsyth told Van Buren that officials were showing too much "tolerance [toward] the wretches scattering fire-brands" and called for a "little more mob discipline of the white incendiaries." He concluded, "A portion of the magician's skill is required in this matter be assured and the sooner you set the imps to work the better." Lt. Gov. Peter V. Daniel wrote that Virginians were angry at these efforts "to bring the whites to a level with the blacks" and wanted Van Buren to stop the "bombs and torpedoes" being sent South.[24]

Jackson and Kendall took advantage of the first opportunity to show their sympathies. On 30 July southerners burned hundreds of abolitionist pamphlets, which had arrived at the post office in Charleston, South Carolina. When asked for a policy, Kendall, who had recently become postmaster general, advised postmasters to "hand out none of the papers." Jackson endorsed the policy, saying that he regretted that abolitionists were trying "to stir up amongst the South the horrors of a servile war."[25]

Other prominent Democrats also showed their colors. Gov. William L. Marcy presided over an antiabolitionist meeting in Albany, and Sen. Isaac Hill addressed another in Concord, New Hampshire. The position of the Democrats was made most clear in fall 1835 when an antislavery convention was planned for Utica, New York. Thomas Ritchie wrote in the *Richmond Enquirer* that Utica had "to choose between two courses." Would Utica "enjoy the honor of repelling the disunionists & fanatics from her gates" or "be degraded" by being hospitable to abolitionism? Under pressure from Van Buren and his Albany Regency, Utica chose the former course. A mob led by Democratic congressman Samuel Beardsley disrupted the convention and assaulted the nearby offices of the abolitionist *Oneida Standard and Democrat,* scattering its type outside the building. Later, Silas Wright boasted in the Senate about the riot, and Marcy defended the rioters in his annual message, saying that they had been forced to act in order to prevent the abolitionists from "excit[ing] insurrection and rebellion in a sister state."[26]

When Congress convened in December 1835, Jackson used his annual message to take a further stand against abolitionism. Denouncing the "wicked attempts" to appeal to the "passions of the slaves," he called on Congress to pass a law prohibiting the circulation of such "incendiary publications." For a supposedly states'-rights, egalitarian president such a proposal for the use of federal power to interfere with freedom of speech was extraordinary. A strange ally, John C. Calhoun, saved Jackson from the consequences of his proposal. When a bill carrying out Jackson's proposals was brought before the Senate, Calhoun said that he could not support such an extension of federal authority. If the federal government was given the power to censor antislavery publications, it might later be given the power to do away with slavery. The bill soon died. In its place Calhoun offered a bill that would allow postmasters to intercept any literature that state laws prohibited. Van Buren was forced to take a position on this bill when Calhoun maneuvered a tie vote on whether to pass his bill for a third reading. Now a candidate for president, Van Buren wooed southern support by voting yea yet suffered no northern backlash, for on 8 June 1836 the bill was defeated, 25 to 19.

While the postal bills were being debated in the Senate, Democrats in both houses were facing the more serious question of how to deal with the many antislavery petitions that were pouring into Congress. The opponents of slavery were following the example of the Sabbatarians and the defenders of the Indians, who had flooded Congress with petitions. Abandoning their efforts to send pamphlets into the South, abolitionists now decided to use petitions to prompt Congress to do away with slavery in the District of Columbia. In the past the House had dealt with similar petitions by tabling them or by burying them in committee. On 18 December 1835 Congressman James Hammond of South Carolina went one step further when he proposed that the House refuse to receive the petitions. Hammond, who had played a major role in the Nullification Crisis, was still only twenty-eight and a freshman member of Congress. His motion touched off a fierce debate in both houses over how to deal with the antislavery petitions.

Since the debate threatened to split the party, Democrats scrambled to find a compromise solution that would satisfy both northerners and southerners. When Calhoun introduced Hammond's proposal in the Senate, James Buchanan of Pennsylvania, who would later become a proslavery president, proposed that the Senate receive the petitions but then immediately reject them. After intense controversy Buchanan's proposal won out. The final vote on 14 March 1836 was 34 to 6, with all northern Democrats voting yea. Democrats in the House looked to Van Buren for a compromise. After prodding from the New Yorker, another South Carolina nullifier, Henry L. Pinckney, proposed that the House receive all antislavery petitions and then immediately table them. As the bill neared the final vote, Georgia congressman George W. Owens confidently called on Van Buren to *"rally the Northern clans."* The bill passed on 26 May by a vote of 117 to 68, with 79 percent of northern Democrats supporting it.[27]

The so-called Gag Rule Controversy had broad implications. At the time the passing of the two gag rules was the capstone of the Democratic policy of opposing abolitionism. Since Hammond and Pinckney were well-known nullifiers, northerners came to believe that a conspiracy had been formed to protect slavery. This concept of a "Slave Conspiracy" played an important part in the coming of the Civil War.

The search for new institutions and the accompanying riots and controversies provides further evidence that Jackson's second term had become a watershed in American history. As they faced the crisis, the Democrats took their stand. Although Jackson appealed to laborers and won the votes of many workers, especially after the Bank veto, he and his administration were more devoted to planters and farmers than to urban workers. Jacksonians were more interested in maintaining party regularity than in helping workers. They also put the interests of the party over the concerns of the abolitionists. In choosing between reform and stability, they chose the latter.

12

★ ★ ★ ★ ★

DEMOCRATIC ADMINISTRATION

Amid the rioting and the new institutions Jackson's presidency had reached a turning point. For over five years he and his men had been fighting a series of campaigns to preserve their ideal of a virtuous agrarian republic. At times they had waged economic battles against the inroads of the new economy, at other times political battles against Jackson's enemies, as in the Peggy Eaton affair. In the process they had often based their emerging party identity on their war against the Bank, an institution that symbolized the social and economic changes brought about by the market revolution. Some victories, perhaps temporary, had been won. They had blocked any overall system of internal improvements and after a long fight had put the Bank in retreat. Jackson had vetoed Clay's distribution bill. The tariff had supposedly been settled for the next eight years. By January 1835 the national debt, another symbol of the unfortunate results of the market revolution, would be completely wiped out. The president, moreover, finally had a cabinet he could trust, and prosperity was returning.

Jackson now felt ready to join those who were building new institutions. Despite the riots, the Old Hero wrote hopefully in his annual message to Congress in December 1834:

> Free from public debt, at peace with all the world, . . . the present may be hailed as the epoch in our history the most favorable for the settlement of those principles in our domestic policy which shall be

best calculated to give stability to our Republic and secure the bless-
ings of freedom to our citizens.

During the next two years he would seek an elusive stability through
constructive efforts to regulate the banks, reorganize the administration
of the government, and reshape the political system.[1]

Jackson began by calling on Congress to pass a bill regulating the
federal funds in the banks receiving federal deposits. The legislation was
needed because banking had expanded so rapidly and because the Bank
was no longer in control. The number of banks had almost doubled since
Jackson took office and the amount of bank notes had risen almost as
fast.[2] As the power of the Bank declined, the importance of the deposit
banks increased proportionately. Between October and December 1833
the number of deposit banks had increased from seven to twenty-two, a
number comparable with the twenty-five branches of the Bank. In January 1834 these twenty-two deposit banks held $9 million in federal de-
posits; the amount at the Bank had dropped to $4 million. Two years
later the deposit banks would have $28 million in federal deposits, and
the Bank, soon to go out of business, would have none. Over the same
period the notes of the deposit banks rose from $8 million (8 percent of
the national total) to $26 million (19 percent).[3]

With such a large share of the nation's funds the deposit banks had
the same power to dominate American banking that had formerly been
held by the Bank. It was up to the government now to take over the
responsibility for regulation that had formerly been exercised by Biddle.
With so much money involved and so much power over the economy,
the opportunities were great. But the decline of the Bank and the need to
build a new system also posed serious problems for the Democrats.
After five years of attacking the old system, they now had to build and
defend one of their own. They would be subject to the same sort of
attacks that they had been leveling against the Bank. Instead of accusing
Biddle of usurping power, they had to answer criticism that the system
gave Jackson, already being called a Caesar, too much executive power.
Without the Bank as an enemy the Democrats were also deprived of their
old party image, which had been based on the Bank War.

Faced with the responsibility for this growing system, the Democrats
made a major effort to see that it was properly run, even though they had
to violate their states'-rights instincts by increasing central power. Soon
after the removal of the deposits Secretary of the Treasury Taney established a set of strict policies to ensure that the banks were operated
conservatively and kept under control. Levi Woodbury continued the
policies when he succeeded Taney in July 1834. The two secretaries de-

manded semimonthly reports and required security bonds. They ordered the banks to go slowly in lending money. On the assumption that a few banks could be controlled more easily than many, they limited the number of banks allowed into the system. Between December 1833 and June 1836 the number rose only from twenty-two to thirty-three. Even though New York, for example, was a wealthy state with a strong Democratic party, it had to be content with its three original deposit banks until 1835.[4]

Needing an agent to carry out these principles, Taney turned first to Kendall, who was not interested, and then considered Reuben M. Whitney. Scholars who have viewed Jacksonians as opportunistic businessmen have sometimes cited Whitney, who had served both Jackson and Biddle, to prove their point. When Taney and then Woodbury hesitated at appointing him, the matter was turned over to Jackson, who suggested, with an eye toward economy, that they let the member banks hire the agent. The persistent Whitney then sent the banks an unsigned letter of recommendation from someone in Washington "high in the confidence of the Executive," who turned out to be Kendall. After twenty of the banks hired Whitney, he provided a number of services such as warning them in advance of government demands for funds. Within strict limits he did an effective job and did not play the role of spoilsman that has been associated with him.[5]

In addition to regulating the system, the president and other Democrats sought to restrain it further by relying more on gold and silver than on paper bank notes. This policy blended nicely with Jackson's long-held hard-money views. In his 1834 annual message, he had urged the states to "prohibit the issue of all small notes," thus ensuring a currency that would not be "liable to fluctuations." Hard money, especially gold, also offered the Democrats a way to solve their problem of identity; the *Globe* asserted, "*Gold* and *paper* will become badges of parties." Benton, often called "Old Bullion," had suggested this sort of party identification in his speech against the Bank in 1830. Instead of attacking the Bank as in the past, the *Globe* now championed hard money and the regulation of state banks.[6]

The administration made its first bid for legislation to carry out these goals at the end of the Panic session in spring 1834. James K. Polk offered a bill based on Taney's conservative policies, which passed the House, 112 to 90, but was not acted upon in the Senate. The administration was more successful with a coinage bill designed to encourage the circulation of gold by increasing the coinage ratio of gold to silver from 15:1 to 16:1. Since the new ratio overvalued gold, producers of the metal would be more inclined to have it coined into money than to sell it on the open market, thus increasing the amount of gold coins in circulation.

The bill passed both houses and was signed by the president on 28 June 1834, two days before the end of the session.

In February 1835 Polk brought his bank-regulating bill back to the House. Among its regulations, the bill made it illegal for United States receivers to accept the notes of banks that issued notes under five dollars and required deposit banks to hold specie equal to one-fourth of their notes in circulation. The reaction to these proposals revealed a split between agrarian-minded hard-money Democrats and commercial-minded paper-money Democrats. The split became so great that the administration was forced to keep its banking bill in committee until March, when Congress adjourned.

With no banking legislation, Jackson had to depend on Secretary Woodbury to maintain the desired stability. Woodbury continued to add as few new banks to the system as possible and forced those already in the system to keep the ultra-hard-money ratio of one to three between specie and circulation. The secretary also devised an arrangement in which the three original deposit banks in New York City could control the state banks in their vicinity in much the same way that the branches of the Bank had operated. The three banks kept balances in the state banks and on order from the Treasury could demand specie, thus forcing the banks to cut back credit. Woodbury strengthened the policy by keeping one-third of all government deposits in the three New York City banks. To encourage an increase in hard money Woodbury issued his own order in March 1835 prohibiting deposit banks from accepting bank notes under five dollars in payment of money owed the government.

An increase in government revenues after the panic made it even more difficult to keep the system in check. In the second half of 1834 Woodbury had coped with the problem by using the surplus to pay off the national debt rather than putting it into the deposit banks, where it would have increased the amount of notes in circulation. As a result United States Treasury deposits in the banks remained at about $9 million throughout the year, and the ratio of specie to note circulation stayed at about two to five, even higher than Woodbury's goal of one to three.

The retirement of the debt in January 1835 and a growing land boom destroyed this stable situation. Annual receipts from the sale of public lands, which had never exceeded $5 million before, suddenly rose to $15 million in 1835 and $25 million in 1836. Hezekiah Niles and Martin Van Buren both believed that the people were "mad." The prosperity that Jackson had bragged about in 1834 had grown into a frightening "rage for speculation," which threatened the cautious banking policy of the administration. During the year 1835 federal deposits in the banks tripled, rising to $28 million by February 1836. Woodbury did what he could to restrain the deposit banks by increasing their specie requirements. As a result the outstanding loans and discounts of the deposit banks, which stood at $47 million in January 1835, rose only to $65 million by February 1836.[7]

In winter 1835–36 the Democrats continued to have difficulty dealing with these monetary problems. As in the previous Congress, hard-money Democrats, who sought stability, wanted to regulate the banks and restrict the issue of small bank notes without increasing the number of deposit banks. Paper-money Democrats accepted the first two goals, but since they sought expansion they insisted on increasing the number of deposit banks. The pressure on the government to give more banks access to federal deposits increased with the speculation in land. There was also the question of what to do about the surplus. For hard-money Democrats the growing surplus, which threatened stability, had become almost as dangerous as the old federal debt. The paper-money Democrats welcomed the surplus, which they proposed to distribute to the states in order to extend the economic boom.

The administration wanted a bill that provided for hard money and bank regulation but knew that it would have to deal with the surplus. Silas Wright introduced a banking bill in the Senate that embodied most of the provisions of Polk's earlier bill and, to avoid distribution, added a provision for the government to invest the surplus in state internal-improvement projects. This plan failed when a combination of Whigs and paper-money Democrats bypassed the bill by referring all banking proposals to a select committee in which the administration was in the minority. The committee produced a bill that called for banking regulation and limits on small bank notes but added distribution and more than doubled the number of deposit banks. There would be at least one deposit bank in every state and territory. The surplus was to be distributed to the states in three annual installments, starting 1 January 1837. Technically, the distribution was a "loan," but no one expected it to be repaid. Badly outmaneuvered, the administration tried feebly to separate the regulation and the distribution parts of the bill, but in June 1836 the bill passed both houses still intact.

Although Jackson disliked the deposit-distribution bill and had Taney prepare a veto, he finally decided to let it pass. He had been warned that if he vetoed the bill, the enormous surplus would be placed in the existing thirty-three deposit banks, allowing the opposition to accuse him of favoring those "pets" at the expense of other banks and the states. Without a presidential veto the hard-money Democrats were left with a law that they found unsatisfactory. Although the law restricted paper money and increased government regulation, the rise in the number of deposit banks from thirty-three to eighty-one made the system unwieldy and harder to control. The additional banks, furthermore, failed to provide as much Democratic patronage as expected because the administration was all too often forced to select a Whig bank in communities where no Democratic bank was available.

As the land boom continued during Jackson's last year in office, it became more and more difficult to hold the banking system in check. Treasury deposits, which had totaled $28 million in February 1836, rose to $45 million by November, five times what they had been in January 1834. It was no longer possible to hold back the loans and discounts at the deposit banks, which almost doubled during the year, reaching $115 million. Much of this federal money went into the very internal improvements that the Old Republicans in the party deplored. And so Jackson's banking policy—like his tariff, internal-improvement, and nullification policies—ended in a compromise.[8]

Worried about the land boom, Jackson sought some way to restrain the economy on his own. On 11 July 1836 he had Woodbury issue a Treasury order, known as the Specie Circular, directing government officials to accept only gold or silver in payment for public lands. With some exceptions the circular went into effect almost immediately. The president said that he was responding to complaints about speculation and insisted that it was his "duty" to "preserve to the labor of our country a solvent uniform specie currency." Taney congratulated Jackson in October, saying that by insisting on hard money in payment for land the Specie Circular had saved many western investors from bankruptcy. Jackson continued to boast about his circular in his annual message.[9]

Scholars, far less generous, have often attacked the Specie Circular, blaming it for the Panic of 1837, which began just as Jackson left office and was followed by a severe depression that lasted until 1843. According to the tradition, Jackson first created the boom by destroying the Bank and replacing it with dozens of "pet wildcat" banks, which lent their funds too recklessly. When the Specie Circular cut off the paper money fueling the boom, bankruptcies and failures followed. In addition the circular overtaxed the large deposit banks in the East by forcing them to send specie west. On 1 January 1837, the first installment of the distribution brought on the panic by draining more funds from the eastern banks.

A more careful study of the data suggests that Jackson does not deserve so much blame. Woodbury kept a heavy hand on the deposit banks and used the three original deposit banks in New York City to control some of the state banks. During most of the land boom there were no more than thirty-three deposit banks, and most of them did not lend recklessly. The Specie Circular did reduce the sale of land, but neither it nor the distribution of the surplus brought about any large-scale transfers of money. The transfers the first year barely reached $20 million, a trivial amount in a gross national product of $1.5 billion.[10]

The Panic of 1837 resulted more from international economic forces than from specific policies of the Jackson administration. Starting in 1831 American imports from Great Britain exceeded exports every year but one, reaching a cumulative deficit of $48 million by the time Jackson left office. The British reinvested so much of this in American projects that there was a large outflow of gold and silver from Great Britain to the United States. Some of this specie had helped ease the Panic of 1834. Alarmed in 1836 by the loss of gold and silver, the Bank of England began to insist on specie from American banks and raised interest rates in order to force British bankers to cut back their American investments. The Panic of 1837 began when American banking houses could not repay their notes to British banks.

But the Jackson administration should not get off scot-free. Beginning with his annual message of 1829, Jackson's rhetoric, first against the Bank, then in support of hard money, and later denouncing the land boom and speculation, had convinced financiers in England and America that Jackson and his successor would do all they could to restrain loans and to contract the currency. With that in mind, bankers and businessmen held back, reduced their loans, and thus helped bring on the panic.[11]

While the Democrats were building the deposit-bank system, they faced constant criticism. One of the major charges was that they used the deposit banks as part of a spoils system by placing the deposits exclusively in Democratic pet banks. As applied to the selection of deposit banks the first few years, the charge was accurate. In making his choices, Kendall pointed out that the deposits would go to "politically friendly" banks but that if a city had no such bank, then banks operated by "opposition men whose feelings [were] liberal," that is, men who would cooperate, would get the funds. Democrats ran five of the seven original banks. The two exceptions, the Girard Bank in Philadelphia and the Bank of America in New York City, were selected because they had close ties with key Democrats. The administration could even be charged with conflict of interest, for Taney had $5,000 invested in the Union Bank of Maryland and Reuben M. Whitney was the brother-in-law of William D. Lewis, the cashier of the Girard Bank in Philadelphia. In adding banks between 1833 and 1836, the administration continued to depend almost exclusively on Democratic banks or banks with Democratic connections.

Political influence was not always applied, however. When Van Buren was asked about a fourth bank for New York City, he made no recommendation, and his Regency bank, the Mechanics' and Farmers' Bank of Albany, had to wait almost two years before it was added to the system and even then received only a small amount of money. Partisanship often took a back seat in 1836 when the system was expanded, and the Democrats frequently had to turn to Whig banks.[12]

There was also the related charge that weak Democratic banks were chosen and that as a group the deposit banks were badly, often recklessly, run. This criticism was unfair. In New York City, for example, the Bank of America was chosen over a more Democratic bank because it was such a strong, well-run institution. The vast majority of the deposit banks were well run, the notorious exception being the Union Bank of Maryland, which so embarrassed Taney during the early stages of deposit removal. Two of the early banks—the Girard Bank and the Bank of Louisville—had to give up their deposits during the panic, but the former took back the deposits five months later and the latter was promptly replaced by the Louisville Savings Bank. Aside from these three unstable situations, the new deposit banks held up well during the panic.[13]

Opponents also claimed that the deposit-bank system was only temporary and that the administration would soon replace it with its own national bank, probably in New York City. According to Biddle, the Jacksonians tried to break the Bank in order to "build up one of their own." It became a battle, he said, between "Van Buren's Government Bank and the present institution," between "Wall St and Chestnut St," between "a Faro Bank and a National Bank." The opposition echoed these charges, and they were revived in the 1950s by the scholars who depicted the Jacksonians as aspiring businessmen.[14]

Some Jacksonians did show an interest in "*a*" national bank, as they put it, to replace "*the*" Bank. In 1831 David Henshaw, the Jacksonian boss of Massachusetts, drew up a petition for a bank capitalized at $50 million, and a group of New York capitalists made a similar proposal. Neither Jackson nor Van Buren repudiated these plans before the election of 1832, hoping to win the support of investors who wanted some form of national bank. Jackson had referred sympathetically to Henshaw's petition in his Bank veto message.[15]

During the panic winter renewed interest grew in a new national bank. In early January 1834, when money was short in New York City, Van Buren received word that plans were afoot to send a memorial to Congress for a bank, but the plan was abandoned. At the same time, however, other New Yorkers, including members of the Albany Regency, were exchanging letters about a national bank. At the end of the month a memorial for such a bank, signed by 6,000 citizens in New York City, was sent to Washington. Concerned that such repeated activity would revive the view that he was the evil genius behind the Bank War, Van Buren called on Regencyman Silas Wright to stand up in the Senate and demonstrate that no New York conspiracy existed. In the speech of his career on 30 January 1834 Wright announced that for constitutional reasons he opposed any bank set up by Congress, "whether to be located at Philadelphia, or New York, or any where else." The stocky, red-faced Wright was so earnest that the Senate fell silent. The speech and the end of the panic settled the matter, and the Democrats never chartered their own national bank.[16]

In the same message in which he asked Congress to regulate the deposit banks, Jackson also called attention to a number of administrative problems. Such attention was needed, for reform was long overdue. In the first forty years of the republic there had been only two formal reorganizations within the government. In 1815 Congress established a Board of Naval Commissioners to provide the secretary of the navy with professional help. Two years later the auditing system of the Treasury Department was overhauled. By 1829 the vast technological and economic changes of the era made wholesale reform imperative. On taking office Jackson showed his awareness of the need by asking each cabinet member to report "what offices [could] be dispensed with, and what improvements made in the economy and dispatch of business." In his first annual message he made almost a dozen suggestions to Congress for administrative reform, with emphasis on the military services and the State Department.[17]

Since Congress reacted slowly and Jackson was preoccupied with political battles, reform was first limited largely to the military. In the War Department Jackson reorganized the Quartermaster's Office, which had been badly run for years, and added an office to cope with the heavy demand for pensions. At the same time he transferred the Coast Survey to the Treasury Department and showed his hostility to federal roads and canals by doing away with the Board of Engineers for Internal Improvements. He was less successful in reforming the navy. In an effort to improve morale, he proposed abolishing the Board of Naval Commissioners, which had usurped power from the secretary of the navy, and setting up a new organization with bureau chiefs responsible to the secretary. Jackson's proposals were not carried out for many years, and his plan to merge the Marine Corps with the army was never implemented.[18]

By 1834 the great expansion of transportation, communication, and land sales had rendered the Post Office, the General Land Office, and the Patent Office almost completely outmoded. Jackson's primary concern was for the Post Office, the size and importance of which, he wrote, "seem to demand its reorganization." During his presidency the Post Office had grown rapidly. The number of local offices, which had risen from 3,000 in 1815 to 8,000 when he took office, had now reached 11,000; since 1827 the amount of postage revenue collected had more than doubled. Despite the resistance of easterners, Jackson had extended the service far into the West; by 1834 New Orleans and Cincinnati ranked among the top ten cities in postage. The expenditures of the Post Office in 1834 totaled $3 million, about one-eighth of the federal budget, providing great opportunities for patronage. Under Jackson the number of clerks in the postmaster general's office alone had climbed from thirty-eight to ninety. The contractors, who did much of the department's work, supported families numbering 20,000 men, women, and children.[19]

Recognizing the importance of the Post Office, Jackson wisely granted his postmaster general, William T. Barry, cabinet status. Unfortunately, however, Barry was incapable of running the department efficiently. A lazy and sloppy record keeper, he made agreements on slips of paper without dates, was slow in collecting money, and never once balanced his books. Under his slovenly regime the mail was arriving later than ever, and more postmasters were opening the letters of rival politicians. Barry and his chief clerk, Obadiah Brown, who handled most of the contracts, were accustomed to receiving gifts from contractors. To ensure maximum profits the contractors devised imaginative ways of making bids. They made bids by private understandings, would bid more than once by using "straw" bidders, and often made "improved" bids, offering services beyond those called for, thus cutting off all competition. Sometimes a bidder would make a low bid, win the contract, and then make a later contract at a much higher sum of money for only slightly increased services. In 1831 James Reeside agreed to deliver mail on two routes in Pennsylvania for $275 a year but was allowed to "improve" the service several times until he was receiving $7,500 a year for routes on which the postage collected was only $600. When Congress began to investigate in 1834, the Post Office suddenly reduced Reeside's fee to $505.[20]

Complaints were numerous. Abraham Bradley, who had been removed as assistant postmaster general in 1829, sent a sharp letter to the *Daily National Intelligencer* in 1834 accusing Barry of incompetence. The eccentric but observant publisher Anne Royall asked whether anything could be done to rid the country of "the cruel oppression" of the Post Office. Another journalist, Hezekiah Niles, protested bitterly against the partisanship and poor service. Painfully loyal to Barry, Jackson might have ignored all this had it not been for the growing deficit. Barry had run up a deficit every year but one, including a shortfall of $313,000 in

1833, and the accumulated deficit had reached at least $500,000 by 1834. As Jackson looked ahead to the crucial elections in the fall, he was warned that he had better make changes in the Post Office or the party would lose.[21]

The situation had become so bad that Barry had considered resigning in February 1834 but had held on. After receiving a critical report in June from a Senate committee dominated by the opposition, Jackson told Barry that he must cut back the number of postal routes. Barry could only reply that he hoped to find savings of $75,000 in the South. Old and ill and desperately trying to get his facts together, Barry lost his head when opposition congressman William Cost Johnson of Maryland called the Post Office "corrupt from head to foot." Barry challenged Johnson, who was twenty-two years younger, to a duel and was saved only when his son, John Barry, intervened and settled the affair with honor. When devastating reports were brought in by another Whig committee in the Senate and a Democratic committee in the House, Jackson had to act. Chief Clerk Obadiah Brown resigned early in 1835, and Barry prepared to follow suit as soon as Jackson could find a replacement.[22]

To replace Barry, Jackson had his mind set on Amos Kendall, who was as good an administrator as he was an adviser. The president pressed him, saying that many men could handle the job, but "*I know you will.*" Mired in debt, Kendall was ready for a new position that would pay more than his fourth auditorship in the Treasury Department. After the failure of his paper mill in the West, he had already asked the president to appoint him subagent for the removal of the Chickasaw Indians, and when that did not come about had considered moving into private business. Kendall accepted the president's offer, but owing to his reputation and the party's weakness in the Senate, he insisted that he not be appointed until after the end of the short session of Congress in March, knowing that otherwise he would be rejected. On 8 April 1835 Barry resigned and was appointed minister to Spain, only to die in Liverpool en route to his new post. Kendall became postmaster general on 1 May, the last of many changes in Jackson's cabinet.[23]

Kendall took over like a whirlwind, moving about the office from desk to desk, examining books and asking countless questions. He made himself familiar with the mail routes and several times brushed aside clumsy efforts at bribery. To get rid of the debt he first set a moratorium on the payment of all obligations incurred before the current quarter and used incoming funds to pay off current debts. By the middle of August all current debts and those for the previous quarter had been settled, and a surplus was on hand to pay off the old debts. The department was solvent by October.

During the following winter and spring, Kendall worked with the new Democratic Congress, fashioning the Post Office Act of 2 July 1836. For the first time the Post Office became a department of the government. Its former financial autonomy was ended; it paid revenues into the Treasury and received appropriations from Congress. An additional auditor in the Treasury Department was provided to keep check on the postal accounts. The postmaster general also lost some of his authority, as his power to appoint the postmasters in the largest offices was transferred to the president. The act carried special provisions to ensure that there would be no more straw bids or improved contracts.

In reorganizing the department further, Kendall deserves most of the credit even though he did draw on innovations already proposed by Barry and John McLean. Kendall's major change was to abandon a cumbersome North-South division of responsibilities and to replace it with a system based on functions. He divided the duties of the department among four offices: an appointments office to set up post offices, a contract office, an inspection office, and the postmaster general's office, which handled miscellaneous functions. And to prevent corruption he designed an intricate system of checks and balances.[24]

While Jackson was depending on Kendall to clean up the Post Office, he was also looking for a successor to Elijah Hayward, the heavy-drinking commissioner of the General Land Office, who was having difficulty dealing with the land boom. After averaging only 2 million acres a year during Jackson's first term, sales of public land jumped to 4 million a year in 1833 and 1834 and a startling 12.5 million acres in 1835. Black Hawk's defeat in 1832 cleared the way for the rise of Chicago and a rush of settlers into the Michigan and Wisconsin territories. "The whole world is bent for Rock River," crowed the *Green-Bay Intelligencer* in Wisconsin, and Harriet Martineau wrote that she had never seen "a busier place than Chicago." A hamlet of only a few huts in 1830, Chicago had grown to 3,400 by 1834, and speculation in city lots reached a peak in 1836. The removal of the southern tribes led to an even greater boom in the Southwest. As Joseph G. Baldwin recalled in *Flush Times of Alabama and Mississippi*, "Emigrants came flocking from all quarters of the Union."[25]

Hayward's main problem was a shortage of help. When he took over as commissioner in 1830, he inherited an office of only eighteen clerks, who even then faced a steadily increasing backlog of land patents. During Hayword's first full year in office, his staff issued 25,000 patents, but the backlog continued to grow. The problem was complicated because the president was required to sign each patent, and even though Jackson signed 10,000 in one six-month stretch, he also fell further behind. The office was so far in arrears that it was said that 5,500 patentees would die before they took possession of their land.

On 2 March 1833, while the compromise bills were ending the Nullification Crisis, Congress took pity on the Old Hero with a bill providing a clerk to sign the president's name on land patents. But even though reports of corruption increased the need for reform, little more was done until September 1835, when Jackson replaced Hayward with former senator Ethan Allen Brown, also of Ohio. Like Kendall, who benefited from the ideas of his predecessors, Brown proposed a tough new system of inspections and checks and balances that had already been suggested by Hayward. Brown also offered a new plan of organization calling for a commissioner's office, five bureaus, and a large new recorder's office, with a total of almost a hundred clerks, accountants, bookkeepers, examiners, package sealers, and draftsmen. With a push from Jackson and Churchill C. Cambreleng on the House Ways and Means Committee the bill creating this new bureaucracy was passed into law on 4 July 1836, just two days after the Post Office Act.[26]

The third office in need of a shake-up in 1835 was the Patent Office, a bureau in the State Department. As American technology grew and inventions multiplied after the War of 1812, the Patent Office began to suffer from a growing workload, inadequate staffing, cramped quarters, and outmoded procedures for granting patents. William Thornton, superintendent of patents between 1802 and 1828, ran the office as intelligently and as efficiently as he could but had been unable to get any assistance from Congress. The need for reform became even more evident when the next two replacements let the office fall into the same sort of disarray that had beset the Post Office. In spring 1835, as he was appointing Kendall, Jackson also named the competent Henry Ellsworth of Connecticut to head the Patent Office. Congress then reorganized the office at the same time that it was dealing with the Post Office and the Land Office. The Patent Office Act of 1836 provided the legislative basis for a new office, still in the State Department, and gave Ellsworth the new title of commissioner of patents. The act also increased the staff, rationalized office procedures, and in general provided a patent system adequate for the new age of manufacturing.[27]

Similar changes were also taking place throughout the rest of the State Department, where officials were overwhelmed by an increase of domestic as well as foreign responsibilities. In his first annual message, Jackson had asked Congress to create a new Home Department to relieve the State Department of its domestic duties. After being rebuffed, he moved ahead on his own and by 1836 had divided the department into eight bureaus, with only two—diplomatic and consular—dealing with foreign affairs. Other bureaus dealt with home affairs such as archives, library, and copyrights. In 1836 Jackson elevated the chief clerk of the department to a position much like that of a twentieth-century undersecretary. Secretary of State John Forsyth added a modern bureaucratic touch by publishing a list of the duties and responsibilities of each position in the department.[28]

A new bureaucracy was also needed to deal with Indian removal, which had been handled by a bureau in the War Department. To replace the bureau Congress in 1834 established the Office of Indian Affairs under a commissioner, adding to it the rapidly growing Indian field service, which hitherto had been entirely at the discretion of the president. The size of the Washington office was doubled in November 1836, when six clerks who dealt with Indian migration were transferred from the commissary general of the army to the Indian commissioner.[29]

Jackson's final reform was in the federal courts. When the Old Hero took office in 1829 the nation was operating under essentially the same federal court system that had been designed for the original thirteen states. Although the number of district courts had been gradually increased to keep up with the admission of new states, no comparable additions had been made to the appeals courts. Appeals in eighteen of the twenty-four states were heard by the seven justices of the Supreme Court, who doubled as circuit judges, each with his own circuit; but there were no such circuits covering Indiana, Illinois, Missouri, Alabama, Mississippi, and Louisiana. Almost as soon as these states entered the Union, they began to clamor for circuit courts but ran afoul of republican suspicion of federal courts. Even though Jackson shared this suspicion, he recognized the "great injustice" and called for court reform in five of his first seven annual messages. The long debate came to a close at the very end of his term when he signed the Judiciary Act of 1837, increasing the membership of the Supreme Court from seven to nine and adding two new appeals circuits for the western states.[30]

Although Jackson did not find the stability he desired, he did make a significant contribution to American government, easing the way for modern bureaucracy. In many cases his reforms were brought on more by necessity than by design. When he first took over, he introduced rotation in office by appointing hundreds of loyal friends and followers, but he let them carry out their tasks in much the same way that administrators had done ever since the days of Washington. He granted his subordinates great independence, giving authority for a department or an agency to one person, with little bureaucratic chain of command. The system was dependent on the ability and the morality of the officials, consistent with Jackson's republican faith in the virtuous individual.

With the decline of old community standards of morality and the rise of new temptations and opportunities in the new market economy, the administrative system proved inadequate. As corruption began to creep in, Woodbury, Kendall, Brown, Ellsworth, and other administrators were forced to turn to a more rationalized system with checks and balances, which became the basis for a burgeoning bureaucracy. At the same time, Jackson's haphazard rotation in office was evolving into a well-organized system of patronage. The same sort of bureaucracy was also beginning to appear in businesses as Americans experimented with new forms of economic arrangements. In seeking to return to virtuous republican ways, Jackson had opened the door to a style of organization compatible with the new free-enterprise capitalist order.[31]

In his own office, however, the Old Hero made no such bureaucratic innovations. Like every president before him, he made do without any official private secretary or any advisers specifically authorized by Congress. He got around this problem by appointing Donelson, Kendall, and Lewis to sinecures in the Treasury Department. When Donelson was in Tennessee during the Eaton affair, Jackson brought in Nicholas Trist from the State Department to be his secretary, and when Donelson resigned in 1836, he was replaced by Andrew Jackson, Jr. The president carried on a large correspondence, writing many letters himself but turning the majority over to Donelson. Jackson read incoming mail carefully, often making written comments indicating the action to be taken. Contrary to myth, he wrote well, sometimes even elegantly, and spelled no worse than many of his better-educated contemporaries. He did occasionally repeat himself, using the same identical phrases in more than one letter on a given subject. After the Maysville veto, for example, he wrote triumphantly on several occasions a version of the sentence, "It works well," and later used the same phrase to describe reactions to the Bank veto.[32]

His advisers often wrote his state papers. According to one study of eighteen major papers, Kendall had a hand in ten, Van Buren and Donelson in five each, and Taney in four. But the president hovered over the authors and often corrected important phrases. In preparing the Nullification Proclamation, for example, he sent Livingston's supposedly final draft back for additional alterations and rejected a last-minute proposal by Lewis. On other occasions, however, such as his statement to the cabinet on deposit removal, he left the final draft in the hands of advisers. A man of strong opinions, he nonetheless respected differing views from his subordinates. The most extreme case occurred when Jackson allowed Louis McLane to publish his report supporting the Bank even though the president was preparing to oppose recharter. He frequently tolerated opposing views from Van Buren. At times Jackson's tolerance was brought on by necessity, as in 1833 when he went to great pains to keep McLane and Cass in the cabinet even though they opposed removal of the deposits.[33]

Jackson cared about details and intervened personally in many situations, often in instances involving moral behavior, that would not be handled by a modern chief executive. In August 1831 he ordered a clerk in the Patent Office dismissed because of insolvency. He refused to reappoint a certain Judge Smith of Florida because he cheated at cards. He removed Jonathan A. Findlay from office because he was "*incompitant* [*sic*] *from intemperance.*" When Leonard Parker, naval officer of Boston, protested that he had not been allowed access to complaints against him, Jackson ordered Secretary of the Treasury Woodbury to show Parker the relevant papers. Jackson interfered so often in pension cases that the commissioner of pensions had to request politely that the president forward all letters to him.[34]

In his search for stability amid the wave of riots, Jackson had created a new banking system and had overhauled much of the executive and judicial branches of the government. In his final year in office he secured congressional legislation reforming the deposit banks, the Post Office, the General Land Office, the Patent Office, the State Department, the Office of Indian Affairs, and the federal courts—more legislation than in all his previous seven years. His accomplishments were made easier by the growing strength of his party in Congress. Whether the party had become strong enough outside of Congress to elect his successor would be determined in the election of 1836.

13

★ ★ ★ ★ ★

A DEMOCRATIC VICTORY

The election of 1836 wrote the final chapter in the central theme of the Jackson presidency—the rise of the Democratic party. Although the Old Hero is better remembered for destroying the Bank and thwarting nullification, those victories proved to be more symbolic than real. The Bank was replaced by a new banking system, and nullification ultimately returned in the form of secession. Party building was more lasting. The Democratic party and the two-party politics that it produced have endured to the present. The issues, personalities, and passions of the Jackson presidency breathed life into the Democratic party and into the Whig party as well. During Jackson's eight years in office his coalition became a party, and a factional system turned into a party system.

The Jackson presidency did not, of course, create the new system singlehandedly. The new concept of political parties as a positive good evolved in state organizations such as the Albany Regency. Reform movements spawned by the Second Great Awakening introduced politicians to new techniques to stir up mass support. The petitions and memorials that flooded Washington during the Panic session were similar to those that had poured in earlier to support the Cherokees or the Sabbatarians. All the reform movements, as well as the new party system, profited greatly from the improved communication and other changes accompanying the market revolution.

A recent study of voting between 1824 and 1852 has shown the importance of the election of 1836 in the development of the two-party system. The first three presidential elections (1824–1832) were similar in

245

many respects. All three were dominated by Jackson's personality, and there was a high correlation between the Jackson vote in any one of the elections and each of the others. They were sectional elections with no national parties and a great variety of political patterns. The turnout for these elections, though far greater than in previous years, still did not match that for most gubernatorial elections. The five elections that followed (1836–1852) were different. There were no overpowering candidates, political sectionalism was greatly diminished, and the turnout of voters in presidential elections reached all-time highs that continued for half a century. A stable two-party political system had emerged, similar in most respects to the system in operation today. Some of the changes were not complete until 1840. Turnout in the election for president in 1836, for example, was still lower than in many state elections. Nonetheless, Jackson's second term and the election of 1836 in particular served as the transition from the old to the new.[1]

By 1835, when the presidential campaign got started, the Democrats were well on the way toward becoming a prototypical political party. At the head of the organization were Jackson, Van Buren, and the president's third cabinet, which was far more homogeneous sectionally and ideologically than in the past. Half the members—Secretary of the Treasury Woodbury, Attorney General Butler, and Secretary of the Navy Dickerson—came from the Northeast, and two more—Secretary of War Cass and Postmaster General Kendall—now from the West, had been raised in the Northeast. The only southerner was the Unionist secretary of state, John Forsyth of Georgia. On the agrarian-commercial spectrum they tended to hug the middle, with Kendall the most agrarian, Cass and Dickerson the most commercial. The cabinet was also more united politically than its predecessors. With the Tennessee clique, the nullifiers, and the pro-Bank men gone, and with no distractions such as the Eaton affair and McLane's quest for power, the cabinet could concentrate on reorganizing the government and on advancing the interests of Jackson and the party. The members of the cabinet had also joined together in supporting Van Buren for president.

Beyond the cabinet the party was held together by an increasingly sophisticated system of patronage that had grown out of the confusion surrounding appointments in 1829. Once indifferent to party considerations, Jackson had been won over. Patronage lay mostly in the hands of Van Buren, Blair, Kendall, who could exploit his position as postmaster general, and Secretary of the Treasury Woodbury, who could select deposit banks and control appointments to land offices, customhouses, and other positions in his department. These men controlled a system that had brought several thousand officeholders into the government.

Historians have long assumed that these new men were markedly differ-ent from the upper-class appointees of previous administrations, but at least for the highest-ranking officials, such was not the case. According to one analysis of cabinet officers, judges, diplomats, territorial gover-nors, and other "elite" officials, Jackson's appointments were not much different from those of John Adams and Thomas Jefferson. Seventy-five percent of Jackson's appointees came from the highest social class com-pared to 80 percent of those appointed by Adams and Jefferson. Ninety percent of the Jacksonians had a high-ranking occupation, almost identi-cal with the 93 percent of the earlier appointees. The 52 percent of Jack-sonians who had attended college was only slightly lower than the 57 percent for the Adams and Jefferson men.[2]

Under these elite officials were the rank and file, the best descriptions of whom came from their foremost critics, Clay and Calhoun. Clay de-scribed "an official corps . . . distributed in every village, city, and ham-let, having daily intercourse with society, and operat[ing] upon public opinion." It was, he cried, "more dangerous than a standing army." Calhoun cited the growing number of government "officers, agents, con-tractors" that made this army possible, calling particular attention to the Post Office, the deposit banks, and "the patronage incident to . . . re-moving the Indians."[3]

Since 96 percent of the federal revenues came from customs and land receipts in 1835 and 1836, the customhouses and land offices played a major role in the Democratic system of patronage. In the years since Jackson had outraged the Albany Regency by appointing Samuel Swart-wout port collector of New York, the office had gradually come under the control of the party. When Swartwout's term expired in 1838, he was replaced by Jesse Hoyt of the Regency, just before Swartwout's defalca-tion was uncovered. The party had exercised much firmer control over the port collector of New Orleans, Martin Gordon, who dispensed the patronage in Louisiana. Gordon was more honest than Swartwout but also more arrogant. When Gordon demanded the removal of District Attorney John Slidell in 1833, Jackson at first sided with the collector for party reasons. William B. Lewis considered Gordon a "true & sincere friend" of the party, and Francis P. Blair reported that Gordon had made a generous gift to the *Globe*. But a year later when Gordon caused a party defeat by antagonizing the Creoles, Jackson promptly dismissed him and returned Slidell to office.[4]

The land offices rivaled the customhouses and post offices as a source of patronage. The head of the party in Mississippi was the un-scrupulous speculator Samuel Gwin, whose appointment as land regis-ter had been confirmed by the Senate at the end of the Nullification

Crisis. The land office was also a source of Democratic patronage in Arkansas, which would enter the Union in time for the election of 1836. Before Arkansas gained statehood, Ambrose H. Sevier, the territorial delegate to Congress, appointed so many Democrats to jobs in the land office that the Little Rock *Advocate* called them "pensioners upon [his] bounty." The land office was especially important in Ohio, since Jackson's first two commissioners of the General Land Office came from that state. The party headquarters in central Indiana was in the office of Land Register James P. Drake of Indianapolis, and Deputy Surveyor Lucius Lyon played a major role in the Michigan party.[5]

By 1835 strong Democratic state organizations existed in all parts of the country. In New England leadership was still centered in New Hampshire, where Levi Woodbury had replaced Isaac Hill as the regional power broker. Democrats had also spread their regime into Maine, calling the first state party convention there in 1829. Although Massachusetts remained in opposition hands, the perennial Democratic candidate for governor, state supreme court justice Marcus Morton, had gradually closed the gap between himself and his Whig opponent. When Democratic patronage director David Henshaw collaborated too openly with Calhoun, the administration shifted patronage to Morton and George Bancroft, whose roots were outside Boston. The Democrats elected their first governor in Connecticut in 1833, but unity was marred by a struggle between party leader John M. Niles, the publisher of the *Hartford Times*, who was antibank, and a rising group of bankers, who had Woodbury's support. The growing strength of the Democrats in Massachusetts and Connecticut produced an effective two-party system in both states, in contrast to New Hampshire and Maine, where the Democrats overwhelmed their opponents.

The Democrats were also well represented in the Middle Atlantic states but were encountering stout Whig opposition. They continued to control New York throughout the Jackson presidency despite the emergence of a capable Whig party, led by Thurlow Weed, the "Wizard of the Lobby." The Whigs were strongest in the Burned-Over District along the western part of the Erie Canal, where many of their supporters were former Anti-Masons. William H. Seward, Millard Fillmore, and other Whig leaders were from this part of the state. In New Jersey the opponents of the Democrats united in August 1834 to form a state Whig party, which produced a viable two-party system. The continued strength of Anti-Masonry, however, slowed the growth of the Whigs in Pennsylvania.

In the Southeast Jackson's policies and his apparent choice of Van Buren as his successor stirred up increasing hostility, but the interplay of issues made it difficult to build a united opposition. It was not easy for nationalistic Clay supporters to work beside states'-rights Democrats, who were angry at Jackson's Nullification Proclamation. In addition Van Buren's popularity varied from state to state. In Virginia, where he was most popular, the Democrats exploited the divisions among the Whigs to regain control of the legislature in 1835. Since the Whigs were more united in North Carolina, they built a strong state party that easily rivaled the Democrats. Farther south the states'-rights issue prevented the use of the term "Whig" by the opposition.[6]

Democrats continued to control the Southwest, but here also the two-party system was beginning to appear. In Kentucky the Democratic organization built by Kendall and Blair competed on even terms with the National Republicans in 1832, winning the governor's seat but losing the presidential election. The newly formed Whig party carried the state in 1834 and maintained its superiority over the Democrats for most of the next two decades. In Mississippi an opposition party formed around Jackson's enemy George Poindexter. Louisiana—less Democratic because of its commercial location at the mouth of the Mississippi—remained in opposition hands during Jackson's first term.[7]

In the Northwest two-party politics came first to Ohio, where Democrats were well organized, but control of the state fluctuated back and forth between them and their opponents. The Democrats made good use of the convention system in Ohio. When they held a convention in Columbus in February 1835, Clay noticed that "a large majority" of the delegates were "office-holders." The Whigs held their own convention later in the year and approached the election ready to challenge the Democrats.

State politics in Illinois and Missouri remained factional until 1835, when the Democrats began to organize. Democratic county representatives met at Vandalia, Illinois, on 7 December 1835 to select presidential electors, after which they debated a resolution to nominate state and county candidates at conventions. Stephen A. Douglas, who had just arrived from the East, spoke in favor of the reform. Although the resolution failed, the Democrats continued to strengthen their party system the next year. In an address written by Douglas they pledged to unite "the friends of democracy" in order to "give effect to the popular will." Responding to protests that party innovations violated true republicanism, Douglas retorted that "the cry of 'no party'" was designed to "disarm the people, and to lull to sleep that eternal vigilance which is the price of liberty." The Missouri Democrats also held a convention in 1835 to prepare for the presidential election. In neither state, however, did the Whigs organize a state party until the election of 1840.[8]

To coordinate with the conventions the Democrats developed an effective system of committees. As early as 1827 Maj. Allan Campbell of Louisville, Kentucky, boasted that he had built a system in Louisville that connected a "Central Committee" with "Sub-Committees" in each ward and was expanding it throughout the state. Within the states, committees were used to elect delegates who then met at conventions, culminating in the national Democratic convention.[9]

The system could not have worked without a party press. By 1835 the original corps of Jacksonian editors had grown into a smooth-running network representing up to 400 newspapers. By exchanging articles they were able to present a united party front during elections and political crises. The administration subsidized the editors with contracts for public printing, and those who were also postmasters had the added advantage of the franking privilege.

Imagine the Democratic press as a wheel with the Washington *Globe* at the center and spokes going out in all directions to hundreds of party organs. A few of the most influential were the *New-Hampshire Patriot*, the *Boston Morning Post*, the *Albany Argus*, the *Richmond Enquirer*, and the *Argus of Western America*. Radiating out from many of the major newspapers were shorter spokes leading to smaller newspapers. In New Hampshire, for example, the *Patriot* in Concord received the word from the *Globe* and then passed it on to the *New Hampshire Gazette* in Portsmouth, the *New Hampshire Argus and Spectator* in Newport, and the *Democratic-Republican* in Haverhill as well as to other newspapers in Maine and Vermont.[10]

A good example of the Democratic administration's coordination of the party press, the post office, and local activists can be seen in a letter to Jackson from John B. Hogan of Fayetteville, North Carolina, in September 1835. Hogan had been asked to provide a list of North Carolina legislators who should receive copies of the *Globe* with a speech by Thomas Hart Benton calling on the Senate to expunge the censure of Jackson from its Journal. In his letter Hogan included a list of the legislators, which had been published in a North Carolina newspaper and republished in the *Globe*. Since Hogan believed the list to be inaccurate, he had marked an N by the names of those who were nullifiers, an X by those for Jackson but against expunging, and an O by those unknown to Jackson who should receive a copy. When criticized for using his franking privilege to send out the *Globes*, Jackson replied that he owed it to his constituents to show them how the resolution of censure had violated the Constitution.[11]

As the Democrats and Whigs prepared for the coming presidential election of 1836, they appealed to different types of voters. In 1828 there had been correlations with past voting, as old habits were hard to break. In states such as New Hampshire, New York, Delaware, and Maryland Federalists became National Republicans, and Jeffersonians became Jacksonians. In Kentucky former Relief party voters turned Jacksonian, the anti-Reliefers National Republican. At the same time the Jacksonian percentage of the vote was highest in the deep South and the frontier West, the National Republican vote highest in New England.

By 1836, however, the electorate had shaken the old habits and the sectionalism. Although no clear-cut pattern of rich versus poor developed, there was a tendency in states such as New Hampshire, New York, Arkansas, and Mississippi for the more prosperous folk to vote Whig, the less so Democratic. The wealthy merchants of New York, for example, were overwhelmingly Whig; the urban poor more often turned to Tammany Hall and the Democratic party. Another determinant was religion. The members of evangelical Protestant denominations—Presbyterians, Baptists, and Methodists—often voted Whig, but those of confessionalist and liturgical faiths—Lutherans, Roman Catholics, and Episcopalians—voted Democratic. This pattern was especially pronounced in the Burned-Over District of western New York, which was as Whiggish as it was evangelical. A similar pattern emerged in New Hampshire, where members of the established Congregational church voted Whig, and Freewill Baptists and other dissenters voted Democratic. An even clearer pattern, however, reflected the market economy. Growing, up-and-coming, commercial regions along major lines of transportation were Whig, but remote, upland areas with small farms and villages tended to be Democratic. In the North this pattern can be traced all the way from New Hampshire, where the seacoast and Merrimack valley regions were Whig, to New York, where the towns along the Erie Canal voted Whig, to the Whiggish prairie land along the Great Lakes, to Missouri, where the Whigs clustered along the Mississippi and Missouri rivers. In the South, upland areas with small farms were Democratic, the commercial towns and rich cotton lands Whig.

These patterns were often interrelated. It is hard to say whether well-to-do Congregationalists in Massachusetts were Whig because of their income or their faith. Irish Democratic voters were often as poor as they were Roman Catholic. Ronald P. Formisano has coined the metaphor of core and periphery to describe the relationship between the evangelicals, who occupied the core of national culture, and the confessionalists, who were in the periphery. He applied the same metaphor to the relationship between the commercial-minded Whigs in the transportation centers and the agrarian-minded Democrats in the back country. In both cases Whigs were comfortably inside, accepting change, and the Democrats uncomfortably outside, resisting the changing world.[12]

To hold their far-flung voters and state organizations together the Democrats turned increasingly to the doctrine of instructions from state legislatures to United States senators. Several legislatures had already used the process to tell senators how to vote on rechartering the Bank and on restoring the deposits. A lively debate ensued on the doctrine between Democrats, who considered it fundamental to republican institutions, and Whigs, who felt it smacked too much of political partyism. Even though Whigs had resorted to instructions in several states, including Virginia and North Carolina, they most often opposed their use. The Whig *Daily National Intelligencer* called the doctrine impractical on the grounds that state legislatures changed so rapidly that their instructions were often out of date. In addition, it claimed, the real power to instruct came from the people who elected the legislatures. The Whig *Southern Literary Messenger*, which engaged in a brisk exchange with the *Richmond Enquirer* on the subject, concluded that legislatures could advise but not instruct.

For the Democratic party the doctrine became a weapon of party discipline. In June 1834 Jackson called on Democratic state legislatures to retaliate against certain senators who had violated instructions by voting to censure him. Pointing out vindictively that their terms would expire the following March, he hoped that they would be replaced, leaving the Democrats with a "virtuous majority." When Jackson talked with Harriet Martineau in January 1835, he was happy to tell her that the state legislatures were helping make his wishes come true. During that winter Benton drew further attention to the doctrine with his Senate resolution to expunge the censure of the president. Although the resolution was tabled, it set off a series of state resolutions instructing senators to vote for expunging.

One of the first senators so instructed was former Democrat Willie Mangum of North Carolina, who had voted to censure Jackson. When told in December 1834 that the instructions were a "broad hint" for him to resign, Mangum refused, arguing that if he resigned, Gabriel Moore of Alabama and John Black of Mississippi, who had also been instructed, would feel that they must do the same. That, concluded Mangum, would give Jackson control of the Senate. After Democrats won back the Virginia legislature in 1835, they started a grassroots campaign to instruct Whig senators John Tyler and Benjamin Watkins Leigh, who had backed censure, to vote for expunging. The resolution passed both Virginia houses in February 1836. In Tennessee, however, an expunging resolution was postponed in 1835 even though Jackson himself sent a draft of a resolution to Gov. William Carroll. Resolutions also failed in Pennsylvania and Maryland.[13]

In some cases the instructions forced senators out of office. When the Virginia legislature instructed Tyler and Leigh to vote for expunging, Tyler refused and resigned in February 1836. Leigh also refused but stayed in office until July, when he also resigned. Mangum resigned in November. Neither Black nor Moore resigned in 1836, but Moore's views cost him his seat when he ran for reelection that year, and Black resigned in January 1838.

The pressure from the legislatures helped the Democrats regain control of the Senate. During Jackson's last three years in office the number of reliable Democrats in the upper house climbed from seventeen to thirty-four. Of the twenty-six senators who voted to censure Jackson in 1834, fifteen were no longer in the Senate when Jackson left office, and two more departed shortly thereafter. The seventeen were replaced by twelve Democrats and only five Whigs. Four of the new Democrats came from the new states of Arkansas and Michigan, which were admitted into the Union in 1836 and 1837. Four more came from New England, which was swinging toward the Democratic camp, and several others replaced Whigs such as Theodore Frelinghuysen, who did not run again. Three were the result of instructions, the most prominent of whom was William C. Rives, who replaced Tyler, two years after having been forced out of the Senate himself. Although legislative instructions were directly responsible for only three of the changes, the Democratic legislatures directly and indirectly played an important role in the transformation of the Senate.[14]

In the winter of 1834–35 the death of Justice William Johnson of the Supreme Court the previous summer and the resignation of Justice Gabriel Duval in January gave the Democrats a chance to test their growing strength in the Senate. Even though still a minority, they won confirmation for Congressman James M. Wayne of Georgia for one seat on 9 January, only two days after he was nominated. Wayne was a devoted Democrat—he had abandoned his quest for the Speakership a year earlier to maintain party unity—but he had also won the favor of many Whigs by supporting the Union during the Nullification Crisis. The Whigs, however, would have none of Jackson's second nominee, Roger B. Taney, whom they had previously rejected as secretary of the Treasury, and his nomination was indefinitely postponed.

The following July the number of vacancies on the Court rose to two when John Marshall died after more than thirty-four years as chief justice. When Congress reconvened in December, Jackson nominated Judge Philip P. Barbour of Virginia, who had run unsuccessfully for vice-president in 1832, and also renominated Taney—this time for chief justice. With the two parties now almost equal, the Senate gave in and confirmed both men on 15 March 1836. After seven years of battling the judiciary, Jackson had won control of the Supreme Court. When the size of the court was increased from seven to nine justices a year later, Jackson and Van Buren added two more Democrats, Judge John Catron of Tennessee and former congressman John McKinley of Alabama.

On the same day that Taney and Barbour were confirmed, the Senate also approved the nomination of Amos Kendall as postmaster general. Then the next day Andrew Stevenson, who had been rejected as minister to Great Britain two years earlier, was confirmed for that post. In addition Benton's expunging resolution crept closer to passing in June but failed when Hugh Lawson White amended the resolution so that it read to "rescind" the censure rather than to "expunge." A number of Democrats, displeased by the wording, joined the Whigs in voting it down. Jackson had anticipated the defeat but looked ahead confidently to the next session when he expected his party to have a safe majority in the Senate. The opposition in that body, he said, was *"broken & disheartened."*[15]

The Democrats also tightened their control of the lower house. At the opening of Congress in December 1835 the House chose James K. Polk for Speaker over incumbent John Bell by the strict party vote of 132 to 84. Polk had failed in June 1834 when he was the secret candidate of the administration, but this time he succeeded as the avowed candidate of the party. And Blair was elected printer for the House over Gales and Seaton of the *Intelligencer* by another party vote, 133 to 59. After five years of waiting, Blair had finally won the congressional patronage that Kendall had promised. The victories of Polk and Blair, Taney and Barbour, Kendall and Stevenson within a span of three months demonstrated the ascendancy of the Democratic party.[16]

Jackson was also determined to have the party nominate Van Buren for president and elect him in 1836. By February 1834 it was apparent that the president and much of the party machine were already behind Van Buren. Willie Mangum noted unhappily that the vice-president's campaign had progressed so well that "the discipline of the Albany school" already held Maine, New Hampshire, New York, Ohio, and Pennsylvania "in chains." Van Buren had some anxiety when the Whigs carried New York City in the spring, but the smashing Democratic victory in the New York state election in the fall made him the obvious candidate. Jackson wanted to hold an early national convention to rally the party behind his candidate.[17]

The Whigs, on the other hand, lacked the organization to hold a convention and nominate a party candidate. The great triumvirate proved to be more a liability than an asset as each man sought the nomination for himself. Of the three only Webster succeeded, and even he lacked broad party support. Black Daniel was nominated by the Massachusetts Whigs in January 1835, but he was unable to win the backing of Anti-Masons or other northern Whigs. William Henry Harrison, however, who had defeated the Indians at Tippecanoe in 1811, was nominated by both the Anti-Masons and the Whigs of Pennsylvania in December 1835 and was soon accepted as the candidate to oppose Van Buren in the North.

The mantle as the southern opposition candidate had already fallen on Sen. Hugh Lawson White of Tennessee. After Bell had defeated Polk to become Speaker in June 1834, the battle was continued in Tennessee during the summer. Although the organizations of both men supported Jackson, only the Polk faction would back Van Buren. Seeking an alternative, the Bell faction turned to White, whose name was already being mentioned. In August Bell tried unsuccessfully to get the Tennessee constitutional convention to nominate the senator. He finally succeeded in December when a majority of the Tennessee congressional delegation asked White to run for president. Only Polk, Felix Grundy, and Cave Johnson of the delegation refused to back the nomination. Shortly afterward White was officially nominated by the Alabama legislature.[18]

Jackson reacted bitterly to White's nomination because he recognized it as an attack on himself. Although the delegation was responding to Van Buren's unpopularity in the South, it was also reacting to the president's Nullification Proclamation, his Force Bill, and his removal of the deposits. He realized that White had been at odds with his administration ever since he had been bypassed for secretary of war in 1829. The nomination of White was all the more pointed because it came out of Jackson's own state and revealed what had always been the case, that he had little influence in Tennessee state politics. Jackson had unsuccessfully spoken out against White's nomination while he was visiting the Hermitage in the summer. On his return that fall he told Van Buren not to worry about any "wavering" in Tennessee, but after White's nomination in December, Jackson himself began to worry. Calling White and his followers "apostates" who had placed their state in a "degraded" position, Jackson admitted that the White movement was a personal "mortification."[19]

During the next two years Jackson was as preoccupied by the White campaign as he had been by the Peggy Eaton affair. As one interested observer, Daniel Webster, noted, the president was paying unusually "close" attention to "the question between White & Van Buren." If only,

Jackson complained, he were an ordinary private citizen so that he could warn the people against White. The president was told several times that White would be hard to stop in Tennessee. After the Nashville *Banner* was taken over by the White forces, all the newspapers in the state except two were supporting him for president. Even when Polk and Donelson managed to set up an administration newspaper, the *Union*, in Nashville, the heavy drinking of its editor, Samuel H. Laughlin, reduced its effectiveness. As the state election of 1835 approached, Jackson poured copies of the *Globe* into Tennessee, but Bell spoke out against this intrusion, and in June Blair complained that he needed more help from those supporters on the scene. Despite the efforts of the administration, the Bell-White faction won the governor's seat and both houses of the legislature by wide margins in August, and pro-Jackson officeholders faced "proscription" in the president's own state.[20]

The White movement made the Democratic National Convention, held several months before the Tennessee election, all the more important as a means of solidifying support for Van Buren. With an eye toward splitting the party, the White faction had decided to boycott the convention. When the Democrats met at Baltimore on 20 May 1835, Blair, who was the president's emissary, boasted that there was a "prodigious turnout," not mentioning that Tennessee, South Carolina, Alabama, and Illinois had sent no delegates. Noting that two-thirds of the 626 delegates came from the states closest to Washington, Whigs called the meeting the "Office-holders Convention." Name-calling turned to ridicule when an unknown Tennessean by the name of Edmund Rucker was allowed to cast the state's votes, a procedure henceforth called to "Ruckerize."[21]

With no White supporters present, Van Buren was nominated unanimously for president, but there was less agreement on the vice-presidency. Early in 1835 party insiders had decided on Kentucky congressman Richard M. Johnson for the nomination, perhaps because of the influence of Blair and Kendall but more likely for broader reasons. With two of the opposition candidates—White and Harrison—from the West, the administration wanted a westerner on the ticket to balance the easterner, Van Buren. Johnson, a western slaveholder who had fought in the War of 1812, filled the bill. He even claimed the distinction of having fired the shot that killed the Indian leader Tecumseh. The Kentuckian also carried strong credentials in parts of the East because of his opposition to Sabbatarianism and his popularity among workers.[22]

Johnson was far less popular in the South, where he was scorned because of his mulatto mistress and two mulatto daughters. According to John Catron, Johnson was not only "positively unpopular" but also "affirmatively odious" in Tennessee. Catron preferred Benton or William

Carroll for vice-president. By the time of the convention the southerners had united behind William C. Rives of Virginia as an alternative. Van Buren was willing to accept Rives because he was a friend and because his nomination would restore the New York–Virginia alliance, but he deferred to Jackson and supported Johnson. Playing the role of party broker, Blair solicited votes for Johnson by explaining to all who would listen "the importance of rallying to Mr. Van Buren . . . the steady Democracy of the West." Still, the southern objections were so great that the party managers were forced to call upon Rucker to cast the fifteen Tennessee votes to ensure Johnson the two-thirds vote necessary for nomination. After the convention Van Buren paid a personal call on Rives at his Castle Hill estate in an attempt to ease the hard feelings, but even then the Old Dominion refused to support Johnson.[23]

In order to avoid divisive debate, the Democrats drew up no official party platform. Instead, they turned the task of stating the party's position over to Andrew Stevenson and a committee that included Van Buren's confidant Silas Wright. The statement, published in the summer, showed how far the Democrats had come as a party. Ignoring the candidate, the committee mentioned Van Buren only once but cited the party thirty-four times. The statement began with a skillful rationale for political parties, which bore the imprint of Wright and the Albany Regency. In a society such as theirs, "collisions of sentiment and interests" made parties "irresistible." Parties had "great public utility" because "they bring into action the greatest talents. They excite a jealousy and vigilance which insures fidelity in public functionaries. They check attempts at the usurpation of power, and thereby preserve the rights of the People." To attain these ends a national convention was indispensable.

Eager to hold as many groups as possible under the party umbrella, the committee ignored specific issues and made no class appeals. Even in a brief attack on the Bank the members of the committee used none of the egalitarian agrarian language of 1832. They relied throughout on the traditional theme of strict construction of the Constitution and balanced states' rights with respect for the Union. Drawing on the past, they mentioned Jackson fifteen times and Jefferson ten and used the term "Republican" twice as often as "Democratic." But at the same time they honored the new democracy with constant references to the rights of "the people," a term that appeared forty-eight times. Van Buren, who had pioneered in party organization, ran comfortably on this platform that balanced old-fashioned republican sentiments with new-style party politics.[24]

Jackson, too, accepted the new politics. The sentimental Old Hero, who had dismayed Van Buren in 1829 by appointing friends rather than party supporters to office, had gradually become more of a party leader. Just before the Nullification Crisis in 1832 he had shown his political awareness in two revealing letters to Van Buren. The first demonstrated how much he had learned about New York politics, as he knowledge-ably discussed the replacement of Samuel L. Gouverneur as New York City postmaster. In the second he said that because of the coming crisis in South Carolina they could not afford to pass over the South in select-ing a new secretary of the Treasury to replace Louis McLane. Unfortu-nately for Jackson, he allowed himself to be talked into appointing William J. Duane instead of a southerner.

The education of the president had continued in his second term. In 1833, while at the Rip Raps preparing to remove the deposits, he wrote that party conventions, "elected by the people themselves," offered the best means of preventing "divisions" and the only way in which "the people" could keep the election of the president "in their own hands." When Tennessee sent no delegates to the Democratic convention in 1835, he denounced the state for "repudiating the republican mode of a national convention fresh from the people." The catchy phrase "fresh from the people" became a Democratic party standby for the rest of the presidential campaign. As he had already indicated in his Protest to the Senate in 1834, Jackson had also become a staunch advocate of the use of legislative instructions. Without the doctrine, he said, "the people be-come . . . hewers of wood and drawers of water for their agents, who have become the sovereign power."

Jackson had begun to play the role of party leader. In the anxious summer of 1834, as the Whigs mounted their challenge in a number of states, Jackson kept in touch with party politics during his stay at the Hermitage. By spring 1835 he had become such a party man that he could write, "Whichever party makes the President, must give direction to his administration. . . . Only by preserving the identity of the [Demo-cratic] party [can] the original rights of the states and the people . . . be maintained." No one, he said, could "carry on this Govt. without support, and the Head of it must rely for support on the party by whose suffrages he [was] elected."[25]

Jackson's strong endorsement of party was an important part of the Democratic shift from dependence on the charisma of the Old Hero to reliance on the Democratic party, the sort of shift that the sociologist Max Weber called "the routinization of charisma." When the Whigs at-tacked the Democrats for blatant partyism, the Democrats replied that only through parties and conventions could the will of the people be expressed. Whig antipartyism, they said, was nothing more than an at-tempt to circumvent the will of the people for the good of a privileged aristocracy. In short, they transferred the charisma of the popular will from Jackson to the party. In so doing they created a new image of party based upon the will of the majority, an image well suited to an egalitarian age that produced few Jacksons and believed in the common man. Though the quintessential personal leader himself, Jackson helped bring about a political system that reduced the emphasis on personality.[26]

A strong antiparty rebuttal appeared in a series of articles in the Whig *Intelligencer* entitled "The Prospect before Us." The Democrats were accused of ushering in a new "ERA" by transforming the republic into a "Monocracy." Under the "tyranny" of the Democrats' spoils system Congress had deteriorated to the point that the members simply expressed the will of the party while the president had acquired powers greater than those of kings. In selecting Van Buren to succeed him, Jackson was only repaying him for the work of his "New York phalanx" in previous Democratic victories. The authors wondered what would have happened in 1824 if James Monroe had designated Calhoun as his successor.[27]

These antiparty views were nothing new, for the National Republicans/Whigs had often opposed the new party system that the Jacksonians/Democrats had embraced. This difference was never more apparent than in the Senate debate on Van Buren's confirmation in 1832, when Clay and Webster attacked the Little Magician for extending New York party politics to Washington and into foreign policy. Whigs were so agitated in 1835 that they prevailed upon the Senate to set up a committee to "inquire into the extent of the executive patronage" and put Calhoun at its head. In its report the committee declared that the spoils system had converted officeholders into "hungry, greedy, and subservient partisans" who had become "corrupt and supple instruments of power," undermining "the foundation of our institutions."[28]

Toward the end of the Jackson presidency and in the years that followed, the Whigs began to adopt the new system. The state elections of 1834 and the state party building in the next two years revealed their abilities. In New York Thurlow Weed, who had lost to the Jacksonians too often, openly copied the techniques of the Albany Regency. When the Whigs carried New York in 1838, even the highly principled Horace Greeley asked Weed for a share of the spoils. In 1840 Daniel Webster also stole a page from the Democratic book by making a series of demagogic partisan speeches on behalf of William Henry Harrison. The Whigs were particularly active in the South, where they often matched the campaign tactics of the Democrats.[29]

But during the Jackson presidency the Whigs lagged behind the Democrats, especially as a national party. Looking back on those years,

Horace Greeley recalled that, nationally, the Whigs had been not a real party but the "undisciplined opponents of a great party." The differences between the Democrats and the Whigs in their acceptance of party undermine the argument that the Whigs were more modern and individualistic than the tradition-minded Democrats. The Democrats did, of course, yearn for the past in their attacks on banks, paper money, and a federal system of internal improvements, but when it came to parties they led the way. And the Whigs, who decried the transformation of their country from a republic to a "Monocracy" and despaired at the decline of Congress, seem traditional on this issue.[30]

In keeping with their antiparty position, the Whigs attacked Van Buren as the archetypal politician during the election of 1836. The New Yorker, they said, considered being a politician a "*trade*" and was good at "gittin all his folks into office." In his letters under the character of Jack Downing, Whig humorist Charles A. Davis called Van Buren a "plaguy cunnin . . . master hand at trippin folks who stand in his way." According to Davy Crockett, soon to die at the Alamo, Van Buren was "all slyness"; Calhoun compared him to "the fox and the weasel." Adding to the devastating caricature was the image of Van Buren as an effeminate dandy, "laced up," according to Crockett, "in corsets, such as women in a town wear." Throughout the campaign Whig writers played on the theme that Van Buren was wholly dependent on Jackson for his nomination. One of the most popular cartoons showed the Little Magician being pulled out of the water holding on to the tail of the Old Hero's horse when the bridge collapsed as Jackson was arriving in New York on his presidential tour. The picture was false because neither Jackson nor Van Buren fell into the water that day, but the image of the sly fox dependent on the Old Hero stuck.[31]

The image of Van Buren as an opponent of slavery also dogged his campaign. The White forces used this theme in hopes of cutting into the Democratic majority in the South, where Jackson had carried all but two states in 1832. The charge lacked any substance, for Van Buren was tolerant of slavery, had once owned a slave himself, and had worked assiduously to cultivate his southern ties. Ever since coming to Washington in 1821 he had directed his energies toward forming a political party uniting New York and Virginia. He expressed his frustration to William C. Rives's wife Judith in April 1835:

> God knows I have suffered enough for my southern partialities. Since I was a boy I have been stigmatized as the apologist of southern institutions, & now, forsooth you good people will have it . . . that I am an abolitionist.[32]

These attacks on Van Buren as antislavery were largely responsible for the strong stand that the Democrats had taken against the abolitionist movement in 1835 and 1836. New York Democrats had responded vigorously to the antislavery convention in Utica in 1835 because it threatened to link Van Buren to abolitionism. The Democrats imposed the gag rule in Congress in 1836 for the same political reason. The antislavery issue was so important during the presidential campaign that it overshadowed others with far more substance. Aware that they must hold on to as much of the South as possible, Van Buren used every opportunity to show his opposition to abolitionism. In March 1836 he published a letter stating that Congress lacked the power to interfere with slavery in the states and insisting that slavery should not be abolished in the District of Columbia. The abolitionist poet John Greenleaf Whittier knew exactly what the Democrats were up to. After the anti-abolitionist riot in Concord, New Hampshire, in September 1835, in which he and George Thompson had to flee for safety, the poet concluded that no "abstract hatred of Abolition principles" was involved. "No," he wrote, the riot was staged "to convince the South that the hard-working *democracy* of New Hampshire was hand in glove with the slave-holding democracy of Virginia and the Carolinas."[33]

With the emphasis on Van Buren's personality and his attitude toward abolitionism, neither side made much effort to address the economic issues of the day—money, banking, internal improvements, the Post Office, Indian removal, the land boom, and other changes that were undermining the old society. Harrison did support federal aid for internal improvements, and Van Buren wrote a number of campaign papers, but each side spent most of its time ridiculing the shortcomings of the other. The *Globe* called the opposition the old "Federal Bank party" and insisted that behind White lay the forces of "bankism, nullification, anti-instructionism, anti-Jacksonianism, and everything . . . anti-republican." White retaliated by attacking partyism and by saying that Jackson's policies led "directly to monarchy." At the end of his most important campaign statement, Harrison denounced the Democrats for their use of the veto power, for their efforts to expunge the censure of Jackson, and for their surrender to "the influence of party spirit."[34]

The differences between the Democrats and the Whigs over party spirit played a major role in the campaign. The extent of the Democratic party system can be seen in the dozens of letters exchanged by Van Buren and party leaders throughout the country. With their superior grassroots organization, the Democrats were better able to exchange editorials, circulate pamphlets, and hold the colorful parades that were then so important in campaigns. Michel Chevalier compared the Democratic parades with Catholic religious processions, both of which offered the faithful the opportunity to identify personally with a mass movement. In describing the Democratic parade in New York City after the great victory in 1834, Chevalier captured the religious fervor of the occasion.

> The procession was nearly a mile long; the Democrats marched in good order to the glare of torches; the banners were more numerous than I had ever seen in any religious festival. . . . On some were inscribed the names of the Democratic societies . . . others bore imprecations against the Bank of the United States. . . . Then came portraits of General Jackson. . . . Portraits of Washington and Jefferson, surrounded with Democratic mottoes, were mingled with emblems. . . . Farther than the eye could reach the Democrats came marching on. I was struck with the resemblance of their air to the train that escorts the Eucharist in Mexico or Puebla. . . . The Democratic procession, also like the Catholic procession, had its halting places; it stopped before the houses of Jackson men to fill the air with cheers and before the doors of the leaders of the Opposition to give three, six, or nine groans.

The parade was the political equivalent of the religious enthusiasm seen in Charles G. Finney's Second Great Awakening. By appealing to this enthusiasm the Democrats were able to win the same sort of loyalty to the party that Jacksonians had once given to the Old Hero. A good example of this loyalty can be seen in the remarks of Democratic congressman Ratliff Boon of Indiana during the 1836 campaign. Whigs had ridiculed Boon for being a "collar man," held by his party on a leash like a dog. To this he replied: "I am a party man, and one of the true collar dogs . . . and am proud to wear the collar of such a man as Andrew Jackson."[35]

Despite their skepticism about the new party politics, the Whigs often tried to copy the Democrats, especially in their local and state organizations. The Whigs, too, established newspapers, issued pamphlets, and held parades. They tried to exploit Harrison's military record as the Democrats had used Jackson's. But nationally there was no overall Whig organization, no overall Whig party, and no overall Whig planning. Only Webster ran solely as a Whig; Harrison ran as a Whig and an Anti-Mason and White as "the southern candidate." A long-held legend maintains that the Whigs united sufficiently at the national level to form a "Whig strategy" to win the election. According to the tradition they agreed to run three candidates in order to force the election into the House of Representatives. Then fearful that two Whig candidates in a given state would throw that state to Van Buren, the Whigs supposedly agreed that they would run only one candidate in each state. This strategy did develop but only as the result of local circumstances and hasty planning in individual states, not as the result of any overall "Whig strategy." The Democrats, however, took advantage of the apparent strategy by accusing the Whigs of a "divide and conquer" conspiracy to thwart the will of the people. Thus Van Buren and the Democratic party appeared to be fighting a Whig conspiracy just as Jackson had fought against the "corrupt bargain" conspiracy of John Quincy Adams and Henry Clay. This image was part of the Democratic strategy of linking Van Buren and the party with Jackson.[36]

Although tired and suffering from a number of ailments, Jackson entered into the campaign with enthusiasm. On the way to the Hermitage in late summer 1836 he described the "great reaction" that he had received as he passed through White country in eastern Tennessee. Two weeks later he told Van Buren with pardonable hyperbole of visiting Nashville and shaking 4,000 hands. The exertion may have been too great because he hemorrhaged so much in the lungs that he was too weak to meet Van Buren at Niagara Falls on his way back from the Hermitage in the fall. Van Buren had hoped that Jackson would detour from Pittsburgh to make a valuable personal appearance in New York. After returning to Washington more directly, the president admitted sadly that Tennessee might go to White, but he still had hope because their friends had "taken the field at last." With typical gusto he recounted gleefully how Robert Burton, who was married to one of Rachel's nieces, had broken two heads when bullies tried to interrupt his speech against Bell and White.[37]

All evidence pointed toward a close election. In the three months before the voting, Whigs had won close elections in North Carolina, New Jersey, and Ohio, states that had previously voted Democratic. Even the usually optimistic Jackson thought that the "ice [was] soft" in these three states as well as in Georgia and Pennsylvania. As the results came in during the month of November, Whig hopes that the election would have to be settled in the House were almost realized. A switch of 2,183 votes in Pennsylvania from Van Buren to Harrison would have kept Van Buren 8 votes short of the needed majority of 148 electoral votes. As it was, he squeaked through in Pennsylvania and won the election with 170 electoral votes to 73 for Harrison, 26 for White, 14 for Webster, and 11 for Willie Mangum, who was chosen by the South Carolina legislature. Van Buren's popular majority was barely 28,000 votes compared with almost 114,000 for Jackson in 1832.[38]

At the state level the election was equally close, with a winning percentage of no more than 55 percent in fourteen of the twenty-five states. It had been that close in only seven states in 1832. To put it another way, in 1832 Jackson swept to victory with over 65 percent of the vote in nine states and was swamped by Clay in two; in 1836 Van Buren swept in only two states and was swamped in none. The average percentage difference in the states between Democrats and their opponents dropped from 36 percent in 1832 to only 11 percent in 1836.

Political sectionalism became a thing of the past. In 1832 the Democrats carried the Southeast and the Southwest with over 60 percent of the vote in each section, and the National Republicans had similar success in New England. Only in the Middle Atlantic states and the Northwest was the balloting close. In 1836 the winning majority was 54 percent or lower in all sections. The Democrats added Connecticut and Rhode Island in New England; the Whigs gained New Jersey in the Middle Atlantic region, Georgia and Tennessee in the South, and Ohio and Indiana in the Northwest. The greatest Democratic losses were in the Southeast and the Southwest, where the party carried about two-thirds of the vote in 1832 and barely one-half of the vote in 1836. The Jacksonians/Democrats, who had lost no southern states in 1828 and two in 1832, lost four in 1836. In Tennessee not even the campaigning of Jackson could prevent a 27,000 majority in 1832 from evaporating into a 10,000 deficit in 1836. The losses might have been greater if Van Buren had not staged his antiabolitionist campaign. His margin was only 270 votes in Louisiana and 291 in Mississippi.[39]

This pattern of close elections and a decline in political sectionalism reflected the growing strength of the second political party system. This new system of Whigs and Democrats, far more extensive than the old system before the Era of Good Feelings, had come about largely because of partisan disagreement over the policies of Jackson's presidency. Although the new system was not completely developed until the election of 1840, it was operating in a majority of the states in 1836 and would continue into the 1850s. The election of 1832 had been a victory for Jackson, but the election of 1836 was a victory for the Democratic party.

With its new majority in the Senate the party continued to flex its muscles after the election. For two years Democratic state legislatures had been instructing their senators to vote for Benton's resolution to expunge the censure of President Jackson. Soon after Congress convened in December Benton moved his resolution once again, and debate began on 12 January 1837. After listening to arguments on both sides, Calhoun rose dramatically at twilight the second day to speak against the resolution. He first stood silently for one or two minutes and then began to speak slowly and softly in short compact sentences. Discounting Democratic claims that the resolution was "the will of the people," Calhoun retorted:

> It is no such thing. We all know how these legislative returns have been obtained. It is by dictation from the White House. The President himself, with that vast mass of patronage which he wields, and the thousand expectations he is able to hold up, has obtained these votes of the State Legislatures.

As Calhoun so clearly understood, the Democratic party, working at every level, had orchestrated the expunging movement.[40]

Sensing that he might have still more orchestrating to do, Benton called a party caucus for Saturday evening, 14 January, at Boulanger's Restaurant. Here, after a great deal of arm-twisting, he won an agreement that the Democrats would not allow the Senate to adjourn on Monday until the expunging resolution had passed. Expecting the Whigs to filibuster, Benton took the precaution of laying in "an ample supply of cold hams, turkeys, rounds of beef, pickles, wines and cups of hot coffee" so that the Democrats could stay up all night. Benton described the scene part way through the debate on Monday:

> As the darkness of approaching night came on, and the great chandelier was lit up, splendidly illuminating the chamber, then crowded with the members of the House, and the lobbies and galleries filled to their utmost capacity by visitors and spectators, the scene became grand and impressive.[41]

Late in the evening, toward midnight, Webster surrendered for his party but only after underlining Calhoun's point that the instructions from the states had originated in Washington. "This resolution is to pass," he conceded. "We expect it. That cause, which has been powerful enough to influence so many State legislatures, will show itself powerful enough, especially with such aids, to secure the passage of the resolution here."[42]

Webster was correct. The resolution to expunge the censure of Jackson passed by a straight party vote, 24 to 19. As soon as the result was announced, "a storm of hisses, groans, and vociferations arose" in the balcony. When the presiding officer ordered the galleries cleared, Benton stopped him, insisting that the sergeant-at-arms expel only "the bank ruffians," who were responsible for the disturbance. The reference to the Bank, which had by this time lost its charter, was a symbolic gesture reminding listeners of an earlier Democratic victory. Then the secre-

265

tary of the Senate drew lines with black ink across the offending passage in the Journal of the Senate and wrote: "Expunged by order of the Senate." On receiving the pen used that night, Jackson replied, "I sincerely thank you for this precious *Pen* which has . . . healed the wound." Although too weak to attend, the president gave a dinner for the twenty-four Democrats. Benton concluded, "That expurgation! it was the 'crowning mercy' of his civil, as New Orleans had been of his military, life."[43]

A few weeks later the Democrats again showed their strength in the Senate in the vote for vice-president. When Virginia refused to vote for Richard M. Johnson in the November election, he had been left with only 147 electoral votes, one short of a majority. The Democrats in the Senate made short work of this problem by electing Johnson over Francis Granger of New York, 33 to 16, with only Garret Wall of New Jersey breaking Democratic party ranks. The two votes for Johnson from the newly elected Democratic senators from Virginia underscored the extent of Democratic party discipline.[44]

But even the newfound party unity could not prevent a Democratic split over the issues of hard money and Texas, issues that would lead to further defections from the party during Van Buren's presidency. In the short session of Congress that met during Jackson's last three months in office, William C. Rives tried to please both paper-money and hard-money Democrats by offering a bill that rescinded the Specie Circular but kept the government from receiving bank notes from banks that issued notes under twenty dollars. He succeeded in holding the party together in the Senate, where the bill passed 41 to 5, but not in the House, where fifty-nine Democrats voted against it. These Democrats voted to retain the Specie Circular either because they were committed hard-money advocates or because they could not bear to vote against a measure that Jackson held so dear. Twenty-two New York Democrats were among the fifty-nine, suggesting that Van Buren wanted to protect his ties with Jackson. After passing both houses, the bill went to the president, who gave it a pocket veto at 11:45 P.M. on 3 March, the day before he left office.[45]

The close tie between Jackson and Van Buren was evident also in the way the president handled the Texas issue. When William H. Wharton arrived in December 1836 seeking recognition and annexation for Texas, Jackson was caught between southern Democrats who wanted both and antislavery northerners who wanted neither. Unwilling to saddle Van Buren with such issues at the start of his administration, Jackson tried to turn the matter over to Congress. In a message on 21 December he ignored annexation and recommended delaying recognition until either

Mexico or a European nation led the way. Pleased as he always was by moderation, Van Buren crowed that the message surprised those "Nullifiers" who had expected Jackson to demand annexation. In the Senate and the House Van Buren's men, Wright and Cambreleng, managed to postpone the issue until March 1837, but then both houses passed resolutions in favor of recognition, though not annexation. On 3 March Jackson recognized the Republic of Texas.[46]

As he cooperated with the president over hard money and Texas, Van Buren showed every indication of continuing Jackson's policies. Seeking stability even more ardently than the Old Hero, Van Buren was anxious to keep the cabinet intact. When Benjamin F. Butler threatened to leave, Van Buren said he dreaded the conflict of interests that would result as Pennsylvania and Virginia vied for the empty seat. Butler agreed to stay as did all the others except Secretary of War Lewis Cass, who had already been appointed minister to France. In replacing Cass, Van Buren tried to placate Virginia by offering the position to Rives, but he refused it. Van Buren then appointed Joel Poinsett, the Union man from South Carolina. Rives's refusal was another omen of future party conflict, for he had already established himself as the leader of the party's paper-money wing.

The sick old president summoned up enough energy to join in Van Buren's inauguration. On a bright warm day, reminiscent of eight years earlier, he and Van Buren rode to Capitol Hill in a carriage made of wood from the USS *Constitution* (a good republican touch) and drawn by four gray horses. After "a murmur of feeling" as they arrived, the crowd remained silent while Van Buren gave his inaugural address. But as the Old Hero started down the steps on the way to the carriage "the deep repressed feeling" of the crowd broke forth. "It was," said Benton, "the affection, gratitude, and admiration of the living age, saluting for the last time a great man." Benton recalled that, "for once, the rising was eclipsed by the setting sun."[47]

14

★ ★ ★ ★ ★

AN AMBIVALENT PRESIDENCY

Near the end of Jackson's regime, observers at both ends of the political spectrum assessed his presidency. Sen. Richard E. Parker of Virginia, still a Jeffersonian Republican, believed that Jackson had remained loyal to the old school. The Union had been preserved, the national debt paid, the Bank put down, the tariff adjusted, internal improvements "confined within reasonable limits," and the Indian question settled "upon just & liberal principles." The Adamses were less favorable. John Quincy Adams wrote sourly that Jackson had succumbed to the demands of the small capitalists and the political spoilsmen around him. The presidency, said Adams, had "fallen into a joint-stock company. . . . the reign of subaltern knaves, fattening upon land jobs and money jobs." According to Charles Francis Adams, Jackson had had "overruling good fortune. . . . Had my father done one half what he has, Impeachment and exile would have been his fate."[1]

Historians too have disagreed about the Jackson years. Like the Adamses, some scholars have viewed Jackson cynically, arguing that he and his party cared little about moral and constitutional ideals and much about winning office and the spoils that went with it. Other writers, more in tune with Parker, have replied that Jackson was devoted to traditional ideas. Richard B. Latner writes that Jackson's goal was "to preserve republican institutions by adjusting and reconciling Jeffersonianism to an increasingly expansive and pluralistic society." For Richard E. Ellis, "Jackson's belief in states' rights was [intertwined] with his belief in social and political democracy."[2]

269

Although Parker and his modern counterparts have sensibly focused attention on Jackson's republican goals, they have not fully considered his presidency in the light of the economic and political revolutions going on around it. When Jackson took office, he had to contend with the massive changes brought on both by the market economy and by the new political party system. Wedded to agrarian states'-rights ideals, Jackson sought to resist the evils of the economic revolution; committed to his own concepts of rotation in office and political reform, he was uneasy about the political party revolution as well. The main theme of Jackson's presidency is his painful adjustment to both.

Just how painful has not been sufficiently appreciated. Nothing came easily for Jackson during his eight years in office. Handicapped by his status as an outsider and the unwieldiness of his coalition, he spent most of his first term defending the Eatons, rearranging his administration, and contending with Congress. Despite it all he achieved some of his agrarian goals by vetoing the Maysville Road, securing the passage of the Indian removal bill, and vetoing the recharter of the Bank. His egalitarian annual message in December 1832 marked the high point of his efforts. From that point on, the Nullification Crisis and the fallout over his removal of the deposits thwarted his efforts. The agrarian tone of his Farewell Address was more a piece of wistful rhetoric than the summation of his presidency.

But more than political battles stood in the way of Jackson's agrarianism, for both the Old Hero and his inner circle had mixed feelings about the market revolution. Even in his Farewell Address, issued as he left office on 4 March 1837, the ambivalence shines through. As he asked Taney to prepare a draft, the president laid out the claim that he had waged a battle to save the old ideals against the onslaught of "privileged monopolies," "the *paper system*," and other evils that were "undermining the purity and . . . simplicity of our virtuous Government." In the address he warned of the danger of an enlarged central government, especially its tendency to overtax, overspend, and accumulate a surplus. Hearkening back to his Bank veto and his fourth annual message, he staked the future of the nation on "the agricultural, the mechanical, and the laboring classes."[3]

At times, however, the Farewell Address evoked a different image. At several points he called attention to America's "rich and flourishing commerce." Toward the end he boasted that American "growth" had been "rapid beyond all former examples in numbers, in wealth, in knowledge, and all the useful arts which contribute to the comforts and convenience of man." Never before had a people "enjoyed so much freedom and happiness as the people of these United States." His enthusiasm was reminiscent of his excitement when he toured the textile mill in Lowell. Although warning of the dangers from the market revolution, Jackson also seemed enthralled by the results.[4]

Jackson's chief advisers shared his ambivalence. In his Central Hickory Club Address in 1832 Amos Kendall spoke out for a Union controlled by the states, with a central government that did little but *"keep off* [the] *evil"* of antirepublicanism. He portrayed an administration that had rooted out corruption and conserved the people's hard-earned money. In another campaign statement the same year, however, he offered a different message, boasting that American "commercial activity" had reached heights "scarcely equalled in our history. The value of shipping, of wharves, of warehouses, of everything connected with commerce, [had] greatly increased," and trade was being "carried on with more spirit and better profit." Kendall's own career reflected the same contradictions. An idealistic schoolteacher who had attacked the Bank for the Panic of 1819 and deplored the excesses of Washington society, he also owned his own paper mill, threatened to leave the administration when his income declined, and later became the wealthy associate of Samuel F. B. Morse in the first telegraph company.[5]

Kendall's rival, Martin Van Buren, provided another example of this ambivalence in his 1837 inaugural address, which was as much a farewell to Jackson's presidency as it was an introduction to his own. Although he began in good republican fashion by pledging to base his policies on the "sovereign power" of the states and the "virtue" of the people, his address was carefully balanced between republican sentiments and enthusiasm over the economic progress of the era. In one nicely balanced sentence he wrote:

Our commerce has been extended to the remotest nations; the value and even nature of our productions have been greatly changed; a wide difference has arisen in the relative wealth and resources of every portion of our country; yet the spirit of mutual regard and faithful adherence to existing compacts has continued to prevail in our councils and never long been absent in our conduct.

Van Buren's career was also balanced. Loyal to Old Republican ideals in the Maysville veto and the Nullification Crisis, he violated them by supporting the Tariff of Abominations and by defending the Bank on several occasions. A successful lawyer and real-estate owner, he too received economic rewards from the market revolution.[6]

The statements of the three party leaders epitomize the rhetoric and position of most of the Democrats. For every states' righter who distrusted the new capitalism—Silas Wright, Francis P. Blair, Thomas Ritchie—there was a nationalist who welcomed the business opportunities—Lewis Cass, Louis McLane, and William L. Marcy. Whether in Blair's elastic phrases, Benton's pompous pronouncements, or Isaac Hill's harsh invective, the Democrats relied on a republican message liberally blended with paeans for the accomplishments of the market revolution.[7]

Those students defending Jackson's ideological consistency argue that he carried out his agrarianism and dismantled Clay's American System of protective tariffs, internal improvements, distribution, and the Bank, but the case does not stand up under close scrutiny. First, there was never a well-established American System for the Democrats to dismantle. Tariff protection was far from complete when Jackson took office. Despite the enthusiasm of John Quincy Adams no federal system of internal improvements existed. Nor was there a policy of distribution. The only part of the American System truly established was the Bank. Second, many Democrats accepted parts of Clay's program. Van Buren and Eaton supported the Tariff of Abominations, McLane and others backed the Bank, and Jackson advocated distribution in his first annual message. And even if we assume that the basis for an American System existed, the administration did not destroy it. Jackson sought no serious tariff reductions until the Nullification Crisis, and the compromise tariff that ensued was not a Jackson measure. Even that bill did not call for substantially lower tariffs until 1842, and many people expected—as actually happened—Congress to return to the higher rates. Jackson did resist a federal system of internal improvements but supported higher expenditures for internal improvements than any of his predecessors. He defeated the Bank but then replaced it with a much larger system of deposit banks based on the same system of paper money that he opposed. After rejecting distribution in 1832 and 1833, he finally accepted a distribution bill near the end of his administration.[8]

Whatever policies Jackson followed, he was powerless to hold back the market revolution. It is often overlooked that the years of Jackson's presidency were among the most prosperous in American history. Disturbed only by the brief Panic of 1834, the market revolution roared on, doubling American exports and imports and producing the great land boom. Despite his often-expressed fears of an expanding central government, Jackson was unable to prevent annual governmental receipts, expenditures, and surpluses from doubling during his tenure.[9]

Jackson not only failed to save the old agrarian republic, but he also contributed to its decline, his efforts to halt change often working in reverse. In getting rid of the Bank, he was forced to give the government added powers to regulate the new banking system. In trying to restore republican virtue to government agencies, he was forced to build an un-republican bureaucracy. By expanding the land available for cotton, his Indian removal stimulated textile manufacturing and foreign commerce. Jackson's new banking system and his outlays for internal improvements, as well as his Indian removal policy, opened opportunities for rising entrepreneurs.

Nor did Jackson's presidency bring an end to the economic changes that were causing so much anxiety when he took office. Spurred on by the expansion of railroads, the transportation revolution went on reshaping America. Jackson arrived in Washington in a carriage in 1829 and left on a train eight years later. One reason for the intensity of the Bank War was the continuing expansion of banks and paper money while Jackson was in office. As more Americans moved west, there was no end in sight for the decline in the political influence of Virginia and New England. The expansion of manufacturing and the start of inflation touched off the labor disorders of the mid-1830s.

Social change also accelerated. As the market revolution expanded, women settled into their separate sphere in the home and found it difficult to pursue careers in business and the professions. The craze for making money and the rise of materialism so impressed Alexis de Tocqueville when he visited America in 1831 that they became two of his themes in his *Democracy in America*. The Nat Turner insurrection, the antiabolitionist riots, and the Gag Rule Controversy revealed how much the hostility over slavery had grown in the Jackson years.

At times Jackson's presidency seems almost irrelevant. His internal-improvement vetoes, his Bank War, and his hard-money policies had less effect—other than symbolic—than people thought at the time. His administration, for example, had less influence on the citizens of Rochester than did either the Erie Canal or the Second Great Awakening. And in New York City the trade union movement had more to say to workers than did Jacksonian Democracy. Both evangelists and labor leaders turned against Jackson, the former because of his opposition to Sabbatarianism, Indian reform, and the antislavery movement, the latter because of his failure to side with the workers. When so many citizens resorted to rioting in the mid-1830s, they exposed the inability of his government to deal with their grievances. The Jackson administration could not understand, much less stop, the wave of violence.

This is not to say that Jackson's presidency was completely out of step with the times. Even in his futile efforts to roll back the clock, Jackson adapted to social and economic changes. On almost every issue his opposition to change helped bring about a workable compromise. Though Jackson did little to help the economic classes with whom he identified, his rhetoric educated Americans about the growing class distinctions. Furthermore, many of his policies looked toward modern America—especially his expansion of foreign commerce, his Indian removal, his administrative reform, and the creation of a patronage system and the Democratic party. In addition, Jackson pointed the way toward the modern presidency by relying on informal advisers, using the press, dramatizing politics, and appealing to the people. He took advantage of the veto and other powers of the chief executive as no president had done before.

Yet to say that he transformed the presidency or became the first modern president is stretching the point. He was not tested by the challenges in foreign policy that have faced almost all presidents since Grover Cleveland, nor was he asked to construct economic programs as have so many presidents in the twentieth century. His assertion of the power of the executive in his veto of the recharter bill was primarily a defensive stand against the Supreme Court. He did make a strong statement of executive power in his Protest against the censure resolution, but he soon retracted much of it. Since he rarely had control of Congress, he was unable to have many bills passed into law—aside from his administrative reforms.

Nor does Jackson's use of the veto power show that he was a strong president. He did veto twelve bills, two more than all the presidents before him, but the vetoes demonstrated more weakness than strength—his inability to prevent Congress from passing bills that he opposed. It was typical of his presidency that when he pocket vetoed Rives's bill to do away with the Specie Circular the day before he left office, he saved it for only one more year. Jackson's use of the veto, furthermore, did not have a great deal of influence on the presidents who immediately followed him. The total of thirty vetoes between Jackson and Lincoln was not particularly large, considering the partisanship and sectionalism of the era. Although Jackson often seemed to be strengthening the presidency, Tocqueville thought otherwise, noting perceptively that the personal "power of General Jackson . . . increases, but that of the President declines." Tocqueville predicted accurately that the power of the presidency would "pass enfeebled into the hands of his successor."[10]

The great achievement of Jackson's presidency was the creation of the Democratic party. During those eight years Jackson's heroic personality, Blair's rhetoric, and the political skills of Van Buren and Kendall made the first modern American political party and the first real two-party system possible. The Democratic party and the Whig party that followed were the first mass political parties in the world, coming half a century before similar parties in Europe. Ever so grudgingly, Jackson's opponents recognized his accomplishment. Calhoun, for example, blamed party patronage for the expunging of the censure. Three years after Jackson left office, John Quincy Adams wrote that—aside from military service and demagoguery—"the art of party drilling" was the "most indispensable element of success" in politics.[11]

One of the legacies of the Democratic party was the policy of accommodating to slavery. Jackson and Van Buren implemented that policy between 1835 and 1837 by appointing five southerners to the Supreme Court, and the policy was an important part of Van Buren's strategy in his election campaign. In the next two decades Democrats trained under Jackson would make every effort to hold their party together by compromising with the South. When the policy began to falter late in the 1850s, old Jackson Democrats were still adhering to it. In the *Dred Scott* decision, for example, a group of aging Democratic justices provided the majority opinion that Congress lacked the power to ban slavery in the territories. Among them were Roger B. Taney, James M. Wayne, and John Catron, all appointed by Jackson, and Peter V. Daniel and Robert C. Grier, appointed by Van Buren and Polk.

While Jackson was president, changes were taking place in the city of Washington that reflected the same struggle between the old republican ideals and the new materialism that had so affected the administration. To perpetuate the republic by glorifying George Washington, two works of art were commissioned. In 1832 Congress chose Horatio Greenough to prepare a statue of the first president, and four years later Robert Mills won a competition to design the Washington Monument. Attention was also given to the Capitol, which had not fully recovered from being burned by the British in 1814, and the President's House, which was shabby inside and unfinished outside. When Charles Bulfinch completed work on the rotunda and the east and west fronts of the Capitol in 1830, the building assumed the form it would retain until the eve of the Civil War. At the President's House the addition of the north portico with its grand columns and the elaborate decoration of the East Room transformed a run-down dwelling into an American temple, called, increasingly, the "White House." To improve the way between these two republican buildings, the government planted trees along Pennsylvania Avenue and macadamized the surface.

But not all the changes in the city recaptured the idealism of the Revolution. The many taverns and cheap stores that sprang up along Pennsylvania Avenue constantly reminded visitors of the less attractive, materialistic side of Jacksonian America. The slums where the German and Irish laborers who worked on the projects lived were a constant reminder of the widening gap between rich and poor. The new East Room of the President's House was not furnished in the chaste Greek revival style of Jefferson but in the more vulgar style of Jackson's era. The new Treasury building, started in 1836, lacked taste in design and blocked the very view from the President's House to the Capitol that the admirers of the Republic were trying to enhance. When Jackson unsuccessfully urged Congress to spend a million dollars to build a new bridge across the Potomac, he was accused of cooperating with land speculators from New York, who hoped to profit from a new port on the Virginia side of the river. Ironically, since Jackson had often attacked such speculators, the port was to be called "Jackson City."[12]

Perhaps in one more way the presidency of Andrew Jackson left an indelible mark—in the image of Jackson himself. One author has argued persuasively that Jackson combined three images that made him the "Symbol for an Age": man returning to nature, the champion of God, and the man of iron will. "Of Andrew Jackson," wrote John William Ward, "the people made a mirror for themselves."[13]

Jackson was indeed a man of iron will. His determination to remove the Indians, to preserve the Union, and to move ahead in the midst of the panic is legendary. Yet there was another—an unsure—Jackson who more accurately reflected the era in which he lived. This was the Jackson who became distraught over the disloyalty of his friends during the Peggy Eaton affair, the Jackson who mumbled that he would be better dead during the dissolution of his cabinet, the Jackson who wrote angry letters to Van Buren over the proclamation and the removal of the deposits and to Grundy during the Nullification Crisis. This was the Jackson who felt the need to placate Duff Green while replacing him with Blair, who allowed McLane to side with the Bank, and who pleaded with William J. Duane to go along with deposit removal. Because of his indecision Jackson failed to take advantage of either of his inaugurations. His policies during his most heroic moment as president, the Nullification Crisis, were in many ways his most uncertain, and yet this man of anxiety as well as of iron will prevailed.

Like no other figure Jackson symbolized the American caught between the ideals of the Revolution and the realities of nineteenth-century liberal capitalism. Only the Old Hero, who had fought so often for the Republic, could convincingly warn his compatriots of the dangers of losing republican virtue. Yet at the same time no one better represented the individualistic, aggressive, mobile man of enterprise in the new age of materialism and opportunity than Jackson, who had made his way up in Tennessee. He came to the presidency at the moment when his country was turning away from its agrarian past and toward its capitalist future. With his strength, his passions, and especially his anxiety, he symbolized the ambivalence of his fellow Americans at this decisive moment. In that way his presidency has made a lasting imprint.

NOTES

ABBREVIATIONS

AHR	*American Historical Review*
JAH	*Journal of American History*
JC	Andrew Jackson, *Correspondence of Andrew Jackson*, ed. John Spencer Bassett and John Franklin Jameson, 7 vols. (1926–35; reprint, New York: Kraus Reprint Co., 1969)
JER	*Journal of the Early Republic*
JP	Andrew Jackson Papers, Library of Congress
JSM	Microfilm Supplement to the Andrew Jackson Papers (Wilmington Del.: Scholarly Resources, 1986)
LC	Library of Congress
MHM	*Maryland Historical Magazine*
MVHR	*Mississippi Valley Historical Review*
THQ	*Tennessee Historical Quarterly*
VBP	Martin Van Buren Papers, Library of Congress

PREFACE

1. James Parton, *Life of Andrew Jackson*, 3 vols. (New York: Mason Brothers, 1860), 1:vii-viii, 3:695; Herman Melville, *Moby Dick*, chap. 26, final paragraph, quoted in Robert V. Remini, *Andrew Jackson and the Course of American Democracy, 1833–1845* (New York: Harper & Row, 1984), p. 530; Arthur M. Schlesinger, Jr., *The Age of Jackson* (Boston: Little, Brown, 1945), p. 43; Richard Hofstadter, *The American Political Tradition and the Men Who Made It* (New York: Alfred A. Knopf, 1948), p. 44.

2. James C. Curtis, *Andrew Jackson and the Search for Vindication* (Boston: Little, Brown, 1976); Marvin Meyers, *The Jacksonian Persuasion: Politics and Belief* (New York: Vintage Books, 1960), p. 15.

CHAPTER 1
AN ANXIOUS REPUBLIC

1. James Parton, *Life of Andrew Jackson*, 3 vols. (New York: Mason Brothers, 1860), 3:154–64; Jackson to John Coffee, 17 Jan. 1829, Andrew Jackson, *Correspondence of Andrew Jackson* (JC), ed. John Spencer Bassett and John Franklin Jameson, 7 vols. (1926–35; reprint, New York: Kraus Reprint Co., 1969), 4:1–2.

2. The term "White House" had begun to appear at this time, but the official name remained the "President's House," which is used throughout this book. William Seale, *The President's House: A History*, 2 vols. (Washington, D.C.: White House Historical Association, 1986), 1:163.

3. Margaret Bayard Smith, *The First Forty Years of Washington Society*, ed. Gaillard Hunt (1906; reprint, New York: Frederick Ungar, 1965), pp. 256, 259, 281.

4. Ibid., p. 253.

5. Jackson was congressman, 1796–97, and senator, 1797–98 and 1823–25. He also visited Washington in 1815 and 1819. Andrew Jackson, *The Papers of Andrew Jackson*, ed. Sam B. Smith, Harold D. Moser, and Sharon MacPherson, 3 vols. to date (Knoxville: University of Tennessee Press, 1980–), 2:102, 104, 108, 172–74, 211–13, 257, 262, 408, 461, 479; Robert V. Remini, *Andrew Jackson and the Course of American Freedom, 1822–1832* (New York: Harper & Row, 1981), p. 123; Smith, *First Forty Years*, p. 259.

6. Jackson to George W. Martin, 2 Jan. 1824, JC, 3:222; Remini, *Jackson and Freedom*, p. 60.

7. Remini, *Jackson and Freedom*, pp. 1–3.

8. John William Ward, *Andrew Jackson—Symbol for an Age* (New York: Oxford University Press, 1955), pp. 13–15, 54 57; Edward Pessen, *Jacksonian America: Society, Personality, and Politics*, rev. ed. (Homewood, Ill.: Dorsey Press, 1978), p. 2.

9. Daniel Webster to Ezekiel Webster, 17 Jan. 1829, Daniel Webster, *The Papers of Daniel Webster: Correspondence*, ed. Charles M. Wiltse and Harold D. Moser, 7 vols. (Hanover, N.H.: University Press of New England, 1974–86), 2:388.

10. For a discussion of the social impact of these changes, see Gordon S. Wood, "The Significance of the Early Republic, JER 8 (1988): 1–20. The first railroad was the Baltimore and Ohio, which was chartered in 1828 and went into operation in May 1830. For statistical data, see George Rogers Taylor, *The Transportation Revolution, 1815–1860* (New York: Harper & Row, 1951), pp. 57, 77, 135–38, 142–43, 150; *Niles' Register* 37 (1830): 339; Alfred M. Lee, *The Daily Newspaper in America* (New York: Macmillan, 1937), pp. 718, 725; *The Statistical History of the United States from Colonial Times to the Present* (Stamford, Conn.: Fairfield Publishers, 1965), p. 14; Census Office, *Statistical Atlas of the United States Based upon Results of the Eleventh Census* (Washington, D.C.: Government Printing Office, 1898), p. 16.

11. *Statistical History,* pp. 239, 623, 625; Taylor, *Transportation Revolution,* p. 325.

12. *Statistical History,* p. 57; Edward Pessen, *Most Uncommon Jacksonians: The Radical Leaders of the Early Labor Movement* (Albany: State University of New York Press, 1967), pp. 9–51; Sean Wilentz, *Chants Democratic: New York City and the Rise of the American Working Class, 1788–1850* (New York: Oxford University Press, 1984), pp. 176–78.

13. Nancy F. Cott, *The Bonds of Womanhood: "Woman's Sphere" in New England, 1780–1835* (New Haven, Conn.: Yale University Press, 1977). For the view that women had more choices than hitherto believed, see Jane H. Pease and William H. Pease, *Ladies, Women, and Wenches: Choices and Constraint in Antebellum Charleston and Boston* (Chapel Hill: University of North Carolina Press, 1990).

14. Russel Blaine Nye, *The Cultural Life of the New Nation 1776–1830* (New York: Harper, 1960), pp. 132–34.

15. *Statistical History,* p. 229; Paul E. Johnson, *A Shopkeeper's Millennium: Society and Revivals in Rochester, N.Y., 1815–1837* (New York: Hill and Wang, 1978).

16. Ely to Jackson, 28 Jan. 1829, JC, 4:3; Bertram Wyatt-Brown, "Prelude to Abolitionism: Sabbatarian Politics and the Rise of the Second Party System," *JAH* 58 (1971): 316–41.

17. *Statistical History,* pp. 11–13, 685; Robert P. Sutton, "Nostalgia, Pessimism and Malaise: The Doomed Aristocrat in Late-Jeffersonian Virginia," *Virginia Magazine of History and Biography* 76 (Jan. 1968): 41–42, 46; *Richmond Enquirer,* 25 Mar., 11 Oct. 1825, 1 Mar., 29 April 1828.

18. Thomas Cooper, "Value of the Union," 2 July 1827, William W. Freehling, ed., *The Nullification Era: A Documentary Record* (New York: Harper & Row, 1967), pp. 20–25.

19. William W. Freehling, *Prelude to Civil War: The Nullification Controversy in South Carolina, 1816–1836* (New York: Harper & Row, 1966), pp. 158–59, 167–68, 175; Jefferson to John Holmes, 22 April 1820, Thomas Jefferson, *The Works of Thomas Jefferson,* ed. Paul L. Ford, 12 vols. (New York: G. P. Putnam's Sons, 1904–5), 12:159.

20. Robert J. Turnbull, "The Crisis," 1827, Freehling, *Nullification Era,* p. 44; "South Carolina Protest," Henry Steele Commager, ed., *Documents of American History* (New York: Appleton-Century-Crofts, 1948), p. 250.

21. Michel Chevalier, *Society, Manners, and Politics in the United States* (1836; reprint, New York: Anchor Books, 1961), p. 268; Louis-Elizabeth Baron de Montlezun, "Voyage Fait dans les Années 1816 et 1817," Oscar Handlin, ed., *This Was America* (New York: Harper & Row, 1949), p. 128; M. M. Noah, *Oration, delivered . . . before Tammany Society* (New York, 1817), p. 3; Lyman Beecher, "The Gospel the Only Security for Eminent and National Prosperity," *American National Preacher* 3 (Mar. 1829): 154. Noah and Beecher are quoted in Fred Somkin, *Unquiet Eagle: Memory and Desire in the Idea of American Freedom, 1815–1860* (Ithaca, N.Y.: Cornell University Press, 1967), pp. 13, 18.

22. *Niles' Register* 38 (1830): 97; Benjamin Brown French, *Witness to the Young Republic: A Yankee's Journal, 1828–1870,* ed. Donald B. Cole and John J. McDonough (Hanover, N.H.: University Press of New England, 1989), pp. 70, 88; Somkin, *Unquiet Eagle,* pp. 40–41, 53.

23. French, *Witness to the Young Republic*, pp. 81–82.

24. *Niles' Register* 27 (6 Nov. 1824): 145, quoted in Somkin, *Unquiet Eagle*, p. 153; Sylvia Neely, "The Politics of Liberty in the Old World and the New: Lafayette's Return to America in 1824," JER 6 (1986): 152–71; Walker Lewis, ed., *Speak for Yourself, Daniel: A Life of Webster in His Own Words* (Boston: Houghton Mifflin, 1969), pp. 118–23.

25. Roger E. Carp, "The Erie Canal Celebration of 1825: Ritual Drama and the Place of Technology in the Early Republic" (paper delivered at meeting of the Organization of American Historians, April 1989), pp. 1–6.

26. In responding to the changing economy Americans were influenced by a variety of intellectual traditions, including liberalism, republicanism, Enlightenment thought, the Scottish moral tradition, and Protestant Christian theology. In recent years historians have overemphasized the clash between liberalism and republicanism. Jack P. Greene, *The Intellectual Heritage of the Constitutional Era: The Delegates' Library* (Philadelphia: Library Company of Philadelphia, 1986). For the early influence of liberalism, see Joyce Appleby, "The Social Origins of American Revolutionary Ideology," JAH 64 (Mar. 1978): 935–58. For the persistence of republican thought, see Richard B. Latner, *The Presidency of Andrew Jackson: White House Politics 1829–1837* (Athens: University of Georgia Press, 1979), pp. 209–12, and Major L. Wilson, "Republicanism and the Idea of Party in the Jacksonian Period, JER 8 (1988): 419–42. See also Daniel T. Rodgers, "Republicanism: The Career of a Concept," JAH 79 (June 1992): 11–38. Lee Benson uses the terms "agrarian-minded" and "commercial-minded" in decribing American attitudes shortly after the Revolution. See Benson, *Turner and Beard: American Historical Writing Reconsidered* (Chicago: Free Press of Glencoe, 1960), pp. 215–28. For the tension between republicanism and liberalism, see Marvin Meyers, *The Jacksonian Persuasion: Politics and Belief* (New York: Vintage Books, 1960), pp. 11–15.

27. Richard P. McCormick, "New Perspectives on Jacksonian Politics," AHR 65 (Jan. 1960): 288–301.

28. Wright to Azariah Flagg, 28 Jan. 1833, Azariah Flagg Papers, New York Public Library.

29. Richard Hofstadter, *The Idea of a Party System: The Rise of Legitimate Opposition in the United States, 1780–1840* (Berkeley: University of California Press, 1969), chaps. 1–2, 6.

30. From this point on I refer to the Bank of the United States as "the Bank." Michael F. Holt, "The Democratic Party 1828–1860," Arthur M. Schlesinger, Jr., ed., *History of U.S. Political Parties*, 4 vols. (New York: Chelsea House, 1973), 1:497–505; Richard H. Brown, "The Missouri Crisis, Slavery, and the Politics of Jacksonianism," *South Atlantic Quarterly* 65 (1966): 55–72.

31. Charlemagne Tower, "Diary," April 1831, Columbia University Library; Van Buren to Ritchie, 13 Jan. 1827, Martin Van Buren Papers (VBP), LC.

32. Robert V. Remini, *The Election of Andrew Jackson* (Philadelphia: J. B. Lippincott, 1963), pp. 61–71.

33. Isaac Hill, *Brief Sketch of the Life, Character and Services of Major General Andrew Jackson* (Concord, N.H.: Manahan, Hoag, 1827).

34. Van Buren to Jackson, 14 Sept., 4 Nov. 1827, VBP; *Albany Argus,* 31 Oct., 4, 7 Nov. 1828.

35. Remini, *Election of Jackson,* pp. 187–88; Hoyt to Van Buren, 21 Mar. 1829, William L. Mackenzie, *The Lives and Opinions of Benjamin Franklin Butler . . . and Jesse Hoyt* (Boston: Cooke, 1845), pp. 51–52.

36. Daniel Webster to Ezekiel Webster, 23 Feb. 1829, Webster, *Papers,* 2:401. Several historians believe that the Jacksonians were more united ideologically than I do. Harry L. Watson views the election as a victory for liberty and agrarianism, Charles Sellers as the emergence of a class party of farmers and urban workers, and Richard B. Latner and Richard E. Ellis see it as the triumph of Old Republicanism. Watson, *Liberty and Power: The Politics of Jacksonian America* (New York: Hill and Wang, 1990), pp. 94–95; Sellers, *The Market Revolution: Jacksonian America, 1815–1846* (New York: Oxford University Press, 1991), pp. 297–300; Latner, *Presidency of Jackson,* pp. 22–23; Ellis, *The Union at Risk: Jacksonian Democracy, States' Rights and the Nullification Crisis* (New York: Oxford University Press, 1987), pp. 13–14. For the economic orientation of Jackson's early backers in Tennessee, see Charles Sellers, "Jackson Men with Feet of Clay," AHR 62 (1957): 537–51. For an analysis of the symbolic Jackson in the election, see Ward, *Jackson,* pp. 41–43, 46–71.

37. Robert V. Remini, *Andrew Jackson and the Bank War: A Study in the Growth of Presidential Power* (New York: W. W. Norton, 1967), pp. 18–19; Martin Van Buren, "The Autobiography of Martin Van Buren," ed. John C. Fitzpatrick, *Annual Report of the American Historical Association for the Year 1918,* vol. 2 (Washington, D.C.: Government Printing Office, 1920), pp. 198, 232–33.

38. Parton, *Jackson,* 3:136; Webster to Ezekiel Webster, 17 Jan. 1829, Webster, *Papers,* 2:388.

39. Heaton to Allen Trimble, 11 Nov. 1828, Heaton to John McLean, 24 Nov. 1828, James Heaton Papers, LC.

40. In this book I have referred to members of the Jackson party as "Jacksonians" until 1832 and thereafter as "Democrats." In like manner I have used "National Republicans" for the opposition until 1834 and then "Whigs." For Niles's quotation, see *Niles' Register* 36 (26 Sept. 1829): 68. For party names, see ibid., 40 (22 Oct. 1831): 149, and Samuel Rhea Gammon, *The Presidential Campaign of 1832* (Baltimore: Johns Hopkins University Press, 1922), pp. 155–62.

41. For party control in Congress, see *Niles' Register* 37 (1829–30): 150, 203, 215, 229.

CHAPTER 2
AN UNCERTAIN PRESIDENT

1. Frances M. Trollope, *Domestic Manners of the Americans* (1832; reprint, London: Folio Society, 1974), p. 113. For a magnificent description of Jackson four years earlier, see Henry A. Wise, *Seven Decades of the Union* (Philadelphia: J. B. Lippincott, 1881), p. 80.

2. Amos Kendall used the term "maneuvering" in Kendall to Francis P. Blair, 14 Feb. 1829, Blair-Lee Papers, Princeton University Library. See also Buchanan to George B. Porter, 22 Jan. 1829, James Buchanan Papers, New-York Historical Society.

3. Philip S. Klein, *Pennsylvania Politics: 1817–1832, A Game without Rules* (Philadelphia: Historical Society of Pennsylvania, 1940), p. 252; Alfred Mordecai to Ellen Mordecai, 11 Feb. 1829, Sarah Agnes Wallace, "Opening Days of Jackson's Presidency as Seen in Private Letters," THQ 9 (1950): 368.

4. *Statistical Atlas of the United States Based upon Results of the Eleventh Census* (Washington, D.C.: Government Printing Office, 1898), p. 16; Wilhelmus B. Bryan, *A History of the National Capital*, 2 vols. (New York: Macmillan, 1914, 1916), 2:16–20, 59–61, 194–212.

5. Jackson to Rachel Jackson, 7 Dec. 1823, Jackson to Swartwout, 27 Sept. 1829, Andrew Jackson, *Correspondence of Andrew Jackson*, ed. John Spencer Bassett and John Franklin Jameson, 7 vols. (1926–35; reprint, New York: Kraus Reprint Co., 1969), 3:216, 4:79.

6. Emily Donelson to Polly Coffee, 27 Mar. 1829, quoted in Pauline Wilcox Burke, *Emily Donelson of Tennessee*, 2 vols. (Richmond, Va.: Garrett and Massie, 1941), 1:178.

7. Amos Kendall, *Autobiography of Amos Kendall*, ed. William Stickney (1872; reprint, New York: Peter Smith, 1949), p. 308.

8. Amos Kendall to Francis P. Blair, 7 Mar. 1829, Blair-Lee Papers; Jackson, fragment, 1831, JC, 6:504.

9. Kendall to Blair, 7 Mar. 1829, Blair-Lee Papers; John Pope to Jackson, 19 Feb. 1829, JC, 4:8.

10. James Parton, *Life of Andrew Jackson*, 3 vols. (New York: Mason Brothers, 1860), 3:174–76; James A. Hamilton, *Reminiscences of James A. Hamilton* (New York: Charles Scribner's Sons, 1869), p. 99.

11. Hamilton, *Reminiscences*, p. 102; Jackson, "Memoranda," Feb., Sept. 1831, JC, 4:235, 343; Kendall to Blair, 7 Mar. 1829, Blair-Lee Papers; Shaw Livermore, *The Twilight of Federalism: The Disintegration of the Federalist Party 1815–1830* (Princeton, N.J.: Princeton University Press, 1962), p. 245.

12. Hamilton, *Reminiscences*, pp. 90–91, 99; Ritchie to Mordecai Noah, 14 Mar. 1829, Andrew Stevenson to Van Buren, 19 April 1829, VBP. Norman K. Risjord points out the lack of dedicated Old Republicans in the cabinet in *The Old Republicans: Southern Conservatism in the Age of Jefferson* (New York: Columbia University Press, 1965), pp. 270–71.

13. Jackson, fragment, 1831, JC, 6:504; Hamilton, *Reminiscences*, p. 101; Kane to Van Buren, 20 Feb. 1829, VBP; Martin Van Buren, "The Autobiography of Martin Van Buren," ed. John C. Fitzpatrick, *Annual Report of the American Historical Association for the Year 1918*, vol. 2 (Washington, D.C.: Government Printing Office, 1920), p. 231.

14. Elias Kent Kane to Van Buren, 19 Feb. 1829, VBP; Van Buren, *Autobiography*, pp. 228–31.

15. Charles Sellers, *James K. Polk, Jacksonian, 1795–1843* (Princeton, N.J.: Princeton University Press, 1957), pp. 135–40.

16. The five members of Congress included Van Buren, who had resigned from the Senate to become governor of New York. William Wirt to William Pope, 22 Mar. 1829, John P. Kennedy, ed., *Memoirs of the Life of William Wirt*, 2 vols. (Philadelphia: Lea and Blanchard, 1850), 2:228; Henry Clay to Charles Hammond, 27 May 1829, Henry Clay, *The Papers of Henry Clay*, ed. James F. Hopkins, Mary W. M. Hargreaves, Robert Seager II, and Melba Porter Hay, 10 vols. to date (Lexington: University Press of Kentucky, 1959–), 8:59.

17. Carl Schurz, *Henry Clay*, 2 vols. (Boston: Houghton, Mifflin, 1899), 1:329–31.

18. Kendall to Blair, 7 Mar. 1829, Blair-Lee Papers; James A. Hamilton to Van Buren, 21, 23 Feb. 1829, VBP.

19. Van Buren to Hamilton, 15 Feb. 1829, Hamilton, *Reminiscences*, p. 93.

20. Edwin A. Miles, "The First People's Inaugural—1829," THQ 37 (1978): 293–94, 299–301; Webster to Achsah Pollard Webster, 4 Mar. 1829, Daniel Webster, *The Papers of Daniel Webster: Correspondence*, ed. Charles M. Wiltse and Harold D. Moser, 7 vols. (Hanover, N.H.: University Press of New England, 1974–86), 2:405.

21. *Niles' Register* 36 (3 Mar. 1829): 39–40; Margaret Bayard Smith, *The First Forty Years of Washington Society*, ed. Gaillard Hunt (1906; reprint, New York: Frederick Ungar, 1965), pp. 291–93.

22. *A Compilation of the Messages and Papers of the Presidents, 1789–1897*, comp. James D. Richardson, 10 vols. (Washington, D.C.: Government Printing Office, 1897–99), 1:322.

23. Ibid., 2:436–38.

24. John Emmett Burke, "Andrew Jackson as Seen by Foreigners," THQ 10 (1951): 33; *Richmond Enquirer* 6, 9 Mar. 1829; Hamilton to Van Buren, 5 Mar. 1829, VBP.

25. Smith, *First Forty Years*, pp. 291, 294–97.

26. The accusations are reviewed in a letter from Ezra Stiles Ely to Jackson, 18 Mar. 1829, Andrew Jackson Papers (JP), LC.

27. David Rankin Barbee, "Andrew Jackson and Peggy O'Neale," THQ 15 (1956): 50–51; Eaton to Emily Donelson, 4 April 1829, JC, 4:29n.

28. Ely to Jackson, 18 Mar. 1829, JP.

29. Jackson to Ely, 23 Mar. 1829, Parton, *Jackson*, 3:186–91.

30. Jackson to John Coffee, 19 Mar. 1829, Jackson to John C. McLemore, 3 May 1829, JC, 4:15, 31.

31. Parton, *Jackson*, 3:191–97, 203–5; Jackson, "Memorandum of interviews with John N. Campbell," 3 Sept. 1829, Andrew J. Donelson, "Memorandum of Jackson's interview with Campbell," 3 Sept. 1829, JP; Salmon P. Chase, "Diary," 5 Sept. 1829, Salmon P. Chase Papers, LC; Samuel D. Ingham to ———, 18 Jan. 1832, Personal Papers, Miscellaneous, LC.

32. Kendall to Blair, 22 Nov. 1829, Blair-Lee Papers.

33. Jackson, "Memorandum," 29 Jan. 1829, Margaret Eaton to Jackson, 9 June 1830, JC, 4:123–24, 145; Van Buren, *Autobiography*, pp. 353–56.

34. John Quincy Adams, *Memoirs of John Quincy Adams*, ed. Charles Francis Adams, 12 vols. (Philadelphia: J. B. Lippincott, 1875–77), 8:185; Barry to Susan Taylor, 16 May, 25 June 1829, William T. Barry, "Letters of William T. Barry,"

William and Mary College Quarterly 13 (1904–5): 239–40, 242; Kendall to Blair, 7 Mar. 1829, Blair-Lee Papers.

35. Jackson to John Coffee, 19 Mar. 1829, Jackson to Richard K. Call, 5 July 1829, Jackson to John C. McLemore, 24 Nov. 1829, Jackson to John Overton, 31 Dec. 1829, JC, 4:13–14, 51–52, 88–89, 108–9; Smith, *First Forty Years*, p. 310; Barry to Susan Taylor, 25 Feb. 1830, "Letters of William T. Barry," *William and Mary College Quarterly* 14 (1905–6): 19.

36. Parton, *Jackson*, 3:287; Henry Wikoff, *Reminiscences of an Idler* (New York: Fords, Howard, and Hulbert, 1880), pp. 27–28.

37. Kendall, *Autobiography*, p. 280; Jackson to Rachel Jackson, 7 Dec. 1823, Jackson to Swartwout, 27 Sept. 1829, JC, 3:215, 4:79.

38. Barry to Susan Taylor, 16 May 1829, "Letters of Barry" (13), p. 239; Smith, *First Forty Years*, pp. 252–53; Jackson to Susan Decatur, 2 Jan. 1830, JC, 4:110. Richard B. Latner does not accept the social interpretation. He believes that Calhoun, Branch, and Berrien attacked Eaton and indirectly Van Buren because they had supported tariff protection. Latner, "The Eaton Affair Reconsidered," THQ 36 (1977): 332–51.

39. Eighty-seven of 167 letters from Jackson between 19 Mar. 1829 and 6 Aug. 1831, JC, 4:13–327, passim.

40. James C. Curtis, *Andrew Jackson and the Search for Vindication* (Boston: Little, Brown, 1976), pp. 94–101; Michael Paul Rogin, *Fathers and Children: Andrew Jackson and the Subjugation of the American Indian* (New York: Alfred A. Knopf, 1975), pp. 268–72; Jackson to Donelson, 24 Mar. 1831, 5 May 1831, JC, 4:251–54, 273–78.

41. Donelson, "Statement," 10 Nov. 1830, JC, 4:200–205.

42. Smith, *First Forty Years*, p. 299; *Daily National Intelligencer*, 9 May 1829; Kendall, *Autobiography*, pp. 307–8; Van Buren, *Autobiography*, p. 231; Jackson to Ralph E. W. Earl, 16 Mar. 1829, Microfilm Supplement to the Andrew Jackson Papers (Wilmington, Del.: Scholarly Resources, 1986) (JSM); Jackson to John Coffee, 22 Mar. 1829, JC, 4:14.

43. Richardson, *Messages and Papers*, 2:448–49.

44. Erik M. Eriksson, "The Federal Civil Service under President Jackson," MVHR 13 (1927): 519–20; Leonard D. White, *The Jacksonians: A Study in Administrative History, 1829–1861* (New York: Macmillan, 1954), p. 106.

45. Jackson, "Outline of Principles Submitted to the Heads of Departments," 23 Feb. 1829, JP; Kendall to Francis P. Blair, 7 Mar. 1829, Blair-Lee Papers; Washington *Globe*, 11 Dec. 1830, 11 Oct. 1832; Kendall, *Autobiography*, p. 298.

46. *Niles' Register* 36 (1829): 235–44, 299.

47. Ibid., pp. 34, 67, 152, 163.

48. Eriksson, "Federal Civil Service," p. 526; Alexis de Tocqueville, *Democracy in America*, ed. Phillips Bradley, 2 vols. (New York: Alfred A. Knopf, 1945), 1:130; Parton, *Jackson*, 3:206–7.

49. The removal rate of deputy postmasters, who made up 80 percent of all officials, was even lower. Postmaster General Barry announced in April 1830 that he had removed only 491 or 6 percent of the 8,050 deputy postmasters. *Niles' Register* 38 (3 April 1830): 104; Eriksson, "Federal Civil Service," pp. 526–29;

Thomas Hart Benton, *Thirty Years' View,* 2 vols. (New York: D. Appleton, 1854), 1:159–62; Carl R. Fish, "Removal of Officials by the Presidents of the United States," *Annual Report of the American Historical Association for the Year 1899,* 2 vols. (Washington, D.C.: Government Printing Office, 1900), 1:73–74.

50. For the argument that Jefferson made a large number of removals, see Carl E. Prince, "The Passing of the Aristocracy: Jefferson's Removals of the Federalists, 1801–1805," JAH 53 (Dec. 1970): 563–75. See also Fish, "Removal," pp. 84–85; Sidney H. Aronson, *Status and Kinship in the Higher Civil Service: Standards of Selection in the Administrations of John Adams, Thomas Jefferson, and Andrew Jackson* (Cambridge: Harvard University Press, 1964), p. 160; *Niles' Register* 38 (3 April 1830): 104; Parton, *Jackson,* 3:210.

51. *The Statistical History of the United States from Colonial Times to the Present* (Stamford, Conn.: Fairfield Publishers, 1965), p. 710; James S. Young, *The Washington Community 1800–1828* (New York: Columbia University Press, 1966), p. 31. The total of 3,000 in 1801 is an extrapolation from the data in these two sources. See also Parton, *Jackson,* 3:214.

52. These men were appointed while they were members of Congress, or within the next six months. United States Constitution, Article 1, section 6; *United States Telegraph,* 11 July 1834; Eriksson, "Federal Civil Service," p. 533; Alvin W. Lynn, "Party Formation and Operation in the House of Representatives, 1824–1837" (Ph.D. diss., Rutgers University, 1972), pp. 258–59.

53. Tyler to Robert W. Christian, 13 May 1830, Lyon G. Tyler, *The Letters and Times of the Tylers,* 3 vols. (Richmond, Va.: Whittet & Shepperson, 1884, 1886), 1:408; Johnston to Henry Clay, 13 April 1830, Clay, *Papers,* 8:191–92; Adams, *Memoirs,* 8:215; Culver H. Smith, *The Press, Politics, and Patronage: The American Government's Use of Newspapers 1789–1875* (Athens: University of Georgia Press, 1977), pp. 79–80; *Niles' Register* 48 (2 May 1835): 147.

54. Smith, *Press, Politics, and Patronage,* pp. 86–88, 258–61; *National Journal,* 3, 8 Dec. 1829, 11 May 1830; *Intelligencer,* 27 Sept. 1832; Ritchie to Van Buren, 27 Mar. 1829, Van Buren, *Autobiography,* pp. 246–48.

55. Since the removals were given only in ten-year intervals, it was impossible to cite precise percentages for each president. Fish, "Removal," pp. 84–85; Carl R. Fish, *The Civil Service and the Patronage* (Cambridge: Harvard University Press, 1904), pp. 158–72; "Diary and Memoranda of William L. Marcy" (1857), AHR 24 (1918–19): 647.

56. In discussing Jackson and the patronage system I have drawn on Paul E. Johnson, "The Spoils System and Party Organization: 1829–1840" (unpublished paper, c. 1970). Jackson to Susan Decatur, 2 April 1829, fragment of a letter in Jackson's handwriting, 1831, JC, 4:22, 6:504.

57. Jackson to Van Buren, 31 Mar. 1829, Van Buren, *Autobiography,* p. 249; Ben: Perley Poore, *Perley's Reminiscences of Sixty Years in the National Metropolis,* 2 vols. (Philadelphia: Hubbard Brothers, 1886), 1:111–12; Hamilton, *Reminiscences,* p. 140.

58. Adams, *Memoirs,* 8:131, 172.

59. Jackson to Ingham, 3 Oct. 1829, Charles Hamilton Galleries, JSM.

60. Hoyt to Van Buren, 21 Mar. 1829, William L. Mackenzie, *The Lives and*

Opinions of Benjamin Franklin Butler . . . and Jesse Hoyt (Boston: Cooke, 1845), pp. 51–52; Hoyt to Van Buren, 11 April 1829, VBP.

61. William Hartman, "The New York Custom House: Seat of Spoils Politics," *New York History* 34 (1953): 149–63; Van Buren, *Autobiography,* p. 266.

62. Van Buren to James A. Hamilton, Mar. 1829, Hamilton, *Reminiscences,* p. 129; Van Buren to Andrew J. Donelson, 14 May 1829, Andrew J. Donelson Papers, LC; John M. Belohlavek, *"Let the Eagle Soar!": The Foreign Policy of Andrew Jackson* (Lincoln: University of Nebraska Press, 1985), pp. 34, 274; John Niven, *Martin Van Buren and the Romantic Age of American Politics* (New York: Oxford University Press, 1983), p. 238.

63. Maxcy to Calhoun, 6 April 1829, James Hamilton, Jr., to Calhoun, 10 May 1829, John C. Calhoun, *The Papers of John C. Calhoun,* ed. Robert L. Merriwether, W. Edwin Hemphill, and Clyde Wilson, 20 vols. to date (Columbia: University of South Carolina Press, 1959–), 11:15–17, 43–44; Parton, *Jackson,* 3:224–25; Lewis to Jackson, 30 Aug. 1839, JC, 6:23.

64. Green to Calhoun, 16 June 1829, Calhoun to Ingham, 26 Sept. 1829, Calhoun, *Papers,* 11:52–53, 78–80; Kendall to Francis P. Blair, 21 June 1829, Blair-Lee Papers.

65. Donald B. Cole, *Jacksonian Democracy in New Hampshire, 1800–1851* (Cambridge: Harvard University Press, 1970), pp. 83–96; Arthur B. Darling, *Political Changes in Massachusetts 1824–1828: A Study of Liberal Movements in Politics* (New Haven, Conn.: Yale University Press, 1925), pp. 59–74; Cambreleng to Jackson, 28 April, 1829, VBP; Adams, *Memoirs,* 8:259.

66. Maxcy to Calhoun, 7 May 1829, Calhoun, *Papers,* 11:30–41. Jackson had offered the positions of secretary of war and minister to Great Britain to Tazewell, but he accepted neither.

67. Kendall to Blair, 9 Jan., 12, 30 April, 21 June 1829, Blair-Lee Papers.

68. Sellers, *Polk, Jacksonian,* pp. 135–40, 142–43, 151-52, 197–98.

CHAPTER 3
FACING CONGRESS

1. James S. Young, *The Washington Community 1800–1828* (New York: Columbia University Press, 1966), pp. 69–71, 89–90, 158–59.

2. Ibid., pp. 98–109, 128–37; Alvin W. Lynn, "Party Formation and Operation in the House of Representatives, 1824–1837" (Ph.D. diss., Rutgers University, 1972), pp. 219, 308, 336, 340–42, 460; Perry M. Goldman and James S. Young, eds., *The United States Congressional Directories, 1789–1840* (New York: Columbia University Press, 1973), pp. 216–20.

3. Daniel Feller, "Andrew Jackson versus the Senate" (unpublished paper, c. 1989), pp. 1–4.

4. Kenneth C. Martis, *The Historical Atlas of Political Parties in the United States Congress 1789–1989* (New York: Macmillan, 1989), pp. 90, 332–36; *Niles' Register* 38 (8 May 1830): 203; Martin Van Buren, "The Autobiography of Martin Van Buren,"

ed. John C. Fitzpatrick, *Annual Report of the American Historical Association for the Year 1918*, vol. 2 (Washington, D.C.: Government Printing Office, 1920), p. 289.

5. Goldman and Young, *Congressional Directories*, pp. 220–25; Martis, *Historical Atlas*, pp. 90, 332–35. For the view that only seven committees had a Jacksonian majority, see Lynn, "Party Formation," pp. 380–81. See also *Register of Debates in Congress, 1825–1837*, 21st Cong., 1st sess., p. 1147, quoted in David J. Russo, "The Major Political Issues of the Jacksonian Period and the Development of Party Loyalty in Congress, 1830–1840," *Transactions of the American Philosophical Society*, n. s., 62, pt. 5 (May 1972): 6.

6. For a useful discussion of the history of selecting committees in the Senate, see *Register of Debates in Congress*, 23d Cong., 1st sess., pp. 19–28. See also Goldman and Young, *Congressional Directories*, pp. 225–27; Martis, *Historical Atlas*, pp. 90, 336.

7. Martis, *Historical Atlas*, pp. 90, 332–36.

8. Samuel Herrick et al. to Jackson, 3 Jan. 1829, Jackson to Judith Rives, 28 June 1829, William C. Rives Papers, LC, JSM; John Brown to Jackson, 10 Mar. 1829, JP; Balch to Jackson, 8 Jan. 1830, Andrew Jackson, *Correspondence of Andrew Jackson*, ed. John Spencer Bassett and John Franklin Jameson, 7 vols. (1926–35; reprint, New York: Kraus Reprint Co., 1969), 4:114–16.

9. *A Compilation of the Messages and Papers of the Presidents, 1789–1897*, comp. James D. Richardson, 10 vols. (Washington, D.C.: Government Printing Office, 1897–99), 2:442–62.

10. *Register of Debates*, 21st Cong., 1st sess., app., p. 103; *The Statistical History of the United States from Colonial Times to the Present* (Stamford, Conn.: Fairfield Publishers, 1965), p. 623.

11. Woodbury to Ingham, 27 June 1829, Ingham to Biddle, 23 July 1829, Biddle to Ingham, 15 Sept. 1829, House of Representatives, *Report on the Bank of the United States* (30 April 1832), no. 460, 22d Cong., 1st sess., pp. 439–40, 446–48, 450–56.

12. Biddle, "Memorandum of a Conversation with A. Jackson," n.d., Nicholas Biddle Papers, LC.

13. Jackson to William B. Lewis, 26 June 1830, JC, 4:156–57.

14. Jackson, "Memorandum on Biddle's Letter," Nov.? 1829, JC, 4:84–85; Jackson to Hamilton, 3 June 1830, James A. Hamilton, *Reminiscences of James A. Hamilton* (New York: Charles Scribner's Sons, 1869), pp. 167–68; Jackson to Dawson, 17 July 1830, JSM.

15. Kentucky and Tennessee were the only western states in which most of the unoccupied land was held by the state and not by the federal government. Daniel Feller, *The Public Lands in Jacksonian Politics* (Madison: University of Wisconsin Press, 1984), pp. 3–9, 77, 105–7.

16. Ibid., pp. 111–13; Charles G. De Witt, "The Great Webster-Hayne Debate," *Olde Ulster* 9 (Nov. 1913): 332–34, quoted in William N. Chambers, *Old Bullion Benton: Senator from the New West* (Boston: Little, Brown, 1956), pp. 161–62.

17. Merrill D. Peterson, *The Great Triumvirate: Webster, Clay, and Calhoun* (New York: Oxford University Press, 1987), pp. 170–79.

18. James Parton, *Life of Andrew Jackson*, 3 vols. (New York: Mason Brothers, 1860), 3:282.

19. Feller, *Public Lands*, pp. 125–26.

20. Ibid., pp. 126–31.

21. Ibid., pp. 131–33.

22. Donald B. Cole, *Martin Van Buren and the American Political System* (Princeton, N.J.: Princeton University Press, 1984), pp. 208–11.

23. Richardson, *Messages and Papers*, 2:311–17; George Rogers Taylor, *The Transportation Revolution, 1815–1860* (New York: Harper & Row, 1951), pp. 20–21.

24. Feller, *Public Lands*, pp. 136–39.

25. Van Buren, *Autobiography*, pp. 320–26.

26. Richardson, *Messages and Papers*, 2:483–93.

27. Ibid.

28. Carlton Jackson, "The Internal Improvement Vetoes of Andrew Jackson," THQ 25 (1966): 268–72.

29. Ibid., pp. 275–77; *Presidential Vetoes 1789–1976* (Washington, D.C.: Government Printing Office, 1978), pp. ix, 5, 9–11.

30. James Hamilton, Jr., to Van Buren, 8 June 1830, Jackson to Van Buren, 26 June 1830, VBP; Jackson to William B. Lewis, 26 June 1830, JC, 4:156; Grundy to Jackson, 31 July 1830, JP; *Richmond Enquirer*, 1 June 1830.

31. Jackson, "Internal Improvement Vetoes," pp. 262–66; Richard E. Ellis, *The Union at Risk: Jacksonian Democracy, States' Rights and the Nullification Crisis* (New York: Oxford University Press, 1987), pp. 19–25; Richard B. Latner, *The Presidency of Andrew Jackson: White House Politics 1829–1837* (Athens: University of Georgia Press, 1979), pp. 98–107.

32. Jackson to Van Buren, 18 Oct. 1830, JC, 4:185–86.

33. For Jackson's interest in the political effects of the Maysville veto, see his letters to Van Buren and Lewis cited in n. 30.

34. After 1833 the road was turned over to the states for maintenance. Jackson, "Internal Improvement Vetoes," pp. 261n, 267, 277; Taylor, *Transportation Revolution*, pp. 20–21; *Niles' Register* 38 (10 April 1830): 123; John Spencer Bassett, *The Life of Andrew Jackson*, 2 vols. in 1 (1911; reprint, Hamden, Conn.: Archon Books, 1967), p. 495.

35. Taylor, *Transportation Revolution*, pp. 372–75. Wholesale commodity prices rose 50 percent, 1834–37. Peter Temin, *The Jacksonian Economy* (New York: W. W. Norton, 1969), p. 69.

36. Francis Paul Prucha, *The Great Father: The United States and the American Indians*, 2 vols. (Lincoln: University of Nebraska Press, 1984), 1:218–20, 225–26, 233, 241, 260; Ronald N. Satz, *American Indian Policy in the Jacksonian Era* (Lincoln: University of Nebraska Press, 1975), pp. 97, 105–6.

37. Robert V. Remini, *Andrew Jackson and the Course of American Freedom, 1822–1832* (New York: Harper & Row, 1981), pp. 66, 221, 227–28, 264; Jackson to Calhoun, 18 Jan. 1821, Jackson, "Talk with Indian Chieftains," 20 Sept. 1821, JC, 3:36–38, 118–21.

38. Jackson to Creek Indians, 23 Mar. 1829, *Niles' Register* 36 (1829): 257–58; Eaton to Cherokee delegation, 18 April 1829, JSM.

39. Bertram Wyatt-Brown, "Prelude to Abolitionism: Sabbatarian Politics and the Rise of the Second Party System," *JAH* 58 (Sept. 1971): 320–29.

40. "Report of the Committee on the Post Office and the Post Roads of the United States Senate," Joseph L. Blau, ed., *Social Theories of Jacksonian Democracy, Representative Writings of the Period 1825–1850* (New York: Liberal Arts Press, 1945), pp. 274–81.

41. Satz, *Indian Policy*, pp. 13–19; Prucha, *Great Father*, pp. 201–5; Herman J. Viola, *Thomas L. McKenney: Architect of America's Early Indian Policy: 1816–1830* (Chicago: Swallow Press, 1974), pp. 206–22.

42. Carroll to Jackson, 29 June 1829, 23d Cong., 1st sess., S. Doc. 512 (Serial 245), pp. 76–77, JSM; *Richmond Enquirer,* 9 June 1829.

43. *Niles' Register* 38 (13 Mar. 1830): 54–55.

44. Goldman and Young, *Congressional Directories,* pp. 222, 226; Jackson, "Indian case," scrap at end of 1829, JP.

45. "Indian Removal Act," 28 May 1830, Francis Paul Prucha, ed., *Documents of United States Indian Policy* (Lincoln: University of Nebraska Press, 1975), pp. 52–53.

46. Frelinghuysen to Evarts, 22 Feb. 1830, Jeremiah Evarts Papers, LC; U.S. Senate, *Speeches on the Passage of the Bill for the Removal of the Indians,* 21st Cong., 1st sess. (1830; reprint, Millwood, N.Y.: Kraus Reprint Co., 1973), pp. 1–78; *Register of Debates,* 21st Cong., 1st sess., pp. 325–39. Of the Jacksonian senators twenty-five voted for the bill and one did not vote; among the opposition nineteen voted against the bill and three for it. *Register of Debates,* 21st Cong., 1st sess., p. 383.

47. Van Buren, *Autobiography,* pp. 288–89.

48. Wilcomb E. Washburn, ed., *The American Indian and the United States: A Documentary History,* 4 vols. (Westport, Conn.: Greenwood Press, 1973), 2:1017–93.

49. Satz, *Indian Policy,* pp. 65–66; *Speeches on Removal of the Indians,* pp. 255–300; *Register of Debates,* 21st Cong., 1st sess., p. 1141.

50. *Register of Debates,* 21st Cong., 1st sess., pp. 1131–35; Van Buren, *Autobiography,* p. 289.

51. This analysis is based on the vote to read the bill for the third time, the results of which were almost identical with the final vote. *Register of Debates,* 21st Cong., 1st sess., p. 1133. Charles Sellers argues that "party lines crystallized in Congress," but 36 of 135 Democrats defied the president by refusing to vote for the bill. Sellers, *The Market Revolution: Jacksonian America, 1815–1846* (New York: Oxford University Press, 1991), p. 311. See also Van Buren, *Autobiography,* p. 289; Latner, *Presidency of Jackson,* p. 93.

52. Erik M. Eriksson, "The Federal Civil Service under President Jackson," *MVHR* 13 (1927): 523–24; Webster to Warren Dutton, 9 May 1830, Daniel Webster, *The Private Correspondence of Daniel Webster,* ed. Fletcher Webster, 2 vols. (Boston: Little, Brown, 1856), 1:501; John Quincy Adams, *Memoirs of John Quincy Adams,* ed. Charles Francis Adams, 12 vols. (Philadelphia: J. B. Lippincott, 1875–77), 8:184.

53. Feller, "Jackson versus Senate," pp. 5–8; Tyler to Robert W. Christian, 13

May 1830, Lyon G. Tyler, *The Life and Times of the Tylers*, 3 vols. (Richmond: Whittet & Shepperson, 1884, 1886), 1:408.

54. Jackson to a committee, Sept. 1832, JC, 4:478–79; Feller, "Jackson versus Senate," pp. 5–6; Adams, *Memoirs*, 8:206; Josiah S. Johnston to Henry Clay, 14 Mar. 1830, Henry Clay, *The Papers of Henry Clay*, ed. James F. Hopkins, Mary W. M. Hargreaves, Robert Seager II, and Melba Porter Hay, 10 vols. to date (Lexington: University Press of Kentucky, 1959–), 8:181–83.

55. Parton, *Jackson*, 3:277–78; Remini, *Jackson and Freedom*, p. 256.

CHAPTER 4
SEEKING HARMONY

1. Webster to Warren Dutton, 15 Jan. 1830, Daniel Webster, *The Private Correspondence of Daniel Webster*, ed. Fletcher Webster, 2 vols. (Boston: Little, Brown, 1856), 1:483; Green to Ninian Edwards, 27 April 1830, Ninian Edwards, *The Edwards Papers, Being a Portion of the Collection of the Letters, Papers, and Manuscripts of Ninian Edwards*, ed. E. B. Washburne, Chicago Historical Society's Collections, vol. 3 (Chicago: Fergus Printing Co., 1884), p. 488.

2. John Williams to Martin Van Buren, 22 Mar. 1831, Andrew Jackson, *Correspondence of Andrew Jackson*, ed. John Spencer Bassett and John Franklin Jameson, 7 vols. (1926–35; reprint, New York: Kraus Reprint Co., 1969), 4:229n–230n.

3. Jackson to Calhoun, 13, 30 May 1830, JC, 4:136, 140–41; Calhoun to Jackson, 29 May 1830, John C. Calhoun, *The Papers of John C. Calhoun*, ed. Robert L. Merriwether, W. Edwin Hemphill, and Clyde Wilson, 20 vols. to date (Columbia: University of South Carolina Press, 1959–), 11:173–91.

4. Calhoun to Maxcy, 6 Aug. 1830, Calhoun, *Papers*, 11:215; Martin Van Buren, "The Autobiography of Martin Van Buren," ed. John C. Fitzpatrick, *Annual Report of the American Historical Association for the Year 1918*, vol. 2 (Washington, D.C.: Government Printing Office, 1920), pp. 376–77; Colt to Nicholas Biddle, 29 Jan. 1831, Nicholas Biddle, *The Correspondence of Nicholas Biddle Dealing with National Affairs, 1807–1844*, ed. Reginald C. McGrane (Boston: Houghton Mifflin, 1919), p. 122.

5. Monroe's biographer, Harry Ammon, believes that Jackson was lying; see Ammon, *James Monroe: The Quest for National Identity* (New York: McGraw-Hill, 1971), pp. 415–17. For Jackson's version, see Jackson, "Memorandum," Feb. 1831, JC, 4:228–36, and Thomas Hart Benton, *Thirty Years' View*, 2 vols. (New York: D. Appleton, 1854), 1:169–74. See also Rhea to Jackson, 4 Jan., 30 Mar. 1831, Jackson to Rhea, 2 June 1831, Rhea to Monroe, 3 June 1831, JC, 4:221–22, 254–55, 288–89; Jackson to Rhea, 23 April 1831, JP.

6. *United States Telegraph*, 17 Feb. 1831; Jackson to Overton, 12 Feb. 1831, JSM; Van Buren, *Autobiography*, pp. 376–87; James Parton, *Life of Andrew Jackson*, 3 vols. (New York: Mason Brothers, 1860), 3:326–27.

7. Van Buren, *Autobiography*, pp. 386–87; Floyd, "Diary," 11 Mar. 1831, Charles H. Ambler, *The Life and Diary of John Floyd* (Richmond, Va.: Richmond

Press, 1918), p. 126; Yell to James K. Polk, 13 Mar. 1831, James K. Polk, *Correspondence of James K. Polk*, ed. Herbert Weaver, Paul H. Bergeron, and Wayne Cutler, 7 vols. to date (Nashville: Vanderbilt University Press, 1969–), 1:402–4; Storrs to Abraham Van Vechten, 22 Feb. 1831, Henry R. Storrs Miscellaneous Papers, New-York Historical Society; *Albany Argus*, 7 Mar. 1831.

8. Jackson to Lewis, 21, 28 July, 7, 15, 17, 25 Aug. 1830, JC, 4:165–66, 167–68, 170–71, 173–74, 176–78.

9. Van Buren, *Autobiography*, pp. 397–406; Donald B. Cole, *Martin Van Buren and the American Political System* (Princeton, N.J.: Princeton University Press, 1984), pp. 218–19.

10. Jackson to Lewis, 25 Aug. 1830, JC, 4:178; Van Buren, *Autobiography*, pp. 406–7; Royce C. McCrary, "The Long Agony Is Nearly Over," *Pennsylvania Magazine of History and Biography* 100 (1976): 231–42.

11. Nineteen men served in the cabinet under Madison, twenty-one under Tyler.

12. Worden Pope to Jackson, 19 Aug. 1831, JP; Samuel D. Ingham to John M. Berrien, 4, 7 May 1831, McCrary, "Long Agony," pp. 239–41.

13. McCrary, "Long Agony," pp. 233–34; Jackson to Van Buren, 23 June 1831, JC, 4:301–2.

14. Jackson to White, 9 April 1830, JC, 4:258–60.

15. For the argument that Jackson appointed "socially acceptable" men to the cabinet, see Lynn L. Marshall, "The Strange Stillbirth of the Whig Party," AHR 72 (Jan. 1967): 460.

16. Van Rensselaer to Clay, 23 June 1831, Henry Clay Papers, LC; Carroll to Jackson, 13 June 1831, JP; Van Buren, *Autobiography*, p. 398; Richard McCall to Thomas Cadwalader, 20 April 1831, Cadwalader Collection, Historical Society of Pennsylvania, Philadelphia; Samuel D. Ingham to John M. Berrien, 4, 7 May 1831, McCrary, "Long Agony," pp. 239–41.

17. Kendall to Francis P. Blair, 25 April 1830, Blair-Lee Papers; Kendall to Lewis, 17 May 1831, Lewis to Kendall, 25 May 1831, "Origin of the Democratic National Convention," *American Historical Magazine* 7 (1902): 267–73.

18. Kendall to Francis P. Blair, 25 April 1830, Blair-Lee Papers; Jackson to William B. Lewis, 26 June 1830, JC, 4:156.

19. Kendall to Blair, 3 Feb., 21 June 1829, 18 Mar., 25, 30 April, 19 July, 22 Aug., 2 Oct. 1830, Blair-Lee Papers; Kendall, *Autobiography of Amos Kendall*, ed. William Stickney (1872; reprint, New York: Peter Smith, 1949), pp. 370–73; Michael W. Singletary, "The New Editorial Voice for Andrew Jackson: Happenstance or Plan?" *Journalism Quarterly* 53 (1976): 672–78; Van Buren, *Autobiography*, p. 377.

20. Circulation figures for the 1830s are unreliable. Elbert B. Smith credits the *Globe* with a circulation of 17,000 in 1835, but Erik M. Eriksson says that it was only 6,000 in 1834, and Frank Luther Mott maintains that the widest circulation of any newspaper in 1833 was 4,500. Smith, *Francis Preston Blair* (New York: Free Press, 1980), pp. 43–48; Eriksson, "President Jackson's Propaganda Agencies," *Pacific Historical Review* 6 (1937): 48–54; Mott, *American Journalism: A History of Newspapers in the United States through 250 Years 1690–1940* (New York: Macmillan, 1941), pp. 202–3. See also Culver H. Smith, *The Press, Politics, and Patronage: The*

American Government's Use of Newspapers 1789–1875 (Athens: University of Georgia Press, 1977), pp. 250–51; Washington *Globe*, 1 July, 5 Nov. 1831.

21. Blair to Maria Gratz, 12 Dec. 1830, 5, 23 Feb., 20 April, 10 May 1831, Thomas H. Clay, ed., "Two Years with Old Hickory," *Atlantic Monthly* 60 (1887): 187–94.

22. *Globe*, 11 Dec. 1830, 12, 15, 19, 22, 29 Jan., 4, 19, 23, 26 Feb., 2 Mar. 1831; William E. Smith, "Francis P. Blair, Pen-Executive of Andrew Jackson," MVHR 17 (1930–31): 543–56; Smith, *Blair*, pp. 71–72.

23. Richard B. Latner, "The Kitchen Cabinet and Andrew Jackson's Advisory System," JAH 65 (Sept. 1978): 371–74; Blair to Maria Gratz, 27 Aug. 1831, Clay, "Two Years with Old Hickory," p. 198; Robert M. Gibbes to Biddle, 11 Dec. 1831, Nicholas Biddle Papers, both quoted in Latner, "Kitchen Cabinet," p. 374.

24. Latner, "Kitchen Cabinet," pp. 374–77. Van Buren, who used the term "sinister" to describe Poindexter, also armed himself after a quarrel with the Mississippian; see Van Buren, *Autobiography*, pp. 755, 761–62.

25. Marshall, "Strange Stillbirth," pp. 450–58; Latner, "Kitchen Cabinet," pp. 377–88; Richard P. Longaker, "Was Jackson's Kitchen Cabinet a Cabinet?" MVHR 44 (1957): 94–108.

26. Longaker, "Was Jackson's Kitchen Cabinet a Cabinet?" pp. 95–96; James C. Curtis, "Andrew Jackson and His Cabinet: Some New Evidence," THQ 27 (1968): 157–64.

27. Levi Woodbury, "Levi Woodbury's 'Intimate Memoranda' of the Jackson Administration," ed. Ari Hoogenboom and Herbert Ershkowitz, *Pennsylvania Magazine of History and Biography* 92 (1968): 513. The quotation was written 10 Jan. 1834. Roger B. Taney, "Roger B. Taney's 'Bank War Manuscript,'" ed. Carl Brent Swisher, MHM 53 (1958): 122–30, 225–26.

28. Woodbury, "Intimate Memoranda," p. 513; Kendall, *Autobiography*, p. 635. Jackson's use of his cabinet did not differ greatly from that of his predecessors.

CHAPTER 5
THE BANK VETO AND INDIAN REMOVAL

1. John A. Munroe, *Louis McLane: Federalist and Jacksonian* (New Brunswick, N.J.: Rutgers University Press, 1973), pp. 302–4; Jackson to Van Buren, 5 Sept. 1831, Andrew Jackson, *Correspondence of Andrew Jackson*, ed. John Spencer Bassett and John Franklin Jameson, 7 vols. (1926–35; reprint, New York, Kraus Reprint Co., 1969), 4:347.

2. Van Buren to Jackson, 11 Oct. 1831, JC, 4:358.

3. *A Compilation of the Messages and Papers of the Presidents, 1789–1897*, comp. James D. Richardson, 10 vols. (Washington, D.C.: Government Printing Office, 1897–99), 2:529; Washington *Globe*, 29 Dec. 1830, 12 Jan., 27, 30 April, 4 May 1831.

4. Thomas Hart Benton, *Thirty Years' View*, 2 vols. (New York: D. Appleton, 1854), 1:187–205.

5. Bray Hammond holds New York responsible for the Bank War in *Banks*

and Politics in America from the Revolution to the Civil War (Princeton, N.J.: Princeton University Press, 1957), pp. 351–56. For a contrasting view, see Frank Otto Gatell, "Sober Second Thoughts on Van Buren, the Albany Regency, and the Wall Street Conspiracy," JAH 53 (1966): 19–40.

6. James L. Crouthamel, "Did the Second Bank of the United States Bribe the Press?" *Journalism Quarterly* 36 (1959): 35–39; James Watson Webb to Van Buren, 12 April 1831, VBP.

7. Pope to Jackson, 19 June, 6 Aug. 1831, JC, 4:297–99, 326–27.

8. Munroe, *McLane*, pp. 304–7.

9. Ibid., pp. 310–13; Louis McLane, "Annual Report," 7 Dec. 1831, Committee on Banking and Currency, United States Senate, *Federal Banking Laws and Reports, 1780–1912* (Washington, D.C.: Government Printing Office, 1963), pp. 188–92.

10. Biddle, "Memorandum," 19 Oct. 1831, Nicholas Biddle, *The Correspondence of Nicholas Biddle Dealing with National Affairs, 1807–1844,* ed. Reginald C. McGrane (Boston: Houghton Mifflin, 1919), pp. 128–35; Jackson to Van Buren, 6 Dec. 1831, JC, 4:379.

11. Roger B. Taney, "Roger B. Taney's 'Bank War Manuscript,'" ed. Carl Brent Swisher, MHM 53 (1958): 121–30, 215–16.

12. Richardson, *Messages and Papers,* 2:544–58.

13. Cambreleng to Jesse Hoyt, 29 Dec. 1831, William L. Mackenzie, *The Life and Times of Martin Van Buren* (Boston: Cooke, 1846), p. 230; McLane to Van Buren, 14 Dec. 1831, VBP; *Globe,* 9, 12 Dec. 1831.

14. C. C. Cambreleng to Van Buren, 4 Feb. 1832, VBP; Montgomery Blair, "Sketch of F. P. Blair, Sr.," 13 May 1858?, pp. 7–8, Blair-Lee Papers; Richard B. Latner, *The Presidency of Andrew Jackson: White House Politics 1829–1837* (Athens: University of Georgia Press, 1979), pp. 114–17.

15. The Calhoun men were Gabriel Moore of Alabama, George Poindexter of Mississippi, and Robert Y. Hayne and Stephen D. Miller of South Carolina. Kenneth C. Martis, *The Historical Atlas of Political Parties in the United States Congress 1789–1989* (New York: Macmillan, 1989), pp. 24, 91, 337–41. According to Alvin W. Lynn, there were only eighty-seven Jacksonian congressmen; see Lynn, "Party Formation and Operation in the House of Representatives, 1824–1837" (Ph.D. diss., Rutgers University, 1972), pp. 162–72.

16. Clay to Biddle, 15 Dec. 1831, Webster to Biddle, 18 Dec. 1831, Biddle, *Correspondence,* pp. 142, 145–46.

17. Cadwalader to Biddle, 20, 21, 22, 23, 25, 26 Dec. 1831, Samuel Smith to Biddle, 17 Dec. 1831, Biddle to Cadwalader, 23, 24 Dec. 1831, Biddle to Samuel Smith, 4 Jan. 1832, Biddle, *Correspondence,* pp. 143–65, 184–85.

18. John M. Belohlavek, "Dallas, Democracy, and the Bank War of 1832," *Pennsylvania Magazine of History and Biography* 96 (1972): 377–82; Benton, *Thirty Years' View,* 1:232–33, 235–36.

19. Benton, *Thirty Years' View,* 1:233–35; *Register of Debates in Congress, 1825–1837,* 22d Cong., 1st sess., pp. 53–55, 58, 113–14.

20. Robert V. Remini, *Andrew Jackson and the Bank War: A Study in the Growth of Presidential Power* (New York: W. W. Norton, 1967), pp. 41–42; Belohlavek, "Dallas," pp. 383–85.

21. Cambreleng to Van Buren, 4, 5 Feb. 1832, VBP; Montgomery Blair, "Sketch of F. P. Blair, Sr.," 13 May 1858?, pp. 7–8, Blair-Lee Papers; Cambreleng to Hoyt, 16 Feb. 1832, William L. Mackenzie, *The Lives and Opinions of Benjamin Franklin Butler . . . and Jesse Hoyt* (Boston: Cooke, 1845), p. 101.

22. House Ways and Means Committee, "Report on Renewal of Charter of Bank of the United States," 9 Feb. 1832, Committee on Banking and Currency, *Federal Banking Laws and Reports*, pp. 193–209; Benton, *Thirty Years' View*, 1:235–42.

23. Ingersoll to Biddle, 23 Feb., 6 Mar. 1832, Biddle, *Correspondence*, pp. 184–85, 188–90; John Quincy Adams, *Memoirs of John Quincy Adams*, ed. Charles Francis Adams, 12 vols. (Philadelphia: J. B. Lippincott, 1875–77), 8:483; James A. Hamilton to Jackson, 7 May 1832, JC, 4:437; Crouthamel, "Second Bank," pp. 35–44.

24. "Bill to Renew Charter of Bank of the United States," Committee on Banking and Currency, *Federal Banking Laws and Reports*, pp. 210–12.

25. *Register of Debates*, 22d Cong., 1st sess., pp. 3851–52.

26. Martin Van Buren, "The Autobiography of Martin Van Buren," ed. John C. Fitzpatrick, *Annual Report of the American Historical Association for the Year 1918*, vol. 2 (Washington, D.C.: Government Printing Office, 1920), p. 625; Taney, "Bank War Manuscript," pp. 224–28; Lynn L. Marshall, "The Authorship of Jackson's Bank Veto Message," MVHR 50 (1963): 466–77.

27. Arthur M. Schlesinger, Jr., *The Age of Jackson* (Boston: Little, Brown, 1945), p. 90; Harry L. Watson, *Liberty and Power: The Politics of Jacksonian America* (New York: Hill and Wang, 1990), p. 147.

28. Richardson, *Messages and Papers*, 2:576–91; Taney to Jackson, 27 June 1832, JP.

29. *Register of Debates*, 22d Cong., 1st sess., pp. 1221–40.

30. Ibid., pp. 1265–74, 1296.

31. William W. Freehling, *Prelude to Civil War: The Nullification Controversy in South Carolina, 1816–1836* (New York: Harper & Row, 1966), p. 247; Richardson, *Messages and Papers*, 2:250, 524, 556.

32. *Globe*, 9 Feb., 25 Mar., 12, 30 May, 25 June 1832; McLane to Jackson, 5 May 1832, JP; Ritchie to Van Buren, 25 June 1832; *Niles' Register* 42 (9 June 1832): 279.

33. F. W. Taussig, *The Tariff History of the United States*, 6th ed. (New York: G. P. Putnam's Sons, 1892), pp. 90–110; Jackson to John Coffee, 17 July 1832, JC, 4:462–63.

34. Frederick Jackson Turner, *The United States 1830–1850: The Nation and Its Sections* (1935; reprint, New York: W. W. Norton, 1965), pp. 399–402.

35. Daniel Feller, *The Public Lands in Jacksonian Politics* (Madison: University of Wisconsin Press, 1984), pp. 143–55; *Register of Debates*, 22d Cong., 1st sess., pp. 1174, 3852–53. My voting analysis is based on the final vote and is thus slightly different from Feller's, which is based on a combination of the final vote and the vote on third reading.

36. *Richmond Enquirer*, 10 July 1832; Richardson, *Messages and Papers*, 2:601–3, 638–39.

37. Ronald N. Satz, *American Indian Policy in the Jacksonian Era* (Lincoln: University of Nebraska Press, 1975), p. 154; Herman J. Viola, *Thomas L. McKenney:*

Architect of America's Early Indian Policy: 1816–1830 (Chicago: Swallow Press, 1974), pp. 223–34.

38. Satz, *Indian Policy,* pp. 66–68, 112, 154–57.

39. Jackson's speech to the Chickasaws, 23 Aug. 1830, quoted in Robert V. Remini, *Andrew Jackson and the Course of American Freedom, 1822–1832* (New York: Harper & Row, 1981), p. 270.

40. Satz, *Indian Policy,* pp. 69–70; Francis Paul Prucha, *The Great Father: The United States and the American Indians,* 2 vols. (Lincoln: University of Nebraska Press, 1984), 1:216–19; "Treaty with the Choctaw Indians," 27 Sept. 1830, Francis Paul Prucha, ed., *Documents of United States Indian Policy* (Lincoln: University of Nebraska Press, 1975), pp. 53–58; Jackson to Coffee, 16 Oct. 1830, JSM.

41. Satz, *Indian Policy,* pp. 65–66, 70–78.

42. Alexis de Tocqueville, *Democracy in America,* ed. Phillips Bradley, 2 vols. (New York: Alfred A. Knopf, 1945), 1:340.

43. Satz, *Indian Policy,* pp. 78–83; Jackson to John Coffee, 6 Nov. 1832, JC, 4:483.

44. Mary Elizabeth Young, *Redskins, Ruffleshirts, and Rednecks: Indian Allotments in Alabama and Mississippi 1830–1860* (Norman: University of Oklahoma Press, 1961), pp. 47–72; Satz, *Indian Policy,* pp. 83–87.

45. Satz, *Indian Policy,* pp. 105–6; Young, *Redskins, Ruffleshirts, and Rednecks,* pp. 73–98; Prucha, *Great Father,* 1:223–26.

46. Satz, *Indian Policy,* pp. 101–4, 113–15. The Seminole population figure was for 1825. Edwin C. McReynolds, *The Seminoles* (Norman: University of Oklahoma Press, 1957), p. 118.

47. "Memorial of the Cherokee Nation," *Niles' Register* 38 (21 Aug. 1830): 454–57.

48. "Resolution and Statements of the Missionaries," Louis Filler and Allen Guttmann, eds., *The Removal of the Cherokee Nation: Manifest Destiny or National Dishonor?* (Boston: D. C. Heath, 1962), pp. 53–60.

49. Richardson, *Messages and Papers,* 2:520, 536–41.

50. Cherokee Nation v. Georgia (1831), 5 Peters 1–80; Van Buren, *Autobiography,* p. 292.

51. Worcester v. Georgia (1832), 6 Peters 515–97.

52. Horace Greeley, *The American Conflict: A History of the Great Rebellion in the United States of America* (Hartford: O. D. Case, 1864), 1:106; Jackson to John Coffee, 7 April 1832, JC, 4:429–30.

53. Edwin Miles, "After John Marshall's Decision: *Worcester* v. *Georgia* and the Nullification Crisis," *Journal of Southern History* 39 (1973): 519–44; Jackson to Lumpkin, 22 June 1832, JC, 4:450–51; Van Buren to Jackson, 22 Dec. 1832, VBP.

54. Williams to William Lenoir, 9 April 1832, quoted in Miles, "After Marshall's Decision," p. 533, n. 32.

55. Kenneth L. Valliere, "Benjamin Currey, Tennessean among the Cherokees: A Study of the Removal Policy of Andrew Jackson," 2 parts, THQ 41 (1982): 140–58, 239–56.

56. Major Ridge and John Ridge to Jackson, 20 June 1836, JSM; Prucha, *Great Father,* 1:233–42.

57. Satz, *Indian Policy*, p. 97; *The Statistical History of the United States from Colonial Times to the Present* (Stamford, Conn.: Fairfield Publishers, 1965), p. 719.

58. Michael Paul Rogin, *Fathers and Children: Andrew Jackson and the Subjugation of the American Indian* (New York: Alfred A. Knopf, 1975), pp. 3–15, 70, 165–69, 179–85; Edward Pessen, *Jacksonian America: Society, Personality, and Politics*, rev. ed. (Homewood, Ill.: Dorsey Press, 1978), pp. 296–301.

59. Robert V. Remini, *The Legacy of Andrew Jackson: Essays on Democracy, Indian Removal, and Slavery* (Baton Rouge: Louisiana State University Press, 1988), pp. 45–82; Prucha, *Great Father*, 1:191; Prucha, "Andrew Jackson's Indian Policy: A Reassessment," JAH 56 (Dec. 1969): 527–39.

60. Prucha, "Jackson's Indian Policy," pp. 533, 536–37; Jackson to Coffee, 6 Nov. 1832, JC, 4:483.

61. Prucha, *Great Father*, 2:911–16.

62. Richardson, *Messages and Papers*, 2:521; Satz, *Indian Policy*, pp. 97, 109.

CHAPTER 6
FOREIGN POLICY

1. Throughout this chapter I have drawn from John M. Belohlavek, *"Let the Eagle Soar!": The Foreign Policy of Andrew Jackson* (Lincoln: University of Nebraska Press, 1985). *The Statistical History of the United States from Colonial Times to the Present* (Stamford, Conn.: Fairfield Publishers, 1965), p. 551.

2. *Statistical History*, p. 551.

3. Martin Van Buren, "The Autobiography of Martin Van Buren," ed. John C. Fitzpatrick, *Annual Report of the American Historical Association for the Year 1918*, vol. 2 (Washington, D.C.: Government Printing Office, 1920), pp. 260–62.

4. *Statistical History*, p. 551.

5. Ibid., pp. 551, 761; Mary W. M. Hargreaves, *The Presidency of John Quincy Adams* (Lawrence: University Press of Kansas, 1985), pp. 92, 111.

6. Hargreaves, *Presidency of John Quincy Adams*, pp. 92–112.

7. *A Compilation of the Messages and Papers of the Presidents, 1789–1897*, comp. James D. Richardson, 10 vols. (Washington, D.C.: Government Printing Office, 1897–99), 2:443; Jackson to Van Buren, 10 April 1830, Andrew Jackson, *Correspondence of Andrew Jackson*, ed. John Spencer Bassett and John Franklin Jameson, 7 vols. (1926–35; reprint, New York: Kraus Reprint Co., 1969), 4:133.

8. Jackson to John Overton, 30 Sept. 1830, JC, 4:181; Hamilton to Jackson, 16 Oct. 1830, James A. Hamilton, *Reminiscences of James A. Hamilton* (New York: Charles Scribner's Sons, 1869), pp. 189–90.

9. Hargreaves, *Presidency of John Quincy Adams*, p. 111; Edward Pessen, *Jacksonian America: Society, Personality, and Politics*, rev. ed. (Homewood, Ill.: Dorsey Press, 1978), p. 319.

10. Richardson, *Messages and Papers*, 2:444, 506.

11. Belohlavek, *"Let the Eagle Soar,"* pp. 99–108; Jackson to Van Buren, 5 Sept. 1831, JC, 4:347.

12. Belohlavek, *"Let the Eagle Soar,"* pp. 108–13.

13. Richardson, *Messages and Papers*, 3:106–7; Belohlavek, *"Let the Eagle Soar,"* pp. 113–20; *Daily National Intelligencer*, 9 Mar. 1835.

14. Belohlavek, *"Let the Eagle Soar,"* pp. 120–22; George W. Erving to Jackson, 25 Sept. 1835, Jackson to Kendall, 31 Oct. 1835, JC, 5:368–70, 374–75.

15. Jackson, "Notes for Annual Message," c. 1 Dec. 1835 (not 7 Dec. as Bassett says), JC, 5:377–79.

16. Richardson, *Messages and Papers*, 3:152–60, 188–93; Belohlavek, *"Let the Eagle Soar,"* pp. 122–25; John Forsyth to Jackson, 4 Feb. 1836, JC, 5:385; *Intelligencer*, 11 May 1836.

17. Hargreaves, *Presidency of John Quincy Adams*, p. 111; Belohlavek, *"Let the Eagle Soar,"* p. 75.

18. Richardson, *Messages and Papers*, 2:549, 3:23–24; Belohlavek, *"Let the Eagle Soar,"* pp. 76–80.

19. Belohlavek, *"Let the Eagle Soar,"* pp. 81, 96–99, 193–94.

20. Ibid., pp. 140–49.

21. Ibid., pp. 130–33.

22. Ibid., pp. 82–88.

23. Ibid., pp. 152–62; *Intelligencer*, 10, 13, 18 July 1832; Washington *Globe*, 11, 16, 19, 25 July 1832.

24. Belohlavek, *"Let the Eagle Soar,"* pp. 162–76.

25. Ibid., pp. 194, 203, 209, 222; *Statistical History*, p. 551.

26. Belohlavek, *"Let the Eagle Soar,"* pp. 60–67.

27. Joe Gibson, "A. Butler: What a Scamp!" *Journal of the West* 11 (1972): 235–37; Jackson to Van Buren, 12 Aug. 1829, Jackson, "Notes on Poinsett's Instructions," 13 Aug. 1829, Jackson to Butler, 19 Oct. 1829, JC, 4:57–61, 79–81.

28. Gibson, "A. Butler," pp. 237–42.

29. Belohlavek, *"Let the Eagle Soar,"* pp. 220–22; Richard R. Stenberg, "The Texas Schemes of Jackson and Houston, 1829–1836," *Southwestern Social Science Quarterly* 15 (1934): 229–50.

30. Belohlavek, *"Let the Eagle Soar,"* pp. 222–24.

31. Butler to Jackson, 21 June 1832, JC, 4:450; Gibson, "A. Butler," pp. 243–45; Jackson to Butler, 27 Nov. 1833, Butler to Jackson, 28, 30 Oct. 1833, 6 Feb. 1834, JC, 5:219–20, 221–22, 228–30, 244–47.

32. Jackson to Butler, 10 Oct. 1829, JC, 4:79–81.

33. Butler to Jackson, 2 Oct. 1833, 7 Mar. 1834, JC, 5:214–16, 249–53; Gibson, "A. Butler," p. 245.

34. Butler to Jackson, 2 July 1834, Forsyth to Jackson, 11 Aug. 1834, JP; Gibson, "A. Butler," pp. 245–47.

35. Austin to Jackson, 15 April 1836, JC, 5:397–98.

36. Jackson to Santa Anna, 4 Sept. 1836, JC, 5:425–26; Austin to Jackson, 4 July 1836, JSM.

37. Dunlap to Jackson, 4 May, 19 July, 6 Aug. 1836, JP.

38. Jackson to Kendall, 12 Aug. 1836, Jackson to Asbury Dickins, 17 Aug. 1836, Jackson to John E. Wool, 23 Aug. 1836, JC, 5:420–22; *Intelligencer*, 11 Mar., 10, 13, 21 May, 19 July, 19 Sept. 1836; Kendall to Jackson, 30 July 1836, Jackson to Gaines, 4 Sept. 1836, JSM.

39. Richardson, *Messages and Papers*, 3:236–39.

40. Belohlavek, *"Let the Eagle Soar,"* pp. 42–51.

41. Hargreaves, *Presidency of John Quincy Adams*, p. 89; *Statistical History*, pp. 551–53; Belohlavek, *"Let the Eagle Soar,"* pp. 22–23.

CHAPTER 7
A JACKSON VICTORY

1. *Niles' Register* 37 (26 Sept. 1829): 68; Webster to Clay, 29 May 1830, Daniel Webster, *The Papers of Daniel Webster: Correspondence*, ed. Charles M. Wiltse and Harold D. Moser, 7 vols. (Hanover, N.H.: University Press of New England, 1974–86), 3:80; Clay to Francis T. Brooke, 1 May 1831, Henry Clay, *The Papers of Henry Clay*, ed. James F. Hopkins, Mary W. M. Hargreaves, Robert Seager II, and Melba Porter Hay, 10 vols. to date (Lexington: University Press of Kentucky, 1959–), 8:342; Richard K. Crallé, "Memorandum," 4 Dec. 1831, John C. Calhoun, *The Papers of John C. Calhoun*, ed. Robert L. Merriwether, W. Edwin Hemphill, and Clyde Wilson, 20 vols. to date (Columbia: University of South Carolina Press, 1959–), 11:523–24.

2. Samuel Rhea Gammon, *The Presidential Campaign of 1832* (Baltimore: Johns Hopkins University Press, 1922), pp. 155–62; David Lee Child to Henry Clay, 11 April 1829, Clay, *Papers*, 8:25; *Niles' Register* 39 (1831): 330; 47 (Sept. 1834): 7, 13; *New-Hampshire Patriot*, 30 May 1825; Jackson to Van Buren, 18 Nov. 1832, Andrew Jackson, *Correspondence of Andrew Jackson*, ed. John Spencer Bassett and John Franklin Jameson, 7 vols. (1926–35; reprint, New York: Kraus Reprint Co., 1969), 4:489; Washington *Globe*, 29 Oct. 1831, 25 Jan., 1 May 1832. Richard P. McCormick warns that even as late as 1836 the name "Democratic" had not been universally adopted. McCormick, "Was There a 'Whig Strategy' in 1836?" JER 4 (Spring 1984): 53n.

3. *The Statistical History of the United States from Colonial Times to the Present* (Stamford, Conn.: Fairfield Publishers, 1965), p. 685.

4. John Quincy Adams, *Memoirs of John Quincy Adams*, ed. Charles Francis Adams, 12 vols. (Philadelphia: J. B. Lippincott, 1875–77), 8:210.

5. Green to Ninian Edwards, 27 April 1830, Ninian Edwards, *The Edwards Papers, Being a Portion of the Collection of the Letters, Papers, and Manuscripts of Ninian Edwards*, ed. E. B. Washburne, Chicago Historical Society's Collections, vol. 3 (Chicago: Fergus Printing Co., 1884), pp. 488–89; Calhoun to Mallett, 7 July 1829, Edward Jones Mallett Papers, LC; H. Petrikin to Jackson, 2 April 1830, JC, 4:131–32.

6. Calhoun to Ingham, 25 May 1831, Green to Calhoun, 18, 25 July, 5 Aug. 1831, Calhoun, *Papers*, 11:390–94, 412–13, 449.

7. Michael F. Holt, "The Antimasonic and Know Nothing Parties," Arthur M. Schlesinger, Jr., ed., *History of U.S. Political Parties*, 4 vols. (New York: Chelsea House, 1973), 1:575–93; Gammon, *Campaign of 1832*, pp. 33–47.

8. Gammon, *Campaign of 1832*, pp. 42–45, 58–62; Clay to Peter B. Porter,

13 June 1830, Clay, *Papers*, 8:222–23; Calhoun to Ingham, 25 May 1831, Calhoun to Christopher Vandeventer, 5 Aug. 1831, Calhoun, *Papers*, 11:391–94, 450–51.

9. Roswell L. Colt to Biddle, 29 Jan. 1831, Nicholas Biddle, *The Correspondence of Nicholas Biddle Dealing with National Affairs, 1807–1844*, ed. Reginald C. McGrane (Boston: Houghton Mifflin, 1919), pp. 122–23; Andrew Beaumont to Van Buren, 4 May 1831, VBP.

10. Holt, "Antimasonic and Know Nothing Parties," pp. 589–90; "Address of the Anti-Masonic Convention," Oct. 1831, Arthur M. Schlesinger, Jr., and Fred L. Israel, eds., *History of American Presidential Elections 1789–1968*, 4 vols. (New York: Chelsea House, 1971), 1:523–39.

11. "Report on the Republican Convention," Dec. 1831, Schlesinger and Israel, *Elections*, 1:540–66.

12. *Globe*, 22 Jan. 1831.

13. Kendall to Lewis, 17 May 1831, "Origin of the Democratic National Convention," *American Historical Magazine* 7 (1902): 267–73.

14. Lewis to Kendall, 25 May 1831, ibid., pp. 270–72; Lewis to Van Buren, 22 April 1859, Martin Van Buren, "Autobiography of Martin Van Buren," ed. John C. Fitzpatrick, *Annual Report of the American Historical Association for the Year 1918*, vol. 2 (Washington, D.C.: Government Printing Office, 1920), pp. 583–86; *Globe*, 6, 19 July 1831.

15. James S. Chase, *Emergence of the Presidential Nominating Convention 1789–1832* (Urbana: University of Illinois Press, 1973), pp. ix–x, 276–95; Van Buren to Ritchie, 13 Jan. 1827, VBP.

16. Gammon, *Campaign of 1832*, pp. 38, 66, 99.

17. Jackson to Van Buren, 23 July, 8 Aug., 5 Sept., 6, 17 Dec. 1831, JC, 4:317, 329, 348, 379, 385; Jackson to Van Buren, 18 Sept. 1831, VBP.

18. Donald B. Cole, *Martin Van Buren and the American Political System* (Princeton, N.J.: Princeton University Press, 1984), pp. 228–30.

19. *Niles' Register* 41 (4, 11, 18 Feb. 1832): 416–34, 453–66; *Register of Debates in Congress, 1825–1837*, 22d Cong., 1st sess., pp. 1325–27.

20. *Niles' Register* 41 (4 Feb. 1832): 416; Thomas Hart Benton, *Thirty Years' View*, 2 vols. (New York: D. Appleton, 1854), 1:214–19.

21. Henry Wikoff, *Reminiscences of an Idler* (New York: Fords, Howard, and Hulbert, 1880), p. 30.

22. Marcy to Azariah Flagg, 6 Feb. 1832, Flagg Papers.

23. Blair to Van Buren, 28 Jan. 1832, Stevenson to Ritchie, 4 Feb. 1832 (copy by James Watson Webb), VBP.

24. Van Buren to Jackson, 20–21 Feb. 1832, VBP.

25. Van Buren, *Autobiography*, pp. 587–91; James Parton, *Life of Andrew Jackson*, 3 vols. (New York: Mason Brothers, 1860), 3:421.

26. Smith to Jackson, 17 June 1832, JP; Lyon G. Tyler, *The Letters and Times of the Tylers*, 3 vols. (Richmond, Va.: Whittet & Shepperson, 1884, 1886), 1:471; Biddle to Clay, 1 Aug. 1832, Clay to Biddle, 27 Aug. 1832, Josiah Johnston to Clay, 29 Sept. 1832, Clay, *Papers*, 8:556, 562–63, 578–79.

27. *Globe*, 12, 13, 19 July, 8, 9, 17, 30 Aug. 1832.

28. Van Buren to Jackson, 29 Aug. 1832, VBP; William T. Barry to Susan

Taylor, 4 July 1832, Barry, "Letters of William T. Barry," *William and Mary College Quarterly*, 14 (1905–6): 233; Jackson to William B. Lewis, 18 Aug. 1832, JC, 4:467; Clay to Daniel Webster, 27 Aug. 1832, Webster, *Papers*, 3:188–89.

29. Ronald N. Satz, *American Indian Policy in the Jacksonian Era* (Lincoln: University of Nebraska Press, 1975), pp. 39–44; Ambrose Spencer to Webster, 14 Mar. 1832, Webster, *Papers*, 3:158–59; Jackson to William B. Lewis, 25 Aug. 1830, JC, 4:177; *New-Hampshire Patriot*, 25 Jan. 1831, 16 Jan., 26 Mar. 1832.

30. *Globe*, 1 Oct., 3 Nov. 1832; Satz, *Indian Policy*, pp. 135–36.

31. John M. Belohlavek, *"Let the Eagle Soar!": The Foreign Policy of Andrew Jackson* (Lincoln: University of Nebraska Press, 1985), pp. 60–67, 140–46, 157–61, 224; *Daily National Intelligencer*, 10, 13, 18 July 1832; *Globe*, 11, 16, 19, 25 July 1832.

32. Webster to Jeremiah Mason, 23 June 1832, G. J. Mason, *Memoir, Autobiography and Correspondence of Jeremiah Mason*, rev. ed. (Kansas City, Mo.: Lawyer's International Publishing Co., 1917), p. 331; William S. Hoffmann, *Andrew Jackson and North Carolina Politics* (1958; reprint, Gloucester, Mass.: Peter Smith, 1971), p. 48.

33. *Register of Debates*, 22d Cong., 1st sess., p. 532; Wirt to Dabney Carr, 25 Oct. 1832, John P. Kennedy, ed., *Memoirs of the Life of William Wirt*, 2 vols. (Philadelphia: Lea and Blanchard, 1850), 2:328–29; *Globe*, 25 Sept. 1832; Erik M. Eriksson, "Official Newspaper Organs and Jackson's Reelection, 1832," THQ 9 (1925): 51–52.

34. *Globe*, 10 May, 8, 17 Oct. 1832; M. J. Heale, *The Presidential Quest: Candidates and Images in American Political Culture, 1787–1852* (London: Longman, 1982), pp. 86–91.

35. Weed to Francis Granger, 11 Nov. 1832, Thurlow Weed Barnes, *Memoir of Thurlow Weed* (1883; reprint, New York: Da Capo Press, 1970), p. 46; Robert V. Remini, "Election of 1831," Schlesinger and Israel, *Elections*, 1:509–14.

36. *Globe*, 13 Oct. 1832. Kendall also published a more positive statement. See Amos Kendall, *Autobiography of Amos Kendall*, ed. William Stickney (1872; reprint, New York: Peter Smith, 1949), pp. 296–303.

37. *Niles' Register* 42 (1832): 354, 371, 389, 404, 408, 419, 450–51.

38. Svend Petersen, *A Statistical History of the American Presidential Elections* (New York: Frederick Ungar, 1963), p. 21; William G. Shade, "Political Pluralism and Party Development: The Creation of a Modern Party System, 1815–1852," Paul Kleppner et al., eds., *The Evolution of American Electoral Systems* (Westport, Conn.: Greenwood, 1981), pp. 82–83.

39. Petersen, *Statistical History*, pp. 20–21, 172–78; Kenneth C. Martis, *The Historical Atlas of Political Parties in the United States Congress 1789–1989* (New York: Macmillan, 1989), pp. 24, 90–91, 332–41.

40. William A. Sullivan, "Did Labor Support Andrew Jackson?"; Edward Pessen, "Did Labor Support Jackson?: The Boston Story," *Political Science Quarterly* 63 (1947): 569–80; 64 (1949): 268.

41. Van Buren, *Autobiography*, pp. 293–94; J. Mills Thornton, *Politics and Power in a Slave Society: Alabama, 1800–1860* (Baton Rouge: Louisiana State University Press, 1978), pp. 28–29.

42. Shade, "Political Pluralism," pp. 80–81.

43. William Nisbet Chambers, "Election of 1840," Schlesinger and Israel, *Elections*, 1:687.

44. Petersen, *Statistical History,* pp. 20–21, 172–78; Martis, *Historical Atlas,* pp. 24, 90–91, 332–41.

CHAPTER 8
DEFENDING THE UNION

1. Louis McLane to Andrew Jackson, 3 Aug. 1832, JP; Alfred Balch to James K. Polk, 6 Jan. 1831, James K. Polk, *Correspondence of James K. Polk,* ed. Herbert Weaver, Paul H. Bergeron, and Wayne Cutler, 7 vols. to date (Nashville: Vanderbilt University Press, 1969–), 1:375; William W. Freehling, *Prelude to Civil War: The Nullification Controversy in South Carolina, 1816–1836* (New York: Harper & Row, 1966), pp. 203–4; Freehling, *The Road to Disunion: Secessionists at Bay 1776–1854* (New York: Oxford University Press, 1990), pp. 213–28; James Banner, Jr., "The Problem of South Carolina," Stanley Elkins and Eric McKitrick, eds., *The Hofstadter Aegis: A Memorial* (New York: Alfred A. Knopf, 1974), pp. 60–93.

2. Freehling, *Road to Disunion,* pp. 229, 257–59; Thomas Cooper, "Value of the Union," Robert J. Turnbull, "The Crisis," John C. Calhoun, "Fort Hill Address," William W. Freehling, ed., *The Nullification Era: A Documentary Record* (New York: Harper Torchbooks, 1967), pp. 20–25, 26–47, 140–47.

3. Freehling, *Prelude,* pp. 147–59, 205–18.

4. Ibid., pp. 221–31; James H. Hammond, Memorandum, 18 Mar. 1831, "Letters on the Nullification Movement in South Carolina," AHR 6 (July 1901): 741–45; George McDuffie, "Speech at Charleston," Freehling, *Nullification Era,* pp. 104–19.

5. Freehling, *Prelude,* pp. 244, 250–52; Mitchell to Jackson, 23 Dec. 1831, JSM (National Archives).

6. Jackson to Hayne, 8 Feb. 1831, Andrew Jackson, *Correspondence of Andrew Jackson,* ed. John Spencer Bassett and John Franklin Jameson, 7 vols. (1926–35; reprint, New York: Kraus Reprint Co., 1969), 4:241–43; Mitchell, "Address," 4 July 1831, Charles Sellers, ed., *Andrew Jackson, Nullification, and the State-Rights Tradition* (Chicago: Rand McNally, 1963), pp. 33–34.

7. Jackson to Van Buren, 18 Nov. 1832, JC, 4:489; Jackson to William B. Lewis, 28 Aug. 1832, JSM.

8. Randolph to Jackson, 26 Mar. 1832; McLane to Jackson, 2 Aug. 1832, JP.

9. Jackson to Robert Y. Hayne, 8 Feb. 1831, Jackson to Andrew J. Donelson, 17 Sept. 1832, Jackson to Cass, 29 Oct. 1832, JC, 4:241–43, 475–76, 483.

10. Jackson to George Breathitt, 7 Nov. 1832 (two letters), Jackson to Poinsett, 7 Nov. 1832, JC, 4:484–86.

11. Freehling, *Prelude,* pp. 149–52, 227–38, 240–41, 252–55, 260–64; Poinsett to Jackson, 29 Nov. 1832, JC, 4:491–92.

12. Washington *Globe,* 26, 29 Nov., 4, 7 Dec. 1832; *A Compilation of the Messages and Papers of the Presidents, 1789–1897,* comp. James D. Richardson, 10 vols. (Washington, D.C.: Government Printing Office, 1897–99), 2:597–99, 606.

13. Richardson, *Messages and Papers,* 2:597–603.

14. Ibid., 3:296–308.

15. Jackson to Livingston, 4 Dec. 1832, JC, 4:494–95.

16. Richardson, *Messages and Papers*, 2:640–56; Kenneth M. Stampp, "The Concept of a Perpetual Union," JAH 65 (June 1978): 32.

17. The proceedings of seventeen state legislatures were published in General Court of Massachusetts, *State Papers on Nullification* (Boston: Dutton and Wentworth, 1834). See also John Quincy Adams, *Memoirs of John Quincy Adams*, ed. Charles Francis Adams, 12 vols. (Philadelphia: J. B. Lippincott, 1875–77), 8:510; Richard E. Ellis, *The Union at Risk: Jacksonian Democracy, States' Rights and the Nullification Crisis* (New York: Oxford University Press, 1987), pp. 85–88; Richard B. Latner, *The Presidency of Andrew Jackson: White House Politics 1829–1837* (Athens: University of Georgia Press, 1979), pp. 154–55.

18. Richardson, *Messages and Papers*, 2:655.

19. Jackson to Poinsett, 9 Dec. 1832, Jackson to Martin Van Buren, 15, 25 Dec. 1832, Jackson to Cass, 17 Dec. 1832, JC, 4:497–98, 500–503, 505–6.

20. Hamilton to Jackson, 13 Dec. 1832, JC, 4:498–99; Philip Hone, *The Diary of Philip Hone 1828–1851*, ed. Allan Nevins (New York: Dodd, Mead, 1936), p. 84; Martin Van Buren, "The Autobiography of Martin Van Buren," ed. John C. Fitzpatrick, *Annual Report of the American Historical Association for the Year 1918*, vol. 2 (Washington, D.C.: Government Printing Office, 1920), p. 547.

21. William H. Haywood to Van Buren, 10 Jan. 1833, Cambreleng to Van Buren, 10? Dec. 1832, VBP; Van Buren, *Autobiography*, p. 547; William F. Gordon to Thomas W. Gilmer, 11 Dec. 1832, "Original Letters," *William and Mary Quarterly Historical Magazine* 21 (1912–13): 1; *Globe*, 17 Dec. 1832–16 Jan. 1833, passim; *Richmond Enquirer*, 13 Dec. 1832; James C. Curtis, *Andrew Jackson and the Search for Vindication* (Boston: Little, Brown, 1976), p. 147.

22. Webster, "Speech to National Republican Convention at Worcester," 12 Oct. 1832, Daniel Webster, *The Writings and Speeches of Daniel Webster*, 18 vols. (Boston: Little, Brown, 1903), 2:124; Silas Wright to Azariah Flagg, 14 Jan. 1833, Flagg Papers; Hoffman to Van Buren, 7 Dec. 1832, Hall to Van Buren, 2 Jan. 1833, VBP.

23. Van Buren, *Autobiography*, pp. 543–48; Jackson to Van Buren, 15 Dec. 1832, Van Buren to Jackson, 22 Dec. 1832, VBP; Jackson to Van Buren, 23, 25 Dec. 1832, Van Buren to Jackson, 27 Dec. 1832, JC, 4:504–8.

24. Hayne, "Inaugural Address," United States Senate, *Message from the President*, 22d Cong., 2d sess., S. Doc. 30, pp. 67–68.

25. Freehling, *Prelude*, pp. 264–78.

26. Perry M. Goldman and James S. Young, eds., *The United States Congressional Directories, 1789–1840* (New York: Columbia University Press, 1973), p. 257; Jackson to Van Buren, 13 Jan. 1833, JC, 5:2–4.

27. Michael J. Birkner, "The New York–New Jersey Boundary Controversy, John Marshall and the Nullification Crisis," JER 12 (Summer 1992): 195–212.

28. *State Papers on Nullification*, pp. 201–2, 222–25, 229–31; Jackson to Andrew Jackson, Jr., 8 Jan. 1833, JSM; Jackson to Van Buren, 13 Jan. 1833, JC, 5:3; Wright to Van Buren, 13 Jan. 1833, VBP.

29. Swartwout to Verplanck, 4 Jan. 1833, Gulian C. Verplanck Papers, New-York Historical Society.

30. James W. Wyly to James K. Polk and James Sandifer, 11 Jan. 1833, Paul H.

Bergeron, ed., "A Tennessean Blasts Calhoun and Nullification," THQ 26 (1967): 383–86.

31. Van Buren to Jackson, 9 Jan. 1833, VBP; Jackson to Van Buren, 13 Jan. 1833, JC, 5:3.

32. Richardson, *Messages and Papers*, 2:610–32.

33. *Register of Debates in Congress, 1825–1837*, 22d Cong., 2d sess., pp. 100–103; Calhoun to Samuel D. Ingham, 16 Jan. 1833, JP; Jackson to Poinsett, 16 Jan. 1833, JC, 5:5–6.

34. *Register of Debates*, 22d Cong., 2d sess., pp. 150, 174–93.

35. McLane to Van Buren, 23 Jan. 1833, VBP; Wright to Azariah Flagg, 20 Jan. 1833, Flagg Papers.

36. Jackson to Van Buren, 25 Jan. 1833, JC, 5:12–13.

37. Carr to Peachey Ridgway Gilmer, 3 Feb. 1833, Peachey Ridgway Gilmer Papers, LC; *State Papers on Nullification*, pp. 195–97.

38. *Register of Debates*, 22d Cong., 2d sess., pp. 244–46, 1653; Ellis, *Union*, pp. 162–65.

39. *Register of Debates*, 22d Cong., 2d sess., pp. 462–78; Robert V. Remini, *Andrew Jackson and the Course of American Democracy, 1833–1845* (New York: Harper & Row, 1984), pp. 39–40; Jackson to Grundy, 13 Feb. 1833, JSM.

40. *Register of Debates*, 22d Cong., 2d sess., pp. 482–83; Jackson to Grundy, 13 Feb. 1833, JSM.

41. *Register of Debates*, 22d Cong., 2d sess., pp. 1653, 1707–22, 1725–26; Ellis, *Union*, pp. 163–65; Benton to Van Buren, 16 Feb. 1833, VBP.

42. Freehling, *Prelude*, pp. 288–91.

43. Norman D. Brown, *Daniel Webster and the Politics of Availability* (Athens: University of Georgia Press, 1969), pp. 16–21; Tyler to John Floyd, 22 Jan. 1833, "Original Letters," p. 11.

44. Glyndon G. Van Deusen, *The Life of Henry Clay* (Boston: Little, Brown, 1937), p. 267; Remini, *Jackson and Democracy*, p. 40.

45. Thomas Hart Benton, *Thirty Years' View*, 2 vols. (New York: D. Appleton, 1854), 1:342–44; *Register of Debates*, 22d Cong., 2d sess., pp. 477–78.

46. *Register of Debates*, 22d Cong., 2d sess., pp. 187–92, 492–587; Brown, *Webster*, p. 21; Webster, "Speech in the Senate," 16 Feb. 1833, Webster, *Writings and Speeches*, 6:197, 238.

47. Jackson to Poinsett, 17 Feb. 1833, JC, 5:18; *Register of Debates*, 22d Cong., 2d sess., pp. 750–84; Charles M. Wiltse, *John C. Calhoun, Nullifier, 1829–1839* (Indianapolis: Bobbs-Merrill, 1949), pp. 189–90, 193–95.

48. *Register of Debates*, 22d Cong., 2d sess., p. 688; Ellis, *Union*, pp. 171–72.

49. Michael C. Hoffman to Azariah C. Flagg, Flagg Papers; Ellis, *Union*, p. 171; *Congressional Globe*, 27th Cong., 2d sess., app., p. 575.

50. Clay told Congressman Nathan Appleton of Massachusetts that "no future Congress would be bound by the act." *Congressional Globe*, 27th Cong., 2d sess., app., p. 575. F. W. Taussig, *The Tariff History of the United States*, 6th ed. (New York: G. P. Putnam's Sons, 1892), pp. 109–12.

51. Benton, *Thirty Years' View*, 1:308–13; *Register of Debates*, 22d Cong., 2d sess., pp. 1772, 1779–80, 1810–11.

52. Benton, *Thirty Years' View*, 1:312; *Congressional Globe*, 27th Cong., 2d sess., app., p. 575.

53. Ellis, *Union*, pp. 170–74; *Richmond Enquirer*, 22 Jan. 1833; Van Buren to Jackson, 20 Feb. 1833, JC, 5:19–21; *Globe*, 16 Feb. 1833; Wright to Azariah C. Flagg, 21, 25 Feb. 1833, Flagg Papers.

54. *State Papers on Nullification*, pp. 133–59; Van Buren, *Autobiography*, 547–53; Ellis, *Union*, pp. 151–56; *New York American*, 4 Feb. 1833; Alexander to Nathaniel Beverley Tucker, 6 Feb. 1833, "Correspondence of Judge N. B. Tucker," *William and Mary College Quarterly Historical Magazine* 12 (1903–4): 85.

55. Ellis, *Union*, pp. 175–76; Daniel Feller, *The Public Lands in Jacksonian Politics* (Madison: University of Wisconsin Press, 1984), pp. 164–68; *Register of Debates*, 22d Cong., 2d sess., pp. 808–9, 1865, 1897, 1903, 1920–21.

56. Force Bill: Democrats, 78 yea, 38 nay and opposition, 71 yea, 10 nay; tariff bill: Democrats, 86 yea, 27 nay and opposition, 33 yea, 58 nay; distribution bill: Democrats, 34 yea, 40 nay and opposition, 62 yea, 0 nay.

57. The Democrats were Hubbard, N.H.; Cambreleng and Beardsley, N.Y.; Mann and Muhlenberg, Pa.; Thomas, Md.; Mason, Va.; McKay, N.C.; Mitchell, S.C.; Wayne, Ga.; R. M. Johnson, Ky.; Polk and C. Johnson, Tenn.; C. C. Clay, Ala.; and Kennon, Ohio.

58. *Register of Debates*, 22d Cong., 2d sess., pp. 808–9.

59. Feller, *Public Lands*, pp. 165–67; Jackson to Poinsett, 6 Mar. 1833, JC, 5:28–29.

60. *Register of Debates*, 22d Cong., 2d sess., p. 1936.

61. Edward A. Miles, *Jacksonian Democracy in Mississippi* (Chapel Hill: University of North Carolina Press, 1960), pp. 48–54.

62. Freehling, *Prelude*, pp. 295–97; *State Papers on Nullification*, pp. 352–75.

63. Freehling omits the statement about Jackson's "great victory" in his more recent treatment of the crisis, which is somewhat less supportive of Jackson than his first. See Freehling, *Prelude*, pp. 293–95, and *Road to Disunion*, pp. 277–85.

64. Freehling, *Prelude*, pp. 293–94.

65. Ellis, *Union*, pp. 78–79, 160–64.

CHAPTER 9

RENEWING THE BANK WAR

1. *A Compilation of the Messages and Papers of the Presidents, 1789–1897*, comp. James D. Richardson, 10 vols. (Washington, D.C.: Government Printing Office, 1897–99), 3:3–5; Washington *Globe*, 4, 8 Mar. 1833. Robert V. Remini argues that unnamed advisers modified the inaugural. Remini, *Andrew Jackson and the Course of American Democracy, 1833–1845* (New York: Harper & Row, 1984), pp. 46–47.

2. Philip Hone, *The Diary of Philip Hone 1828–1851*, ed. Allan Nevins (New York: Dodd, Mead, 1936), pp. 88–89, 96–97; Charles Francis Adams, *Diary of Charles Francis Adams*, ed. Aida DiPace Donald, David Donald, Marc Friedlaender, and L. H. Butterfield, 8 vols. (Cambridge: Harvard University Press, 1964–86), 5:44, 106, 110.

3. Charles Francis Adams, *Diary,* 4:406–7.

4. McLane to Van Buren, 25 April 1833, Barry to Van Buren, 7 July 1833, Silas C. McClary to Van Buren, 28 June 1833, VBP; Seba Smith, *My Thirty Years out of the Senate by Major Jack Downing* (New York: Oaksmith, 1859), p. 201; *Albany Argus,* 8 Mar. 1833; *New-Hampshire Patriot,* 18 Feb. 1833; Norman D. Brown, *Daniel Webster and the Politics of Availability* (Athens: University of Georgia Press, 1969), pp. 29–44.

5. *The Statistical History of the United States from Colonial Times to the Present* (Stamford, Conn.: Fairfield Publishers, 1965), pp. 13, 57, 302, 428, 445; George Rogers Taylor, *The Transportation Revolution, 1815–1860* (New York: Harper & Row, 1951), pp. 325, 339.

6. William G. Shade, "Political Pluralism and Party Development: The Creation of a Modern Party System," Paul Kleppner et al., eds., *The Evolution of American Electoral Systems* (Westport, Conn.: Greenwood Press, 1981), pp. 78–79.

7. Claude Moore Fuess, *Daniel Webster,* 2 vols. (Boston: Little, Brown, 1930), 2:4. Webster to Nicholas Biddle, 21 April 1833, Nicholas Biddle Papers, quoted in Brown, *Webster,* p. 38; Jackson to Polk, 16 Dec. 1832, JC, 4:501; James Parton, *Life of Andrew Jackson,* 3 vols. (New York: Mason Brothers, 1860), 3:500–504; Amos Kendall, *Autobiography of Amos Kendall,* ed. William Stickney (1872; reprint, New York: Peter Smith, 1949), p. 376.

8. Richard P. Longaker, "Was Jackson's Kitchen Cabinet a Cabinet?" MVHR 44 (1957): 103–4.

9. Kendall to Van Buren, 2, 10 Nov. 1832, VBP.

10. Kendall, *Autobiography,* p. 376.

11. Jackson to cabinet, 19 Mar. 1833, Andrew Jackson, *Correspondence of Andrew Jackson,* ed. John Spencer Bassett and John Franklin Jameson, 7 vols. (1926–35; reprint, New York: Kraus Reprint Co., 1969), 5:32–33.

12. Jackson to _____, 24 Mar. 1833, JC, 5:47–48.

13. Woodbury to Jackson, 2 April 1833, Barry to Jackson, April 1833, JP; William J. Duane, *Narrative and Correspondence Concerning the Removal of the Deposites* (1838; reprint, New York: Burt Franklin, 1965), pp. 5–6; McLane to Jackson, 20 May 1833, JC, 5:75–101.

14. Ellicott to Jackson, 6 April 1833, Taney to Jackson, 29 April 1833, JC, 5:49–52, 67–71.

15. Woodbury and Kendall were among those who believed that McLane sought to control two departments. Levi Woodbury, "Levi Woodbury's 'Intimate Memoranda' of the Jackson Administration," ed. Ari Hoogenboom and Herbert Ershkowitz, *Pennsylvania Magazine of History and Biography* 92 (1968): 510; Kendall, *Autobiography,* p. 377; Kendall to Jackson, 11 Aug. 1833, JC, 5:152.

16. Jackson to Van Buren, 12 May 1833, JC, 5:74–75; *Niles' Register* 44 (18 May 1833): 117; Jackson to Van Buren, 25 April 1833, VBP.

17. *New-Hampshire Patriot,* 5 May 1833; Fletcher M. Green, "On Tour with President Jackson," *New England Quarterly* 36 (1963): 209–28.

18. Duane, *Narrative,* pp. 5–11.

19. McLane to Van Buren, 4 June 1833, Martin Van Buren, "Autobiography of Martin Van Buren," ed. John C. Fitzpatrick, *Annual Report of the American His-*

torical Association for the Year 1918, vol. 2 (Washington, D.C.: Government Printing Office, 1920), p. 602; Kendall to Van Buren, 9 June 1833, Jackson to Van Buren, 6 June 1833, VBP; Jackson to Duane, 26 June 1833 (two letters), JC, 5:111–28.

20. Duane, *Narrative,* pp. 36–83.

21. Those institutions showing interest included banks in New York, Philadelphia, Baltimore, and Natchez. Duane, *Narrative,* pp. 84–92; Kendall, *Autobiography,* pp. 378–80.

22. Woodbury, "Intimate Memoranda," p. 513; Kendall to a Baltimore bank, 30 July 1833, JP; Kendall to Jackson, 2, 11, 14, 25 Aug. 1833, JC, 5:145–47, 150–53, 156, 169–70; Kendall, *Autobiography,* 380–83.

23. Kendall to Jackson, 11, 14 Aug. 1833, JC, 5:150–53, 156.

24. Blair to Van Buren, 13 Nov. 1859, Van Buren, *Autobiography,* pp. 607–8.

25. Jackson to Van Buren, 24 July, 16 Aug. 1833, JC, 5:142–43, 158–59; Van Buren to Jackson, 29 July 1833, VBP.

26. Wright to Azariah Flagg, 8 Aug. 1833, Flagg Papers; Wright to Van Buren, 28 Aug. 1833, JP; Van Buren to Jackson, 19, 30 Aug., 4 Sept. 1833, JC, 5:171–72, 179–82.

27. Frank Otto Gatell, "Spoils of the Bank War: Political Bias in the Selection of Pet Banks," AHR 70 (Oct. 1964): 35–52; Jackson to Hamilton, 8 Sept. 1833, James A. Hamilton, *Reminiscences of James A. Hamilton* (New York: Charles Scribner's Sons, 1869), p. 260.

28. Duane, *Narrative,* pp. 97–98; Jackson, "Memorandum," 10 Sept. 1833, JP.

29. Duane, *Narrative,* pp. 98–100; Jackson, "Memorandum," 19 Sept. 1833, JP.

30. Jackson, "Draft of Paper Read to the Cabinet," 18 Sept. 1833, JC, 5:192–203; Richardson, *Messages and Papers,* 3:5–19; Blair to Van Buren, 13 Nov. 1859, Van Buren, *Autobiography,* p. 608.

31. *Globe,* 20 Sept. 1833.

32. Jackson to Van Buren, 8 Sept. 1833, Taney to Jackson, 17 Sept. 1833, JC, 5:182–83, 191–92; Duane, *Narrative,* p. 100; Remini, *Jackson and Democracy,* p. 99.

33. Jackson to Van Buren, 24, 25 Sept. 1833, Blair to Van Buren, 13 Nov. 1859, Van Buren, *Autobiography,* pp. 603–4, 608; Richardson, *Messages and Papers,* 3:19.

34. Van Buren to Jackson, 11, 14 Sept. 1833, Jackson to Van Buren, 8, 19, 22, 23, 29 Sept., 5 Oct. 1833, JC, 5:182–86, 203–7, 212–13, 216–17; Jackson to Van Buren, 15, 26 Sept. 1833, VBP; Jackson to Van Buren, 24, 25 Sept. 1833, Van Buren, *Autobiography,* pp. 603–4.

35. Van Buren to Jackson, 22 Sept. 1833, JP; Van Buren to Jackson, 26 Sept., 2 Oct. 1833, JC, 5:211–12, 214; Van Buren to Jackson, 11, 27 Sept. 1833, Van Buren, *Autobiography,* pp. 605–7; Van Buren to Jackson, 28 Sept. 1833, VBP.

36. Lynn L. Marshall, "The Strange Stillbirth of the Whig Party," AHR 72 (Jan. 1967): 450n. Richard B. Latner argues that westerners, Kendall in particular, had the most influence over Jackson. Latner, *The Presidency of Andrew Jackson: White House Politics 1829–1837* (Athens: University of Georgia Press, 1979), pp. 4, 17–22. Harriet Martineau, *Retrospect of Western Travel,* 3 vols. (London: Saunders and Otley, 1838), 1:258. Silas Wright, William L. Marcy, and others had been born in New England.

NOTES TO PAGES 197–203

37. Kendall to Blair, 3 Feb., 7 Mar. 1829, Blair-Lee Papers.

38. *Statistical History,* pp. 623, 625, 711; Jacob P. Meerman, "The Climax of the Bank War: Biddle's Contraction," *Journal of Political Economy* 71 (Aug. 1963): 381; Walter B. Smith, *Economic Aspects of the Second Bank of the United States* (Cambridge: Harvard University Press, 1953), pp. 47, 50.

39. Roger B. Taney, "Roger Brooke Taney's Account of His Relations with Thomas Ellicott in the Bank War," MHM 53 (1958): 58–60, 131–52; Meerman, "Climax of Bank War," pp. 378–80.

40. Biddle to Robert Lenox, 30 July, 1 Oct. 1833, Biddle to Daniel Webster, 13 Aug. 1833, Nicholas Biddle, *The Correspondence of Nicholas Biddle Dealing with National Affairs, 1807–1844,* ed. Reginald C. McGrane (Boston: Houghton Mifflin, 1919), pp. 212–13, 214–16; Smith, *Economic Aspects,* pp. 160, 163.

41. Swartwout to Biddle, 23 Nov. 1833, Biddle, *Correspondence,* p. 217; Hone, *Diary,* pp. 106, 111, 112.

42. John Tyler to Littleton W. Tazewell, 25 Dec. 1833, Lyon G. Tyler, *The Letters and Times of the Tylers,* 3 vols. (Richmond, Va.: Whittet & Shepperson, 1884, 1886), 1:485; *Niles' Register* 46 (24 May 1834): 204.

43. Biddle to William Appleton, 27 Jan. 1834, Biddle to John G. Whatmough, 8 Feb. 1834, Biddle to Joseph Hopkinson, 21 Feb. 1834, Biddle, *Correspondence,* pp. 219, 221, 222.

44. Jackson to Van Buren, 5 Oct. 1833, 3 Jan. 1834, JC, 5:216, 238.

CHAPTER 10
TWO-PARTY POLITICS

1. According to Kenneth C. Martis, the House was made up of 143 Democrats and 97 members of the opposition. Alvin W. Lynn, however, sets the figures at 124 Democrats, 105 opposition, and 11 unknown. Martis, *The Historical Atlas of Political Parties in the United States Congress 1789–1989* (New York: Macmillan, 1989), pp. 24, 92, 342–48; Lynn, "Party Formation and Operation in the House of Representatives, 1824–1837" (Ph.D. diss., Rutgers University, 1972), p. 191.

2. Lynn, "Party Formation," p. 298; Jackson to Blair, 30 Nov. 1833, Andrew Jackson, *Correspondence of Andrew Jackson,* ed. John Spencer Bassett and John Franklin Jameson, 7 vols. (1926–35; reprint, New York: Kraus Reprint Co., 1969), 5:230.

3. *A Compilation of the Messages and Papers of the Presidents, 1789–1897,* comp. James D. Richardson, 10 vols. (Washington, D.C.: Government Printing Office, 1897–99), 3:19–35.

4. *Register of Debates in Congress, 1825–1837,* 23d Cong., 1st sess., pp. 20–29.

5. Clay to Clayton, John M. Clayton Papers, LC, quoted in Norman D. Brown, *Daniel Webster and the Politics of Availability* (Athens: University of Georgia Press, 1969), p. 59.

6. Martin Van Buren, "Autobiography of Martin Van Buren," ed. John C.

Fitzpatrick, *Annual Report of the American Historical Association for the Year 1918*, vol. 2 (Washington, D.C.: Government Printing Office, 1920), pp. 677–79.

7. Perry M. Goldman and James S. Young, eds., *The United States Congressional Directories 1789–1840* (New York: Columbia University Press, 1973), pp. 274–76; Webster to Biddle, 21 Dec. 1833, Nicholas Biddle, *The Correspondence of Nicholas Biddle Dealing with National Affairs, 1807–1844*, ed. Reginald C. McGrane (Boston: Houghton Mifflin, 1919), p. 218.

8. *Register of Debates*, 23d Cong., 1st sess., p. 24.

9. Ibid., pp. 2166–71.

10. Ibid., pp. 2206–7; Charles Sellers, *James K. Polk, Jacksonian, 1795–1843* (Princeton, N.J.: Princeton University Press, 1957), pp. 215–16.

11. Thomas Hart Benton, *Thirty Years' View*, 2 vols. (New York: D. Appleton, 1854), 1:415–25.

12. *Register of Debates*, 23d Cong., 1st sess., pp. 14, 23, 26, 29, 37; Benton, *Thirty Years' View*, 1:400.

13. *Register of Debates*, 23d Cong., 1st sess., pp. 58–94; John Quincy Adams, *Memoirs of John Quincy Adams*, ed. Charles Francis Adams, 12 vols. (Philadelphia: J. B. Lippincott, 1875–77), 9:62; James Parton, *Life of Andrew Jackson*, 3 vols. (New York: Mason Brothers, 1860), 3:542.

14. Benton, *Thirty Years' View*, 1:406–10, 420; *Register of Debates*, 23d Cong., 1st sess., pp. 829–31, 834–36, 1187.

15. *Register of Debates*, 23d Cong., 1st sess., p. 1187.

16. Ibid., pp. 2265–89.

17. Throop to Martin Van Buren, 1 Feb. 1834, VBP; Sellers, *Polk, Jacksonian*, p. 221; Clay to Biddle, 2 Feb. 1834, Binney to Biddle, 4 Feb. 1834, Biddle, *Correspondence*, pp. 220–21.

18. *Register of Debates*, 23d Cong., 1st sess., pp. 2735–40, 2868–69.

19. Ibid., pp. 2869, 3475–77, 4467–69; Jackson to Andrew Jackson, Jr., 6 April 1834, JC, 5:259.

20. Jackson to Andrew Jackson, Jr., 6, 15 April 1834, Jackson to John D. Coffee, 6 April 1834, JC, 5:258–61.

21. Richardson, *Messages and Papers*, 3:69–93.

22. *Register of Debates*, 23d Cong., 1st sess., pp. 1336–40, 1711–12; Richardson, *Messages and Papers*, 3:93–94.

23. Sellers, *Polk, Jacksonian*, pp. 234–42, quotation of doorkeeper, p. 242.

24. Jacob P. Meerman, "The Climax of the Bank War," *Journal of Political Economy* 71 (Aug. 1963): 381–85; Peter Temin, *The Jacksonian Economy* (New York: W. W. Norton, 1969), pp. 59–64.

25. Meerman, "Climax of Bank War," pp. 385–88; Temin, *Jacksonian Economy*, pp. 64–68.

26. Sellers, *Polk, Jacksonian*, p. 222.

27. For the vote on the resolution against the Protest, see *Register of Debates*, 23d Cong., 1st sess., p. 1171. For the vote on the Taney nomination, see "Votes on the nominations of Taney, St. Clair, and Stevenson," Senate Journal, 24 June 1834, JP. For the other votes see Benton, *Thirty Years' View*, 1:385–86, 395–96, 423.

28. See Lynn, "Party Formation," pp. 413–45, especially the table, p. 441;

David J. Russo, "The Major Political Issues of the Jacksonian Period and the Development of Party Loyalty in Congress, 1830–1840," *Transactions of the American Philosophical Society*, n. s., 62, pt. 5 (May 1972): 34–35, 48; Benton, *Thirty Years' View*, 1:398.

29. Daniel Feller, "Andrew Jackson versus the Senate" (unpublished paper, c. 1989), pp. 14–16; Richardson, *Messages and Papers*, 3:87–90; Russo, "Major Political Issues," pp. 31, 34–35.

30. Glyndon G. Van Deusen, "The Whig Party," Arthur M. Schlesinger, Jr., ed., *History of U.S. Political Parties*, 4 vols. (New York: Chelsea House, 1973), 1:336–39.

31. Michael F. Holt, "The Democratic Party 1828–1860," Schlesinger, *Parties*, 1:507–10.

32. *New-Hampshire Patriot*, 18 June 1832.

33. Summary of Clay, "Speech in Senate," 14 April 1834, Henry Clay, *The Papers of Henry Clay*, ed. James F. Hopkins, Mary W. M. Hargreaves, Robert Seager II, and Melba Porter Hay, 10 vols. to date (Lexington: University Press of Kentucky, 1959–), 8:714–15; Van Buren to Judith Rives, 6 April 1834, William C. Rives Papers; James Love to John J. Crittenden, 27 May 1834, John J. Crittenden Papers, LC.

34. Lewis to Jackson, 25 July 1834, Jackson to Van Buren, 16 Aug. 1834, Jackson to Lewis, 8 Sept. 1834, JC, 5:276, 282–83, 289.

35. Van Buren to Jackson, 23 Oct. 1834, John Bigler to Jackson, 24 Oct. 1834, JSM; Cornelius Van Ness to John P. Van Ness, 7 Nov. 1834, JP.

CHAPTER 11
A VIOLENT DEMOCRACY

1. Carl E. Prince, "The Great 'Riot Year': Jacksonian Democracy and Patterns of Violence in 1834," JER 5 (Spring 1985): 4–8.

2. Peter Temin, *The Jacksonian Economy* (New York: W. W. Norton, 1969), p. 69.

3. For the institutional decline, see Stanley Elkins, *Slavery: A Problem in American Institutional and Intellectual Life*, 2d ed. (Chicago: University of Chicago Press, 1968), pp. 27–34, 140–57.

4. Thomas Roderick Dew, *Review of the Debate on the Abolition of Slavery in the Virginia Legislature of 1831 and 1832* (1832; reprint, Westport, Conn.: Negro University Press, 1970). William W. Freehling rejects the assumption that the Virginia debates "spawned a Great Reaction" in Virginia in favor of "permanent" slavery in *The Road to Disunion: Secessionists at Bay 1776–1854* (New York: Oxford University Press, 1990), pp. 190–93.

5. Louis Filler, *The Crusade against Slavery 1830–1850* (New York: Harper & Brothers, 1960), pp. 60–67.

6. Paul E. Johnson, *A Shopkeeper's Millennium: Society and Revivals in Rochester, N.Y., 1815–1837* (New York: Hill and Wang, 1978). The theme of revivalism as a form of social control has been challenged by Lawrence Frederick Kohl in "The

Concept of Social Control and the History of Jacksonian America," JER 5 (Spring 1985): 21–34.

7. Sean Wilentz, *Chants Democratic: New York City and the Rise of the American Working Class, 1788–1850* (New York: Oxford University Press, 1984), pp. 172–254; Edward Pessen, *Most Uncommon Jacksonians: The Radical Leaders of the Early Labor Movement* (Albany: State University of New York Press, 1967), pp. 37, 44.

8. Leonard L. Richards, *"Gentlemen of Property and Standing": Anti-Abolition Mobs in Jacksonian America* (New York: Oxford University Press, 1970), pp. 10–19; Charles Francis Adams, *Diary of Charles Francis Adams*, ed. Aida DiPace Donald, David Donald, Marc Friedlaender, and L. H. Butterfield, 8 vols. (Cambridge: Harvard University Press, 1964–86), 5:293; John Quincy Adams, *Memoirs of John Quincy Adams*, ed. Charles Francis Adams, 12 vols. (Philadelphia: J. B. Lippincott, 1875–77), 9:162.

9. Richards, *"Gentlemen,"* pp. 63–64, 75n, 113–22; Philip Hone, *The Diary of Philip Hone 1828–1851*, ed. Allan Nevins (New York: Dodd, Mead, 1936), pp. 134–37.

10. Prince, "Great 'Riot Year,'" pp. 18–19.

11. Jackson, "Memorandum," April 1834, Jackson to Levi Woodbury, 6 Oct. 1834, JSM; Francis P. Blair to George Bancroft, 24 June 1845, Andrew Jackson, *Correspondence of Andrew Jackson*, ed. John Spencer Bassett and John Franklin Jameson, 7 vols. (1926–35; reprint, New York: Kraus Reprint Co., 1969), 5:238n; Washington *Globe*, 14 Feb. 1834, 4 Feb. 1835.

12. Richard C. Rohrs, "Partisan Politics and the Attempted Assassination of Andrew Jackson," JER 1 (Summer 1981): 149–56; Carlton Jackson, "—Another Time, Another Place—The Attempted Assassination of President Andrew Jackson," THQ 26 (1967): 184–90.

13. Arthur M. Schlesinger, Jr., *The Age of Jackson* (Boston: Little, Brown, 1945), especially pp. 339–44; *A Compilation of the Messages and Papers of the Presidents, 1789–1897*, comp. James D. Richardson, 10 vols. (Washington, D.C.: Government Printing Office, 1897–99), 2:590; Jackson to Committee on Behalf of Cabinet Makers, Pianoforte Makers and Others of the Mechanics of Philadelphia, 17 Dec. 1834, JSM; *Globe*, 1 June 1831.

14. *Niles' Register* 46 (30 Aug. 1834): 441; Richardson, *Messages and Papers*, 3:164.

15. Pessen, *Most Uncommon Jacksonians*, p. 19.

16. Richard B. Morris, "Andrew Jackson, Strikebreaker," AHR 55 (Oct. 1949): 54–68, quotations pp. 61, 67.

17. Frank Otto Gatell, ed., "Roger B. Taney, the Bank of Maryland Rioters, and a Whiff of Grapeshot," MHM 59 (1964): 262–67.

18. Donald B. Cole, *Martin Van Buren and the American Political System* (Princeton, N.J.: Princeton University Press, 1984), pp. 173–75.

19. Wilentz, *Chants Democratic*, pp. 236, 286–89.

20. Kendall to Jackson, 7 Aug. 1836, JSM; Robert V. Remini, *Andrew Jackson and the Course of American Democracy, 1833–1845* (New York: Harper & Row, 1984), pp. 340–41.

21. For a summary of the debate from the anti-Schlesinger point of view, see

Edward Pessen, *Jacksonian America: Society, Personality, and Politics*, rev. ed. (Homewood, Ill.: Dorsey Press, 1978), pp. 253–58. For the New York working-men and Jackson, see Wilentz, *Chants Democratic*, pp. 174, 189–90, 198–99, 208–10. The link between the Democrats and labor grew stronger in the 1840s.

22. Fletcher M. Green, "On Tour with President Jackson," *New England Quarterly* 36 (1963): 226–28; *Niles' Register* 44 (6 July 1833): 316.

23. *Dover Gazette*, 25 Aug. 1835; *New-Hampshire Patriot*, 23 May 1836; *Congressional Globe*, 24th Cong., 1st sess., app., p. 91; 31st Cong., 1st sess., app., p. 798. For the original view, see Gerald S. Henig, "The Jacksonian Attitude toward Abolitionism," THQ 28 (Spring 1969): 42–56. For the revisionist view, see John M. McFaul, "Expediency vs. Morality: Jacksonian Politics and Slavery," JAH 62 (June 1975): 24–39, quotation, p. 39.

24. Forsyth to Van Buren, 5 Aug. 1835, William A. Butler, *A Retrospect of Forty Years 1825–1865* (New York: Charles Scribner's Sons, 1911), pp. 78–79; Daniel to Van Buren, 25 Sept. 1835, VBP.

25. Kendall to Alfred Huger, 4 Aug. 1835, quoted in *Globe*, 12 Aug. 1835; Kendall to Jackson, 7 Aug. 1835, Jackson to Kendall, 9 Aug. 1835, JC, 5:359–61.

26. *Albany Argus*, 31 Aug., 5, 7 Sept. 1835; *New-Hampshire Patriot*, 21 Sept. 1835. For Ritchie's statement, see Howard Alexander Morrison, "Gentlemen of Proper Understanding: A Closer Look at Utica's Anti-Abolitionist Mob," *New York History* 62 (Jan. 1981): 71. See also *Congressional Globe*, 24th Cong., 1st sess., pp. 120–21; Marcy, "Annual Message," 5 Jan. 1836, Charles Z. Lincoln, ed., *Messages from the Governors*, 11 vols. (Albany, N.Y.: J. B. Lyon, 1909), 3:570–84.

27. Richardson, *Messages and Papers*, 3:175–76; Freehling, *Road to Disunion*, pp. 308–36; Owens to Van Buren, 16 May 1836, VBP.

CHAPTER 12
DEMOCRATIC ADMINISTRATION

1. *A Compilation of the Messages and Papers of the Presidents, 1789–1897*, comp. James D. Richardson, 10 vols. (Washington, D.C.: Government Printing Office, 1897–99), 3:108.

2. George R. Taylor, *The Transportation Revolution 1815–1860* (New York: Harper & Row, 1951), p. 325.

3. Jacob P. Meerman, "The Climax of the Bank War: Biddle's Contraction," *Journal of Political Economy* 71 (Aug. 1963): 381; Harry N. Scheiber, "The Pet Banks in Jacksonian Politics and Finance, 1833–1841," *Journal of Economic History* 23 (June 1963): 202; *The Statistical History of the United States from Colonial Times to the Present* (Stamford, Conn.: Fairfield Publishers, 1965), p. 623.

4. Scheiber, "Pet Banks," pp. 197–200.

5. Jackson to Woodbury, 8 July 1834, JSM; Whitney to Jackson, 6 Oct. 1834, JP.

6. Richardson, *Messages and Papers*, 3:112; John M. McFaul, *The Politics of Jacksonian Finance* (Ithaca, N.Y.: Cornell University Press, 1972), pp. 71–77; Washington *Globe*, 15 July 1834.

7. McFaul, *Politics*, pp. 78–79, 112–23, 147–64; *Register of Debates in Congress, 1825–1837*, 23d Cong., 1st sess., pp. 4602–22, 4760; Scheiber, "Pet Banks," pp. 200–202; *Statistical History*, p. 712; *Niles' Register* 48 (9 May 1835): 167–68; Van Buren to Churchill C. Cambreleng, 10 May 1835, VBP.

8. McFaul, *Politics*, pp. 130–38, 143–48; Taney to Jackson, 27 June 1836, Andrew Jackson, *Correspondence of Andrew Jackson*, ed. John Spencer Bassett and John Franklin Jameson, 7 vols. (1926–35; reprint, New York: Kraus Reprint Co., 1969), 5:404–11; Scheiber, "Pet Banks," pp. 202–6.

9. Scheiber, "Pet Banks," p. 206; Jackson to Amos Kendall, 8 July 1836, JSM; Taney to Jackson, 27 Oct. 1836, JC, 5:431–32; Richardson, *Messages and Papers*, 3:249–50.

10. Scheiber, "Pet Banks," 206–7; Peter Temin, *The Jacksonian Economy* (New York: W. W. Norton, 1969), pp. 120–36.

11. Scheiber, "Pet Banks," pp. 207–9; *Statistical History*, pp. 551, 553.

12. Frank Otto Gatell, "Spoils of the Bank War: Political Bias in the Selection of Pet Banks," AHR 70 (Oct. 1964): 35–58; Kendall is quoted on p. 36. Van Buren to Jackson, 21 April, 28 Sept. 1833, VBP; Van Buren to Jackson, 4, 14 Sept. 1833, JC, 5:181–82, 187. For Whig banks in 1836, see Scheiber, "Pet Banks," pp. 203–4.

13. Gatell, "Spoils," pp. 38–39, 41–42, 55.

14. In his statement Biddle became confused and put "Chestnut St," where the Bank was located in Philadelphia, before "Wall St," which destroyed the meaning of the statement. Biddle to J. S. Barbour, 16 April, 11 July 1834, Biddle to Thomas Cooper, 6 May 1834, Nicholas Biddle, *The Correspondence of Nicholas Biddle Dealing with National Affairs, 1807–1844*, ed. Reginald C. McGrane (Boston: Houghton Mifflin, 1919), pp. 207, 209–11.

15. Richardson, *Messages and Papers*, 2:577; McFaul, *Politics*, pp. 44–45.

16. *Register of Debates*, 23d Cong., 1st sess., pp. 397–405, 464.

17. Matthew Crenson, *The Federal Machine: Beginnings of Bureaucracy in Jacksonian America* (Baltimore: Johns Hopkins University Press, 1975), pp. 2–3; Albert Somit, "Andrew Jackson as Administrative Reformer," THQ 13 (1954): 204–5; Jackson, "Outline of Principles Submitted to the Heads of Departments," 23 Feb. 1829, JP. Jackson made few requests for administrative reform in his annual messages of 1830–33 but made numerous suggestions in the messages of 1834 and 1835.

18. Somit, "Jackson as Administrative Reformer," pp. 207–10.

19. Richardson, *Messages and Papers*, 3:116–17; *Statistical History*, pp. 497, 711; *Niles' Register* 48 (25 May 1835): 215; Leonard D. White, *The Jacksonians: A Study in Administrative History, 1829–1861* (New York: Macmillan, 1954), pp. 266–67.

20. White, *Jacksonians*, pp. 257–63; Crenson, *Federal Machine*, pp. 93–98.

21. Anne Royall to Willie Mangum, 16 Jan. 1835, Willie P. Mangum, *The Papers of Willie Person Mangum*, ed. Henry T. Shanks, 5 vols. (Raleigh, N.C.: State Department of Archives and History, 1950–56), 2:282–83; *Niles' Register* 43 (13 Oct. 1832): 97 and 44 (23 Mar. 1833): 49; *Statistical History*, p. 497; White, *Jacksonians*, p. 266.

22. White, *Jacksonians*, p. 253; Jackson to Barry, 16 June 1834, JSM; Barry to Jackson, 28 Aug. 1834, JP; Barry to Susan Taylor, 4 Jan. 1835, William T. Barry, "Letters of William T. Barry," *William and Mary Quarterly* 14 (1905–6): 240–41.

23. Lewis Cass resigned as secretary of war on 5 October 1836 to become minister to France, but there was no replacement until the next administration. Amos Kendall, *Autobiography of Amos Kendall*, ed. William Stickney (1872; reprint, New York: Peter Smith, 1949), p. 335; Kendall to Jackson, 19 July, 21 Aug. 1834, Thomas P. Moore to Jackson, 28 Aug. 1834, JP.

24. Kendall, *Autobiography*, pp. 337–46; White, *Jacksonians*, pp. 274–76; Gerald Cullinan, *The United States Postal Service* (New York: Praeger, 1973), p. 61; Crenson, *Federal Machine*, 105–10.

25. Malcolm J. Rohrbough, *The Land Office Business: The Settlement and Administration of American Public Lands, 1789–1837* (New York: Oxford University Press, 1968), pp. 221–48.

26. Crenson, *Federal Machine*, pp. 115–30; Rohrbough, *Land Office Business*, pp. 252–70.

27. Daniel Preston, "The Administration and Reform of the U.S. Patent Office," JER 5 (Fall 1985): 331–53.

28. Somit, "Jackson as Administrative Reformer," pp. 206–7.

29. Ronald N. Satz, American Indian Policy in the Jacksonian Era (Lincoln: University of Nebraska Press, 1975), pp. 154–55, 165–66.

30. Charles Warren, *The Supreme Court in United States History*, 2 vols., rev. ed. (Boston: Little, Brown, 1926), 2:39–40.

31. Crenson, *Federal Machine*, pp. 51–55, 66–70, 131–39. Lynn L. Marshall, "The Strange Stillbirth of the Whig Party," AHR 72 (Jan. 1967): 465.

32. For details on Jackson's private secretaries, see JC, 5:433n. For examples of Jackson's repetition, see Jackson to Van Buren, 26 June 1830, VBP, and Jackson to William B. Lewis, 26 June 1830, JSM.

33. Richard P. Longaker, "Was Jackson's Kitchen Cabinet a Cabinet?" MVHR 44 (1957): 103–4.

34. Jackson to Asbury Dickins, 6 Aug. 1831, Leonard M. Parker to Jackson, 15 Jan. 1835, Jackson to Levi Woodbury, c. 15 Jan. 1835, J. H. Hook to Jackson, 4 July 1836, JSM; Jackson to Felix Grundy, 21 Mar. 1832, JP; Jackson to Samuel D. Ingham, 16 Mar. 1830, JC, 4:127.

CHAPTER 13
A DEMOCRATIC VICTORY

1. Richard R. John, "Taking Sabbatarianism Seriously: The Postal System, the Sabbath, and the Transformation of American Political Culture," JER 10 (Winter 1990): 517–67; William G. Shade, "Political Pluralism and Party Development: The Creation of a Modern Party System, 1815–1852," Paul Kleppner et al., eds., *The Evolution of American Electoral Systems* (Westport, Conn.: Greenwood Press, 1981), pp. 82–93, 104–5.

2. Sidney H. Aronson, *Status and Kinship in the Higher Civil Service: Standards of Selection in the Administrations of John Adams, Thomas Jefferson, and Andrew Jackson* (Cambridge: Harvard University Press, 1964), pp. 31, 195.

3. Clay, "Senate Speech on the Appointing and Removing Power," 18 Feb.

1835, Henry Clay, *The Works of Henry Clay*, ed. Calvin Colton, 10 vols. (New York: G. P. Putnam's Sons, 1904), 8:23, quoted in Paul E. Johnson, "The Spoils System and Party Organization: 1829–1840" (unpublished paper, c. 1970), p. 4; "Report of a Senate Committee to Inquire into the Extent of the Executive Patronage," 9 Feb. 1835, Robert V. Remini, ed., *The Age of Jackson* (New York: Harper & Row, 1972), pp. 45–51.

4. *The Statistical History of the United States from Colonial Times to the Present* (Stamford, Conn.: Fairfield Publishers, 1965), p. 712; Gordon to Lewis, 27 Mar. 1833, Jackson to Gordon, 9 April 1833, Lewis to Jackson, 26 April 1833, JP; William J. Duane to Jackson, 22 July 1833, JSM; Van Buren to Jackson, 6 Aug. 1833, VBP.

5. "Report of Senate Committee," Remini, *Age of Jackson*, p. 45; Malcolm J. Rohrbough, *The Land Office Business: The Settlement and Administration of American Public Lands, 1789–1837* (New York: Oxford University Press, 1968), pp. 273–83.

6. Richard P. McCormick, *The Second American Party System: Party Formation in the Jacksonian Era* (Chapel Hill: University of North Carolina Press, 1966), pp. 35–99, 103–47, 166–73, 177–209, 236–54.

7. Ibid., pp. 209–36, 295–303, 310–26.

8. McCormick, *Second Party System*, pp. 257–87, 304–10, 320–26; Clay, "Senate Speech," *Works*, 8:15; Douglas et al., "To the Democratic Republicans of Illinois," 31 Dec. 1835, Stephen A. Douglas, *The Letters of Stephen A. Douglas*, ed. Robert W. Johannsen (Urbana: University of Illinois Press, 1961), pp. 24–31.

9. Campbell to Jackson, 4 Feb. 1827, JP; Thomas Ford, *A History of Illinois* (New York: Ivison & Phinney, 1854), pp. 313–15, 316–22, Remini, *Age of Jackson*, pp. 7–12.

10. The number of 400 is taken from Elbert B. Smith, *Francis Preston Blair* (New York: Free Press, 1980), pp. 71–72.

11. Hogan to Jackson, 27 Sept. 1835, JP; Jackson to Alfred O. P. Nicholson, 18 Dec. 1835, JSM.

12. Harry L. Watson, *Liberty and Power: The Politics of Jacksonian America* (New York: Hill and Wang, 1990), pp. 236–48; Edward Pessen, *Jacksonian America: Society, Personality, and Politics,* rev. ed. (Homewood, Ill.: Dorsey Press, 1978), pp. 241–47; Daniel Walker Howe, "The Evangelical Movement and Political Culture in the North during the Second Party System," JAH 77 (Mar. 1991): 1216–39; Ronald P. Formisano, *The Transformation of Political Culture: Massachusetts Parties, 1790s–1840s* (New York: Oxford University Press, 1983), pp. 3–23, 149–54, 268–80.

13. *Daily National Intelligencer,* 12 Jan., 10, 19 Sept. 1836; Jackson to Edward Livingston, 27 June 1834, Jackson to Felix Grundy, 24 Sept. 1835, Andrew Jackson, *Correspondence of Andrew Jackson,* ed. John Spencer Bassett and John Franklin Jameson, 7 vols. (1926–35; reprint, New York: Kraus Reprint Co., 1969), 5:271–72, 367; Harriet Martineau, *Restrospect of Western Travel,* 3 vols. (London: Saunders and Otley, 1838), 1:254; Benjamin S. King to Mangum, 15 Dec. 1834, Mangum to William A. Graham, 16, 17 Dec. 1834, North Carolina Legislature "Resolutions," 27 Dec. 1834, Willie P. Mangum, *The Papers of Willie Person Mangum,* ed. Henry T. Shanks, 5 vols. (Raleigh, N.C.: State Department of Archives and History, 1950–56), 2:238–39, 240–47, 269–70.

14. Kenneth C. Martis, *The Historical Atlas of Political Parties in the United States Congress 1789–1989* (New York: Macmillan, 1989), pp. 24, 93–94, 349–60.

15. Charles Warren, *The Supreme Court in United States History,* 2 vols., rev. ed. (Boston: Little, Brown, 1926), 1:795–96, 2:39–42; *Intelligencer,* 16, 17 Mar. 1836; Jackson to Arthur P. Hayne, 17 April 1836, JSM.

16. *Niles' Register* 49 (12 Dec. 1835): 218. Blair lost the House printing in 1837 but regained it for the years 1839–41 and 1843–45. He was printer for the Senate, 1837–41. Culver H. Smith, *The Press, Politics, and Patronage: The American Government's Use of Newspapers 1789–1875* (Athens: University of Georgia Press, 1977), p. 250.

17. Mangum to Duncan Cameron, 7 Feb. 1834, Mangum, *Papers,* 2:74.

18. Charles Sellers, *James K. Polk, Jacksonian, 1795–1843* (Princeton, N.J.: Princeton University Press, 1957), pp. 253–62.

19. Burton W. Folsom III, "Party Formation and Development in Jacksonian America: The Old South," *Journal of American Studies* 7 (1973): 217–29. See also Jackson to Van Buren, 5 Oct. 1834, JSM; Jackson to Joseph Conn Guild, 24 April 1835, Jackson to James K. Polk, 12 May 1835, JC, 5:338–41, 345–46; Jackson to Samuel Gwin, 25 April 1834, JSM.

20. Jackson to Polk, 12 May 1835, JC, 5:345–46; Webster to Jeremiah Mason, 1 Feb. 1835, Daniel Webster, *The Letters of Daniel Webster,* ed. C. H. Van Tyne (1902; reprint, New York: Haskell House Publishers, 1969), p. 195; Blair to Felix Grundy, 10 June 1835, JP; Jackson to Andrew J. Donelson, 4 May 1835, JSM.

21. Blair to Jackson, 19 May 1835, JC, 5:348–49; *Intelligencer,* 25 May 1835.

22. Blair to Jackson, 19 May 1835, JC, 5:348–49. For the influence of Blair and Kendall, see Richard B. Latner, *The Presidency of Andrew Jackson: White House Politics 1829–1837* (Athens: University of Georgia Press, 1979), pp. 198–99.

23. Catron to Jackson, 21 Mar. 1835, Blair to Jackson, 19 May 1835, JC, 5:330–32, 348–49; Alfred Balch to Jackson, 3 Feb. 1835, JP; Van Buren to Rives, 3 Nov. 1835, William C. Rives Papers.

24. "Statement by the Democratic Republicans of the United States," in Joel H. Silbey, "Election of 1836," Arthur M. Schlesinger, Jr., and Fred L. Israel, eds., *History of American Presidential Elections 1789–1968,* 4 vols. (New York: Chelsea House, 1971), 1:616–38.

25. Jackson to Van Buren, 18 Nov. 1832, Jackson to Tilghman A. Howard, 20 Aug. 1833, Jackson to Joseph Conn Guild, 24 April 1835, Jackson to James K. Polk, 12 May, 3 Aug. 1835, JC, 4: 489–90, 5:165–66, 338–41, 345–46, 359; Jackson to Van Buren, 25 Nov. 1832, Martin Van Buren, "The Autobiography of Martin Van Buren," ed. John C. Fitzpatrick, *Annual Report of the American Historical Association for the Year 1918,* vol. 2 (Washington, D.C.: Government Printing Office, 1920), pp. 495–96.

26. Thomas Brown, "From Old Hickory to Sly Fox: The Routinization of Charisma in the Early Democratic Party," JER 11 (Fall 1991): 339–69.

27. *Intelligencer,* 24 April, 16, 27 May, 11, 13, 17, 20, 24, 27 June, 1, 8 July 1835.

28. "Report of Senate Committee," Remini, *Age of Jackson,* pp. 45–51.

29. Sydney Nathans, *Daniel Webster and Jacksonian Democracy* (Baltimore: Johns Hopkins University Press, 1973), pp. 1–7, 130–47.

30. Lynn L. Marshall argues that the Whigs resisted partyism in "The Strange Stillbirth of the Whig Party," AHR 72 (Jan. 1967): 445–68, as does Paul E. Johnson in "Spoils System," pp. 1–5. William J. Cooper, Jr., finds southern Whigs as well organized as Democrats, but most of his evidence comes from the period after Jackson left office. See Cooper, *The South and the Politics of Slavery 1828–1856* (Baton Rouge: Louisiana State University Press, 1978), pp. 23–42. Greeley's statement is from Horace Greeley, *Recollections of a Busy Life* (New York: J. B. Ford, 1868), p. 137, quoted in Johnson, "Spoils System," p. 5. For the view that Democrats feared change and sought to keep the old world while Whigs looked ahead confidently, see Lawrence Frederick Kohl, *The Politics of Individualism: Parties and the American Character in the Jacksonian Era* (New York: Oxford University Press, 1989).

31. Charles A. Davis, *Letters of J. Downing, Major, Downingville . . . to Mr. Dwight* (New York: Harper and Bros., 1834), pp. 112, 230; David Crockett, *The Life of Martin Van Buren* (Philadelphia: Robert Wright, 1835), pp. 30, 80–81, 167; John C. Calhoun, speech in the Senate, *Congressional Globe*, 24th Cong., 1st sess., p. 113.

32. Van Buren to Judith Rives, 1 April 1835, Rives Papers.

33. Haverhill, Mass., *Essex Gazette*, 12 Sept. 1835; Van Buren to Junius Amis et al., 4 Mar. 1836, VBP.

34. Washington *Globe*, 12, 23 Sept. 1836; William Henry Harrison to Sherrod Williams, 7 April 1836, in Silbey, "Election of 1836," pp. 608–13. The *Globe's* "bankism" attack is quoted in Silbey, p. 588. For the White campaign see Jonathan M. Atkins, "The Presidential Campaign of Hugh Lawson White in Tennessee, 1832–1836," *Journal of Southern History* 58 (Feb. 1992): 27–56.

35. Michel Chevalier, *Society, Manners, and Politics in the United States: Letters on North America* (1839; reprint, New York: Anchor Books, 1961), p. 307; *Register of Debates in Congress, 1825–1837*, 24th Cong., 1st sess., p. 3552, quoted in Alvin W. Lynn, "Party Formation and Operation in the House of Representatives, 1824–1837," (Ph.D. diss., Rutgers University, 1972), p. 129.

36. Richard P. McCormick, "Was There a 'Whig Strategy' in 1836?" JER 4 (Spring 1984): 47–70.

37. Jackson to Kendall, 5 Aug. 1836, Jackson to Van Buren, 22 Aug., 19 Sept. 1836, JSM; Jackson to Van Buren, 2 Oct. 1836, JC, 5:428.

38. Jackson to Hardy Cryer, 13 Nov. 1836, JSM; *Intelligencer*, 7, 26 Nov., 13 Dec. 1836; Svend Petersen, *A Statistical History of the American Presidential Elections* (New York: Frederick Ungar, 1963), pp. 21–23, 172, 178.

39. Petersen, *Statistical History*, pp. 21–23, 172, 178; Silbey, "Election of 1836," pp. 577–83, 595–600.

40. Thomas Hart Benton, *Thirty Years' View*, 2 vols. (New York: D. Appleton, 1854), 1:728–29; Nathan Sargent, *Public Men and Events from the Commencement of Mr. Monroe's Administration in 1817, to the Close of Mr. Fillmore's Administration in 1853*, 2 vols. (Philadelphia: J. B. Lippincott, 1874), 1:332–35.

41. Sargent, *Public Men and Events*, 1: 336; Benton, *Thirty Years' View*, 1:727–28.

42. Benton, *Thirty Years' View*, 1:730.

43. Ibid., 1:730–31; Jackson to Benton, 17 Jan. 1837, JC, 5:451.

44. Benton, *Thirty Years' View,* 1:683–84.

45. *A Compilation of the Messages and Papers of the Presidents, 1789–1897,* comp. James D. Richardson, 10 vols. (Washington, D.C.: Government Printing Office, 1897–99), 3:282–83.

46. Van Buren to John Van Buren, 22 Dec. 1836, VBP; Richardson, *Messages and Papers,* 3:265–69.

47. Benton, *Thirty Years' View,* 1:735. The "murmur" quotation is from the writer Nathaniel P. Willis, quoted in James Parton, *Life of Andrew Jackson,* 3 vols. (New York: Mason Brothers, 1860), 3:628.

CHAPTER 14
AN AMBIVALENT PRESIDENCY

1. Richard E. Parker to Jackson, 26 Feb. 1836, JP; Charles Francis Adams, *Diary of Charles Francis Adams,* ed. Aida DiPace Donald, David Donald, Marc Friedlaender, and L. H. Butterfield, 8 vols. (Cambridge: Harvard University Press, 1964–86), 6:333; John Quincy Adams, *Memoirs of John Quincy Adams,* ed. Charles Francis Adams, 12 vols. (Philadelphia: J. B. Lippincott, 1875–77), 9:311.

2. Those historians arguing that Jackson and his party were primarily interested in winning office include Richard P. McCormick, *The Second American Party System: Party Formation in the Jacksonian Era* (Chapel Hill: University of North Carolina Press, 1966), and Edward Pessen, *Jacksonian America: Society, Personality, and Politics,* rev. ed. (Homewood, Ill.: Dorsey Press, 1978). Those who believe that they had ideological goals include Richard B. Latner, *The Presidency of Andrew Jackson: White House Politics 1829–1837* (Athens: University of Georgia Press, 1979), quotation p. 212, and Richard E. Ellis, *The Union at Risk: Jacksonian Democracy, States' Rights and the Nullification Crisis* (New York: Oxford University Press, 1987), quotation p. 40.

3. Jackson to Taney, 13 Oct. 1836, Andrew Jackson, *Correspondence of Andrew Jackson,* ed. John Spencer Bassett and John Franklin Jameson, 7 vols. (1926–35; reprint, New York: Kraus Reprint Co., 1969), 5:429–30; *A Compilation of the Messages and Papers of the Presidents,* comp. James D. Richardson, 10 vols. (Washington, D.C.: Government Printing Office, 1897–99), 3:298–301, 305.

4. Richardson, *Messages and Papers,* 3:294–95, 307.

5. Washington *Globe,* 13 Oct. 1832; Amos Kendall, *Autobiography of Amos Kendall,* ed. William Stickney (1872; reprint, New York: Peter Smith, 1949), pp. 297–99.

6. Richardson, *Messages and Papers,* 3:313–20.

7. A good example of a lesser Jacksonian with a similar message is John Coffee. In a letter to Jackson he first reminded the president that his duty was to "settle our Gov't down on honest and republican principles." He then spent the rest of the letter discussing the cotton crop. Coffee to Jackson, 18 Dec. 1830, JP. Five years later Stephen A. Douglas praised Jackson for following "strict construction" and for "extending our commercial prosperity." Douglas et al., "To The Democratic Republicans of Illinois," 31 Dec. 1835, Stephen A. Douglas, *The*

Letters of Stephen A. Douglas, ed. Robert W. Johannsen (Urbana: University of Illinois Press, 1961), p. 29.

8. Two months after the reduced rates of the compromise tariff went into effect on 1 July 1842, they were replaced by the protective duties of the Tariff of 1842. F. W. Taussig, *The Tariff History of the United States*, 6th ed. (New York: G. P. Putnam's Sons, 1892), pp. 112–13.

9. *The Statistical History of the United States from Colonial Times to the Present* (Stamford, Conn.: Fairfield Publishers, 1965), pp. 538, 711.

10. Alexis de Tocqueville, *Democracy in America*, ed. Phillips Bradley, 2 vols. (New York: Alfred A. Knopf, 1945), 1:414.

11. John Quincy Adams, *The Diary of John Quincy Adams 1794–1845*, ed. Allan Nevins (New York: Longmans, Green, 1928), p. 503.

12. Wilhelmus B. Bryan, *A History of the National Capital*, 2 vols. (New York: Macmillan, 1914, 1916), 1:237–50.

13. John William Ward, *Andrew Jackson—Symbol for an Age* (New York: Oxford University Press, 1955), p. 208.

BIBLIOGRAPHICAL ESSAY

Despite the attention lavished on the Age of Jackson the only other book-length study of the Old Hero's presidency is Richard B. Latner's excellent *The Presidency of Andrew Jackson: White House Politics 1829–1837* (Athens: University of Georgia Press, 1979), which stresses the influence of republican ideology and western advisers on Jackson. The best broad surveys of the era are Arthur M. Schlesinger, Jr., *The Age of Jackson* (Boston: Little, Brown, 1945); Edward Pessen, *Jacksonian America: Society, Personality, and Politics,* rev. ed. (Homewood, Ill.: Dorsey Press, 1978); Harry L. Watson, *Liberty and Power: The Politics of Jacksonian America* (New York: Hill and Wang, 1990); and Charles Sellers, *The Market Revolution: Jacksonian America, 1815–1846* (New York: Oxford University Press, 1991). The first deserves its reputation as a classic, but it overstates the parallels between Jacksonian Democracy and the New Deal. Pessen depicts a less than egalitarian era in which the gap between rich and poor widened. Watson portrays the Jackson movement as an effort to roll back the inroads of the market revolution, and Sellers uses Marxian and religious concepts to synthesize the economy, culture, and politics of the age. Robert H. Wiebe offers an even broader overview in *The Opening of American Society: From the Adoption of the Constitution to the Eve of Disunion* (New York: Alfred A. Knopf, 1984). Frederick Jackson Turner's *The United States 1830–1850: The Nation and Its Sections* (1935; reprint, New York: W. W. Norton, 1965), is still worth consulting. For a Whiggish interpretation, see Glyndon G. Van Deusen, *The Jacksonian Era, 1818–1848* (New York: Harper & Brothers, 1959).

The most comprehensive bibliography for the period is Robert V. Remini and Edwin A. Miles, *The Era of Good Feelings and the Age of Jackson, 1816–1841* (Arlington Heights, Ill.: AHM Publishing Corp., 1979). An excellent bibliography for Jackson is Robert V. Remini and Robert O. Rupp, eds., *Andrew Jackson: A Bibliography* (Westport, Conn.: Meekler, 1991). Review essays include: Ronald P. Formisano, "Toward a Reorientation of Jacksonian Politics: A Review of the Literature, 1959–1975," *Journal of American History* 63 (June 1976): 42–65; Edward Pessen, *Jacksonian America*, pp. 329–67; Sean Wilentz, "On Class and Politics in Jacksonian America," *Reviews in American History* 10 (1982): 43–63; and Daniel Feller, "Politics and Society: Toward a Jacksonian Synthesis," *Journal of the Early Republic* 10 (Summer 1990): 135–61.

For the social changes of the early Republic, see Gordon S. Wood, "The Significance of the Early Republic," *Journal of the Early Republic* 8 (1988): 1–20. The market revolution in New England is analyzed in Christopher Clark, "The Household Economy, Market Exchange, and the Rise of Capitalism in the Connecticut Valley, 1800–1860," *Journal of Social History* 13 (1979): 169–90. The concept of the transportation revolution was introduced by George Rogers Taylor in *The Transportation Revolution, 1815–1860* (New York: Harper & Row, 1951). Mary P. Ryan describes the rise of the middle class in western New York in *Cradle of the Middle Class: The Family in Oneida County, New York 1790–1865* (Cambridge: Cambridge University Press, 1981). Paul E. Johnson presents the Second Great Awakening as a form of social control in *A Shopkeeper's Millennium: Society and Revivals in Rochester, N.Y., 1815–1837* (New York: Hill and Wang, 1978); for a contrary view, see Lawrence Frederick Kohl, "The Concept of Social Control and the History of Jacksonian America," *Journal of the Early Republic* 5 (Spring 1985): 21–34. Two articles that relate Sabbatarianism to politics are Bertram Wyatt-Brown, "Prelude to Abolitionism: Sabbatarian Politics and the Rise of the Second Party System," *Journal of American History* 58 (1971): 316–41; and Richard R. John, "Taking Sabbatarianism Seriously: The Postal System, the Sabbath, and the Transformation of American Political Culture," *Journal of the Early Republic* 10 (Winter 1990): 517–67. Daniel Walker Howe links evangelism and politics more broadly in "The Evangelical Movement and Political Culture in the North during the Second Party System," *Journal of American History* 77 (Mar. 1991): 1216–39.

A convenient introduction to the intellectual traditions influencing America after the Revolution is Jack P. Greene, *The Intellectual Heritage of the Constitutional Era: The Delegates' Library* (Philadelphia: Library Company of Philadelphia, 1986). The best survey of American thought in the early Republic is Jean V. Matthews, *Toward a New Society: American Thought and Culture, 1800–1830* (Boston: Twayne, 1991). For the theme of republicanism, start with Robert E. Shalhope, "Republicanism and Early American Historiography," *William and Mary Quarterly*, 3d series, 39 (April 1982): 334–56. Valuable modifications of the republican interpretation are Joyce Appleby, *Capitalism and a New Social Order: The Republican Vision of the 1790s* (New York: New York University Press, 1984); James T. Kloppenberg, "The Virtues of Liberalism: Christianity, Republicanism, and Ethics in Early American Political Discourse," *Journal of American History* 74 (June 1987): 9–33; and Daniel T. Rodgers, "Republicanism: The Career of a Concept," *Journal of American History* 79 (June 1992): 11–38. For two works expressing the Jacksonian longing for a lost utopia see Marvin Meyers, *The Jacksonian Persuasion: Politics and Belief* (New York: Vintage Books, 1960), and Fred Somkin, *Unquiet Eagle: Memory and Desire in the Idea of American Freedom, 1815–1860* (Ithaca, N.Y.: Cornell University Press, 1967). John William Ward describes Jackson as an American symbol in *Andrew Jackson—Symbol for an Age* (New York: Oxford University Press, 1955).

Richard P. McCormick provides the best survey of the new political system in *The Second American Party System: Party Formation in the Jacksonian Era* (Chapel Hill: University of North Carolina Press, 1966). For a briefer analysis see William G. Shade, "Political Pluralism and Party Development," Paul Kleppner et al., eds., *The Evolution of American Electoral Systems* (Westport, Conn.: Greenwood, 1981), pp. 77–112. Michael Wallace discusses the Albany Regency's ideas concerning party in "Changing Concepts of Party in the United States: New York, 1815–1828," *American Historical Review* 74 (Dec. 1968): 453–91. Richard Hofstadter has written a broader treatment of the subject in *The Idea of a Party System: The Rise of Legitimate Opposition in the United States, 1780–1840* (Berkeley: University of California Press, 1969). Ronald P. Formisano argues that antipartyism and old-style deference politics continued much longer than students originally thought. See "Political Character, Antipartyism and the Second American Party System," *American Quarterly* 21 (Winter 1969): 683–709, and "Deferential-Participant Politics: The Early Republic's Political Culture, 1789–1840," *American Political Science Review* 68 (1974): 473–87. For two valuable studies of party formation in Congress, see Alvin W. Lynn, "Party Formation and Operation in the House of Representatives, 1824–1837" (Ph.D. dissertation, Rutgers University, 1972), and David J. Russo, "The Major Political Issues of the Jacksonian Period and the Development of Party Loyalty in Congress, 1830–1840," *Transactions of the American Philosophical Society,* new series, vol. 62, part 5 (May 1972). For the techniques and culture of American political campaigns, see M. J. Heale, *The Presidential Quest: Candidates and Images in American Political Culture, 1787–1852* (London: Longman, 1982).

Interpretations of Jacksonian Democracy have shifted repeatedly. Arthur M. Schlesinger, Jr.'s, thesis that Jackson represented the working class was sharply attacked by "consensus" historians, who considered Jacksonians as entrepreneurs. Richard Hofstadter led the way with his chapter, "Andrew Jackson and the Rise of Liberal Capitalism," in *The American Political Tradition and the Men Who Made It* (New York: Alfred A. Knopf, 1948), pp. 44–66. Both of these views were challenged by Lee Benson and the "ethnocultural" historians, who argued that politics was mainly influenced by ethnic and religious considerations: Benson, *The Concept of Jacksonian Democracy: New York as a Test Case* (Princeton N.J.: Princeton University Press, 1961). For a skillful review of this interpretation, see Richard L. McCormick, "Ethno-Cultural Interpretation of Nineteenth-Century American Voting Behavior," *Political Science Quarterly* 89 (June 1974): 351–77. Other historians, including Richard B. Latner and Marvin Meyers in the works already cited, have portrayed Jacksonians as yearning for republican ideals of the past. See also Major L. Wilson, "Republicanism and the Idea of Party in the Jacksonian Period, *Journal of the Early Republic* 8 (1988): 419–42. The pendulum has now swung back toward Schlesinger with the works by Watson and Sellers previously cited and with John Ashworth, *"Agrarians and Aristocrats": Party Political Ideology in the United States, 1837–1846* (Cambridge: Cambridge University Press, 1987). Lawrence Frederick Kohl paints a picture of Democrats as outer-directed traditionalists and Whigs as inner-directed individualists in *The Politics of Individualism: Parties and the American Character in the Jacksonian Era* (New York: Oxford University Press, 1989).

The best short history of the Democratic party is Michael F. Holt, "The Democratic Party 1828–1860," Arthur M. Schlesinger, Jr., ed., *History of U.S. Political Parties*, 4 vols. (New York: Chelsea House, 1973), 1: 497–571. See also Jean H. Baker, *Affairs of Party: The Political Culture of Northern Democrats in the Mid-Nineteenth Century* (Ithaca, N.Y.: Cornell University Press, 1983). Two explanations of southern antebellum politics are William J. Cooper, *The South and the Politics of Slavery, 1828–1856* (Baton Rouge, Louisiana State University Press, 1978), which stresses the importance of slavery, and Burton W. Folsom III, "Party Formation and Development in Jacksonian America: The Old South," *Journal of American Studies* 7 (1973): 217–29, which puts more emphasis on Jackson's policies.

Glyndon G. Van Deusen offers a brief history of the Whig party in "The Whig Party," Schlesinger, *U.S. Political Parties*, 1:333–493; and Daniel Walker Howe assesses the Whig culture in *The Political Culture of the American Whigs* (Chicago: University of Chicago Press, 1980). The view that Whigs took part reluctantly in the new party politics appears in Lynn L. Marshall, "The Strange Stillbirth of the Whig Party," *American Historical Review* 72 (Jan. 1967): 445–68. Charles Sellers cites economic differences between southern Whigs and southern Democrats in "Who Were the Southern Whigs?" *American Historical Review* 59 (Jan. 1954): 335–46. Anti-Masonry, once considered a fanatical movement, is now presented as a popular reaction against what was thought to be a corrupt privileged organization. See Michael F. Holt, "The Antimasonic and Know Nothing Parties," Schlesinger, *U.S. Political Parties*, 1:575–93; and Kathleen S. Kutolowski, "Antimasonry Reexamined: Social Bases of the Grass-Roots Party," *Journal of American History* 71 (Sept. 1984): 269–93.

Among the better recent studies of state politics are Paul Goodman, "The Social Basis of New England Politics in Jacksonian America," *Journal of the Early Republic* 6 (Spring 1986): 23–58; Ronald P. Formisano, *The Transformation of Political Culture: Massachusetts Parties, 1790s–1840s* (New York: Oxford University Press, 1983); Harry L. Watson, *Jacksonian Politics and Community Conflict: The Emergence of the Second American Party System in Cumberland County, North Carolina* (Baton Rouge: Louisiana State University Press, 1981); and J. Mills Thornton III, *Politics and Power in a Slave Society: Alabama, 1800–1860* (Baton Rouge: Louisiana State University Press, 1978).

For the rise of national nominating conventions, see James S. Chase, *Emergence of the Presidential Nominating Convention 1789–1832* (Urbana: University of Illinois Press, 1973). The election of 1828 is colorfully described by Robert V. Remini in *The Election of Andrew Jackson* (Philadelphia: J. B. Lippincott, 1963). The standard account of the election of 1832 is Samuel Rhea Gammon, *The Presidential Campaign of 1832* (Baltimore: Johns Hopkins University Press, 1922). For the election of 1836, see Richard P. McCormick, "Was There a 'Whig Strategy' in 1836?" *Journal of the Early Republic* 4 (Spring 1984): 47–70, and Jonathan M. Atkins, "The Presidential Candidacy of Hugh Lawson White in Tennessee, 1832–1836," *Journal of Southern History* 58 (Feb. 1992): 27–56. Thomas Brown explains how the Democrats weaned their party away from its dependence on the charisma of Jackson in "From Old Hickory to Sly Fox: The Routinization of Charisma in the Early Democratic Party," *Journal of the Early Republic* 11 (Fall 1991): 339–70. For shorter accounts of the four elections in which Jackson was involved, see James F. Hopkins, "Election of 1824," Robert V. Remini, "Election of 1828" and "Election of 1832," and Joel H. Silbey, "Election of 1836," Arthur M. Schlesinger, Jr., and Fred L. Israel, eds., *History of American Presidential Elections 1789–1968*, 4 vols. (New York: Chelsea House, 1971), 1:349–640.

Valuable Democratic newspapers are the Washington *Globe*, the Concord *New-Hampshire Patriot*, the *Albany Argus*, and the *Richmond Enquirer*. *Niles' Register* of Baltimore and the Washington *Daily National Intelligencer* speak for the opposition. For the official executive and legislative record, see *A Compilation of the Messages and Papers of the Presidents, 1789–1897*, comp. James D. Richardson, 10 vols. (Washington, D.C.: Government Printing Office, 1897–99); *Register of Debates in Congress, 1825–1837;* and *Congressional Globe, 1833–1873*. Other useful sources are Perry M. Goldman and James S. Young, eds., *The United States Congressional Directories 1789–1840* (New York: Columbia University Press, 1973); Kenneth C. Martis, *The Historical Atlas of Political Parties in the United States Congress 1789–1989* (New York: Macmillan, 1989); and *The Statistical History of the United States from Colonial Times to the Present* (Stamford, Conn.: Fairfield Publishers, 1965).

Among the many accounts by foreign travelers the most perceptive remains Alexis de Tocqueville, *Democracy in America*, ed. Phillips Bradley, 2 vols. (New York: Alfred A. Knopf, 1945). Two other Europeans who left vivid records are Michel Chevalier, *Society, Manners, and Politics in the United States* (1836; reprint, New York: Anchor Books, 1961), and Harriet Martineau, *Retrospect of Western Travel*, 3 vols. (London: Saunders and Otley, 1838). Diaries, letters, and reminiscences written by Americans with sharp eyes and ears include Benjamin Perley Poore, *Perley's Reminiscences*, 2 vols. (Philadelphia: Hubbard Brothers, 1886); Philip Hone, *The Diary of Philip Hone 1828–1851*, ed. Allan Nevins (New York: Dodd, Mead, 1936); Benjamin Brown French, *Witness to the Young Republic: A Yankee's Journal, 1828–1870*, ed. Donald B. Cole and John J. McDonough (Hanover, N.H.: University Press of New England, 1989); and Margaret Bayard Smith, *The First Forty Years of Washington Society*, ed. Gaillard Hunt (1906; reprint, New York: Frederick Ungar, 1965).

Jackson's papers are easily accessible in the microfilm edition of his correspondence at the Library of Congress, in the National Archives microfilm series, and in the microfilm supplement of other Jackson papers published in 1986. The new and selective letterpress edition of the Jackson papers has reached 1815. Jackson, *The Papers of Andrew Jackson*, ed. Sam B. Smith, Harold D. Moser, and Sharon MacPherson, 3 vols. to date (Knoxville: University of Tennessee Press, 1980–). Historians are still well served by Andrew Jackson, *Correspondence of Andrew Jackson*, ed. John Spencer Bassett and John Franklin Jameson, 7 vols. (1926–35; reprint, New York: Kraus Reprint Co., 1969).

For the Van Buren papers, scholars can choose between the microfilm edition of his papers at the Library of Congress and a microfilm edition including the Library of Congress series and other Van Buren papers, published in 1987. Still an invaluable source is Martin Van Buren, "The Autobiography of Martin

Van Buren," ed. John C. Fitzpatrick, *Annual Report of the American Historical Association for the Year 1918,* vol. 2 (Washington D.C.: Government Printing Office, 1920).

The other Jacksonians left much less of a record. There are interesting letters from Amos Kendall to Francis P. Blair in the Blair-Lee Papers at the Princeton University Library, but Kendall's *Autobiography of Amos Kendall,* ed. William Stickney (1872; reprint, New York: Peter Smith, 1949) is unreliable. Other published sources include William T. Barry, "Letters of William T. Barry," *William and Mary College Quarterly* 13 (1904–5): 236–44; 14 (1905–6): 19–23, 230–41; Thomas Hart Benton, *Thirty Years' View,* 2 vols. (New York: D. Appleton, 1854); James A. Hamilton, *Reminiscences of James A. Hamilton* (New York: Charles Scribner's Sons, 1869); James K. Polk, *Correspondence of James K. Polk,* ed. Herbert Weaver, Paul H. Bergeron, and Wayne Cutler, 7 vols. to date (Nashville: Vanderbilt University Press, 1969–); and Levi Woodbury, "Levi Woodbury's 'Intimate Memoranda' of the Jackson Administration," ed. Ari Hoogenboom and Herbert Ershkowitz, *Pennsylvania Magazine of History and Biography* 92 (1968): 507–15.

The Whig sources include three major letterpress series: John C. Calhoun, *The Papers of John C. Calhoun,* ed. Robert L. Merriwether, W. Edwin Hemphill, and Clyde Wilson, 20 vols. to date (Columbia: University of South Carolina Press, 1959–); Daniel Webster, *The Papers of Daniel Webster: Correspondence,* ed. Charles M. Wiltse and Harold D. Moser, 7 vols. (Hanover, N.H.: University Press of New England, 1974–86); and Henry Clay, *The Papers of Henry Clay,* ed. James F. Hopkins, Mary W. M. Hargreaves, Robert Seager II, and Melba Porter Hay, 10 vols. to date (Lexington: University Press of Kentucky, 1959–).

The writings of two Democrats who turned Whig may be found in Willie P. Mangum, *The Papers of Willie Person Mangum,* ed. Henry T. Shanks, 5 vols. (Raleigh, N.C.: State Department of Archives and History, 1950–56), and Lyon G. Tyler, *The Letters and Times of the Tylers,* 3 vols. (Richmond, Va.: Whittet & Shepperson, 1884, 1886). For many events the most penetrating and acerbic comments can often be found in John Quincy Adams, *Memoirs of John Quincy Adams,* ed. Charles Francis Adams, 12 vols. (Philadelphia: J. B. Lippincott, 1875–77). Two younger Whigs are represented by Charles Francis Adams, *Diary of Charles Francis Adams,* ed. Aida DiPace Donald, David Donald, Marc Friedlaender, and L. H. Butterfield, 8 vols. (Cambridge: Harvard University Press, 1964–86), and Thurlow Weed, *Autobiography of Thurlow Weed,* ed. Harriet A. Weed (Boston: Houghton, Mifflin, 1883). Some of the correspondence of the Anti-Masonic presidential candidate, William Wirt, may be found in John P. Kennedy, ed., *Memoirs of the Life of William Wirt,* 2 vols. (Philadelphia: Lea and Blanchard, 1850).

Biographies of Jackson have appeared regularly. James Parton, *Life of Andrew Jackson,* 3 vols. (New York: Mason Brothers, 1860) is still valuable because of its anecdotes and the author's interviews with surviving Jacksonians. The Progressive interpretation of Jackson as the leader of democracy is set forth in John Spencer Bassett, *The Life of Andrew Jackson,* 2 vols. in 1 (1911; reprint, Hamden, Conn.: Archon Books, 1967), and in Marquis James, *Andrew Jackson: The Border Captain* and *Andrew Jackson: Portrait of a President* (Indianapolis: Bobbs-Merrill, 1933, 1937). In his *Andrew Jackson and the Search for Vindication* (Boston: Little,

Brown, 1976), James C. Curtis offers a psychological study of Old Hickory. The definitive biography of Jackson is Robert V. Remini's three-volume work: *Andrew Jackson and the Course of American Empire, 1767–1821; Andrew Jackson and the Course of American Freedom, 1822–1832;* and *Andrew Jackson and the Course of American Democracy, 1833–1845* (New York: Harper & Row, 1977, 1981, 1984). These volumes have been conveniently condensed into one volume in Remini, *The Life of Andrew Jackson* (New York: Harper and Row, 1988). See also Remini, *The Legacy of Andrew Jackson: Essays on Democracy, Indian Removal, and Slavery* (Baton Rouge: Louisiana State University Press, 1988).

There have been two recent biographies of Van Buren: John Niven's *Martin Van Buren and the Romantic Age of American Politics* (New York: Oxford University Press, 1983), and Donald B. Cole, *Martin Van Buren and the American Political System* (Princeton, N.J.: Princeton University Press, 1984). Both give Van Buren much of the credit for the rise of the American two-party system. For Van Buren's presidency, see James C. Curtis, *The Fox at Bay: Martin Van Buren and the Presidency, 1837–1841* (Lexington: University Press of Kentucky, 1970), and Major L. Wilson, *The Presidency of Martin Van Buren* (Lawrence: University Press of Kansas, 1984). For James K. Polk, see the excellent biography by Charles Sellers, *James K. Polk, Jacksonian, 1795–1843,* and *James K. Polk, Continentalist, 1843–1846* (Princeton, N.J.: Princeton University Press, 1957, 1966). Other biographies of Jacksonians include John A. Munroe, *Louis McLane: Federalist and Jacksonian* (New Brunswick, N.J.: Rutgers University Press, 1973); Elbert B. Smith, *Francis Preston Blair* (New York: Free Press, 1980); William N. Chambers, *Old Bullion Benton: Senator from the New West* (Boston: Little, Brown, 1956); Carl B. Swisher, *Roger B. Taney* (New York: Macmillan, 1935); and Frances F. Wayland, *Andrew Stevenson Democrat and Diplomat 1785–1857* (Philadelphia: University of Pennsylvania Press, 1949). For William B. Lewis, see Louis R. Harlan, "Public Career of William Berkeley Lewis," *Tennessee Historical Quarterly* 7 (1948): 3–37, 118–51.

Studies of the great Whig triumvirate abound. For Webster's rapprochement with Jackson, see Norman D. Brown, *Daniel Webster and the Politics of Availability* (Athens: University of Georgia Press, 1969); for the influence of Jacksonian Democracy on Webster, see Sydney Nathans, *Daniel Webster and Jacksonian Democracy* (Baltimore: Johns Hopkins University Press, 1973). Irving H. Bartlett has explored "The Black Dan–Godlike Man Paradox" of Daniel Webster in his *Daniel Webster* (New York: W. W. Norton, 1978), and Maurice G. Baxter has presented the traditional view of Webster as the savior of the Union in his *One and Inseparable: Daniel Webster and the Union* (Cambridge: Harvard University Press, 1984). Charles M. Wiltse's magisterial but overly-sympathetic life of Calhoun has been challenged by John Niven. See Wiltse, *John C. Calhoun, Nationalist, 1782–1828; John C. Calhoun, Nullifier, 1829–1839;* and *John C. Calhoun, Sectionalist, 1840–1850* (Indianapolis: Bobbs-Merrill, 1944, 1949, 1951), and Niven, *John C. Calhoun and the Price of Union* (Baton Rouge: Louisiana State University Press, 1988). For half a century the only modern full-length biography of Clay was Glyndon G. Van Deusen's *The Life of Henry Clay* (Boston: Little, Brown, 1937), but Robert V. Remini has recently completed a new study: *Henry Clay: Statesman for the Union* (New York: W. W. Norton, 1991). Merrill D. Peterson has woven together the careers of the three Whigs in *The Great Triumvirate: Webster, Clay and Calhoun* (New York: Oxford University Press, 1987). For John Quincy Adams, see Samuel Flagg Bemis, *John Quincy Adams and the Union* (New York: Alfred A. Knopf, 1956); and Mary W. M. Hargreaves, *The Presidency of John Quincy Adams* (Lawrence: University Press of Kansas, 1985).

Richard B. Latner gives a new twist to the Eaton affair in "The Eaton Affair Reconsidered," *Tennessee Historical Quarterly* 36 (1977): 330–51. The most comprehensive analyses of the origins of the spoils system are still Carl R. Fish, "Removal of Officials by the Presidents of the United States," *Annual Report of the American Historical Association for the Year 1899*, 2 vols. (Washington, D.C.: Government Printing Office, 1900), 1:65–86; Carl R. Fish, *The Civil Service and the Patronage* (Cambridge: Harvard University Press, 1904); and Erik M. Eriksson, "The Federal Civil Service under President Jackson," *Mississippi Valley Historical Review* 13 (1927): 517–40. For the argument that the spoils system began with Thomas Jefferson, see Carl E. Prince, "The Passing of the Aristocracy: Jefferson's Removal of the Federalists, 1801–1805, *Journal of American History* 53 (Dec. 1970): 563–75. Sidney Aronson makes the case that the social and economic status of those appointed to office did not change much between 1797 and 1837 in *Status and Kinship in the Higher Civil Service: Standards of Selection in the Administrations of John Adams, Thomas Jefferson, and Andrew Jackson* (Cambridge: Harvard University Press, 1964).

Arthur M. Schlesinger, Jr.'s, emphasis on the Bank War has made it a staple of Jacksonian historiography. Schlesinger's most vocal critic, Bray Hammond, blamed the war on rival bankers, particularly those from New York, in *Banks and Politics in America from the Revolution to the Civil War* (Princeton, N.J.: Princeton University Press, 1957), a view that has been successfully rebutted by Frank Otto Gatell in "Sober Second Thoughts on Van Buren, the Albany Regency, and the Wall Street Conspiracy," *Journal of American History* 53 (1966): 19–40. Robert V. Remini has defended the Jacksonians in *Andrew Jackson and the Bank War: A Study in the Growth of Presidential Power* (New York: W. W. Norton, 1967). Roger B. Taney claimed credit for writing the Bank veto in "Roger B. Taney's 'Bank War Manuscript,'" ed. Carl Brent Swisher, *Maryland Historical Magazine* 53 (1958): 103–31, 215–37, but Lynn L. Marshall has convincingly given the credit to Amos Kendall in "The Authorship of Jackson's Bank Veto Message," *Mississippi Valley Historical Review* 50 (1963): 466–77. The best study of the Bank remains Ralph C. H. Catterall, *The Second Bank of the United States* (Chicago: University of Chicago Press, 1903). For a selection of Nicholas Biddle's correspondence, see Nicholas Biddle, *The Correspondence of Nicholas Biddle Dealing with National Affairs, 1807–1844*, ed. Reginald C. McGrane (Boston: Houghton Mifflin, 1919). The story of the removal of the deposits from the Bank, the panic that followed, and the establishment of the deposit-bank system is told in William J. Duane, *Narrative and Correspondence Concerning the Removal of the Deposites* (1838; reprint, New York: Burt Franklin, 1965); Jacob P. Meerman, "The Climax of the Bank War: Biddle's Contraction," *Journal of Political Economy* 71 (Aug. 1963): 378–88; Harry N. Scheiber, "The Pet Banks in Jacksonian Politics and Finance, 1833–1841," *Journal of Economic History* 23 (June 1963): 196–214; Frank Otto Gatell, "Spoils of the Bank War: Political Bias in the Selection of Pet Banks," *American Historical Review* 70 (Oct. 1964): 35–58; John M. McFaul, *The*

Politics of Jacksonian Finance (Ithaca, N.Y.: Cornell University Press, 1972); and Peter Temin, *The Jacksonian Economy* (New York: W. W. Norton, 1969).

William W. Freehling gives Jackson credit for saving the Union in *Prelude to Civil War: The Nullification Controversy in South Carolina, 1816–1836* (New York: Harper & Row, 1966), and Richard E. Ellis argues that Jackson almost split his party during the crisis in *The Union at Risk: Jacksonian Democracy, States' Rights and the Nullification Crisis* (New York: Oxford University Press, 1987). In his recent first volume of a two-volume study of the movement of the South to secession, Freehling argues that the South was far from monolithic. See *The Road to Disunion: Secessionists at Bay 1776–1854* (New York: Oxford University Press, 1990). The role of republican ideology in the Nullification Crisis is shown in Richard B. Latner, "The Nullification Crisis and Republican Subversion," *Journal of Southern History* 43 (1977): 19–38. The proceedings of most of the state legislatures on the Nullification Crisis have been gathered in General Court of Massachusetts, *State Papers on Nullification* (Boston: Dutton and Wentworth, 1834).

The most evenhanded discussion of Indian removal is Ronald N. Satz, *American Indian Policy in the Jacksonian Era* (Lincoln: University of Nebraska Press, 1975). Francis Paul Prucha defends Jackson in "Andrew Jackson's Indian Policy: A Reassessment," *Journal of American History* 56 (Dec. 1969): 527–39, and *The Great Father: The United States and the American Indians*, 2 vols. (Lincoln: University of Nebraska Press, 1984); Michael Paul Rogin and Mary Elizabeth Young are more critical in *Fathers and Children: Andrew Jackson and the Subjugation of the American Indian* (New York: Alfred A. Knopf, 1975) and in *Redskins, Ruffleshirts, and Rednecks: Indian Allotments in Alabama and Mississippi 1830–1860* (Norman: University of Oklahoma Press, 1961). Edwin A. Miles sets the record straight on Jackson's alleged refusal to back up John Marshall's decision in the Cherokee case in "After John Marshall's Decision: *Worcester* v. *Georgia* and the Nullification Crisis," *Journal of Southern History* 39 (1973): 519–44. Documents relating to Indian removal are to be found in Francis Paul Prucha, ed., *Documents of United States Indian Policy* (Lincoln: University of Nebraska Press, 1975), and U.S. Senate, *Speeches on the Passage of the Bill for the Removal of the Indians*, 21st Cong., 1st sess. (1830; reprint, Millwood, N.Y.: Kraus Reprint Co., 1973).

The history of an underrated political issue is told well in Daniel Feller, *The Public Lands in Jacksonian Politics* (Madison: University of Wisconsin Press, 1984), and in Malcolm J. Rohrbough, *The Land Office Business: The Settlement and Administration of American Public Lands, 1789–1837* (New York: Oxford University Press, 1968). Carlton Jackson takes the position that Jackson had political motives in opposing federal internal improvements in "The Internal Improvement Vetoes of Andrew Jackson," *Tennessee Historical Quarterly* 25 (1966): 261–79.

The standard overview of Jacksonian administration is Leonard D. White, *The Jacksonians: A Study in Administrative History, 1829–1861* (New York: Macmillan, 1954). For a more thematic study, see Matthew Crenson, *The Federal Machine: Beginnings of Bureaucracy in Jacksonian America* (Baltimore: Johns Hopkins University Press, 1975). To put Jackson's use of the veto in perspective, see *Presidential Vetoes 1789–1976* (Washington, D.C.: Government Printing Office, 1978). Albert Somit considers Jackson a competent administrator in "Andrew Jackson as Administrative Reformer," *Tennessee Historical Quarterly* 13 (1954): 204–23. Jackson's cabinet and kitchen cabinet are examined in Richard P. Longaker, "Was Jackson's Kitchen Cabinet a Cabinet?" *Mississippi Valley Historical Review* 44 (1957): 94–108; James C. Curtis, "Andrew Jackson and His Cabinet: Some New Evidence," *Tennessee Historical Quarterly* 27 (1968); and Richard B. Latner, "The Kitchen Cabinet and Andrew Jackson's Advisory System," *Journal of American History* 65 (Sept. 1978): 371–74. For two key services, see Gerald Cullinan, *The United States Postal Service* (New York: Praeger, 1973), and Daniel Preston, "The Administration and Reform of the U.S. Patent Office," *Journal of the Early Republic* 5 (Fall 1985): 331–53. The party press is described in Culver H. Smith, *The Press, Politics, and Patronage: The American Government's Use of Newspapers 1789–1875* (Athens: University of Georgia Press, 1977).

The best history of Jackson's foreign policy is John M. Belohlavek, *"Let the Eagle Soar!": The Foreign Policy of Andrew Jackson* (Lincoln: University of Nebraska Press, 1985). A useful general account is Paul Varg, *United States Foreign Relations, 1820–1860* (East Lansing: Michigan State University Press, 1979). See also the brief studies of the diplomacy of Jackson's four secretaries of state in Samuel Flagg Bemis, ed., *The American Secretaries of States and the Diplomacy*, 10 vols. (1927–29; reprint, New York: Cooper Square Publishers, 1963), 4:161–343. For a narrative of Anthony Butler's fumbling diplomacy in Mexico, see Joe Gibson, "A. Butler: What a Scamp!" *Journal of the West* 11 (1972): 235–47.

Carl E. Prince relates the rioting of the 1830s to the traumatic social and economic changes of the era in "The Great 'Riot Year': Jacksonian Democracy and Patterns of Violence in 1834," *Journal of the Early Republic* 5 (Spring 1985): 1–19. Leonard L. Richards ties the rioting to the abolitionist movement in *"Gentlemen of Property and Standing": Anti-Abolition Mobs in Jacksonian America* (New York: Oxford University Press, 1970); David Grimsted shows the connection between the riots and Jackson's anarchic style in "Rioting in Its Jacksonian Setting," *American Historical Review* 77 (April 1972): 361–97. For the attempted assassination of Jackson, see Richard C. Rohrs, "Partisan Politics and the Attempted Assassination of Andrew Jackson," *Journal of the Early Republic* 1 (Summer 1981): 149–53. Two articles showing Jacksonian lack of concern for the labor movement are Richard B. Morris, "Andrew Jackson, Strikebreaker," *American Historical Review* 55 (Oct. 1949): 54–68; and Frank Otto Gatell, ed., "Roger B. Taney, the Bank of Maryland Rioters, and a Whiff of Grapeshot," *Maryland Historical Magazine* 59 (1964): 262–67. Edward Pessen finds the workers less than radical in *Most Uncommon Jacksonians: The Radical Leaders of the Early Labor Movement* (Albany: State University of New York Press, 1967). Sean Wilentz, however, cites evidence of radical republicanism and class warfare in *Chants Democratic: New York City and the Rise of the American Working Class, 1788–1850* (New York: Oxford University Press, 1984). Although Gerald S. Henig and John M. McFaul agree that the Jacksonians were in sympathy with slavery, the former accuses them of racism, but the latter argues that they were simply trying to preserve the Union. See Henig, "The Jacksonian Attitude toward Abolitionism," *Tennessee Historical Quarterly* 28 (Spring 1969): 42–56, and McFaul, "Expediency vs. Morality: Jacksonian Politics and Slavery," *Journal of American History* 62 (June 1975): 24–39.

INDEX

Bank of the United States, *continued*
207–8; investigation of, 1832, 102–3; as
an issue, 1829–32, 54–55, 56–59, 96–106;
and Panic of 1819, 13; recharter bill for,
97–98, 100–106; rejection of directors of,
208–9; removal of deposits from, 186–
200
Baptists, 69–70
Barbour, Philip P., 141, 145, 253–54
Barry, John, 239
Barry, William T., 31, 85, 92, 164, 197, 239;
cabinet appointment, 27–28, 31–32; and
Eaton affair, 36–38; and 1832 election,
145, 146; and Post Office, 238–40; and
removal of deposits, 188, 193; and spoils
system, 47, 48; starting *Globe*, 89, 90
Barton, David, 75–76
Beardsley, Samuel, 169, 226
Beaumarchais family, 125
Beaumont, Andrew, 13
Beecher, Lyman, 13
Bell, John, 65, 71, 169; backs White for
president, 255–56; defeated for Speaker,
254; elected Speaker, 209–10
Bell, Samuel, 43, 212
Belohlavek, John M., 135
Benton, Thomas Hart, 56, 60, 71, 93, 142,
214, 256–57, 267, 272; backs internal
improvements, 63, 64; brawl with
Jackson, 5, 148; and 1832 election, 146,
148; expunging resolution, 250, 252–54,
264–66; on hard money, 96, 231; in
Jackson coalition, 19, 54; and land
policy, 59–60; and Nullification Crisis,
170, 172; opposes Bank, 58, 96, 101–2;
and Panic of 1819, 17; in Panic session,
204–6; proposes South-West alliance,
55; and spoils system, 41
Berrien, John M., 36, 48, 83, 85, 87, 92,
213; and Bank, 58; cabinet appointment
of, 28–29, 31; daughter of, 36
Bibb, George, 54, 144
Biddle, Nicholas, 59, 81, 95, 230, 236; and
Bank recharter, 97–98, 100–103; early
career, 57; and 1832 election, 145;
interview with Jackson, 58; and Panic of
1834, 198–99, 207–8; and Portsmouth
branch, 58; relations with McLane, 97–
98; and removal of deposits, 186–88,
193, 198–200
Binney, Horace, 101, 102, 207
Black, John, 211, 212, 252–53
Black Hawk War, 112, 146, 240
Blair, Francis P., 18, 184, 197, 221–22, 225,
272; on the Bank, 96, 145–46; becomes
editor of *Globe*, 88–91; in Democratic

party, 246, 247, 249, 256–57; efforts to
become congressional printer, 89, 100,
170, 201, 254; in elections, 19, 141–50;
fight with McLane, 99, 102, 143; and
kitchen cabinet, 91, 93; and Nullification
Crisis, 157, 159, 160, 162, 166, 170, 174,
178; and Panic of 1819, 17; in Panic
session, 201, 209, 210; and patronage,
89–90; on removal of deposits, 186, 192–
94; and spoils system, 48
Blount, Willie, 71
Boardinghouses, congressional, 51–52
Board of Engineers for Internal
Improvements, 237
Board of Naval Commissioners, 237
Boston Morning Post, 250
Boulanger's Restaurant, 265
Bradley, Abraham, 238
Branch, John, 34, 36, 74–75, 83, 87, 92,
213; cabinet appointment of, 28–29, 31
Branch, Mrs. John, 34, 36
Breathitt, George, 157
Breathitt, John, 146
Brent, Daniel, 46
Brent, Thomas L. L., 128
Brown, Bedford, 169
Brown, Ethan Allen, 241, 243
Brown, Obadiah, 69–70, 238–39
Buchanan, James, 24, 44, 129, 227; and
Indian removal, 74
Buckner, Alexander, 172
Bunker Hill monument, 14
Bunner, Rudolph, 97
Burned-Over District, 10, 218, 248, 251
Burr, Aaron, 46, 145
Burton, Robert, 263
Butler, Anthony, 130–33, 136
Butler, Benjamin F., 209, 246, 267
Butler, Benjamin F., 209, 246, 267; and
Nullification Crisis, 165, 174

Cabinet, 189, 315n23; criticism of
appointments, 1829, 29–31; first, 27–32;
Jackson's use of, 93; reorganization,
1831, 83–87
Cadwalader, Thomas, 100
Calhoun, Floride, 34, 36
Calhoun, John C., 21, 24, 30, 52, 53, 56,
62, 91, 100, 186, 213, 222, 259; and
abolitionist tracts, 227; breaks tie votes,
74, 143–44; and cabinet breakup, 85, 86;
and Eaton affair, 34, 36–38; in 1832
election, 88, 137–41; on expunging
resolution, 264–65; in Florida
controversy, 79–83, 93; in Jackson